What Justice? Whose Justice?

WITHDRAWN

What Justice?
Whose Justice?

Fighting for Fairness in Latin America

Edited by Susan Eva Eckstein
and Timothy P. Wickham-Crowley

UNIVERSITY OF CALIFORNIA PRESS
Berkeley · Los Angeles · London

HM
671
.W47
2003

RECEIVED

SEP 29 2004

Kennedy School Library

University of California Press
Berkeley and Los Angeles, California

University of California Press, Ltd.
London, England

© 2003 by
The Regents of the University of California

Library of Congress Cataloging-in-Publication Data

What justice? whose justice? : fighting for fairness in
Latin America / edited by Susan Eva Eckstein and
Timothy P. Wickham-Crowley.
        p.   cm.
    Includes bibliographical references (p.) and index.
    ISBN 0-520-23744-7 (cloth)—ISBN 0-520-23745-5
(paper)
    1. Social justice—Latin America.
2. Democratization—Latin America.
3. Free trade—Social aspects—Latin America.
I. Eckstein, Susan, 1942–   II. Wickham-Crowley,
Timothy P., 1951–
HM671 .W47   2003
303.3′72′098—dc21   2002009718

Manufactured in the United States of America

12 11 10 09 08 07 06 05 04 03

10 9 8 7 6 5 4 3 2 1

The paper used in this publication is both acid-free and
totally chlorine-free (TCF). It meets the minimum
requirements of ANSI/NISO Z39.48-1992 (R 1997)
(Permanence of Paper). ♾

To John Coatsworth and Steve Reifenberg
and the entire staff of
Harvard's David Rockefeller Center for Latin American Studies
and Georgetown's Center for Latin American Studies
in appreciation of their support
for the LASA Congress we organized together.
—Susan and Tim

Contents

Illustrations

Preface

SUSAN EVA ECKSTEIN AND
TIMOTHY P. WICKHAM-CROWLEY

Social justice: it is an age-old preoccupation of the materially poor and the politically weak. But what justice, for whom, and why?

As universal and as morally grounded as the human concern for justice is, we know surprisingly little about it. Some preeminent philosophers have sought to understand the moral precepts that govern a just society, but we believe that the topic begs for societally grounded historical and comparative study. Conceptions of justice, efforts to reduce or eliminate perceived injustices, and the success of such efforts vary over time and among groups. They also vary among persons differently located within social structures and among persons embracing different values, which themselves are not free-floating but embedded in local, national, and international structures of everyday life and practice. Given such variations within and across human societies, we do not overreach ourselves in asserting that one group's sense of justice may be viewed by others as unfair or unprincipled. Such varied human perceptions also underlie a core assertion that animates this work: if people define social situations as unjust, then such perceived injustices are real in their consequences.

The book focuses on Latin America from a variety of perspectives and scholarly disciplines, precisely because conceptions of and responses to injustices are variable and structurally and culturally contingent. The Latin American Studies Association (LASA), the most internationally preeminent organization of Latin American specialists, is deeply committed to interdisciplinary research on the region. We, the community of scholars, know that we do not all think alike. Different disciplines selectively focus on different features of society, and often employ different levels of analysis, some more micro, some more macro. Scholars of different disciplines as well as different analytical perspectives accordingly create a broad tapestry of pertinent (and often poignant) information about justice and injustice, the study of which has everything to gain from region-specific, interdisciplinary cross-fertilization.

Aware of how pervasive feelings of injustice are, how understudied they are, how various scholarly disciplines together can improve our understanding of the conditions in which perceived injustices are rooted, and how an improved understanding might reduce injustices in the future, we chose the theme of social justice for the Latin American Studies Association International Congress we oversaw and organized. At the time, we were president of the association and program chair of the congress (Susan Eckstein and Timothy Wickham-Crowley, respectively). The essays that follow are largely substantially revised versions of papers, presented at the congress, that touch upon this theme.

Given limited space and the variety in the essays gathered here, any generalizations we or others draw about the politics of justice and injustice in the region must be considered provisional. The contribution of the studies is mainly at the level of description, albeit always analytically grounded description. Their richness of detail can provide us with building blocks for a more general theory of justice. So too can they inform philosophical discussions about how ordinary people actually perceive injustices and why they perceive them in specific ways.

Of course, recurrent themes that arise in this volume do not in themselves constitute evidence that the most important features of Latin American political injustices have been delineated. They may merely reflect a common set of interests or biases among the contributors. We selected contributors not merely because they are knowledgeable about particular cases of perceived injustices and efforts to correct them, but also because we knew that they would address a similar range of structurally and culturally grounded issues related to the topic at hand. At the same time, we also insist that recurrent themes across chapters cannot be attributed to a single overarching theory that induced authors to focus on certain features to the exclusion of others. The chapters were not written, nor were they selected by us, in order to "prove" this or that predefined theory.

While these essays focus on Latin American experiences, we believe that their theoretical and practical lessons are of much broader import. Ideally, the book will enlighten readers not merely about the patterning of injustices in Latin America, but also about parallel and differing ways in which the regional phenomena contrast with those found in other world regions. An understanding of both the historically specific and the generalizable features of injustices will ideally help make for a future in which more people in the world enjoy lives that they view as just.

In this assemblage of essays we also try to "give voice" to many Latin Americans whose voices have gone unheeded in the rush toward neo-liberal market reforms and in the complacent satisfaction with recurrent elections as "enough" democracy for one and all. Giving voice should be considered to be one of the basic goals of good social-science research, and not something that only anthropologists routinely pursue. We frankly recognize that there always will be slippage between the actual voices and views of those whose lives we focus on here and the translation of those into the prose of this book; the goal of presenting their voices remains a compelling one, even when we fall short of it. As our essays collectively demonstrate, we hope, many Latin Americans under different circumstances *have* given voice: they have pressed for the restoration of rights that they felt were denied, sought retribution for past injustices, and asserted rights that they previously did not enjoy but to which they have come to feel entitled.

In the end, we believe that these essays are of political, not merely empirical and theoretical, significance. Although not all were necessarily written with a political agenda in mind, they suggest that actual and perceived experiences are not mechanistically determined by formal political institutions or by macroeconomic forces. In demonstrating instances where Latin Americans have pressed to correct injustices, the authors show that the politically weak and meek are not doomed to a life of privation and degradation. A better understanding of the concerns of the weak and the limits of current institutional politics should contribute to a more enlightened and just use of power in the years to come.

For assistance in organizing our LASA Congress, we are indebted to staff of the LASA Secretariat at the time, Reid Reading, Sandy Klinzing, Stacy Maloney, and Mirna Kolbowski. We are also indebted to the David Rockefeller Center for Latin American Studies at Harvard, which hosted the LASA presidency, and to the Center for Latin American

Studies at Georgetown University, which hosted the LASA Program Office, respectively, during our terms of office. At Harvard we are especially indebted to John Coatsworth and to Steve Reifenberg, who helped make the affiliation possible, smooth-running, and enjoyable; at Georgetown we thank Graduate Dean Bruce Douglass and Arturo Valenzuela of the Center for Latin American Studies for willing financial support. We would also like to acknowledge the generosity of the Ford Foundation and the William and Flora Hewlett Foundation for LASA support that helped in this project. We thank, in turn, our good colleagues Walter Goldfrank, Daniel Levine, and Philip Oxhorn for sage advice on parts of the manuscript. And, finally, we wish to thank, at the University of California Press, Naomi Schneider for again confirming her reputation as a deft hand in helping to shape better scholarly work on Latin America, as well as Laura Harger for overseeing the book production process from start to finish, and Andrew Frisardi for his careful copy editing of the manuscript.

CHAPTER ONE

Struggles for Justice in Latin America

SUSAN EVA ECKSTEIN AND
TIMOTHY P. WICKHAM-CROWLEY

The new millennium began with the triumph of democracy over dictatorship, the removal of fetters believed to have obstructed economic advancement in poor countries, and new global concern with human rights. But for whom is life now more just, in what ways, and why? And what can people do to correct remaining injustices?

How can we answer such questions? Preeminent philosophers, from Aristotle and Plato to John Rawls and Amartya Sen, though long preoccupied with the meaning and bases of social justice, have arrived at no consensus. Does justice imply freedom, as Sen (1999) suggests? Or equality, as Rawls (1971) argues? Since ideas of justice necessarily involve values, we cannot look mainly to philosophical reasoning for an adequate understanding of what people in different times and places have thought just or for conditions accounting for the injustices they perceived. Conceptions of the just and the unjust vary with historical circumstances and with people's positions in social hierarchies and group identities. A full understanding of justice requires empirically grounded analyses, not mere philosophical theorizing.

If people define social situations as unjust, then such perceived injustices are real in their consequences. This thesis of ours is the guiding principle of our book, which is designed to launch a much-needed, long-overdue interdisciplinary concern with injustices and how they might be mitigated.[1] It is also our contention that, even though situationally defined, conceptions of justice are sociologically explicable in terms of people's values and their institutionally grounded, real-life experiences. With the aim of deepening our understanding of conditions considered just and unjust (both empirically and analytically), this book includes essays on the political dimensions of injustice, addressing different institutional practices, the uses and abuses of power, and different cultural repertoires that have contributed to felt injustices and efforts to redress them. Although they focus on Latin America, the chapters aim to deepen our understanding of the various ways through which both local and translocal forces generate inequities, shape perceptions of them, and induce efforts to create more favorable situations. We firmly believe that messages of broader import will emerge from a close look at one world region.

With these objectives, this chapter is designed to highlight (1) how social-scientific understandings of politically grounded injustices themselves vary, depending on a priori assumptions embedded in analysts' frames of analysis; (2) how and why citizen rights have been historically contingent and different in Latin America than in the first industrial countries; (3) how and why political institutions central to justice differ in form and function, and in ways that partially contrast with their counterparts in industrial countries; (4) the nature of the state's implicit social contract with its people, the conditions under which that contract has been violated, why it has been violated, and with what effects; (5) which institutionalized structures allow people to exercise their political rights (or not), including people's (in)ability to organize collectively to redress political grievances; and (6) how formal and informal grassroots processes may make political institutions and processes more democratic and responsive.

The chapter accordingly focuses on the different institutional structures, processes, and cultural features that pattern *political* bases of justice and injustice in general and in Latin America in particular.[2] In so doing it ties the relevance of the following chapters to a broader context useful for the comparative and historical understanding of the politics of injustice. We will discuss these issues in general and with reference to specific contributors to the volume, contributors who through perceptive in-depth analyses shed light on the issues at hand.

FRAMES AND DISCIPLINES

What social scientists see, highlight, and prioritize depends on their prior assumptions and analytic frames, not merely on the "facts" on which they focus. Contemporary mainstream economists, for example, see the world through lenses shaped by modernization theory, and accordingly presume that the world is increasingly following a Western developmental course, and that such a path is normatively preferred. One virtue of looking at macroeconomic forces, as such scholars routinely do, is to follow the causal pathways from the introduction of deeply consequential market reforms that mimic rich-country economic structures and to ask questions most of the economists leave unasked: Who have been the winners and who the losers from such transformations? Which groups have seen their economic-linked powers wax or wane as a result, such as with the retraction of state economic involvements in Latin America in the closing years of the twentieth century? The answers to these questions are sometimes obvious, sometimes not, as we shall see. Whether or not neoliberal-biased economists focus specifically on issues of justice, their conceptual frame presumes that people will be best off with a bourgeois-democratic capitalist order that gives priority to market features and minimizes state involvement, and an order premised on individuals' civic, political, and property rights. Yet scholars from a wide variety of perspectives, and not merely the radical Left, have criticized the assumption that unfettered capitalism can produce a just society (Moore 1972; Heilbroner 1974; and Berger 1974, although Berger 1986 retreats from much of that critique).

Postmodernists, in contrast, do not see a unilinear path of development or universal value consensus, including about standards of justice, that transcends time and place (see Alvarez, Dagnino, and Escobar 1998), and accordingly do not see people in the Third World uniformly accepting or wanting modernizing practices and ideas imposed from "above" and abroad. Focusing on what they call "decentered" particularities, postmodernists highlight local variability, in line with people's individual "bundles" of beliefs, norms, and wants. Conceptions of justice and conditions generating injustices, in their view, can only be situationally understood.

Marxists and neo-Marxists, meanwhile, focus on class dynamics on the local, national, and international levels and see social change as driven first and foremost by class interests. They highlight the economic roots of injustice, especially in relations of production but also in market forces. Thus, their conceptual frame leads them to highlight the unequal benefits accruing to different social classes with the global neoliberal reforms modernization proponents prioritize, inequities concealed at the macroeconomic level.

Feminist scholars, in turn, focus on gendered variations in human experience, independently and in conjunction with class and sometimes with race/ethnicity. Across a vast array of feminist theorizing, two questions are consistently repeated, according to the synthesis by Lengermann and Niebrugge-Brantley (1992: 448–50): "And what about the women?" and "Why so?" To which we could add a third: "What is to be done about the situation?" By its very nature, therefore, feminist theorizing raises issues of unjust practices weighted against women, variations of which several contributors to this volume address.

State-centered analysts, meanwhile, highlight how the state, institutionally and ideologically, may mediate between globalization tendencies on the one hand and civil society on the other, even in market-driven economies (see, for example, Evans, Rueschemeyer, and Skocpol 1985; and Evans 1995). Justice, from their vantage point, focuses on laws, legal and political institutions, political rights, and uses and abuses of power and authority. Injustices include instances where subordinate peoples perceive power holders to have no legitimate claims to rule, to impose unfair demands (e.g., taxes), and to exercise power in illegitimate, uncustomary, arbitrary, and discriminatory ways.

Finally, "moral economists" argue that people's views of just and unjust arrangements are likely to vary not only with their economic or other standing in social hierarchies, but also with their cultural understandings, and that ordinary people are especially likely to view as morally unacceptable any economic situation threatening their subsistence (see Thompson 1971; Scott 1976). Views of injustice, however, are not necessarily overtly transparent. For one thing, hegemonic groups typically propagate ideology and discourse in a manner that presents their own views as the generalized views of society. Second, people in subordinate positions may feel the risks are too great to challenge publicly the conditions they consider unjust (see Scott 1985, 1990). The more the economically and politically weak perceive that overt challenges may be met with punishment, the more likely they are to turn instead to "everyday forms of resistance," to borrow Scott's by now famous terminology: that is, to foot-dragging, passive noncompliance, deceit, pilfering, slander, sabotage, arson, and the like. Since such covert activity signals felt injustices, it should be central to the study of the issue. Over time, such disobedience may do more to bring about change than overt challenges to authority, since covert noncompliance may undermine productivity and legitimacy to the point that elites feel compelled to institute significant reforms or lose their stakes in society.

Thus each analytic perspective throws light on certain features of a complex world, while leaving others unnoticed, undocumented, and unanalyzed. Taken collectively rather than singly, they may deepen our understanding both of conditions considered unjust and of attempts to correct them. While drawing on a variety of analytic frames, some common features guide the volume as a whole. First, we focus on *institutional arrangements,* including those that affect how people define rights, norms, values, ideologies, preexisting and emergent identities, and perceived options. Institutionally based activity provides a window through which to unravel the relationship between structure and agency, as well as between structure and culture, fundamental counterpoints that haunt basic theory in the social sciences. Historically rooted social conditions and cultural practices will be seen here to shape, but not in themselves to strictly predetermine, people's lived experiences and their perceptions of how just those experiences are; they also will be shown to shape collective responses to injustices. We argue that within structural and cultural parameters human agency does indeed mediate. Marx remains correct in his argument that men (and women) make history, but not under conditions of their choosing. Second, our approach captures the *interplay between* macropolitical, social, cultural, and economic dynamics at the national and international levels, and the more microsocial relations in which justice and injustice are experienced.

POLITICAL INSTITUTIONS AND POLITICAL RIGHTS

Constitutions provide an obvious first point of entry into legal approaches to the study of politically grounded justice. They specify for a given nation the form of authority considered legitimate, who is entitled to what formal rights (and obligations), and the criteria for protection under the law. In so doing they particularly address which persons have access to the polity as voters and as office holders, and under what conditions.

Latin American countries have installed new constitutions with much greater frequency than the United States. Their greater efforts at rewriting constitutions reflect not merely greater political instability, but also their changing conceptions of citizen rights and the fundamental laws of the land, including, of course, issues of political legitimacy. Conceptions and claims have changed with both shifts in domestic political thinking and power and the borrowing of ideas from abroad.

Citizens' Rights

"Democratization" and "democratic deepening" have (justifiably) become frequently used words in the study of Latin American politics since countries in the region in the 1980s shifted, one after another, from military to civilian rule. New constitutions laid the bases of new forms of governance and the rights and obligations of citizens, including specifically targeted groups such as women and indigenous peoples (see PDBA 1999). Since earlier (if more exclusionary) periods of formal democratic rule in the region had seen such constitutional protections swept away by coups d'etat, the Latin American experience suggests that broad-based documents provide a legal base but no guarantee of political justice.

The Western European and North American experiences give further reason for caution in believing that constitutions ensure democracy. Democracy in those places did not burst fully formed onto the political stage, like some populist Athena emerging from the head of Zeus. Rather, full democracy occurred through the gradual extension of rights, in a predictable sequence, to ever more of the population. Propertied white men (as the dominant ethnic group), for example, received the vote first, with the right subsequently extended "downward" through the class structure to other men, and later to nondominant ethnic groups and women (Rokkan 1966; Ochoa 1987; Ramirez, Soysal, and Shanahan 1997).

In chapter 2, Philip Oxhorn shows that the historical sequence in the extension of rights, the nature of those rights, and the retention of rights in Latin America differ from the experience of industrial countries, and that the quality of democracy and the extent of inequities in the two regions vary as a consequence. While in Europe (Marshall 1950; Bendix 1964) the ordering of rights proceeded from civil rights (e.g., protection before the law and property rights) to political rights (e.g., the vote) to social rights—the last including extensive labor and welfare-state protections—in Latin America political rights have ebbed and flowed and have not expanded in the unilinear manner of the early industrializers (where, in point of fact, there was one period of reversal, under fascism and Nazism in the twenties, thirties, and early forties). Moreover, the initial extension of political rights in Latin America preceded effective civil rights, to the point that civil society has been more at the state's mercy than it has in the European democracies. Moreover, social rights have been extended selectively and unevenly, resulting in social inequalities on a scale unknown in Europe and the U.S., and social rights have been reversed, even under democratic rule. Indeed, even though those political rights lost in the 1960s and 1970s were restored with subsequent redemocratization, the accompanying market reforms resulted in cutbacks in social rights and, paradoxically, a weakened civil society.

Oxhorn adduces evidence showing that, under such conditions, there has ensued a concomitant and widespread decline of Latin Americans' confidence in democratic institutions. Such disillusionment surely underlies mass support for impeachment of presidents in several Latin American countries, as Aníbal Pérez-Liñán describes in chapter 4, and the successive resignations of multiple Argentine presidents in late 2001 and early 2002. Declines in democratic confidence are perhaps also connected to soaring crime rates and corruption, and to a "thinning" of wage- and salary-workers' effective (not legal) ability to strike to protect or improve their earnings, job rights, and access to subsidized health and other benefits. As democratic governments have proven unable or unwilling to address the principal concerns of their citizens, democracy itself risks becoming irrelevant. The return to populist sentiments and governments (e.g., Hugo Chávez in Venezuela) has not solved the problem of fiscal constraints that *all* rulers face in the new, neoliberal age.

The Juridical System and Law Enforcement

All democratic constitutions in Latin America, building in part on the U.S. experience, formally specify not only citizen rights but also the separation of federal powers. However, since both judiciaries and legislatures in the region tend to be subservient to the executive branch, we see how constitutions alone do not dictate political practices; nor do they mimic the actual practices of the industrial democracies.

Discretionary juridical subordination to the executive has a historical precedent in Latin America, with the judiciary either accepting or tolerating that subordination. Lisa Hilbink, in chapter 3, documents such subordination in what might be considered a "least likely case," Chile, one of the countries in the region with the longest history (until 1973) of uninterrupted formal democratic rule. She examines the evolution of the national judiciary and the rule of law in Chile, mainly but not exclusively prior to the 1973 military coup d'etat of Augusto Pinochet, who ruled until 1990. Despite Chile's good "judicial reputation," Hilbink documents how and explains why the judiciary rarely acted independently of the executive branch. Courts often refused to challenge patently illegal executive and legislative activity, for example in denying habeas corpus and granting "states of exception" from the normal rule of law. Upon taking power, and then overseeing the transition to democracy (begun in the late 1980s), General Pinochet built on and deepened the subordination of the judiciary to the executive. He insisted on legal measures to prevent the courts from exercising independence, in order to ward off the possibility that they might bring him and other officers to trial for atrocities committed under his rule.

Under the veneer of democracy, civilian presidents elsewhere in the region also took de jure steps to restrict juridical autonomy. This was especially true of Alberto Fujimori in Peru and Hugo Chávez in Venezuela in the 1990s. Chávez initially had mass support for concentrating power in the presidency, owing to his stated efforts to end government corruption in a political system ordinary citizens had come to discredit. Yet Fujimori faced thousands of prodemocracy protesters when he dismantled the Constitutional Court in June 1997, and the contrast shows that ordinary people in different contexts vary in their views of and responses to such extralegal concentration of power in the executive.

By the turn of the new century, though, some courts in the region began coming into their own (Weissert 2000). In Chile, as well as in Argentina, Guatemala, and Mexico, judiciaries showed signs of asserting their powers and government officials ceased to operate "above the law" with impunity. The Supreme Court of Chile, for example, finally removed the legal immunity Pinochet had crafted for himself and ruled that he could be brought to trial for crimes against humanity committed while he was head of state. In Mexico the high court ordered Ernesto Zedillo, at the end of his presidential term (1994–2000), to give bank documents to Congress that might reveal illegal contributions to his 1994 campaign; the court also overruled the executive's claims that turning over the documents would violate bank secrecy. In Argentina, courts closely investigated a Senate bribery scandal, while Nobel peace laureate Rigoberta Menchú filed genocide charges in Spain against former Guatemalan president Efraín Ríos Montt (1982–83), who was responsible for many of the estimated two hundred thousand Guatemalans killed during that nation's civil war.[3] Such changes in juridical practices have come via Congress as well as the executive branch, and are rooted in (although not alone caused by) nascent, international, human-rights legal standards. Contributing to such changes were foreign legal initiatives, in particular the willingness of Spanish and British courts to consider prosecution of the former Chilean dictator when Pinochet went to London for medical care. Chilean removal of Pinochet's legal immunity followed the overseas cases and was clearly emboldened by them.

Growing autonomy notwithstanding, the judicial system remains corrupt and submissive, both to privileged-class interests within their societies and to the executive branch of government. This is true from the highest judges down to police on the streets. Brazil provides two apt examples: a police colonel was convicted (a decade later!) of ordering a 1992 *post*riot massacre of 111 prisoners and was sentenced to 632 years in jail, but was let out on appeal; and a judge was accused of embezzling eighty-seven million dollars from funds for construction of a court building (*Economist*, July 7, 2001: 38). Furthermore, macroeconomic dynamics affect how class forces impinge on court systems. For example, in maximizing the role of market forces and slimming down the economic role of the state, neoliberal reforms around the turn of the century had the unintended effect of exacerbating corruption within the legal system and strengthening the elite bias of law enforcement. With the privileging of market forces, as Philip Oxhorn notes in his chapter, there came a "marketization" of the law: in part through the privatization of law enforcement itself (with the growth of elite, hired, private-security forces), but mainly through the sheer ability of the prosperous to purchase effective legal services and hence "real" access to the judicial process. Indicative of how money continues to corrupt the system of justice, Colombian judges seeking judicial independence in the late twentieth century were offered the option of *plata o plomo* (silver or lead; i.e., a bribe or a bullet) by the *narcotraficantes* (drug dealers) who were under their purview, a scenario subsequently repeated in Mexico.

Meanwhile, police have become part of a mounting crime problem in the region, and are perceived as such. The World Values Surveys confirmed the impression of "no confidence" in the region's police (Inglehart, Basañez, and Moreno 1998: V278). Rates of theft, pilfering, looting, illicit dealings, and kidnappings rose to unprecedented levels. So too did homicide rates, to the point that Latin America became the most murder-prone region in the world (for homicide rates, see Archer and Gartner 1984: pt. 3; *SALA* 1992: pt. 1, 460–61; Newman 1999: 285–88). Indeed, violence and the threat of violence, along with payoffs, have completely corroded the administration of justice in Colombia, as Marc Chernick details in chapter 7—and this in a regime that remained formally democratic.

Against this backdrop, the urban poor, even under Hugo Chávez's populist regime, became impatient with mounting street crime (partly the result of increased arms and drug trafficking) and the failure of the government and police to protect them. Cases of mob justice around the turn of the new century suggested that many Venezuelans had given up on the government taking control. Mobs in one case killed eight alleged murderers, in early 2001, in the crowded hillside slums that surround much of the capital city (*Boston Globe,* January 17, 2001: 15). Violent vigilante justice meted out to common thieves also became commonplace in Mexican society (*Washington Post,* July 31, 2001: A1), perhaps reflecting a similar disgust with the absence of effective and honest policing.

The Legislature, Separation of Powers, and Presidential Accountability

Despite official autonomy, in Latin America legislatures as well as judiciaries have tended to defer to the presidency, even under the democracies. Legislatures often "rubber stamp" executive legal initiatives, giving a democratic legislative veneer to presidentialism.

Illustrative of de facto subordination of legislators to the presidency rather than to their official constituencies, in Mexico the legislature for decades exercised negligible control over the federal budget and ratified almost all laws backed by the executive (see González Casanova 1970: 17–18, 201). Indeed, so strong were the de facto powers of many presidents in the region, especially in ruling by decree, that Gláucio Soares (2000) dubbed such trends "imperial presidentialism."

By the turn of the century Mexico illustrated how, more generally, Latin American legislatures and judiciaries were asserting themselves as never before, even if Venezuela under Chávez remained an important counterexample. Yet democratization, as such, contributed less to this upsurge in autonomy than did the region's neoliberal reforms, which shrank the state's role in the economy and in society and called for decentralization—changes that had unanticipated effects. In this changed political-economic context, congressmen and the business interests with which they were associated simply became less beholden to the central government. Thus neoliberalism generated new channels whereby powerful class interests could informally influence the law and its implementation, and in so doing "decentered" power away from the executive branch.

Aníbal Pérez-Liñán, in chapter 4, describes and analyzes how Congress-based impeachments by the turn of the century had become a Latin American commonplace. He explores the comparative regional pattern wherein congressional autonomy contributed to this regionally unprecedented mode of correcting perceived executive-branch injustices, as impeachments replaced coups d'etat as the most common way of ousting presidents. President Fernando Collor de Mello was the first democratically elected president in Brazil after two decades of military rule, but his flagrant corruption elicited a mass, multiclass, and multi-institutional opposition movement, and he became the first president in the world to be removed from office by impeachment. The Brazilian events stirred an impeachment movement that came to inspire others in the region.

Impeachment hearings reflect an emergent and unprecedented respect for the law in Latin America, as well as a new consensus that legal means can and should be used to remove presidents perceived to be abusing their authority. The mass popularity of such proceedings, in turn, leaves little doubt that the term "social justice" applies here. Concomitantly, though, impeachments ironically reveal the failure of the new, formally constituted democratic regimes to bring to office leadership with de facto as well as de jure legitimacy. And they reveal that mere mimicking of Western political institutions, or modernizing politically in the Western mode, does not necessarily bring to power leaders who respect the law of the land or governments with widespread support.

Pérez-Liñán finds that impeachment movements occur where there is a highly publicized scandal accompanied by great public outrage against a president with a narrowly based group of clientelistic supporters. They also occur in a context, at the turn of the new century, in which coups d'etat no longer are viewed as viable options because the militaries discredited themselves both economically and politically when they ruled in the 1960s, 1970s, and 1980s. Democratization itself indirectly contributed to the impeachment trends because political transformations increased press freedoms (allowing for exposés of scandals) and broke down former sociopolitical controls, thereby making expression of outrage easier and more probable. Meanwhile, the outrage fed on the new economic hardships that accompanied neoliberal reforms. While these conditions appear to be "necessary," impeachment initiatives ended in a president's removal from office only when, in addition, that president lacked sizable backing in the legislature. The presence of both "necessary" and "sufficient" factors led to successful impeachments in Ecuador and Venezuela, as well as in Brazil, but Ernesto Samper in Colombia managed to escape an impeachment effort because of his stronghold in the legislature.

In the context of legislatures' growing readiness to take on presidents whom they perceive to abuse power or rule incompetently, some presidents opted, when they were publicly shamed, to resign rather than face congressional efforts to depose them. In 2000 in Peru, for example, Fujimori escaped a legislative call for impeachment—his government lost legitimacy as corruption scandals surfaced—by fleeing the country and resigning from office overseas. In Argentina, in contrast, two democratically elected presidents, Raúl Alfonsín (1983–89) and Fernando de la Rúa, took it upon themselves to resign from office (the latter in 2001, barely into his term) when their inability to manage the economy caused widespread unrest. De la Rúa, in particular, faced national protests that paralyzed the country, and he and a short-lived string of successors resigned the presidency as Argentina's dollarized economy faltered, the peso-dollar linkage was scrapped, the government defaulted on international loans, and a major peso devaluation followed (*Boston Globe,* January 6, 2002: A6). Although the military under such circumstances in times past would have staged a coup d'etat, they did not even threaten to do so, given redemocratization processes begun in the 1980s.

Thus political institutions in Latin America have often functioned differently than their outward form suggests. Democratization did not necessarily end executive domination of the judiciary and the legislature. Actual practices instead reflect the permeation of class and informal political dynamics in the society in which those political institutions are embedded, and also the autocratic use and abuse of power. Accordingly, no purely "statist" analysis can explain such trends, even within state institutions. Societal forces, de facto if not de jure, shape the formation and implementation of laws and the treatment of those who evade the law.

THE STATE'S IMPLICIT SOCIAL CONTRACT

In addition to constitutionally based rights and institutions designed to ensure justice through the juridical system and elected legislatures, there exists in Latin American countries, as elsewhere, an underlying and tacit social contract between governments and their people. Barrington Moore (1978) argued that such "contracts" entail a commitment of those who govern to provide defense against external enemies, to maintain internal peace and order, and to contribute to the material security of their people. The governed, in turn, are duty-bound to obey legitimate directives from authorities and to provide surplus for the maintenance of state activity. Claudio Véliz (1980) traces the Latin American variant to (bureaucratic) centralism, linked to a worldview premised on hierarchy and inequality. Corporatist depictions, in which the state plays a mediating role between groups with varying rights and responsibilities, similarly characterize the Latin American variant (see Schmitter 1972; Stepan 1978; Wiarda 1981). Such close involvement of the state in both society and the economy has been enshrined in constitutions in the region.

Mid-twentieth-century processes through much of Latin America deepened the populations' moral-economic, material expectations of their states. Building on the region's centralist tradition were governments that promoted a development model after World War II known as import substitution industrialization (ISI). Under ISI, the strategy of choice in most of the region until fully discredited by debt crises of the 1980s, governments became yet more deeply involved in the economy and society: in ownership of productive property, in public investment, and (most significantly from the vantage point of justice) in public regulation and subsidization of subsistence, through, for example, caps placed on the price of basic foods and mass transit. The approach was worlds apart from the (neo)liberal, laissez-faire view that "the state which governs least governs best," the policy imposed on the region since the mid-1980s, under the influence of economists associated with leading U.S. universities as well as international institutions and the U.S. government, policies that came to be known as the "Washington Consensus."

Although first imposed under colonial rule, the everyday meaning of the centralist tradition of Latin America was redefined over the years, in ways that usually served to reinforce a state's strong hold over society. The state shaped the socioeconomic order defined as just, as well as how different social groups envisioned state responsibilities. While states in the region never instituted or sanctioned a society of equals, their policies became closely tied to people's perceptions of material fairness. When subsistence minima have been infringed upon, those deprived have viewed the violations as morally unjust, a source of indignation, even rage, especially where they lack other material options (such as easy migration).

What, then, should the analyst expect in such a context? First, one would expect state-linked justice issues to be more wide-ranging in Latin American countries than in other nations, especially the United States, where the laissez-faire state has stronger roots. Second, insofar as governments in the region, under foreign pressure, have become mimic laissez-faire economies—for example, through the "structural adjustments" and "neoliberal reforms" that Washington and the International Monetary Fund (IMF) have imposed—one would expect citizen responses to retractions of state protections to be stronger and deeper than in countries without such a heritage, given the region's cultural and statist legacy (see Walton 2001). And such cutbacks especially flourished as the neoliberal age came to the region.

State-Based Material Protections

Following the debt crises in the region, both the IMF and the U.S. government pressed Latin American countries to privatize their economies, to eliminate state subsidies that had directly benefited the citizenry, and to reduce state-imposed barriers to trade that stood in the way of would-be importers, exporters, and foreign investors. Policymakers associated with what has been referred to as the "Washington Consensus" had become convinced that neoliberalism was the economic strategy of choice, for both theoretically grounded and practical reasons. Rewarding efficiency, the removal of market barriers opened up global economic opportunities, especially for rich-country businesses that could best compete where state restrictions did not stand in the way. But in Latin America the structural changes had the effect of dramatically altering domestic state/society and state/economy relations associated with the implicit social contract, also "squeezing out" firms and farms unable to compete without state protections. In sharp contrast to the preceding history of the region, the neoliberal reforms led resolutely to a new era entailing a substantial state withdrawal from virtually all forms of economic involvements, as Marcelo Cavarozzi (1992) noted earlier than most. The impact of the leaner, meaner state policies on inequality and material well-being has been profound, as several of the contributors in this book will show. Sometimes they have stirred such mass rage that even elected officials have been pressured to leave political office. The political fate of Fernando de la Rúa, the Argentine president who presided over the increasing material *in*security of the Argentine populace, is a case in point.

While the material aspects of political justice in Latin America do not center around claims to equality, we should note the inherent tension between equality and the principle of freedom, in this case economic freedom rooted in economic (neo)liberalization (for a discussion of this tension already in the 1960s, see Dahrendorf 1968: chap. 7). In the absence of equality, even state material protections undermine true democracy, as both Karl Marx and Max Weber, founding fathers of the social sciences, noted long ago.[4]

In chapter 5 of this book, Terry Karl addresses the political as well as social and economic costs of Latin America's "vicious cycle of inequality," which continued even under the nominally democratic systems prevailing in the region since the mid-1980s. Karl argues that historically high levels of inequality—which had for centuries been associated with elite-skewed policymaking—reached perhaps record levels during the 1980s and 1990s, due to the neoliberal-linked changes in the region. In this context, she argues, democratically elected officials regularly have failed to be responsive in their policies to the democratic forces that brought them to high office. There is evidence instead that the political class often remains "captured" by the economic elites of their nations, with states as a result failing to fulfill their tacit material contract with their citizenry. As Karl might put it, newly enhanced *political inclusion* (namely, elections) have continued to coexist with deep *social exclusion,* evidenced by the skewing of spending, taxing, and regulatory policies so that the wealthy win the alliance of the middle classes at the expense of the poor. Even Peruvian president Alejandro Toledo, who touted his own humble origins and was elected to office in 2001 on the promise that he would champion the interests of the common man (and woman), within a year faced major strikes and protests by groups ranging from professionals, doctors, and nurses to peasants and street vendors as he reneged on his campaign claims and initiated neoliberal reforms, such as privatization of utility companies, that threatened job losses and higher utility prices for consumers.

The State's Protective Political Duties

Nor have governments in the region always fulfilled their tacit duty to maintain internal peace and order. Indeed, governments have at times turned the weapons and personnel of public protection violently upon the very populace they are charged to protect, and in so doing lost the trust of their citizens. Evidence unfortunately abounds in Latin America of state-directed and -sanctioned violence pursued in the name of maintaining or establishing peace and order. Such violence against the citizenry was especially widespread under the military governments that ruled in the region from the 1960s through the 1980s. Resistance to such state betrayal initially was timid, episodic, and isolated, for the risks of overtly challenging the regimes were great. Some three hundred thousand Latin Americans died at military gunpoint during this period, in Argentina, Chile, Uruguay, El Salvador, and especially Guatemala.

Discredited economically (by the debt crises of the 1980s) and politically (with gathering domestic and international outrage over crimes
against humanity), governing militaries gradually reinstituted civilian
rule. But widespread state-incited violence left unanswered the question
of how to deal justly with officials responsible for homicidal crimes. Military governments had violated the most basic of human rights, the right
to live, and even the right to die, when refusing to acknowledge the
killings, admitting only "disappearances." Under the new democracies
efforts were undertaken to achieve *some* type of restorative justice, even
if pure retribution—"an eye for an eye"—was ruled out.

In chapter 6, Leigh Payne takes the reader on an extraordinary tour,
showing how former torturers have created a range of narratives to "explain" or account for their actions. One of the narrative tactics was
avoidance, refusing to recognize or talk about having committed crimes
against humanity. Another strategy she discusses focuses on a redefinition by torturers of those they murdered. In Argentina, for example, perpetrators of state violence framed their victims as not truly Argentine,
premised on the conception that those outside the body politic fall outside protections guaranteed by the state and therefore are treatable as
enemy outsiders. Labels of "communist," "subversive," "red," and "terrorist" reflected attempts by states and state-linked actors to remove entire groups from the protections embedded and promised in the implicit
social contract, just as they also constituted attempts to justify "cleansing" the society of such "foreign bodies" (cf. Wickham-Crowley 1991:
chap. 3). The parallels to ethnic cleansing in the former Yugoslavia are
evident.

Payne's work leaves us with a conundrum: are rights to justice and to
just retribution against torturers the best goal to pursue in such national
circumstances? Or is the society's overall "mending" best served by simply dropping the issue and moving on, or merely by removing torturers
and murderers from public office without subjecting them to punishment? The latter eventuated from "truth commissions" in Guatemala,
Uruguay, and Brazil, not to mention the highly public "accounting,"
without punishment, to which the former apartheid criminals of South
Africa were subjected. The combined pursuit of truth and reconciliation
at least entails a break with official versions of the past and public acknowledgment by state actors of past wrongs. While confessions are crucial to the process, they do not help in accomplishing either retributive
or restorative justice, since confessors come forth only with immunity.

Nonetheless, they are important in the effort to come to terms with the past and to assuage, in part, the memories haunting the living.

In chapter 7, Mark Chernick touches directly on certain themes found in Leigh Payne's discussion of torturers, while more obliquely blending with Lisa Hilbink's concerns about the judiciary. Chernick's focus is on the violations of the political rights and expectations held by Colombians, including elementary concerns about physical safety and life itself. In this context, we encounter again the state's failure to provide its citizenry with the basic protections incumbent on state officials in the implicit social contract. Chernick argues that Colombia's sui generis pattern of violence is intelligible neither in terms of economic "justice"— areas of intense poverty have not correlated with areas of greatest violence—nor simply in terms of the weakness of the state's political "presence" in certain locations or during certain eras. Instead, he argues that the problem is rooted in the state's failure to deliver justice in the face of more than fifty years of horrific and numerous politically motivated murders. The state's recurrent response to such awesome violence has been a repeating cycle of "amnesty, rehabilitation, assassination [of those amnestied], insurgency." Rather than making any systematic attempt to bring violators to just punishment, Colombian governments chose to do nothing. This "response" was well illustrated already in the 1950s when the leadership of the two main political parties, whose members were responsible for the mass murders associated with the civil strife known as La Violencia, formed a state-sanctioned political pact. The Frente Nacional (National Front) coalition governments that resulted chose the path of "reconciliation and forgetting." When viewed in that historical context, the more recent wave of rampant violence, in the 1990s, linked to the growing drug economy, a guerrilla movement, and the militarization of the countryside, proves to build on a preexisting national repertoire of socially and politically grounded murders. It does not represent a break with patterns of the past.

Around the turn of the new century, governments in Latin America (and other Third World regions) increasingly privatized the means of violence. Privatization was consistent with the notion of a slimmed-down neoliberal state, but inconsistent with the view that the modern state, by definition, has a territorial monopoly on the means of force (see Weber 1946: 77–78). In privatizing access to and control over weaponry, authorities freed themselves from the critique that they were violating their implicit responsibility for protecting their citizenry. Indeed, as Chernick illustrates, paramilitaries with close connections to the military and to economic elites were responsible for most of the tens of thousands of murders in Colombia in the 1990s, when it was the most violent country in Latin America. Reflecting common people's perceptions of the growing privatization of repression, Colombian villagers whose menfolk were massacred identified their assailants in January 2001 as paramilitaries supported directly by government troops deploying intelligence flyovers and *cordon sanitaire* tactics (Wilson 2001). Stepped-up U.S. military aid, designed to fight the drug problem "at its source," also provided the means, both intentionally and not, for this new "decentered" militarization.

DEEPENING DEMOCRATIZATION AT THE GRASSROOTS LEVEL: FORMAL AND INFORMAL PATHS

The right of people to be consulted, let alone to be crucial in constituting the authority of the central polity, is far from universal. It is a modern right associated with democracy. Following the lead of Rueschemeyer, Stephens, and Stephens (1992: 43–44), we define "full formal democracy" as entailing (1) regular, free, and fair elections of representatives with universal and equal suffrage; (2) freedom of expression and association, including the liberty to campaign and debate issues competitively and openly and to organize for particularized interests; and (3) recognition and respect for the legal authority of democratically elected governments by the state apparatus, especially by potential adversaries of democratic outcomes, like coup-minded soldiers. "Full democratization," in our view, however, entails not merely formal guarantees of individual (and, possibly, as discussed below, certain collective) rights, but the democratization of sociopolitical processes within the formal institutions of the state, starting at the grassroots level, and the mobilization of informal political power among those not well served by formal political institutions.

Respect for Formal Electoral Rights

"Full" formal democratization is premised on citizens' rights to elect their representatives. Thus the right to vote is essential. But so too are the right to put forth candidates for political office, the right of those selected to campaign, and respect for electoral outcomes essential. For legally specified political rights to be effectively actuated, persons and

parties must be able to campaign freely for votes, something that has frequently been impossible in Latin America. While politically popular candidates of the Left have experienced the greatest abuse, Left-leaning guerrillas have at times sabotaged elections as well.

This was true of the Peruvian guerrillas, Sendero Luminoso (Shining
Path), in the 1980s and early 1990s and then of Colombian guerrillas in
the late 1990s. These groups kidnapped election officials, burned ballots, and threatened prospective voters in local and congressional elections. Colombian guerrillas claimed they did so in protest against state
prevention of free and fair party activity and elections, and cited government and party corruption and attacks on candidates of the Left as
reasons for their electoral sabotage. Deepening the assault on electoral
rights, despite the continued formal facade of Colombian democracy,
military and paramilitary forces in turn killed thousands of guerrillas
and the leaders of one political party (among others) the guerrillas had
launched, Unión Patriótica (Patriotic Union; UP), until the rebel-formed
party eventually fell apart and the rebels abandoned electoral politics.

Formal political justice rooted in electoral rights also rests on respect
for outcomes at the polls. The "veto coups" that have recurrently swept
Latin America clearly reflect a fundamental disrespect for citizens' political rights (see Huntington 1968: 219–37), even when the military has
usurped power with some civilian backing. While such coups in the main
disappeared from the Latin American political repertoire in the closing
years of the twentieth century, the military and its growing paramilitary
allies continued on occasion to turn their guns on elected authorities.
This occurred at the grassroots level, and not only in countries, such as
Colombia, that were ripped apart by civil wars. Several mayors associated with the Partido dos Trabalhadores (Workers' Party; PT) in the state
of São Paulo in Brazil, for example, lost their lives at gunpoint in the
first years of the new century, and in Guatemala a similar fate befell public authorities and activists committed to the defense of human rights. At
the national level in Venezuela disaffected military, businessmen,
shopowners, and privileged workers destabilized the economy to try to
drive the elected populist leader Hugo Chávez from office.

Less violently, state-engineered electoral fraud covertly served to sabotage citizen rights while retaining a democratic veneer. To illustrate, the
outcomes of the presidential elections in Mexico in 1988 and in Peru
twelve years later were widely believed to be fraudulently manipulated.
Yet unlike years past, when electorates had publicly tolerated results they
privately questioned, in both countries ordinary voters and candidates

who felt unjustly deprived of the "right to win" publicly challenged state electoral manipulation. Anger over state disregard for electoral rights and outcomes stirred antifraud mobilizations after the 1988 Mexican balloting, with demonstrators arguing that the ruling Partido Revolucionario Institucional (Institutional Revolutionary Party; PRI) stole the election. Church-affiliated base communities inspired by Liberation Theology played an important role in mobilizing the campaign for citizen respect. In Mexico as elsewhere in the region clergy inspired by the new theology came to be key agents who spoke out against state violations of a broad range of human rights, not merely electoral injustices. Although the antifraud movement failed to change the official 1988 Mexican voting results, it planted the seeds for civic concern that made subsequent elections more transparent and opened the door for the year 2000 victory of the opposition Partido Acción Nacional (National Action Party; PAN) candidate Vicente Fox, the first non-PRI president elected to office in over seventy years.

In Peru that year the main opponent to Fujimori's effort to get himself reelected to a third term was Alejandro Toledo, who claimed state computer manipulation of the first-round electoral results. Initially he pressed for an electoral runoff, but then withdrew his candidacy. With the backing of international observers, consonant with the growing transborder concern with political and other human rights, Toledo challenged Fujimori's abuse of voter rights. In so doing he stirred widespread domestic unrest, including a major anti-Fujimori "demonstration of the four corners" in Lima. The latter reference to the four divisions of the ancient Inca empire illustrates how claims for modern political rights may be deliberately grounded by leaders in indigenous beliefs, customs, and claims to be the "authentic" representative of the popular will. While Fujimori survived the public challenge, he resigned shortly thereafter, when the widespread corruption in his administration was publicly revealed. And Toledo finally was elected to the presidency in mid-2001 in the election following Fujimori's resignation.

Societally Embedded Democratization

Social structures, with deep roots in class as well as in racial and ethnic inequities, generally change more gradually than the more episodically inclined polity, and thus they did not change concomitantly and automatically with Latin America's formal (re)democratization wave of the 1980s. Yet in the new political milieu, people in the region asserted themselves in new ways, partly through the party system and partly independently of it, and often in conjunction with nongovernmental organizations (NGOs).

Sybil Rhodes, in chapter 8, examines the region's most serious and exemplary effort at deepening democratic participation and institutional accountability and responsiveness through institutions of formal governance at the municipal level: in Porto Alegre, capital of the Brazilian state of Rio Grande do Sul. In her careful examination of the experience of "progressive pragmatism" and consultative community participation there, Rhodes highlights how the PT's pattern of governance broke the two previous modes of "doing politics," clientelism and populism. She shows a real deepening of the "implicit social contract," a deepening that was made to stick not just by extending more political rights to the populace, such as participation in municipal budgeting, but also by delivering collective goods such as roads, education, and health care more effectively and widely than had previous governments. Such performance seems to explain the government's ability both to impose new taxes and to collect old ones with more success, in a region of the world notoriously resistant to taxation. The city, in turn, has seen falling crime rates and a noticeably more equal distribution of income than other Brazilian cities. As a consequence, PT governments there could pursue socially progressive agendas while still practicing fiscal responsibility, an unusual pairing indeed. Although other municipalities attempted to reproduce the Porto Alegre model, they have done so typically with less success. Rhodes argues that a conjuncture in Porto Alegre of a relatively rich economy with a labor-friendly political culture and history was a condition conducive to the deepening of grassroots, administrative-governmental justice there.

In chapter 9, and in contrast to Rhodes, David Scott Palmer shows us how Latin Americans who lack access to such responsive political structures may invent their own ways of "doing politics," and thereby make the political system more responsive to their wants and needs. Palmer shows how, even in a multiparty and formally democratic regime, political parties and institutions have left poor people's needs untended. Instead of merely acquiescing to the situation or pressing for radical change, Peruvians in the areas he studied turned to "informal politics." Palmer makes a political parallel to the "informal economy" analysis of the Peruvian Hernando de Soto (1989). De Soto depicted how in the interstices of the regulated and so-called formal economy a more vibrant pattern of unregulated, informal business activity emerged. In like fashion, Palmer

observes that informal politics evolved to provide, through grassroots efforts, what formal political institutions could not or would not provide.
As responsive to societal concerns as informal politics may be, however,
it offers no guarantee of institutionalized justice, just as the informal economy provides no guaranteed labor protections for workers.

THE RISE OF ETHNIC CLAIMS TO JUSTICE

By the dawn of the twenty-first century, groups who until then had been at
the margins of society and whom elites presumed would either remain that
way or assimilate selectively and individually into the mainstream began
to claim new rights on a collective as well as individual basis. This was especially true of indigenous peoples; less so of racial minorities. Under the
new democracies and the few long-standing civilian regimes—for example, Mexico and Colombia—indigenous groups began to make claims associated with a newly framed concept of justice. These claims centered on
issues of equity, to be sure, but also on the right to be different.

The ethnic solidarities that came to the fore toward the end of the
twentieth century were partly premised on an articulation of previously
latent and repressed identities, which elites in the past had effectively
compelled subordinate ethnic groups either to conceal or to express only
in tolerated, transmuted forms, such as *indigenismo. Indigenismo* had
allowed indigenous groups symbolic national representation but had
provided them with no institutionalized rights. Scott's (1985, 1990)
analyses of acts of domination on the one hand and everyday forms of
resistance on the other help us understand how and why shifts from latent to manifest identities come about.

The newly conceived rights found expression in a new global legitimation of indigenous and other minority rights, just as the previously
discussed drives to hold authorities responsible for injustices they committed were grounded in new international conceptions of justice. With
respect to indigenous peoples we see how evolving universal values contributed, paradoxically, to the generation of claims premised on the right
to be distinctive.

Global dynamics influenced indigenous claims through the work of
NGOs, which gained a footing in the region during the economically
austere years of the 1980s. The NGOs provided ethnic groups with relevant material resources, skills, and social networks conducive to asserting ethnic claims. They also framed local movements in ways that
attracted international support (see Keck and Sikkink 1998). And so too

did the NGOs bring new conceptions of rights and spark new identities. In the changed context new ethnic identities, new objectives, and new bases of organization and communication all contributed to new indigenous claims, including by previously quiescent women.

But the new indigenous claims were rooted also in changed domestic circumstances, what Tarrow (1998) would call changed opportunity structures. In political terms, aside from newly specified constitutional rights, indigenous peoples faced fewer risks in asserting claims under the new democracies than under the previous authoritarian regimes. The new, more inclusionary governments were more tolerant of indigenous movements and claims, if for no other reason than opportunistic interest in the ethnic vote. Indeed, in countries with large Indian populations political parties sought to champion the concerns of newly politicized indigenous communities. Economically, neoliberal reforms had the unintended effect of stirring ethnic politicization when they eroded indigenous people's livelihoods. This occurred when governments rescinded long-standing community land rights, retracted social supports, and attracted investments to indigenous regions with dislocating effects. And socially and culturally, the Internet gave inspiration to indigenous claims, in providing access to new information and means to coordinate concerns with sympathetic groups worldwide.

Chapters 10, 11, and 12—by John Peeler, June Nash, and Beatriz Manz, respectively—highlight different aspects of these emergent indigenous trends in the region. Peeler focuses on the diversity of new claims made by indigenous peoples and movements in Ecuador, Bolivia, Peru, and Guatemala, the countries with the largest indigenous populations, but also on the Zapatista movement in Chiapas, Mexico. He points both to cross-national similarities and differences in claiming of rights. At one extreme, Ecuadorian indigenous communities have asserted claims for ethnic autonomy; at the other extreme, Peru's indigenous Quechua-speaking citizens have made more individualistically grounded claims to rights. The Ecuadorian community-based concept of citizenship is premised on collective rights as members of specific ethnic groups, with a kind of "plurinational" relation to the national government. The Peruvian indigenous variant, by contrast, identifies with the state and is associated with a quest for the extension of individual citizenship rights already enjoyed by others in society. While some Peruvian parties clearly have sought votes through targeting indigenous peoples, including Fujimori in 1990 and Toledo in 2000 and 2001, they have combined ethnic with nonethnic concerns. The Peruvian variant is at least partly a consequence of how the guerrilla group Shining Path politicized the country, through fear and force, along nonethnic lines in the 1980s and early 1990s, and then of how the state sought to rein in the movement through state-promoted, community-based *rondas campesinas* (community self-defense organizations) and a concomitant militarization of the countryside. The joint processes submerged collective, pan-village ethnic identities. Peru's Amazonian Indians bear a greater resemblance to the Ecuadorian *indigenistas,* but they are less mobilized, more isolated, and far fewer in number (see Brysk and Wise 1995: 25–29). The two indigenous perspectives, individual and collective, refract differently through national political life. Ecuadorian indigenous peoples, with their claims to autonomy, seek *particularized* treatment in ways that differentiate them from the national citizenry. The Peruvian indigenous peoples, by contrast, seek a more *universalized* participation and equality of treatment as citizens of a nation.

Meanwhile, in contrast to both the individualistic and collectivistic conceptions, Bolivian indigenous claims tend to be couched in terms of class, namely *campesino* (peasant farmer) claims to power, influence, and rights. Bolivia's 1952 revolution in part accounts for this framing. In official discourse that revolution led to a cultural redefinition of the *indio* as *campesino,* a redefinition associated with reforms that gave *campesinos* land and electoral rights. Even on the fiftieth anniversary of the revolution, presidential candidates understood that their appeal to the indigenous and *mestizo* majority rested mainly on appeals to populist themes and rights to coca-growing, which Washington, preoccupied with the U.S. domestic drug-consumption problem, sought to bring to heel.

Central to the emergence of the new indigenous claims and their different variants has been an emergent indigenous leadership, or, as in Chiapas, a nonindigenous leadership with a strong indigenous component and commitment. The leadership has the social capital to function in the national and international as well as indigenous arenas (see Warren 1998). In Guatemala, for example, where a pan-Mayan movement arose, well-educated indigenous advocates typically experienced partial but blocked socioeconomic mobility at the same time that they maintained ties with their roots. With the capacity to express and disseminate ideas about indigenous peoples bilingually, they helped create and remake indigenous culture in a manner that built bridges among indigenous communities, which often do not speak the same Indian language as one another, and also between these communities and other lower-, working-, and middle-class people in their countries. The leadership also sought to make visible a history that the dominant class had suppressed but which indigenous peoples had kept covertly alive over the years through what Scott (1990) refers to as "hidden transcripts." The changes approximate what Habermas (e.g., 1970, 1971) referred to as the "ideal speech situation," in which only the power of reason, uncorrupted by inequalities of power, wealth, and the like, prevails in establishing common understandings of social life. Far more than the previous, Hispanic-dominated discourse systems, the new indigenous-generated discourses began to approximate—however limited their reach—"unconstrained discourses," as Habermas termed them.

In chapter 11, June Nash highlights how state violence against indigenous peoples—directly and through its privatized counterparts—contributed to the rise of a major social movement in the Mexican state of Chiapas. Yet such violence did not alone "produce" that movement, because it was fostered by an astute leadership combining indigenous, feminist, and other demands for justice. The Zapatista movement burst onto the public stage there on January 1, 1994, timed deliberately with the day the North American Free Trade Agreement (NAFTA) went into effect. Nash documents how the movement had the unintended effect of activating new perceptions and demands with a feminist and not merely indigenous cast. She shows that resistance to male-hegemonic practices emerged as conditions in the region changed. Never-married, separated, and widowed women, less subject to strong male counterpressures, were especially drawn into the new forms of organizing, notably via the Ejército Zapatista de Liberación Nacional (Zapatista Army of National Liberation; EZLN), the Zapatistas' armed wing. With 30 percent of the EZLN's commanders women, the insurgent leadership issued an unprecedented "Declaration of the New Law for Women." This document expressed a newfound commitment to feminist principles, including demands for women's control of their own fertility and a call for an end to all hierarchies, including men's authority in the home. Social forces, however, blocked implementation of such principles. Military and paramilitary violence "militarized" everyday life at the community as well as family level: Nash notes a rise in wife and child abuse, erosion of trust among community members, increased threats to subsistence, and a retraction of the state's (already minimal) commitment to its tacit social contract.

Meanwhile, Beatriz Manz provides us in chapter 12 with an in-depth portrayal of indigenous people in one town in the Ixcán region of Guatemala, which experienced the pervasive violence that so much of the nation suffered. Manz shows how the experience of repression may deeply "define" social life in the absence of a leadership able to transform identities and/or channel demands for social justice. She conveys in microcosm how the indigenous people experienced events that ripped families and communities apart, and also recounts people's attempts to remember and make discursive sense of what transpired. Manz's attempt to gain people's trust and unearth their "real" feelings and interpretations of those events shows us some of the special challenges both prosecutors and scholars face in trying to make state actors accountable for terroristic actions—already noted in the above summary of Leigh Payne's chapter. Such testimonies are exceptionally hard to elicit in the quasi- (or fully) paranoid postwar situation in Guatemala, where one astonished man, who had tried to present to Manz answers that he thought she wanted to hear, finally said to her, "You want to hear what I *really* think?" (emphasis added). Manz also detects divergent responses among those who fled and those who stayed in the village as the army militarized it, yet there remained a shared consensus among all that their interests were not represented nationally by the military.

Looking back across the diversity of emergent ethnic claims in Latin America, we can confidently conclude that the varied indigenous movements were structurally patterned but not strictly predetermined. The variety emerged under somewhat similar cross-border macroeconomic and political conditions, revealing how even common ethnic identity and a similar history of ethnic oppression do not in themselves generate a singular conception of justice and perceived rights or a single movement to redress grievances.

Democratization also surely contributed to the new public concern with race-based rights in certain countries in the region, although that turn also was not inevitable. On a much more reduced scale in countries with African populations, race (or color) also has newly become a basis for making racialized claims. This has been true in both Colombia and Brazil. Colombia's 1991 constitution extended collective rights to black communities there and advanced the goal of a pluriethnic and multicultural nation (Gureso, Rosero, and Escobar 1998). The new national vision consecrated in that document served as the basis for incipient black-community mobilizing for cultural, ethnic, and territorial demands in the Pacific portion of the country. Leaders framed the movement partly in terms of the government's redefinition of citizenship, but they had difficulty getting support that cut across the class divide. Uninterested in being singled out as a social minority, few black elites supported efforts to make such racialized claims.

Race-based movements in Brazil, as well, tended to be class-specific, owing to the continued significance of class. Long working against race-based movements there, the dominant discourse speaks of race as a cultural, not a biological, phenomenon, implying an ability to "pass," that is, improve one's social standing with education and presentation of self (more so than in contrast to the United States and South Africa [cf. Marger 1994]). Yet, for the first time in the country's history, under President Fernando Henrique Cardoso, in 2001 the government publicly acknowledged racial injustices and announced efforts to redress them. Among other things, it announced race-based affirmative employment action for blacks in state ministries. Faced with inevitable elite political resistance, with difficulties in defining race in a society where racial differences had long been denied, and with no guarantee that future governments would honor Cardoso's public commitment, the long-term effects remain to be seen.

The various social efforts to redefine ethnic and, to a limited extent, race-based rights reveal the limitations of frames of analysis other than the contextual institutional approach applied and advanced here. Reflecting back on the frames briefly summarized at the start of this chapter, modernization theory would predict ethnicity to wither away as Third World peoples were exposed to modern ideas and culture, gained command of Western languages, and were schooled in Western ways. Supposedly, exposure to Western ideas and practices would contribute to—not to mention actively call for—assimilation and the suppression of ethnicity. But these very conditions were shown here to give rise to ethnic-based claims, including the right to be different. In essence, the effects of exposure to westernization are historically contingent.

Feminist analyses, in turn, reveal that even a frame that accounts for and explains ethnic claims needs to be sensitive as well to women's-rights issues, which may intersect in odd ways with ethnic grievances and ethnic claims to justice. Yet, feminist analyses cannot alone explain when and why concern about gender justice has varied at different times and in different places and taken different forms quite independently of discrimination against women. While postmodernists offer a frame sensitive to the importance both of ethnicity and gender, especially their localized variants, they tend to essentialize such identities, especially among marginalized social groups whose worldviews are declared inaccessible to outsiders.[5] Hence, they do not analytically account for the complex cultural borrowings, diffusions, and outright hybridities visible among groups who have never undergone experiences of post-modernity (García Canclini 1995). Unlike the Marxists they have so deeply criticized, they also lack an analytic frame that accounts for and explains how broader macroeconomic forces and class dynamics become locally consequential. Yet class analyses, for their part, miss the important new ways that marginalized groups, such as indigenous peoples, independent of their relationship to the means of production, have come to conceive justice, sometimes in ways shared among members across class lines.

THE ORGANIZATION OF THIS BOOK

The chapters in this book are grouped according to the main political bases of injustice outlined in this introduction, although a number of contributors admittedly speak to more than one set of issues. The book starts—in chapters by Oxhorn, Hilbink, and Pérez-Liñán—with a focus on the foundations of political rights and on those political institutions forming the structural pillars of democracy. Chapters address how and why societal dynamics have subverted, transformed, and transmuted democratic processes, in function if not in form. The next section is composed of chapters—by Karl, Payne, and Chernick—that shed light on contradictions between extreme societal inequalities and principles of equality embedded in political citizenship and on the nature and impact of state violations of the implicit social contract between those governing and those governed. The next set of chapters, by Rhodes and Palmer, concern societal efforts to embed democracy more fully within the social order, so as to involve the citizenry more directly in governance and to foster mobilization that would engender more responsive government. In the final set of chapters, that same thematic continues, but with an ethnic focus. The authors of these chapters, Peeler, Nash, and Manz, examine efforts by previously excluded indigenous peoples to be treated justly and to have their own conceptions of justice honored.

Each section starts with the most general, broad-based, and comparative chapter, then moves to chapters with rich, detailed case studies. Taken together, the chapters should make transparent how conceptions of justice are socially constructed and contested, and historically contingent. People often have disparate views of what is and what is not just, but the views of the privileged are often the more visible and honored ones. Nonetheless, at the same time that the socially and politically disprivileged may not feel free to make their voices and views publicly known, covertly they may seek to correct injustices. And when they feel conditions no longer tolerable, or when established social controls break down, we see them capable of fighting for their standards of justice. An improved understanding of people's views of a just political order—and of those social forces that obstruct or facilitate the broadest access to such a just, if not ideal, world—should be of both academic and practical import.

NOTES

1. This thesis is inspired by W. I. Thomas (in Coser 1971: 521), a founding father of American sociology, who perceptively argued that situations defined as real are real in their consequences.

2. See Eckstein and Wickham-Crowley (2002) for an analysis of economic and social injustices, and struggles for associated rights, in Latin America.

3. The massacres occurring under his regime continue to haunt the memory of survivors, as Beatriz Manz vividly depicts in chapter 12.

4. The Marxian view of "bourgeois democracy," in which business concedes the "right to rule" for the "right to make money," entrusting a political class to protect and defend its economic interests at the same time that citizen rights formally expand, is the most famous conceptualization of this. But perhaps the most pithy version of this tension comes from Max Weber (1946: 230), who suggested that under bureaucratized, industrial-capitalist systems there would be strong pressures (amid countervailing forces) for "crypto-plutocracies" to emerge; that is, rule by the wealthy, albeit in hidden form.

5. Thus Lyotard (2000: 428), one of the key founders of postmodern theory, simply asserts the "heteromorphous nature of language games" and the fact of mutual unintelligibility. This entire formulation of multiple (sub?)groups, each with its own perspective that cannot be known by outsiders, presumes the factual separation of humankind into strictly segmented groupings, which is factually false.

REFERENCES

Alvarez, Sonia E., Evelina Dagnino, and Arturo Escobar, eds. 1998. *Cultures of Politics/Politics of Cultures: Re-Visioning Latin American Social Movements.* Boulder, Colo.: Westview Press.

Archer, Dane, and Rosemary Gartner. 1984. *Violence and Crime in Cross-National Perspective.* New Haven, Conn.: Yale University Press.

Bendix, Reinhard. 1964. *Nation-Building and Citizenship: Studies of Our Changing Social Order.* New York: John Wiley and Sons.

Berger, Peter L. 1974. *Pyramids of Sacrifice: Political Ethics and Social Change.* New York: Basic Books.

———. 1986. *The Capitalist Revolution: Fifty Propositions about Prosperity, Equality, and Liberty.* New York: Basic Books.

Brysk, Alison, and Carol Wise. 1995. *Economic Adjustment and Ethnic Conflict in Bolivia, Peru, and Mexico.* Working paper 216. Latin American Program, Woodrow Wilson International Center for Scholars, Washington, D.C.

Cavarozzi, Marcelo. 1992. "Beyond Transitions to Democracy in Latin America." *Journal of Latin American Studies* 24, no. 3 (October): 665–84.

Coser, Lewis. 1977. *Masters of Sociological Thought: Ideas in Historical and Social Context.* 2d ed. New York: Harcourt Brace Jovanovich.

Dahrendorf, Ralf. 1968. *Essays in the Theory of Society.* Stanford, Calif.: Stanford University Press.

Eckstein, Susan, and Timothy P. Wickham-Crowley, eds. 2002. *Struggles for Social Rights in Latin America.* New York: Routledge.

Evans, Peter. 1995. *Embedded Autonomy: States and Industrial Transformation.* Princeton, N.J.: Princeton University Press.

Evans, Peter, Dietrich Rueschemeyer, and Theda Skocpol, eds. 1985. *Bringing the State Back In.* New York: Cambridge University Press.

García Canclini, Néstor. 1995. *Hybrid Cultures: Strategies for Entering and Leaving Modernity.* Trans. Christopher L. Chiappari and Silvia L. López. Minneapolis: University of Minnesota Press.

González Casanova, Pablo. 1970. *Democracy in Mexico.* New York: Oxford University Press.

Gureso, Libia, Carlos Rosero, and Arturo Escobar. 1998. "The Process of Black Community Organizing in the Southern Pacific Coast Region of Colombia." In *Cultures of Politics/Politics of Cultures: Re-Visioning Latin American Social Movements,* ed. Sonia E. Alvarez, Evelina Dagnino, and Arturo Escobar, pp. 196–219. Boulder, Colo.: Westview Press.

Habermas, Jürgen. 1970. "Toward a Theory of Communicative Competence." In *Recent Sociology No. 2,* ed. Hans Peter Dreitzel, pp. 115–48. New York: Macmillan.

———. 1971. *Knowledge and Human Interests.* Trans. Jeremy J. Shapiro. Boston: Beacon Press.

Heilbroner, Robert. 1974. *An Inquiry into the Human Prospect.* New York: W. W. Norton.

Huntington, Samuel P. 1968. *Political Order in Changing Societies.* New Haven, Conn.: Yale University Press.

Inglehart, Ronald, Miguel Basañez, and Alejandro Moreno. 1998. *Human Values and Beliefs: A Cross-Cultural Sourcebook.* Ann Arbor: University of Michigan Press.

Keck, Margaret, and Kathryn Sikkink. 1998. *Activists beyond Borders.* Ithaca, N.Y.: Cornell University Press.

Lengermann, Patricia Madoo, and Jill Niebrugge-Brantley. 1992. "Contemporary Feminist Theory." In *Sociological Theory,* 3d ed., ed. George Ritzer, pp. 447–96. New York: McGraw-Hill.

Lyotard, Jean-François. 2000 [1984]. "The Post-Modern Condition: A Report on Knowledge." In *Readings in Social Theory,* 3d ed., ed. James Farganis, pp. 418–32. New York: McGraw-Hill.

Marger, Martin. 1994. *Race and Ethnic Relations: American and Global Perspectives*. 3d ed. Belmont, Calif.: Wadsworth.

Marshall, T. H. 1950. *Citizenship and Social Class, and Other Essays*. Cambridge: Cambridge University Press.

Moore, Barrington, Jr. 1972. *Reflections on the Causes of Human Misery, and upon Certain Proposals to Eliminate Them*. Boston: Beacon Books.

———. 1978. *Injustice: The Social Bases of Obedience and Revolt*. White Plains, N.Y.: M. E. Sharpe.

Newman, Graeme, ed. 1999. *Global Report on Crime and Justice*. United Nations Office of Drug Control and Crime Prevention. New York and Oxford: Oxford University Press.

Ochoa, Enrique C. 1987. "The Rapid Expansion of Voter Participation in Latin America: Presidential Elections, 1845–1986." In *Statistical Abstract of Latin America*, vol. 25, ed. James W. Wilkie and David Lorey, pp. 861–904. Los Angeles: UCLA Latin American Center Publications, University of California.

PDBA. 1999. Political Database of the Americas: Constitutions. Georgetown University web site, http://www.georgetown.edu/pdba (September).

Ramirez, Francisco O., Yasemin Soysal, and Suzanne Shanahan. 1997. "The Changing Logic of Political Citizenship: Cross-National Acquisition of Women's Suffrage Rights, 1890 to 1990." *American Sociological Review* 62, no. 5 (October): 735–45.

Rawls, John. 1971. *A Theory of Justice*. Cambridge, Mass.: Harvard University Press, Belknap Press.

Rokkan, Stein. 1966. "Mass Suffrage, Secret Voting, and Political Participation." In *Political Sociology*, ed. Lewis Coser, pp. 101–31. New York: Harper and Row.

Rueschemeyer, Dietrich, Evelyne Huber Stephens, and John D. Stephens. 1992. *Capitalist Development and Democracy*. Chicago: University of Chicago Press.

SALA (Statistical Abstract of Latin America). 1992. Vol. 29. Ed. James W. Wilkie. Los Angeles: UCLA Latin American Center Publications, University of California.

Schmitter, Philippe. 1972. "Paths to Political Development in Latin America." In *Changing Latin America: New Interpretations of Its Politics and Society*, ed. Douglas Chalmers, pp. 83–105. New York: Academy of Political Science, Columbia University.

Scott, James C. 1976. *The Moral Economy of the Peasant: Rebellion and Subsistence in Southeast Asia*. New Haven, Conn.: Yale University Press.

———. 1985. *Weapons of the Weak: Everyday Forms of Peasant Resistance*. New Haven, Conn.: Yale University Press.

———. 1990. *Domination and the Arts of Resistance: Hidden Transcripts*. New Haven, Conn.: Yale University Press.

Sen, Amartya. 1999. *Development as Freedom*. New York: Alfred A. Knopf.

Soares, Gláucio Ary Dillon. 2000. "Programas de estabilización y presidencialismo imperial: Argentina, Brasil, y Perú." *Estudios Sociológicos* (Mexico) 18, no. 52 (January–April): 3–23.

Soto, Hernando de, with Instituto de Libertad y Democracia. 1989. *The Other Path: The Invisible Revolution in the Third World.* Trans. June Abbott. New York: Harper and Row.

Stepan, Alfred. 1978. *The State and Society: Peru in Comparative Perspective.* Princeton, N.J.: Princeton University Press.

Tarrow, Sidney. 1998. *Power in Movement: Social Movements, Collective Action, and Politics.* 2d ed. Cambridge: Cambridge University Press.

Thompson, E. P. 1971. "The Moral Economy of the English Crowd in the Eighteenth Century." *Past and Present* 50 (February): 76–136.

Véliz, Claudio. 1980. *The Centralist Tradition of Latin America.* Princeton, N.J.: Princeton University Press.

Walton, John. 2001 [1989]. "Debt, Protest, and the State in Latin America." In *Power and Popular Protest: Latin American Social Movements,* ed. Susan Eckstein, pp. 299–328. Berkeley: University of California Press.

Warren, Kay. 1998. "Indigenous Movements as a Challenge to the Unified Social Movement Paradigm for Guatemala." In *Cultures of Politics/Politics of Cultures: Re-Visioning Latin American Social Movements,* ed. Sonia E. Alvarez, Evelina Dagnino, and Arturo Escobar, pp. 165–95. Boulder, Colo.: Westview Press.

Weber, Max. 1946. *From Max Weber: Essays in Sociology.* Ed. and trans. Hans H. Gerth and C. Wright Mills. New York: Oxford University Press.

Weissert, Will. 2000. "Courts Gain Power in Latin America." *Boston Globe* (September 7), p. 9.

Wiarda, Howard. 1981. *Corporatism and National Development in Latin America.* Boulder, Colo.: Westview Press.

Wickham-Crowley, Timothy. 1991. *Exploring Revolution: Essays on Latin American Insurgency and Revolutionary Theory.* Armonk, N.Y.: M. E. Sharpe.

Wilson, Scott. 2001. "Chronicle of a Massacre Foretold: Colombian Villagers Implicate Army in Paramilitary Strike." *Washington Post* (January 28), pp. A1, A24.

PART ONE

Political Institutions, Rights, and Injustice

Social Inequality, Civil Society, and the Limits of Citizenship in Latin America

PHILIP OXHORN

At least since Aristotle, the existence of social inequality has posed a central problem for the theory and practice of democracy. Although political democracy may ultimately be undermined by socioeconomic inequality, a certain level of inequality is inevitable given the reality of modern democratic politics. This is because socioeconomic inequality is unavoidable in market economies, as Marx recognized (albeit in an exaggerated way) so long ago. Efforts at social "leveling" will meet with stiff resistance. In Latin America, there may even be a direct correlation between the level of inequality and the resistance to equity-enhancing measures. Extremes in socioeconomic inequality can raise the stakes of the politics of (re)distribution, making substantial reforms least likely in precisely those countries where they are most needed for maintaining democratic stability.

Here lies the principal insight of T. H. Marshall (1950): socioeconomic inequality could be legitimized in Western democracies only through the gradual extension and expansion of the universal rights of citizenship. In what would prove to be a truly virtuous circle over the course of some three hundred years of British and, by extension, European history, the evolution of citizenship rights began with the establishment of civil rights, defined as "the rights necessary for individual freedom—liberty of person, freedom of speech, thought and faith, the right to own property and to conclude valid contracts, and the right to justice" (Marshall 1950: 10–11). Once civil rights were recognized, citizenship would then continue to expand to include, first, political rights in the form of universal suffrage and, later, the social rights of citizenship associated with the modern welfare state (access to health care, various state policies to ensure a minimal standard of living, and so on). In the process, the social inequality associated with capitalism was legitimated, as the social and political foundations upon which modern capitalism could thrive were successfully put into place.

It is precisely this insight that is often overlooked in debates on social justice in Latin America, despite the resurgence of free-market capitalism. The unprecedented ascendance of political democracy, with its concomitant guarantees of political rights, has shifted attention away from Marshall's original focus on the evolution of citizenship rights. The focus is now more on trying to understand the *quality* of existing democratic regimes. Aside from the high social costs implied by severe limits on effective citizenship rights (crime, poverty, economic insecurity, and so on), there is always the danger that growing levels of social frustration will be vented in either a resurgence of demagogic populism or the reemergence of extremism on both the Right and Left (Oxhorn 1998b). In a pattern that is very different from the one described by Marshall half a century ago, the granting of political rights in many new democracies has been accompanied by the increasingly precarious nature of civil rights and the increasing limits—if not actual reversals—of the social rights of citizenship.

In this chapter, I attempt to apply certain insights from Marshall, which deal with the interrelationship between distinct types of citizenship rights and social inequality, in order to understand some of the principal challenges facing Latin American democracies today. Going beyond Marshall, I propose to understand the development of citizenship rights as a process intimately linked to the development of civil society. For the purposes of this argument, civil society is defined as "the social fabric formed by a multiplicity of self-constituted territorially- and functionally-based units which peacefully coexist and collectively *resist subordination* to the state, at the same time that they *demand inclusion* into national political structures" (Oxhorn 1995b: 251–52). In the first part, I argue that citizenship rights are socially constructed and that where civil society is weak, the social construction of citizenship rights is correspondingly narrower. More specifically, I reinterpret Marshall's arguments about the evolution of citizenship rights by suggesting that the process he described reflected the accumulation of power resources by Britain's working class. I briefly contrast the British experience with that of Latin America, where a similar process of power accumulation historically did not occur, and highlight the implications of alternative paths in the development of citizenship rights for the emergence of strong civil societies.

The second part of this chapter looks at some current problems in Latin American democracies. In most cases, political rights preceded the effective guarantee of basic civil rights, which generally remain notoriously weak. I argue that the popular struggles against authoritarian regimes in the 1970s and 1980s did not lead to the same cumulative process described by Marshall. This is because the elitist nature of these transitions cut short the process by which civil society developed. It also reflects parallel processes of economic change that have fragmented and disarticulated civil society. In the conclusion, I explore possible alternatives for strengthening civil society as an essential mechanism for expanding citizenship rights by making existing democratic regimes more inclusionary.

CIVIL SOCIETY AND THE
SOCIAL CONSTRUCTION OF CITIZENSHIP

In his classic study of the historical evolution of modern citizenship rights, T. H. Marshall argued that citizenship was that status of equal rights and duties shared by all full members of a political community. The traditional social divisions originating in Europe's feudal past were becoming increasingly untenable as the spread of capitalism gave rise to the emergence of new social classes defined by their productive role in market economies. To ameliorate growing social tensions created by rising socioeconomic inequality, "[the] differential status, associated with class, function and family, was replaced by the single uniform status of citizenship, which provided the foundation of inequality on which the structure of [capitalist] inequality could be built" (Marshall 1950: 34). Using Britain as his model, Marshall saw that the emergence of modern universal rights of citizenship paralleled the growth of the market economy. The specific content of the rights and duties of citizenship would continue to evolve in tandem with the requirements of capitalist accumulation. As a consequence, Marshall argued, political rights in the now established liberal democratic regimes were necessarily preceded by guarantees of basic civil rights to the working class. Once political rights were extended to all citizens, the evolution of citizenship rights could enter a new phase characterized by the extension of the social rights of citizenship associated with the modern welfare state.

This process began in the eighteenth century, because the emerging capitalist economy required the institutionalization of property rights through the enforcement of basic civil rights, and because the new capitalist society had to legitimate the resultant social inequality with a new principal: citizenship. Civil rights thus became the cornerstone of modern conceptions of citizenship. The formative period for political rights then began in the nineteenth century. Without the newly created status of "citizen," political rights that were independent of economic status were inconceivable. This is because, unlike the earlier creation of civil rights, the evolution of political rights of citizenship entailed the "granting of old rights to new sections of the population. . . . Political rights were defective, not in content, but in distribution—defective, that is to say, by the standards of democratic citizenship" (Marshall 1950: 19). Civil rights, in effect, created a new standard for evaluating political rights. Industrial change and the new conception of civil rights made old conceptions of rights obsolete. The process of establishing the political rights of citizenship culminated, in the 1918 British Reform Act, with the adoption of universal manhood suffrage.[1]

With political rights extended to all (male) adults, the evolution of citizenship rights could reach its full potential with the addition of social rights. Workers' right to vote translated into new social policies that began to narrow the gap between one's salary and one's real standard of living, including state subsidies. For Marshall, decreased economic inequality due to economic development, combined with the social integration achieved through universal civil and political rights, generated a new social consensus for the minimization of social inequality. The modern welfare state was born and a three-hundred-year historical process appeared (at least in retrospect) as a virtuous arc along which the cumulative rights of the lower classes had continued to grow until a democratic class compromise between representatives of big business and workers could be reached. While not eliminated, social inequality was significantly reduced, so that "citizenship itself became, in certain respects, the architect of legitimate social inequality" (Marshall 1950: 9).

With increasing demands for the expansion of citizenship rights to include dimensions Marshall never contemplated (including gender, ethnicity, ecology, and community), as well as the curtailing of social rights in many democracies (particularly Britain) that suggests a reversibility he did not anticipate, the limits to Marshall's understanding of citizenship are evident (Turner 1992). These limits are the result of the inadequacies of Marshall's essay as a *causal* theory of citizenship rights. Despite some isolated references, the role of class conflict and social struggle in defining and expanding citizenship rights is largely ignored. Marshall adopts a deterministic, almost functionalist view of the evolution of citizenship rights from the perspective of capitalist economic development and political stability.[2] There is an implicit assumption that the interests of the working class and of capitalists are complementary rather than contradictory. In the first instance, capitalists required civil rights in order to protect their interests. This, in turn, was portrayed as unleashing a seemingly inevitable teleological process in which economic development created a new societal consensus surrounding universal rights of citizenship. The institutionalization of citizenship rights in Britain was able to keep pace with changing public attitudes, in large part because continued economic prosperity raised levels of economic equality independently of state redistributive policies. Ultimately, British economic prosperity and the new social consensus that it created allowed for an increasingly direct attack by the state on any remaining sources of social inequity.

In Latin America, the historical tendency has been the exact opposite: economic growth has generally exacerbated economic inequality, while state redistributive policies have met with fierce, frequently violent opposition (Oxhorn and Ducatenzeiler 1999). Marshall's economic determinism and his focus on a single path for the development of universal citizenship rights in many ways anticipated the modernization theories of socioeconomic development of the 1960s and 1970s. These theories also envisioned a single, conflict-free, and more or less inevitable developmental path, loosely based on the experiences of the first countries to industrialize in the West.

Unlike modernization theories, however, Marshall's account of the evolution of citizenship rights is not necessarily inconsistent with approaches stressing the role of conflict and contingency in the social construction of citizenship. British capitalists may have enjoyed economic prosperity and relative political stability for centuries, but this is better understood as the consequence of concessions brought about by social struggles initiated by workers, rather than as the outcome of any teleology of capitalist development. Capitalists elsewhere have also done extraordinarily well by following distinct paths of political and economic development, in which limited social rights of citizenship were in effect given to workers as a way of co-opting or controlling worker mobilization in the absence of effective political and civil rights (Oxhorn 1995b, 1998b; Mann 1996).

Rather than being the outcome of the functional requirements of capitalism or a consequence of a new social consensus associated with modernity, a causal theory of citizenship rights should focus on the development of civil society within particular countries and civil society's interaction with the state. To understand this, civil society is defined so as to stress the power relations within a given society by emphasizing the centrality of organization and struggle. The dual dynamic of resistance and inclusion that is characteristic of civil societies implies that strong civil societies reflect a relative dispersion of political power throughout entire polities.[3] The ability of distinct groups to organize themselves contributes to the dispersion of political power in their favor. The existence of multiple self-constituted organizations based on social class, gender, religion, ethnicity, culture, language, community, shared collective identity, and so on, allows these groups to define and defend their collective interests in interactions with other actors, including the state, to improve their position within a given society. This dispersion of political power helps mitigate the tendency in capitalist societies for the interests of dominant actors and social classes to subordinate the interests of less powerful actors and social classes. While civil society's full potential can be reached only within the space that a democratic regime can provide, the emergence of civil society historically has preceded the advent of democratic regimes in Western Europe and is to a certain extent independent of the existence of a democratic political regime. In contrast to Marshall, the argument here is that stable democratic rule is the contingent outcome of successful struggles by civil-society actors to achieve and maintain it. In societies where political power is more concentrated, civil society is weaker and the prospects for long-term democratic stability are correspondingly lower, as political stability is maintained by suppressing civil society's autonomy.

By focusing on power relations, it becomes clear how civil society as a concept is distinct from economic structure. In particular, civil society is characterized more by "institutionalized societal pluralism" (Schmitter 1986: 6) than by the relative strength of class-based organizations such as employers groups, trade unions, and peasant organizations. Other civil-society actors may include economic sectors and professions, independent territorial communities, ethnic and linguistic groups, religions and sects, voluntary associations, and gender and generational groupings, among others. Shared identities, the ability for self-organization, and a history of collective struggle are sources of power that can enable disadvantaged groups to challenge the status quo.

While civil society is distinct from economic structure, economic structure conditions civil society's potential in important ways. In particular, economic structure creates shared interests that can serve as a basis for the emergence of important collective actors (e.g., workers, professionals, business groups, peasants). It also affects the availability of resources for sustaining different forms of organizational activity, and may affect the ability of different groups to engage in collective action (for example, the difficulties of organizing workers in the informal sector of the economy, as compared to organizing those in the formal sector). As economic structures evolve over time (due, for example, to periods of prolonged economic growth, processes of industrialization or de-industrialization, changes in state development policies, and/or changes in a particular country's insertion in the international economy), the potential for civil society to continue to develop may also be affected. To the extent that economic change contributes to a greater dispersal of power resources and increases the capacity of distinct groups to organize themselves, it should facilitate greater levels of social inclusion and democratization. Conversely, if economic change increases the level of economic concentration or is accompanied by the erection of new barriers to collective action on the part of distinct groups, it would tend to undermine civil society and allow for a greater contraction of social inclusion and democratization. The former scenario is essentially what happened in England, as described by Marshall. As we shall see, the latter scenario is more typical of Latin America.

As Tilly (1996: 9) notes, historically it was the "struggle and bargaining between expanding states and their subjects [that] created citizenship where it had not previously existed." While today there is perhaps greater consensus than ever before on the normative content of democratic citizenship rights, these rights are still contested in practice, as a consequence of their uneven coverage and their ambiguous impact on important aspects of a given society (gender relations, landowning patterns, indigenous cultures, and the environment, for example). There is still no consensus about how to implement specific rights of citizenship. In most new democracies, conflicts over basic citizenship rights were central but unresolved issues in the transition process. The failure of democratic institutions to address these shortcomings after the transition, as will be discussed below, is often the principal source of their fragility. Agency is a key to understanding how citizenship rights actually evolve or stagnate. The pressures for expanding citizenship rights that emerge (or fail to emerge) from within civil society, and how those

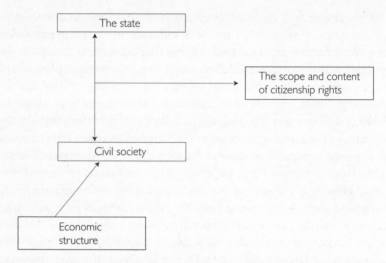

Figure 2.1. The social construction of citizenship rights.

pressures are dealt with by the state, are central to any causal theory of citizenship.

These arguments are summarized schematically in figure 2.1. The scope and content of citizenship rights are determined in specific countries by the interaction between the state and civil society. It is through the struggles (or lack thereof) of different organized groups within civil society vis-à-vis each other and the state that citizenship rights are socially constructed. Civil society's contours and relative strengths, in turn, are conditioned by the nature of a particular country's economic structure. In societies characterized by weak civil societies and/or closed, authoritarian regimes that deliberately seek to control (if not destroy) civil society, citizenship rights are severely constrained. Conversely, the strength of civil society is reflected in the breadth and multifaceted content of citizenship rights through civil society's capacity to expand citizenship rights and check authoritarian tendencies at the level of the state.

It is important to highlight the collectivist dimension of citizenship rights. Citizenship rights are obviously individual rights, yet the struggle for them can only be carried out collectively, and collective demands for citizenship rights are essential to make them effective. There is a certain paradox in this observation: the liberal ideal of individual freedom, so closely associated with the ideal of universal citizenship, cannot be achieved unless individuals organize collectively to demand respect for the rights such freedom requires. "Individual" rights are in effect granted to entire classes of people (workers, women, illiterates, etc.), even if their normative justification rests on liberal premises. Marshall (1950: 43) recognized this paradox, noting that "civil rights were in origin intensely individual, and that is why they harmonised with the individualistic phase of capitalism....[Yet] groups were enabled to enact legally as individuals," particularly trade unions. Citizenship rights are collective rights in practice, regardless of the intent of liberal reformers.

Social rights, in particular, have a collective dimension that blurs the distinction between individual and collective rights of citizenship. Social security and public health care, for example, are classic examples of the social rights of citizenship that are group based. Moreover, many of the social rights of citizenship demanded by social movements that are not class based are not reducible to individualist premises. Formal rights intended to create more equal gender relations, promote cultural autonomy, and protect the environment, for example, may even challenge the narrow liberal basis of citizenship that Marshall envisioned as culminating in social rights of citizenship in England. This is because their normative basis may not rest on *individual* rights and freedom, but rather on the autonomy and freedom of entire groups, if not the human race more generally.

This collectivist dimension of citizenship rights is in many ways the essence of strong civil society. What distinguishes civil society from other social formations is the nature of its collective actors and their specific demands or objectives. A good example of this is the working class. In societies that have experienced a minimal level of industrialization, the working class is an important potential actor. Whether or not the organized working class will be part of civil society will depend on how the movement is organized and establishes its goals. In nineteenth-century Western Europe and early-twentieth-century Latin America, the organized working class was a key actor in democratization processes (Rueschemeyer, Stephens, and Stephens 1992). As Bendix (1964) argued for Western Europe, the socialist (and nationalist) movements of the nineteenth century should be seen as political, reflecting the political alienation of the working class seeking *integration* into the sociopolitical system. Only rarely did the working class organize as a revolutionary force, with goals that were explicitly antithetical to the existence of a strong civil society.

Turning to Latin America through the 1970s, working-class demands for integration into the sociopolitical system proved historically much less successful, owing to processes of *controlled inclusion* (see Oxhorn 1995b, 1998b). In many countries, the working class was organized by the state in order to limit its political and economic power by undermining any autonomous working-class organization that could challenge the privileged position of the dominant classes. At the same time, organized labor became a relatively privileged actor among the popular sectors more generally. This further segmented the population hierarchically into distinct groups with limited opportunities for upward social mobility, given organized labor's relatively small size compared to the working classes in the industrialized economies of Western Europe. This was a key characteristic of Latin American populism and corporatist institutions in countries such as Brazil and Mexico. In some cases, most notably Chile, a strong working-class movement emerged that was closely tied to leftist parties. But even here, the development of civil society was constrained by the dominant classes, who remained in effective control of the state until the socialist government of Salvador Allende was installed in 1970, and by the predominance of political parties that severely limited the autonomy of organizational activity within civil society (including the autonomy of workers' organizations) by subordinating it to narrow partisan interests (Oxhorn 1995a). Throughout Latin America, civil society emerged but remained weak and at the mercy of the state. When the institutions of controlled inclusion failed to contain demands for integration, authoritarian rule was violently imposed in countries as diverse as Argentina, Bolivia, Brazil, Chile, and Uruguay.

There is an important group of countries—most notably Mexico, Venezuela, Colombia, and Costa Rica—where the institutions of controlled inclusion did not collapse into a downward spiral of violence. As a result, these countries have enjoyed more stable (but not necessarily democratic) political regimes, while civil society was stymied in fundamental respects. In Mexico, controlled inclusion was achieved through a social revolution that resulted in strong corporatist state institutions dominated by a single political party that subordinated organized labor and other sectors of society (Eckstein 1988; Zapata 1998). The regime remained authoritarian through most of the 1990s, with restrictions on political competition and the autonomy of civil-society groups, but growing pressure from civil society, beginning in the mid-1980s, has led to important political openings.[4]

Two other examples, Venezuela and Colombia, have had democratic political regimes since the late 1950s in terms of relatively free and fair competitive elections for government positions. Elite consensus in both countries was institutionalized through political agreements, or "pacts," which ushered in their respective democratic regimes by protecting the vital interests of the principal political actors represented in the pacts. Yet they both share with Mexico serious problems of inequality and social exclusion that reflect weak civil societies and high levels of official corruption. Their democratic regimes are under increasing strain, as democratic institutions appear incapable of addressing pressing social problems. In Colombia, society is increasingly being torn apart by the violence associated with the drug trade and an ongoing civil war between the state, paramilitary groups and powerful guerrilla movements that control over 50 percent of the national territory (*El Nuevo Herald,* April 11, 1999 [web site, http://www.elherald.com/]). In 1992, Venezuela faced its first attempted military coup in a generation, when middle-level officers sought to take advantage of growing popular discontent with rising poverty, high levels of social inequality, and rampant political corruption that appeared to have squandered the country's vast oil wealth. While the coup attempt failed, its leader, Hugo Chávez Frías, became president with a landslide electoral victory in early 1999 by promising to completely revamp Venezuela's democratic institutions. However, he narrowly escaped elite-backed movements to depose him in 2002 and early 2003.

Costa Rica in many ways epitomizes the potential and limits of controlled inclusion. Its democratic regime, which dates to 1948, is the oldest in the region and its stability is directly tied to a welfare state. While often characterized as a transition by "imposition," in which elite actors reached political pacts that laid the foundation for democratic rule (Karl 1991: 174–75), Paige (1997) argues that the nascent agro-industrial bourgeoisie that dominated this process only reluctantly accepted a democratic regime based on important social rights as a consequence of earlier popular mobilization. Paradoxically, after a brief civil war that preceded the installation of the democratic regime, the victors implemented the reform agenda of the defeated president, who was allied with the Communist Party and enjoyed the support of working-class organizations and the Catholic Church. As Paige argues, the viability of reform reflected the inability of the coffee agrarian elite to displace small and medium-sized farmers during the nineteenth century. This led to cooperative relations between them, and served as a foundation for the national "myths" of equality and class cooperation that Costa Rica's social democracy only reinforced.

From the perspective of civil society, as a result of landowning patterns power was relatively more dispersed in Costa Rica than in the rest of the isthmus. This necessitated compromises among elite and important middle-class groups that were foreclosed in countries where the hegemony of agrarian coffee elites was more firmly established. A working-class/leftist coalition could then emerge, which, although defeated militarily, effectively set the political agenda for a reformist government bent on stopping the spread of communism in the 1950s. As Paige concludes, "It was pressure from below, not simply enlightenment from above, that established the Costa Rican welfare state" (Paige 1997: 249). Costa Rica thus avoided the more violent, protracted civil wars that wracked the region in the 1980s, even though its underlying social structure of socioeconomic exclusion for large segments of the population was remarkably similar to the rest of Central America.

Elsewhere in Central America, prerevolutionary Bolivia, Cuba, and Mexico, as well as Paraguay under Stroesner and Peru prior to the 1968 military government, were important exceptions to this general pattern of controlled inclusion. The working class was small and weakly organized. Popular-sector inclusion was minimal, if not nonexistent, and elite agrarian interests were dominant in politics and society. Civil society was very weak. The resultant concentration of economic and political power led to extremes of social polarization. Lacking any other avenues for achieving integration into the sociopolitical system, the relatively weak working class could only ally with the much larger peasantry to form revolutionary movements. To varying degrees and with different levels of success, these movements came to represent strong, well-organized popular-sector actors. But their goals and methods were not compatible with civil society. Fundamentally, the emergence of such revolutionary movements reflects the *weakness* of civil society and the concomitant lack of alternatives to violent conflict for pursing popular-sector interests.[5]

While the discussion in this section has been limited to social classes, the analysis is equally applicable to understanding other potential actors. As already noted, citizenship is a social construction in which a variety of actors potentially participate. These actors are the constitutive elements of strong civil societies. Their absence in national political processes reflects the weakness of civil society and/or repressive state policies. It inevitably results in limited citizenship rights.

In sum, the expansion of citizenship to include civil, political, and, ultimately, social rights as described by Marshall should be reinterpreted to recognize the conflictual nature of the process and the central role played by civil society. These struggles are also constitutive of the growing strength of civil society. Through collective struggle, collective identities are created and redefined as new sources of political power. When rights are granted as a result of social struggle, a certain prior distribution of power resources is recognized and institutionalized by the state, contributing to a further relative dispersion of power resources and concomitantly strengthening civil society. From this perspective, the path followed by Britain as described by Marshall may be "ideal," but it is also unique. When the evolution of citizenship rights follows alternative paths, the consequences for democracy and civil society can be dramatic. In other contexts, including most of Latin America, social rights of citizenship historically have often been a substitute for civic and political rights. This was the sine qua non of controlled inclusion. Rather than redistributing power in favor of the working class, as happened in Western Europe, the segmented, limited expansion of social rights institutionalized social inequalities by creating a new, relatively small group of privileged workers among the popular sectors, stymieing civil society's continued development.

CITIZENSHIP RIGHTS IN LATIN AMERICA'S NEW DEMOCRACIES

In contrast to Marshall's teleological view of citizenship rights and the alternative pattern of limited (as opposed to universal) social rights granted to particular groups in society (e.g., the working class) in the absence of universal political and civil rights, the transitions to democracy in Latin America since the mid-1970s represent a third path: the provision of universal political rights in the absence of universal civil rights and with social rights in decline. While generally stable (with the partial exceptions of Peru, under Fujimori; Venezuela, beginning with the failed coup attempt in April 2002; and Ecuador), these regimes possess severe limits on the *quality* of democratic rule that pose significant challenges to their consolidation. This particular sequence reflects the elitist nature of these transitions to democracy, over which militaries retained a disproportionate influence, as well as the consequences of the neoliberal economic development policies that became dominant throughout the region in the 1980s. Both of these factors have affected

the capacity of civil society to engage in the collective struggles necessary to define citizenship in a more inclusionary fashion.

Latin Americans throughout the region currently enjoy an unprecedented level of political rights exercised through reasonably free and fair
elections. The principal exception remains Cuba, now that Mexico has
elected an opposition candidate to the presidency, where social rights of
citizenship have preceded political rights. Somewhat paradoxically, given
that widespread human-rights abuses were a principal motivation for opposition to the military regimes that ceded power to elected civilian governments in the 1970s and 1980s, the civil rights of citizenship remain
extremely precarious for the majority in most countries (NACLA 1996;
Oxhorn 1998a; Méndez, O'Donnell, and Pinheiro 1999). Significant restrictions on civil rights were found in all Latin American democratic
regimes during the 1990s (with the exception of Uruguay and Chile), according to Freedom House (1999) surveys.[6] Such surveys, however, ob-
scure how the limits on civil rights disproportionately affect the majority
of Latin American citizens. As Pinheiro (1999: 2) explains, "The poor
continue to be the preferred victims of violence, criminality, and human
rights violations." For example, even though transitions to democracy
have contributed to a reduction in the systematic violation of human
rights by the state (except in Guatemala and Peru against indigenous peoples, and in Colombia against guerrillas), state violence in these countries
has generally not declined. Instead, it has undergone a qualitative change,
as it is no longer directed against the political opposition, but rather
against the poor (Méndez 1999a: 19–20).

In Latin America, civil rights historically have been very precarious.
This has been the direct result of the politicization of the state, as state
institutions fall prey to rent-seeking and become dominated by narrow
special interests (including class interests) that deprive them even of the
appearance of neutrality in the design and implementation of policy. The
limits of controlled inclusion also have resulted in various forms of state
repression when social pressures threaten to surpass those limits. Juxta-
posed with the universal political rights of citizenship under democratic
regimes, however, the lack of civil rights threatens to undermine democratic legitimacy, if not the relevance of democratic government to people's everyday lives. Moreover, in the current context, several factors
have combined to exacerbate the problems associated with limited civil
rights.

Abuse of the legal system by elites, corruption, and widespread perceptions that officials enjoy a certain impunity regardless of what they

do has also undermined trust in legal institutions. Throughout Latin America, with the exception of Chile, public confidence in the judiciary is alarmingly low. This is particularly true for low-income groups, including the poor in Chile (Garro 1999: 279). This is one of the principal institutional legacies of authoritarian rule that new democracies must confront. It reflects not only the continued distrust of state institutions caused by high levels of abuse by authoritarian regimes, but also the fact that such practices do not end with the transition to democracy. Laws and personnel are held over from the authoritarian regime and are difficult to change. People become accustomed to pursuing extralegal remedies for their grievances and assume that any reforms will fail in practice, even if enacted by an elected government. Moreover, elected officials have contributed to the pervasive lack of confidence in judicial institutions due to their own political intervention in the courts (Méndez 1999b). Unless trust in the legal order can be created, democratic reforms will be undermined, as many will assume that reforms will be ineffective.

Civil rights in many new democracies are further undermined by a de facto marketization of the rule of law, in which civil rights are allocated according to people's "buying power." Equal protection under the law exists on paper, but the poor cannot access it. The state is incapable, because of corruption and its own lack of resources, of filling the void. Instead, legal systems serve to further reinforce structural problems of inequality and social exclusion. As Pinheiro (1999: 4) argues, "Police and other institutions of the criminal justice system tend to act as 'border guards,' protecting the elites from the poor." "Middle class and elite crimes," including corruption, fraud, tax evasion, and the exploitation of child or slave labor, are ignored by judicial systems, which focus on the crimes committed by the poor (Pinheiro 1999: 5). Law enforcement remains an instrument for corruption and repression, rather than for enforcing universal civil rights. In a vicious circle, ineffective remedies for corruption and ensuring official accountability further undermine trust in the legal and political systems, making it more difficult to curb abuses.

The situation is further exacerbated by a substantial increase in crime rates throughout Latin America after countries experienced transitions to democracy (NACLA 1996). Not only are the poor the primary victims of crime, but they are often targeted by police efforts to control crime, in what amounts to a criminalization of poverty (Méndez, O'Donnell, and Pinheiro 1999). For example, the dramatic rise in the crime rate after the transition to democracy in El Salvador led to the passage of the Ley

de la Emergencia contra la Delincuencia (Emergency Law against Delinquency) and the Ley para la Defensa Social (Law for Social Defense), on
March 19, 1996. The laws, portions of which were eventually declared
unconstitutional, stipulated that individuals could be considered potential criminals, subject to imprisonment and the loss of basic rights, simply because law-enforcement officials felt they looked suspicious. The
unemployed, the poor, young people, or simply people who dressed differently were targeted by laws that ignored the equally serious (but
largely white-collar) problems of organized crime and official corruption (*Proceso* 16 [March 27, 1996]: 702). Yet because the poor are also
the principal victims of crime, these laws enjoyed overwhelming popular support—a phenomenon that is not unique to El Salvador (Méndez
1999a: 22). At the same time, particularly among the relatively well-off,
there is an increasing privatization of law enforcement, as people pay
for private security against kidnapping as well as theft.

In sharp contrast to the development of citizenship rights in Britain,
business interests have been able to cope successfully with—if not actually profit from—the limits of civil rights in much of the region. The marketization of the rule of law, the criminalization of poverty, and the privatization of law enforcement are all at least partial solutions to rising
crime rates and ineffective legal systems that are available only to people with economic resources. Moreover, business interests are enjoying
growing political influence in Latin America (Mahon 1996; Oxhorn and
Ducatenzeiler 1998). This influence is often through informal, undemocratic channels and is a major source of the precariousness of civil rights.
Because business interests may benefit from such irregularities—something Marshall did not anticipate—they will not necessarily provide any
impetus for change. As Mahon (1996: 200) wryly observed, "Those who
move markets may have no objection to formally unaccountable state
power, as long as it is informally accountable to them."

The growing influence of business interests in Latin America reflects
the adoption of a new set of neoliberal development policies that has
had a significantly negative impact on the social rights of citizenship.
These development policies rely on the market for determining the best
allocation of resources and opportunities for the poor. The state retains
only a limited role in providing certain public goods and income transfers directly to those most in need. In contrast to earlier periods, when
business interests were directly dependent upon various state subsidies
or rents, including those resulting from protectionist trade policies that
sheltered them from foreign economic competition, states are much more

dependent upon the business interests that dominate their market economies for securing resources and continued economic success (Oxhorn 1998a).

The implications of this change in development policy for social rights are most evident in the new social-welfare policies of *targeted assistance*. First developed under the military regime of Augusto Pinochet in Chile, these policies have become increasingly dominant throughout the region. They are premised on the assumption that the solution to poverty is at the micro level, by channeling minimal state welfare provisions directly to those most in need until they can find regular employment. The emphasis is on short-term palliatives for poverty until these people can become self-supporting through their participation in the labor market. General subsidies to all citizens and the overly bureaucratic welfare policies that formerly, under controlled inclusion, provided social rights to select groups (including organized labor) are replaced by strictly needs-based direct payments (both cash and in kind, to users or to service providers) in areas such as health care, education, nutrition, employment, and housing. The efficiency of social-welfare expenditures is allegedly increased by limiting the amount of leakage to middle- and upper-class groups. In health care, for example, the state's role is minimized by making it the provider of last resort. Only those who cannot afford private health insurance will be channeled into a public health service that is supposedly more efficient and streamlined compared to the vast bureaucratic public health apparatuses of the period of controlled inclusion. A similar pattern occurs regarding public housing. While the state never was deeply committed to such provisioning, it has renounced public housing in principle in favor of providing limited mortgage subsidies to those who qualify, and screening for eligibility. The state thus attempts to supplement the savings of the segment of the poor who can save, leaving it to the market to ensure an adequate supply of low-cost housing.

As a result of this policy shift, poverty reduction in the region in the 1990s has been due almost entirely to economic growth and a concomitant increase in employment opportunities for the poor, despite increases in state social expenditures in a number of countries (ECLAC 1994; Helwege 1995). Even in Chile, where social expenditure increased 21 percent in real terms between 1990 and 1992, more than 80 percent of the increased income received by the poorest 40 percent of all households during this period was from increases in earned income (ECLAC 1994: 8). Yet while growth may be necessary for poverty reduction, the

empirical evidence clearly demonstrates that it is not enough. Despite a
6 percent increase in per capita GDP in the region between 1990 and
1995, the poverty level declined only marginally from what it was in
1989, while the number of poor people actually increased by fifty million compared to the average for the 1980s (Fluery 1998: 6; Korzeniewicz and Smith 2000: 15). Moreover, this shows that the state has refrained from filling a significant redistributive role. Social expenditures
still remain largely regressive, despite the promise of targeting. Tax reforms and minimum wage polices have not been used to redistribute income to any significant degree by increasing relative national income
shares for the poor (Helwege 1995). Policies designed to reverse the
structural causes of poverty and inequality, particularly through investments in human capital such as education and health care, are sacrificed
to the short-term priorities of maintaining low levels of inflation, bal-
anced state budgets, and external balance of payments equilibrium,
under the assumption that targeted programs for the neediest will provide the necessary time for the economy to provide more jobs. Basic
social "rights" of citizenship, such as health care and education (which
were never very significant for the poor in any case), have been cut back
for the working and middle classes, in comparison to the period of controlled inclusion. The working and middle as well as lower classes increasingly all must rely on the underfinanced and deteriorating public
sector. The well-to-do, in contrast, can afford recourse to the private
sector.

These policy changes have severely affected social equity in the region, further compounding the growing problem of soaring crime rates.
Despite sometimes significant reductions in poverty, the resumption of
economic growth in Latin America after the international debt crisis and
economic recession in the 1980s has generally failed to bring levels of
inequality back to those experienced in the 1970s (Altimir 1994 and
1995).[7] The long-term outlook this suggests is quite bleak for the region's poor. As Enrique Iglesias, president of the Inter-American Development Bank, warned, "In conditions of stable growth, it could take the
continent many years—between 50 and more than a century, depending
on the country—to give all citizens a minimum level of well-being on
current distribution trends" (*New York Times,* March 25, 1998: A7).

Many of the social problems discussed here are not new in Latin
America. Social exclusion and inequality have long plagued the region.
What is unique in the 1990s is the coincidence of limited civil rights, de-
clining social rights (at least compared to periods of controlled inclu-

sion), and nearly universal political rights of citizenship. The juxtaposi-
tion of universal political rights with such sharp limits to other aspects
of citizenship will have important consequences for the *quality* of democracy in the region, ultimately threatening its future. It reflects the
weakness of civil society that stems both from the nature of the transitions that established democratic regimes in Latin America and the shift
to neoliberal economic development policies. In particular, the dominance of political parties and elite actors in these transitions has stymied
the development of Latin American civil societies, at the same time that
economic trends have weakened organized labor, the principal actor that
in the past had struggled for the limited social rights associated with controlled inclusion.[8]

Popular mobilization generally played an important role in precipi-
tating democratic transitions, as people from virtually all sectors engaged
in organized protest activity, demanding that incumbent authoritarian
regimes cede power to elected governments. The extent of such mobilization, accompanied by the emergence of a wide variety of human-rights
organizations and self-help groups, seemed to portend the strengthening
of civil society through the spread of autonomous organizational activities among the popular sectors. This so-called resurrection of civil society, however, proved short-lived, as elite actors and political parties ultimately determined the final course of the transitions (O'Donnell and
Schmitter 1986; Oxhorn 1995a and 1995b). The clearest expression of
this is the political pacts that in many cases determined not only the rules
of the game for the future democratic regime and the kinds of actors who
could participate, but set limits on the substantive issues that elected governments could address (Karl 1986). Among those limits were concessions to outgoing authoritarian regimes regarding future prosecutions for
human-rights abuses, and the preservation of various "authoritarian enclaves" within the institutions of the new democracy (Garretón 1989).
These enclaves often included new institutionalized channels of political
influence for nonelected officials, particularly the military and intelligence
community, and well-entrenched civilian bureaucracies that were held
over from the previous regime.

The process by which elite actors and political parties came to dominate the political process during the transition necessarily entailed a demobilization of mass actors and their subordination to the interests of
ensuring a successful democratic transition. This demobilization appeared necessary to avoid a potential authoritarian backlash by depriv-
ing extremists within the authoritarian regime of any pretense for halt-

ing the transition process (O'Donnell and Schmitter 1986). Regardless, demobilization was not without tensions. Fundamentally, demobilization cut short the process of building civil society that had started as a prelude to the transition. This problem was only exacerbated by the continued dominance of elite actors, particularly party elites, after the transition and a widespread perception of a growing distance between party leaders and the population at large. The available "space" for popular participation often seemed circumscribed to the electoral process by the kind of democratic institutions that were erected during the transition process. Even women's movements that played a critical role in mobilizations against authoritarian regimes defused (Waylen 1994), although in some countries women benefited from new, guaranteed political representation (through quotas) and new laws against domestic violence. Moreover, in many countries frustration with the few changes democracy brought about led men as well as women to withdraw from civil society organizational involvement.

Several other factors have affected the degree to which civil society appears to have receded under democratic rule. In a number of countries, autonomous organizational activity among large segments of the population was a relatively new phenomenon, which emerged, paradoxically, during periods of intense repression and economic hardship. It was often a direct result of the exigencies of trying to survive under brutal authoritarian rule (Oxhorn 1995a, 1995b). Once the transition had been completed, the organizational experiences acquired under an authoritarian regime had to be translated into a democratic environment (with all of its shortcomings), if the momentum that civil society's development had achieved in the absence of political democracy was to continue. This proved to be no easy task. Many of the members of the organizations that had emerged during the period of authoritarian rule, particularly the young, had no experience with democratic politics. Organizational styles and the kinds of demands that were being articulated had to be adapted to a very different setting if they were to be effective in influencing political processes.

A good example was the fact that there no longer was an unambiguous "enemy" against whom to mobilize, as the dictatorship now had been replaced with an elected civilian government. Without a clear enemy to catalyze activism, such popular mobilization often became elusive. Moreover, most of the people actively involved in the various organizations that had emerged during the period of authoritarian rule still viewed democracy, in terms of universal political rights of citizenship, as an end in itself, regardless of its shortcomings. Ironically, this commitment to political democracy actually may have complicated the problem of autonomous popular-sector organizational activity. Potential leaders of such mobilization often remained unsure of how to express their growing frustration. Many did know how to take advantage of the opportunities for participation that democratic politics might offer. At the same time, they feared that mobilization could create destabilizing pressures that would threaten the viability of the new democratic regime—the same fear that contributed to their demobilization during the transition. Under an authoritarian regime, these people either did not think about the potentially destabilizing effects of their activities or they had them as their explicit goal. Now the fear (often echoed by political elites) is that any autonomous mobilization would be counterproductive.

There were important exceptions in a number of countries, particularly among segments of organized labor and human-rights organizations. Yet the ability of these groups to mobilize support beyond their immediate memberships, in order to influence political outcomes, generally remained limited compared to the period of authoritarian rule. There also were mass mobilizations to deepen democratization. Brazilians, for example, mobilized for direct presidential elections in 1984 and for the impeachment of President Fernando Collor de Mello in 1992. And Peruvians mobilized in the early years of the new century against perceived infringements of political (as well as socioeconomic) rights.

Movements of indigenous peoples are the most important exception from the perspective the social construction of citizenship rights. In sharp contrast to most of the social movements that were prominent during periods of authoritarian rule, indigenous groups in a number of countries, particularly Bolivia, Ecuador, Guatemala, and Mexico, have been able to take advantage of the opportunities for political participation provided by democratic regimes in order to create new organizations based on indigenous identity (Yashar 1998). Such organizations draw on preexisting networks to resist "state reforms which restricted access to state resources and jeopardized pockets of local political, material, and cultural autonomy that indigenous communities had carved out" (Yashar 1998: 24). As a result, significant constitutional and other legal reforms have been enacted throughout the region in an effort to institutionalize important new collective social rights of citizenship (Dandler 1999).

Within civil society, preexisting networks and strong cultural identities represent an important aspect of power dispersion; they provide indigenous peoples with a certain capacity to organize themselves and to project their influence onto national political agendas when their self-defined interests are threatened. The importance of this is underscored by the experience of Peru. There, the ability of nonindigenous groups to co-opt important symbols of indigenous culture into their own societal projects has meant that indigenous Peruvians have been more effectively mobilized on the basis of social class and national citizenship—including the activities of violent, class-based revolutionary groups like Sendero Luminoso (Shining Path) (Degregori 1998; see also chapter 10 in this volume).

Despite the important gains by indigenous groups throughout much of the region, "there is still a great distance to go before we can confidently say that the 'rule of law' reigns in relationships between nation-states and indigenous peoples in Latin America" (Davis 1999: 158). Continued indigenous mobilization will be necessary to close this gap, yet the severe disadvantages that indigenous peoples have historically suffered (high rates of poverty, poor education, racial discrimination, to list but a few) suggest this will be a daunting challenge. The May 1999 rejection in Guatemala of constitutional reforms that would have officially recognized the country's twenty-four indigenous groups and institutionalized important channels for them to influence public policy is a poignant example (*New York Times,* May 18, 1999: A8). In a country where over 60 percent of the population is indigenous, the historic constitutional reforms were rejected in a national referendum in which only 18.5 percent of registered voters cast ballots.

It is also important not to forget that some successful mobilizations of mass support in Latin America during the 1990s were *against* what were deemed to be fundamentally flawed democratic regimes. Examples included violent revolutionary movements in Peru and Colombia. They also included populist leaders like Alberto Fujimori in Peru and Hugo Chávez in Venezuela, who both won the presidency of their respective countries by appealing specifically to popular frustrations with the corruption of elected leaders and the inability of existing democratic institutions to address pressing concerns of poverty and lawlessness. This only serves to underscore the problems posed for democratic regimes by restricted citizenship rights and relatively weak civil societies.

This general experience contrasts sharply with the working-class mobilization in Britain referred to by Marshall. There, mobilization was deliberately intended to change an existing (according to the standards of the day) democratic regime, rather than overthrow a violent authoritarian one. Because regime change was the dominant, if not only, demand of the actors involved in recent transitions, there was a tendency to view political rights as almost a panacea for resolving a variety of social ills rather than as an indispensable starting point. The break with the past was not only less dramatic in the British case; it was *deliberate*. Whereas the Latin American transitions cut short a process of building civil society, in Britain the process was continuous and cumulative—hence the teleology of Marshall's analysis.

The contrast is even sharper when we look specifically at organized labor in Latin America. The British labor movement was significantly strengthened through its struggles to win important civil rights, and went on to help create the British Labour Party and secure its political integration. In most Latin American countries, organized labor played an important role in the mobilizations that helped bring about transitions to democracy (Drake 1996), yet its situation remains considerably weakened in virtually every country in the region.[9] Labor movements throughout Latin America suffered significant declines in membership as a result of severe repression and the economic depression caused by the debt crisis in the 1980s. Processes of economic globalization, which have affected trade-union strength throughout the world, and neoliberal economic policies have helped ensure that organized labor in Latin American could not regain its former strength. As a result, with the adoption of neoliberal economic policies labor unions were hard hit by the rolling back of the social rights that they had been granted (often through struggle) in earlier periods (Oxhorn 1998a).

The overall result has been an extreme fragmentation of civil society in most countries of the region. The growing social inequality, pronounced demobilization of mass actors compared to the period preceding recent transitions, and the weakening of organized labor, in particular, have dampened pressures that otherwise might have come from within civil society for the expansion of citizenship rights. In a process that is almost the inverse of the virtuous arc in Marshall's account of citizenship rights, Latin American democracy has continued to constrain civil society's potential despite the universalization of political rights in recent years.

CONCLUSIONS

Returning to the key insight of Marshall—that socioeconomic inequality could be legitimized in Western democracies only through the gradual extension and expansion of the universal rights of citizenship—it is clear that Latin American democracy faces severe challenges. Not only has inequality increased in terms of income distribution, but the state has come to play a decreasing role in compensating for material inequalities by providing social rights of citizenship in a region long considered among the most unequal in the world. Far from legitimizing social inequality, the incapacity of political rights of citizenship to reverse these trends risks undermining the legitimacy of political democracy, opening the way to undemocratic alternatives from below, or from above (as, e.g., populist leaders like Alberto Fujimori in Peru and Hugo Chávez in Venezuela sought to take advantage of growing popular-sector frustrations). Already a decade following the transitions, as noted the Inter-American Development Bank president, public opinion polls showed that only 27 percent of Latin Americans had confidence in existing democratic institutions (*New York Times,* March 25, 1998: A7). As democratic governments proved incapable and/or unwilling to address the principal concerns of their citizens, democracy itself risked becoming irrelevant as people searched for ways to create better lives for themselves (Garréton 1999; Méndez 1999a).

In attempting to analyze the role of civil society in the social construction of citizenship rights, it becomes clear that the weakness of civil society in Latin America is both a consequence and a cause of the particular paths the region has followed in the evolution of universal citizenship rights. In Britain, a greater dispersal of power resources within civil society permitted a series of struggles in which there was a cumulative increase both in the substance of citizenship rights and the strength of civil society. Earlier in the twentieth century in Latin America, social rights of citizenship were often granted only to relatively privileged groups (particularly organized labor), in the context of limited political and civil rights, as a mechanism of social control that deliberately obstructed the kind of cumulative processes implicit in Marshall's description. More recently, both social and civil rights remain restricted rather than universal, despite the existence of substantial political rights. The effect has been to further stymie civil society's development, leaving the future of democracy in the region open to significant doubts.

While it is beyond the scope of this chapter to develop specific solutions, I will briefly sketch out three possible starting points. The investment of more resources in law enforcement and judicial processes, including legal reform, is one. As Marshall correctly argued, civil rights are essential for effective political rights (not to mention social rights) of citizenship. Ironically, Marshall's championing of public-defenders offices (to ensure access to the legal system for society's disadvantaged) as the ultimate stage in the development of social rights is particularly relevant to Latin America today, where social rights have a long way to go before they could even begin to rival those of postwar Britain.

Second, the possibility of utilizing the immense national and international human-rights apparatus that emerged during the period of authoritarian rule for securing civil rights and building stronger civil societies under democratic rule should be explored. "Human rights" might even be best understood as citizenship rights in a democratic context. Past efforts to curtail state political repression could be redirected toward helping to universalize citizenship rights by curbing police and judicial abuse. The expertise gained in organizing the myriad human-rights groups under dictatorships similarly could be applied to help distinct groups within civil society organize themselves so that they can begin to define and defend their interests through democratic institutions.

Finally, the state has an important role to play. In the first instance, effective civil and social rights of citizenship will require reforms (sometimes quite substantial) of state institutions. Beyond that, the state may have a role in providing material and technical assistance to emerging groups within civil society. The temptation to use such resources for partisan gain is obviously a real danger, but Western democracies—including Marshall's Britain—have developed mechanisms to ensure some measure of impartiality. More generally, if it is to be successful, state involvement would have to allow for a much greater level of autonomy on the part of the societal organizations than was the case in Latin America in the past.

The challenges are clearly quite daunting, especially given the fragility of many new democratic regimes. Given the stakes, however, they cannot be ignored.

NOTES

This chapter previously appeared in different form in English as part of the series *Documentos de discusión sobre el tercer sector,* no. 9 (2000), and in Spanish as "Desigualdad social, sociedad civil y los límites de la ciudanía en América Latina," *Economía, Sociedad, y Territorio* (Mexico) 3 (January–June 2001): 153–95, both published by El Colegio Mexiquense, A.C. I would like to thank Manuel Antonio Garretón, Nancy Thede, and, in particular, Susan Eckstein for their comments on earlier versions of this chapter.

    1. Interestingly, Marshall only noted that the status of women was "peculiar" (Marshall 1950: 18).

2. For Marshall, political stability *requires* democratic citizenship under capitalism and is synonymous with democratic stability.

3. "Power" and "power resources" refer to economic resources and organizational capacity to autonomously pursue group interests. The latter can be based on a shared collective identity, ideology, and organizational skill. It can also derive from the availability of selective incentives for members. Coercive strength is not relevant because it typically undermines civil societies.

4. Electoral reforms and setbacks for the ruling Partido Revolucionario Institucional (Institutional Revolutionary Party; PRI) suggest that the political rights Mexicans have had since the 1920s are increasingly effective in the late 1990s. The culmination of this was the election of Vicente Fox, from the Partido Acción Nacional (National Action Party; PAN), as president in 2000.

5. This is why movements like Peru's Sendero Luminoso (Shining Path) brutally attack other popular-sector actors. This group sought to undermine civil society and eliminate alternatives to violent revolution. Guerrilla movements can change their goals and participate in democratic politics—as happened in El Salvador and Guatemala with the signing of peace accords in the 1990s, for example.

6. On a scale of one to seven, with one representing the highest degree of freedom, Freedom House characterizes countries with a civil liberties score of three to five and one-half as being only "partly free." Both Uruguay and Chile scored two, while most other Latin American democracies scored three.

7. The principal exception is Colombia, although this has not led to greater civil and social rights.

8. I am not suggesting that there was any alternative, or that political rights have not been of tremendous importance for most people. I am only analyzing the limitations of these transitions.

9. Brazil is an exception. Rapid industrialization helped strengthen unions, which achieved high levels of autonomy from the state in the late 1970s and 1980s. Workers won important concessions from employers and the state, and contributed to the rise of the Partido dos Trabalhadores (Workers' Party; PT), which won the presidency in a landslide victory in 2002.

REFERENCES

Altimir, Oscar. 1994. "Income Distribution and Poverty through the Crisis and Adjustment." *CEPAL Review* 52 (April): 7–31.

———. 1995. "Inequality, Employment, and Poverty in Latin America: An Overview." Paper presented at the conference Poverty in Latin America: Issues and New Responses, Kellogg Institute for International Studies, University of Notre Dame, Notre Dame, Ind., September 30–October 1.

Bendix, Reinhard. 1964. *Nation-Building and Citizenship: Studies of Our Changing Social Order.* New York: John Wiley and Sons.

Dandler, Jorge. 1999. "Indigenous Peoples and the Rule of Law in Latin America: Do They Have a Chance?" In *The (Un)Rule of Law and the Underprivileged in Latin America,* ed. Juan E. Méndez, Guillermo O'Donnell, and Paulo Sérgio Pinheiro, pp. 116–51. Notre Dame, Ind.: University of Notre Dame Press.

Davis, Shelton H. 1999. "Comment on Dandler." In *The (Un)Rule of Law and the Underprivileged in Latin America,* ed. Juan E. Méndez, Guillermo O'Donnell, and Paulo Sérgio Pinheiro, pp. 152–59. Notre Dame, Ind.: University of Notre Dame Press.

Degregori, Carlos Iván. 1998. "Ethnicity and Democratic Governability in Latin America: Reflections from Two Central Andean Countries." In *Fault Lines of Democracy in Post-Transition Latin America,* ed. Felipe Agüero and Jeffrey Stark, pp. 203–34. Miami: North-South Center Press of the University of Miami.

Drake, Paul. 1996. *Labor Movements and Dictatorships: The Southern Cone in Comparative Perspective.* Baltimore: Johns Hopkins University Press.

Eckstein, Susan. 1988. *The Poverty of Revolution: The State and Urban Poor in Mexico.* Princeton, N.J.: Princeton University Press.

Economic Commission for Latin America and the Caribbean (ECLAC). 1994. *Social Panorama of Latin America.* Santiago: ECLAC.

Fleury, Sonia. 1998. "Política social, exclusión y equidad en América Latina en los años noventa." Paper presented at the Conference Política Social, Exclusión y Equidad en Venezuela durante los años 90: Balance y Perspectiva, Caracas, Venezuela, May.

Freedom House. 1999. *Annual Survey of Freedom: Country Scores, 1972–73 to 1998–99.* Web site, http://www.freedomhouse.org/.

Garretón, Manuel Antonio. 1989. *The Chilean Political Process.* Boston: Unwin Hyman.

———. 1999. "Social and Economic Transformations in Latin America: The Emergence of a New Political Matrix?" In *Markets and Democracy in Latin America: Conflict or Convergence?* ed. Philip Oxhorn and Pamela K. Starr, pp. 61–78. Boulder, Colo.: Lynne Rienner.

Garro, Alejandro M. 1999. "Access to Justice for the Poor in Latin America." In *The (Un)Rule of Law and the Underprivileged in Latin America,* ed. Juan E. Méndez, Guillermo O'Donnell, and Paulo Sérgio Pinheiro, pp. 278–302. Notre Dame, Ind.: University of Notre Dame Press.

Helwege, Ann. 1995. "Poverty in Latin America: Back to the Abyss?" *Journal of Interamerican Studies and World Affairs* 37 (Fall): 99–123.

Karl, Terry Lynn. 1986. "Petroleum and Political Pacts: The Transition to Democracy in Venezuela." In *Transitions from Authoritarian Rule: Southern Europe,* ed. Guillermo O'Donnell, Philippe Schmitter, and Laurence Whitehead, pp. 196–219. Baltimore: Johns Hopkins University Press.

———. 1991. "Dilemmas of Democratization in Latin America." In *Comparative Political Dynamics: Global Research Perspectives,* ed. Dankwart A. Rustow and Kenneth Paul Erickson, pp. 163–91. New York: Harper-Collins.

Korzeniewicz, Roberto, and William Smith. 2000. "Poverty, Inequality, and Growth in Latin America: Searching for the High Road to Globalization." *Latin American Research Review* 35, no. 3: 7–54.

Mahon, James. 1996. *Mobile Capital and Latin American Development.* University Park: Pennsylvania State University Press.

Mann, Michael. 1996. "Ruling Class Strategies and Citizenship." In *Citizenship Today: The Contemporary Relevance of T. H. Marshall,* ed. Martin Bulmer and Anthony Rees, pp. 125–44. London: UCL Press.

Marshall, T. H. 1950. *Citizenship and Social Class, and Other Essays.* Cambridge: Cambridge University Press.

Méndez, Juan E. 1999a. "The Problems of Lawless Violence: Introduction." In *The (Un)Rule of Law and the Underprivileged in Latin America,* ed. Juan E. Méndez, Guillermo O'Donnell, and Paulo Sérgio Pinheiro, pp. 19–24. Notre Dame, Ind.: University of Notre Dame Press.

———. 1999b. "Institutional Reform, Including Access to Justice: Introduction." In *The (Un)Rule of Law and the Underprivileged in Latin America,* ed. Juan E. Méndez, Guillermo O'Donnell, and Paulo Sérgio Pinheiro, pp. 221–26. Notre Dame, Ind.: University of Notre Dame Press.

Méndez, Juan E., Guillermo O'Donnell, and Paulo Sérgio Pinheiro, eds. 1999. *The (Un)Rule of Law and the Underprivileged in Latin America.* Notre Dame, Ind.: University of Notre Dame Press.

NACLA. 1996. "Report on Crime and Impunity." *NACLA Report on the Americas* 30, no. 3 (September–October): 17–43.

Nuevo Herald. 1999. Web site, http://www.elherald.com/ (April 11).

O'Donnell, Guillermo, and Philippe Schmitter. 1986. *Transitions from Authoritarian Rule: Tentative Conclusions about Uncertain Democracies.* Baltimore: Johns Hopkins University Press.

Oxhorn, Philip. 1995a. *Organizing Civil Society: The Popular Sectors and the Struggle for Democracy in Chile.* University Park: Pennsylvania State University Press, 1995.

———. 1995b. "From Controlled Inclusion to Reactionary Exclusion: The Struggle for Civil Society in Latin America." In *Civil Society: Theory, History, and Comparison,* ed. John Hall, pp. 250–77. Cambridge: Polity Press.

———. 1998a. "Is the Century of Corporatism Over? Neoliberalism and the Rise of Neopluralism." In *What Kind of Democracy? What Kind of Market? Latin America in the Age of Neoliberalism,* ed. Philip Oxhorn and Graciela Ducatenzeiler, pp. 195–217. University Park: Pennsylvania State University Press.

———. 1998b. "The Social Foundations of Latin America's Recurrent Populism: Problems of Class Formation and Collective Action." *Journal of Historical Sociology* 11 (June 1998): 212–46.

Oxhorn, Philip, and Graciela Ducatenzeiler. 1999. "The Problematic Relationship between Economic and Political Liberalization: Some Theoretical Considerations." In *Markets and Democracy in Latin America: Conflict or Convergence?* ed. Philip Oxhorn and Pamela K. Starr, pp. 13–41. Boulder, Colo.: Lynne Rienner.

———, eds. 1998. *What Kind of Democracy? What Kind of Market? Latin America in the Age of Neoliberalism.* University Park: Pennsylvania State University Press.

Paige, Jeffery M. 1997. *Coffee and Power: Revolution and the Rise of Democracy in Central America.* Cambridge, Mass.: Harvard University Press.

Pinheiro, Paulo Sérgio. 1999. "The Rule of Law and the Underprivileged in Latin America: Introduction." In *The (Un)Rule of Law and the Underprivileged in Latin America,* ed. Juan E. Méndez, Guillermo O'Donnell, and Paulo Sérgio Pinheiro, pp. 1–15. Notre Dame, Ind.: University of Notre Dame Press.

Proceso (newsletter). 1996. Vol. 16 (March 27).

Rueschemeyer, Dietrich, Evelyne Huber Stephens, and John D. Stephens. 1992. *Capitalist Development and Democracy.* Chicago: University of Chicago Press.

Schmitter, Philippe. 1986. "An Introduction to Southern European Transitions from Authoritarian Rule." In *Transitions from Authoritarian Rule: Southern Europe,* ed. Guillermo O'Donnell, Philippe Schmitter, and Laurence Whitehead, pp. 3–10. Baltimore: Johns Hopkins University Press.

Tilly, Charles. 1996. "Citizenship, Identity, and Social History." In *Citizenship, Identity, and Social History,* ed. Charles Tilly, pp. 1–17. International Review of Social History Supplement 3. Cambridge: Press Syndicate of the University of Cambridge.

Turner, Bryan. 1992. "Outline of a Theory of Citizenship." In *Dimensions of Radical Democracy: Pluralism, Citizenship, Community,* ed. Chantal Mouffe, pp. 33–62. London: Verso.

Waylen, Georgina. 1994. "Women and Democratization: Conceptualizing Gender Relations in Transition Politics." *World Politics* 46 (April): 327–54.

Weyland, Kurt. 1993. "The Rise and Fall of President Collor and Its Impact on Brazilian Democracy." *Journal of Interamerican Studies and World Affairs* 35 (July): 1–37.

Yashar, Deborah. 1998. "Contesting Citizenship: Indigenous Movements and Democracy in Latin America." *Comparative Politics* 31, no. 1 (October): 23–42.

Zapata, Francisco. 1998. "Trade Unions and the Corporatist System in Mexico." In *What Kind of Democracy? What Kind of Market? Latin America in the Age of Neoliberalism,* ed. Philip Oxhorn and Graciela Ducatenzeiler, pp. 151–67. University Park: Pennsylvania State University Press.

CHAPTER THREE

An Exception to Chilean Exceptionalism?

The Historical Role of Chile's Judiciary

LISA HILBINK

In the 1960s and early 1970s, leading intellectuals and political actors in Latin America defined social justice in contrast to and in conflict with formal justice. Social justice, it was understood, could derive only from a radical restructuring of socioeconomic relations; and formal justice— that is, justice administered by courts according to law—was condemned as bourgeois and epiphenomenal. Indeed, from the 1930s onward, most social conflicts in Latin America were addressed by elected officials or regulated by administrative agencies. The judiciary was viewed as, at best, irrelevant to the pursuit of democratic justice (Peña González 1994: 11; Frühling 1998: 245).

However, in the wake of massive and systematic human-rights violations by the region's authoritarian regimes in the 1970s and 1980s, many citizens of Latin American countries and theorists of democratization have embraced the "bourgeois" concepts of rights and the rule of law as necessary to support and sustain democratic rule (Schmitter and Karl 1991; Mainwaring 1992; Greenberg et al. 1993; Przeworski 1995; Jelin and Hershberg 1996; Linz and Stepan 1996; Becker 1997; Frühling 1998; Correa Sutil 1999a; O'Donnell 1999; Schedler, Diamond, and Plattner 1999). Scholars and activists now maintain that modern democracy must involve much more than majority rule expressed through regular and clean elections. To be legitimate, and thus sustainable, a democratic regime must incorporate mechanisms designed to check and limit governmental action; that is, it must couple strictly democratic institutions with liberal or constitutionalist institutions.[1]

This requires, among other changes, that the judiciary take on a more central role in Latin American polities. While courts are not the only institutions responsible for cultivating and upholding constitutionalism (Whittington forthcoming), many theorists agree that an independent, effective, and accessible judiciary is what "give[s] teeth to the principle" of the rule of law (Ehrmann 1976: 48).[2] A strong judiciary is now deemed "essential" for sustaining accountable government and nurturing a strong democratic culture (Prillaman 2000: 1). For this reason, over the past decade and a half judicial reform has swept Latin America (Hammergren 1998; Prillaman 2000).

With this perspective in mind, this chapter is devoted to the analysis of the historical role of the judiciary in Chile, a country generally considered at an advantage in the region in terms of its prospects for consolidating both the rule of law and democracy. In a continent plagued by political violence and instability, Chile has often been celebrated for its "strong...tradition of respect for the rule of law" and its stable "constitutional framework of presidential government" (Valenzuela 1995: 31). In addition to its historically (i.e., pre-1973) "high level of party competition and popular participation, open and fair elections, and strong respect for democratic freedoms," Chile has been said to have had independent, vigilant, and neutral courts that "provided an important safety valve from the hyper-politicization of most of public life" (Valenzuela 1989: 171; see also Gil 1966). Of course, all of this was attacked and radically distorted by the brutal regime of General Augusto Pinochet, which respected neither democracy nor legality (Cavallo Castro, Salazar Salvo, and Sepúlveda Pacheco 1989; Valenzuela 1995). However, with Pinochet having been stripped of his senatorial immunity by Chilean high courts in 2000, some are led to think that, "after more than a decade of sluggishness," the Chilean judiciary is back on track, ready to "rise above political obstacles" and impose the rule of law (Weissert 2000).[3]

In this chapter, I offer empirical evidence to challenge these conventional views. My argument will consist of four main points: first, that Chile's judiciary played neither a vigilant nor a neutral role in Chilean politics before 1973; second, and focusing on the period 1964–94, that the role played by the courts was consistently illiberal under both democratic and authoritarian regimes; third, that this continuity can be attributed to long-standing institutional features of the judiciary; and fourth, that therefore any transition to a more liberal judicial role in Chile will come about only gradually, as institutional reforms take effect, and will depend on persistent social and political support.[4]

Specifically, I will argue that the long-standing institutional structure and ideology of the judiciary, namely tight hierarchical control by the Supreme Court over judicial careers and a strict, positivist-inspired distinction between law and politics, served to reproduce conformity and conservatism in the judicial ranks.[5] That is, the professional incentives and ideology of this institutional setting combined generally to discourage judges from taking "political" stands to limit government authority, while permitting exceptions to this rule in the name of traditional (conservative) values and interests, which were deemed natural or necessary and not "political." Thus, the courts played an active role in challenging the progressive government of Eduardo Frei Montalva and discrediting the socialist administration of Salvador Allende, and then acquiesced to and supported the Pinochet regime, whose explicit project was to depoliticize society and restore traditional Chilean values (chilenidad). Even after the transition to civilian rule in 1990, judges, with few exceptions, failed to take stands in defense of greater liberality; conservatism and conformity continued to reign within the judicial hierarchy. Indeed, it is only since institutional reforms of the mid-1990s have taken effect that more than a few maverick judges have proven willing and able to defend liberal principles.

To make these points, the chapter is organized as follows. First, I provide an historical background explaining the political views and events that informed the construction of the judiciary in Chile. Then I offer four sections, three of which analyze the role of the judiciary under different regimes: the previous democratic regime (1964–73); the authoritarian regime (1973–90); and the first administration of the new civilian regime (1990–94); and a closing section that discusses reforms to the judiciary that came later in the 1990s.[6]

HISTORICO-INSTITUTIONAL BACKGROUND: THE CONSTRUCTION OF THE JUDICIAL ROLE IN CHILE

Nineteenth-century Chilean state builders, concerned above all with securing order and building a rule of law to promote economic progress, created a system that concentrated power in the hands of the president, limiting the possibility of challenges to his authority (Collier 1967; Frühling 1984; Loveman 1988; Jaksić 1997a). Thus, in the 1833 constitution, they neither established the judiciary as an equal branch of government nor entrusted the courts with constitutional interpretation. Instead, they granted the legislature the duty to "oversee the observance of the constitution and the laws" (Kinsbrunner 1967: 60).[7] The most influential legal thinker of the period, Andrés Bello, was a strong believer in legal positivism.[8] He argued that judges were to be "slaves of the law" or "delegates of the executive." The Civil Code of 1855, which Bello authored, thus forbade judges from interpreting laws according to their spirit or purpose when their literal content was clear (Article 19), and otherwise sought to minimize judicial discretion (Navarro Beltrán 1988; Bravo Lira 1991; Jaksić 1997b). Statesman Diego Portales, for his part, held that the key to a just and effective rule of law rested in the judges themselves, and that it was the duty of the president of the republic to ensure that judges were good agents of the sovereign will (Bravo Lira 1991). To ensure this, the 1833 constitution granted the president strong control over the appointments of judges at all levels and the responsibility to oversee the prompt and adequate administration of justice, including the official behavior of judges. Judges were thus discouraged both ideologically and institutionally from articulating any legal interpretation at odds with those of the president (Loveman 1993: 393).

During the era of the parliamentary republic (1891–1924), in which Congress wrested significant power from the president, party elites secured judicial deference by appointing party loyalists to the bench (Gil 1966; Cumplido and Frühling 1980; De Ramón 1989). As Federico Gil (1966: 128) writes, under the parliamentary republic the "allegiance of judges was given to the political parties to which they owed their appointments, just as it had formerly been given to the chief executive in the preceding period."

In the first decades of the twentieth century, then, as new social sectors began organizing and questioning the legitimacy of this oligarchic regime as a whole, the prostrate judiciary drew increasing scorn (Gil 1966: 128; De Ramón 1989: 34). The legal edifice of the nineteenth century did not appear neutral, impersonal, or apolitical to important sectors of society. Thus, after the military seized power in 1924, reform-minded politicians, led by Arturo Alessandri Palma, drafted a new constitution that aimed at adapting the political system to meet some of the demands of the middle and working classes.[9] In addition to shifting the balance of power from the Congress back to the president, and instituting a new interventionist role for the state in the economy, the reformers also sought to restore the legitimacy and efficiency of the civil service by professionalizing state agencies, including the judiciary.[10]

In view of the fragility of the political and social consensus of the period, the reformers, mostly lawyers themselves, thought it necessary to ensure, at least formally, the impartiality of the courts (Frühling 1984: 101).[11] To this end, the constitutional architects placed the power of nomination for judicial vacancies completely in the hands of the judiciary; that is, they ended formal government intervention in judicial nominations. From 1925 onward, the Supreme Court itself drew up the five-person lists of nominees for vacancies in its own ranks, as well as the lists of three nominees for openings on any appellate court. Appellate courts, in turn, became responsible for composing the lists of three nominees for any open district-level magisterial post under their jurisdiction.[12] The president of the republic was to select appointees from these lists and could not remove them from their posts except through a formal impeachment process. The Supreme Court, by contrast, retained the right, upon a two-thirds vote of its membership, to remove any judge for "bad behavior." An internal evaluation system, instituted in 1927, made the threat of removal more serious by giving the Court the power, every three years, to review and classify (in lists of descending merit) all judicial employees for the efficiency, zeal, and morality of their work.[13] In short, the drafters of the 1925 constitution made the Supreme Court a virtually self-generating body and gave the justices increased power over the careers of their subordinates.

In addition, the reformers officially made the judiciary a power of the state, and gave the Supreme Court the power of judicial review for the first time (via the *recurso de inaplicabilidad por inconstitucionalidad*). Although this power was limited by the fact that a ruling on unconstitutionality would only apply to the case in question (i.e., would only have *inter partes* effects), it was a significant innovation (Gil 1966: 125). On appeal from a party in a case before any court in the country, or *de oficio*, the Supreme Court could now declare any law unconstitutional either in form (i.e., due to unconstitutional procedure in the passage of the law) or in substance (due to the unconstitutionality of the content of the law). In addition, the constitution gave the judiciary the power to decree the immediate liberty of those detained or imprisoned with infractions of constitutional principles, and it placed the protection of essential rights and constitutional guarantees definitively in the courts for the first time.

Crucially, however, the reformers did not carry out a purge of the judiciary to rid its ranks of the conservative lackeys appointed under the parliamentary republic. Colonel Carlos Ibáñez, who seized the presidency in 1927, did attempt to rid the judiciary of those judges he viewed as most venal and corrupt (Matus Acuña 1999: 108), but the move was viewed as scandalous by the traditional political elite, and Ibáñez finished by expelling only a small fraction of judicial personnel (De Ramón 1989: 53). Thus, the sociopolitical composition of the judiciary remained basically the same as it had been for at least thirty-five years, with those at the top of the hierarchy vested with more power than ever over their subordinates. At the same time, the memory of the purge made it unlikely that any ideological innovators in the judicial ranks would assert their new powers against Ibáñez's policies. Indeed, during the four years of Ibáñez's dictatorship, judges declined to raise legal or constitutional objections to labor repression, widespread censorship, restricted political party activity, and the torture, imprisonment, and exile of the political opposition (Cumplido and Frühling 1980; Tavolari 1995).

Even after democratic government was restored in 1932,[14] judges refused to assert their new powers of judicial review and rights protection. Secondary accounts reveal that judges—who increasingly came not from elite families but from lower-middle- and middle-class backgrounds[15]—failed to cultivate and develop a constitutionalist orientation during this period (Caffarena de Jiles 1957; Bertelsen 1969; Frühling 1984; Mera, González, and Vargas 1987; González 1989; Verdugo Marinkovic 1989). Instead, in cases involving the alleged abuse of state power to limit civil and political rights, such as habeas corpus, due process, freedom of expression, freedom of association, and freedom of assembly, the courts continued to defer to, and hence uphold, the absolute authority of the executive.[16] They did so by offering a strict interpretation of the separation of powers, that is, by arguing that the courts had no authority to rule on issues of a "political" (as opposed to strictly legal) nature. In their unwillingness to review, evaluate, and (when appropriate) challenge the decisions and acts of the executive in such cases, they demonstrated a greater commitment to public order than to the rights of individual citizens.

THE JUDICIAL ROLE DURING THE HEYDAY OF CHILEAN DEMOCRACY, 1964–1973

After 1932, Chile underwent a process of significant social and political democratization. The electorate shifted leftward, forcing the gradual decline of the nineteenth-century conservative political parties. New par-

ties of the Center and Left, with strong ties to groups in civil society, established themselves as major contenders in the political game, and even
the Right produced somewhat reformist candidates (Drake 1978; Cea
1987; Aylwin et al. 1996). Participation and contestation evolved gradually, such that by the 1960s Chile was considered among the most democratic countries in the world (Dahl 1971). Indeed, a 1965 index that
ranked countries in terms of democratic performance placed Chile in the
top 15 percent, above the United States, France, Italy, and West Germany (Bollen 1980).

Under the rules established by the 1925 constitution, state intervention in the economy had been a hallmark of this social and political development. However, the degree of intervention and the pace of change
were stepped up significantly with the election of Christian Democrat
Eduardo Frei Montalva in 1964 and Socialist Salvador Allende in 1970.
Frei instituted a major agrarian reform, increased public housing, and
encouraged rural unionization and mass-level political activity. (Loveman 1988; Collier and Slater 1996). Allende attempted to pursue a legal
path to socialism via the acceleration of agrarian reform and, in the
name of the proletariat, state takeover of major industries. Unlike Frei,
however, he lacked majority support in Congress for most of his program, and so he sought to implement his policies using special powers
reserved (by law) to the executive. As time went by, many of his supporters took matters into their own hands. The tactics of both the extreme Left and the extreme Right grew ever more radical (Garcés 1973;
Sigmund 1977; Valenzuela 1978).

During these years of rapid change and social conflict, the public paid
great attention to how the courts resolved important cases brought before them. Despite significant critiques of the formal legal system (Novoa
Monreal 1964; Figueroa 1978), the discourse of law remained a powerful one in Chilean political life, and it was important for most players
in the system to be able to claim that the law was on their side (Arriagada 1974; Cea 1978). For the government, such a claim had traditionally been easy to make. First, the political system was heavily presiden-
tialist; that is, it concentrated much decision-making power in the hands
of the executive (Silva Cimma 1977). Moreover, and as noted in the previous section, the courts had long deferred to and upheld the absolute
authority of the executive, on the grounds that judges had no authority
to intervene in "politics." Thus, Presidents Frei and Allende both expected the courts to rule in their favor.

Instead, during this period Chilean judges demonstrated an increasingly strong willingness to challenge the executive in the name of the civil and political rights of individual citizens. However, they extended such rights protection very unevenly, actively defending conservative values and interests but reverting to positivist and even formalist reasoning in cases involving defendants of the ideological Left. When the Left called attention to this practice, the judges claimed that such critiques were motivated by narrow "political" passions, which audaciously challenged the sober and objective reasoning of the courts. The courts and their supporters portrayed themselves as servants of transcendent and immutable principles and public values, while they accused their critics of wallowing in the bogs of *politiquería* (petty partisan politics). They thus antagonized the Left, emboldened the Right, and eroded the possibility that more moderate forces would prevail on either side of the burgeoning political battle.

In a landmark case of 1967, for example, the Supreme Court ruled that a lower court had the constitutional authority to review presidential decrees for constitutionality and to apply or refuse to apply the decree based on that review. The ruling, in the case *Juez de Letras de Melipilla con S.E. el Presidente de la República,* shattered a tradition of deference to presidential authority. This deference had held even in cases (such as this one) involving a "decree of insistence," a legal instrument allowing a decree to go forth, despite legal objections, with the official assent of all cabinet members.[17] In this case, by contrast, the Court invoked the duty of the judiciary "to protect the fundamental rights of the human person," even in cases where the constitution seemed to give the last word to the executive (RDJ 64 [1967] 2.1: 109–20).[18] The "fundamental rights" in question were the property rights of an agricultural estate owner, whose farm had been seized temporarily by the government after a labor struggle and who suspected he would be forced to give up his land for the agricultural reform.

The Court thus endorsed the idea that judges had the authority and the duty to defend constitutional rights. It did so, however, in a case that directly challenged the prerogative of the Frei government, taking a stand in favor of traditional property rights even as the whole concept of property was being rethought and redefined, with majority support, by the country's elected leaders.[19] Moreover, because the decision departed from the deference that the courts had traditionally shown toward the government, it appeared to reflect a bias in favor of conservative forces.

This perception was enhanced by the judiciary's inconsistent treatment of two suits brought by the Frei government that were quite similar in their general facts. Both cases involved alleged violations of the Law of Internal State Security, which extended significant powers to the president to preserve societal order, broadly defined. In the first case, the defendants were members of the right-wing National Party, who, in the national and international press, had attacked the "weak and vacillating" foreign policy of the Frei government, and whose party platform called for the imposition of a "regime of iron authority" to stem the "period of disorder" that the Frei government had initiated. In the second case, the defendant was Socialist Party senator Carlos Altamirano, who at an academic conference criticized the Frei government in the context of a speech that celebrated and encouraged the emulation of the Cuban revolutionary model.

In the National Party case, both the Santiago Appeals Court and the Supreme Court ruled that the politicians had "the right to publicly express the judgment which the acts of the Government deserve and to criticize its actions, unless these opinions constitute an incitation to subversion... or an insult to His Excellency, the President of the Republic or to his Cabinet Ministers, *which in the present case has not been established from their text.*" They also concluded that there had been no grave offense to patriotic sentiment, "an offense...*which must be a matter of fact and not of simple declarations.*"[20] Thus, the courts clearly saw fit the evaluation of the facts of the case against the claims of the government, and were willing to take a stand in defense of the constitutional right of free expression.

By contrast, in the Altamirano case *(Carlos Altamirano O.)* the same courts abandoned any commitment to the constitutional protection of free speech and gave full justification to the government's position, arguing that

> the constitutional precept that consecrates the freedom of expression without previous censorship has left free the determination of the cases in which people incur responsibility for crimes and abuses committed in the exercise thereof to the law, such that it is incumbent upon the legislator, and not upon the judge, who is limited simply to applying it, to prevent that right from being unjustifiably spoiled. The legislator makes a political appraisal; the judge, a juridical one. (RDJ 64 [1967] 2.4: 274)

In other words, the Court argued that legal limits to the constitutionally protected freedom of expression were not subject to judicial evaluation. In contrast to the ruling in the National Party case, this ruling placed special emphasis on the textual legal limits to the freedom of speech and on the limited responsibility of the judiciary to defend against these. The courts thus sent the message that aggressive right-wing speech was legitimate dissent, protected by the constitution, but aggressive left-wing speech was not.

In similar political rights cases under President Allende, the courts, led by the Supreme Court, also ruled in favor of the political Right, extending protection to individuals critical of the executive but not to those critical of the opposition in Congress. For example, when the Allende government prosecuted far-right journalist Rafaél Otero for public libel and an attack on public order (i.e., violations of the Law of Internal State Security), the Supreme Court ruled that Otero had not demonstrated any libelous intent nor any intent to disrupt public order (*Contra Rafaél Otero Echeverría*, RDJ 68 [1971] 2.4: 77–81).[21] By contrast, a few weeks later, when four opposition congressmen filed a suit against the director and owner of a pro-Allende newspaper, *Puro Chile*, for repeated acts of "defamation and contumelious insult" that threatened public order, the Santiago Appeals Court upheld the charges.[22] Arguing that the text of the Law of Internal State Security did not permit them to review the subjective factors surrounding the case, and ignoring the fact that the executive (who had traditionally decided such matters) did not deem public order to be threatened, the judges ruled to convict (*Contra José Antonio Gómez López*, RDJ 68 [1971] 2.4: 46–56).

As in the past, judges claimed that all of these decisions were completely apolitical. Indeed, the Supreme Court reserved the term "political" as a derogatory term to refer to behavior supportive of left-wing causes. In his annual speech inaugurating the judicial year in both 1970 and 1971, for example, then-president of the Supreme Court, Ramiro Méndez Brañas, claimed that the Left's charge of class bias in the judiciary was unreasonable; judges could not be blamed for the outcomes of the cases they decided, since they simply applied the laws in force in the country.[23] He felt so strongly about this that in 1970 he appeared with a fellow justice on a national television program to rebut the charge that the courts administered "class justice." In his 1972 speech, Méndez defended this action as an effort to protect the judiciary from insidious efforts from the Left to "politicize" the judicial system. "Just as doctors opine on issues of public health or engineers on the problems of the nation's bridges and roads, it is the business of judges to opine on [juridical] matters," he asserted. However, to those judges who opined in support of the Allende administration (which sought dramatic reform of the judiciary), Méndez issued a stern warning, announcing that the Supreme Court would "adopt the appropriate measures to prevent members of the judiciary from listening" to the voices of political "proselytizers," bent on "destroying our crystalline tradition of respect for the rule of law" (RDJ 69 [1972] 1: xv).[24]

The seriousness of these statements became clear in the following year, when the Supreme Court threatened to remove a justice from the La Serena Appeals Court. The judge, Oscar Álvarez, had been a member of the judiciary for nineteen years and had been serving on a commission of judges that worked closely with the Ministry of Justice under Allende to help draft bills on judicial reform. The Supreme Court formally accused Álvarez of instructing the executive to fill a vacancy in his court, rather than notifying the Supreme Court that the post had gone unfilled. Álvarez claimed that these were trumped-up charges, for all he had done was notify the minister of justice, whose legitimate concern it was, that the post had gone unfilled for five months. The true reason the Court sought to punish him, he argued, was because of his cooperation with the Allende administration in drawing up proposals to democratize the justice system. This same interpretation had been offered by the right-wing newspaper *El Mercurio*, which viewed such cooperation as inappropriate and legitimately punishable. And indeed, Judge Álvarez and five of his colleagues who had served on Allende's judicial commission had already been denounced to the Supreme Court by rightist congressmen.[25]

In the end, Álvarez was suspended for only five days,[26] but the action taken against him had a chilling effect on the rest of the judicial hierarchy. Although a significant percentage of judges were open to the idea of making the legal and judicial system more representative of and more accessible to the nonelite, it became clear that if they expressed excessive enthusiasm for Allende's policies, they would be subject to disciplinary measures. As Álvarez claimed in an interview, after this, "what else could we do [but remain silent]?" (Harnecker and Vaccaro 1973: 32).

Over the course of 1972 and 1973, relations between the Supreme Court and Allende's Unidad Popular (Popular Unity) government grew increasingly acrimonious. In situations where citizens carried out illegal and sometimes destructive or violent seizures of farms or factories, Allende's policy was to prohibit the police from executing judicial commands to use force against the perpetrators. Judges and many lawyers interpreted this as general disrespect for the law and an attack on judicial independence and power. In addition, Allende permitted unprecedented acts of protest against the judiciary, and the language used to critique the judges in the pro-Allende press was often crass and offensive (Echeverría and Frei 1974; Gardner 1980). However, it was equally true that the Supreme Court applied much stricter standards to and launched far more criticisms of the Allende government than they had against any previous administration (DeVylder 1974; Athey 1978; Kaufman 1988). Moreover, when Allende supporters pointed this out, the Supreme Court responded by reasserting their objectivity and dismissing the critics as impassioned, self-interested, ignorant, and unethical (RDJ 70 [1973]: 169–71). This rigid and aggressive stance, as Allende himself remarked, certainly never "favored social peace or the reestablishment of democratic dialogue" (RDJ 70 [1973]: 226).

THE JUDICIAL ROLE UNDER
AUTHORITARIANISM, 1973–1990

When the military overthrew the Allende government and seized power on September 11, 1973, it did so in the name of the rule of law *(el estado de derecho)*. In its first official statement justifying the coup, Bando 5, the governing junta declared that the Allende administration had violated all of the most fundamental rights of Chile's citizens and had thereby fallen into "flagrant illegitimacy." The armed forces had thus seized power with the objective of reestablishing "normal economic and social conditions in the country, with peace, tranquillity, and security for all" (Loveman and Davies 1989: 238–39).

Immediately after the coup had begun, the junta began issuing "decree laws" to give their actions a formal legal backing. On September 11 itself, they issued Decree Law 1, declaring the constitution of the governing junta with the "patriotic commitment to restore Chilean national identity *[chilenidad]*, justice, and the country's institutional structure *[institucionalidad]*." Decree Law 1 further declared that the junta would "guarantee the full effectiveness of the judiciary's attributes" and would "respect the Constitution and the laws of the Republic, *insofar as the country's present situation permits*" (Frühling, Portales, and Varas 1982: 85, my emphasis).

As this last clause suggests, the junta's definition of the rule of law was, from the start, no more than a version of *quod principi placuit legis habet vigorem* ("what pleases the emperor has the force of law"). As James Gardner (1980: 272) puts it, under the military regime in Chile, "policy was law and law was policy." Moreover, all policy (and hence all law) of the military regime was rooted in national-security doctrine, that is, in the belief that the primary mission of the armed forces, "singular representatives of the Nation and of the State" (Frühling, Portales, and Varas 1982: 51), was to protect society from internal "enemies."[27] Indeed, it was the necessary "war" against communism that Pinochet used to justify the regime's permanent restrictions on civil and political liberties, as well as the construction of a "new institutionality."[28]

In the face of Pinochet's illiberal and antilegalist project, the courts reacted far differently than they had under Allende. Instead of asserting themselves as a modest but immovable bulwark against attacks on basic civil and political liberties, judges turned a blind eye to the new regime's massive human-rights violations. Rather than challenging the government's abuse of police power and standing up for the rule of law, the courts, and especially the Supreme Court, justified the regime's brutal policies. Those few judges who did take stands in defense of liberal principles were censured by the Supreme Court for their inappropriate "political" behavior, while those who cooperated with the regime were rewarded (via promotion) for their professionalism and patriotism.

Most members of the legal community in Chile insist that the military regime did not rob the judiciary of its formal independence. Unlike the juntas in Argentina, Brazil, and other countries, the Chilean junta did not purge the judiciary after the coup or systematically threaten judges into submission. Indeed, as I demonstrate here and elsewhere, such a move was not necessary in Chile, given the general ideological sympathy of the highest judicial authorities with the authoritarian leaders and their power over the judicial hierarchy. In interviews, many judges emphasized the strong control the Supreme Court maintained over their subordinates under the dictatorship, and spoke of how this discouraged them from rendering any decision unfavorable to, or even expressing any displeasure with, the government. This feeling was particularly strong after the Supreme Court dismissed or forced the retirement of forty judges (15 percent of the total) in 1974, either by giving them poor evaluations for 1973 or by transferring them to geographically isolated posts (Hilbink 1999a).

The courts thus offered almost no resistance to the military's arbitrary and brutal policies. Between 1973 and 1983, the courts rejected all but ten of fifty-four hundred petitions for habeas corpus filed by the Vicaría de la Solidaridad (Vicariate of Solidarity), the Church-sponsored organization that provided legal defense (and other services) for regime victims (Velasco 1989: 60). Judges unquestioningly accepted the explanations offered by the government regarding the fate of the disappeared, ignored legal rules that protected due process, and found a host of legal technicalities for dismissing pleas for intervention. Indeed, the Supreme Court repeatedly instructed lower courts, albeit indirectly, to ignore the letter of the law so as not to disrupt the work of the generals.

The carte blanche that the Supreme Court granted the military government in its pursuit of "antipatriots" is particularly evident in a ruling of March 21, 1974, which denied habeas corpus to a minor.[29] One week earlier, the Santiago Appeals Court had accepted the petition, arguing that the traditional legal precepts governing habeas corpus, found in the constitution and the Penal Code, were still in effect, and that even the junta's own legislation, namely Decree Laws 1 and 128, recognized the powers of the judiciary to process this writ. Moreover, international human-rights treaties signed by Chile obligated the Chilean state to maintain courts that could offer protection to anyone considered to be arbitrarily detained. In addition, the junta itself had declared that all arrests and transfers under a state of siege had to be ordered by means of supreme decrees signed by the Ministry of the Interior. However, in the case of fifteen-year-old Luis Adalberto Muñoz Mena, the proper decrees had not been issued. Finally, the extended detention of a minor, who couldn't be prosecuted as an adult no matter what his crimes, appeared excessive, since it would be difficult to argue that someone so young could gravely infringe on the nation's defense or threaten the political order.

Dismissing all of these arguments, the Supreme Court overturned the ruling. The high court's decision stated that under a state of siege the executive had the exclusive right to determine who could be arrested and that no court had the right to evaluate the motives underlying the arrest. Moreover, procedural norms governing the trial of minors only applied in criminal trials, not in cases such as this one. In short, the Court argued that "measures of protection for minors...cannot take priority over the dispositions adopted by the authorities during a state of siege" (RDJ 71 [1974] 2.4: 197–200). This reasoning was reiterated in October 1975, when the Supreme Court overturned an appeals-court ruling granting habeas corpus to Celso Rosario Calfallán. This latter decision stated explicitly that in any conflict "between legal precepts that govern, on the one hand, the superior end of social regulation, and on the other, the rights of certain individuals or groups,...the former must necessarily take priority over the latter" (*Fallos del Mes* 203: 215–16). That the Court approved of the military's sociopolitical project could hardly be clearer.

Even after the "state of war" ended (1978) and the new constitution went into effect (1980), judges, especially higher-court judges, continued to justify and support the expansive police powers of the military government (Garretón 1987, 1989). For example, in 1982 and 1983 the government prosecuted members of the human-rights community for "favoring political tendencies aimed at the destruction of the security of the state and the established government" (Vicaría de la Solidaridad 1982 [August]: 42–45; RDJ 80 [1983] 2.4: 74–76). The courts accepted the government's claims about and interpretations of the defendants' activities in these cases, denying that the information these groups collected and disseminated was based on fact, and supporting the idea that the suppression of human-rights groups was part of a legitimate political project. Between 1983 and 1986, when public protest against the regime increased dramatically, the courts did little to protect the populace from the government's repressive response. They ruled that abusive search operations that the government conducted in shantytowns were justified as "a normal police function," designed to protect law-abiding citizens from "antisocial elements." At the same time, they accepted the legal restriction of citizens' rights, ruling, for example, that a law penalizing "those who without authorization foment or convoke public collective acts in the streets, plazas, and other public places, and those who promote or incite demonstrations of any other type which allow or facilitate the alteration of public tranquillity," did not violate the constitutional right to free assembly (Vicaría de la Solidaridad 1985 [June]; *Fallos del Mes* 326: 980–92).

By 1986, the judiciary began to look increasingly isolated in its legal defense of the authoritarian regime. In July of that year, the first national congress of lawyers under the dictatorship issued a statement declaring that the rule of law did not exist in Chile; that the 1980 constitution was illegitimate; and that nobody could be obligated to obey unjust laws. The lawyers thus resolved to "assume the moral and patriotic duty of promoting, from this moment, political and social democracy and the exercise of rights and liberties that are universally consecrated." The jurists also strongly criticized the country's judges, contending that "a diligent and responsible judicial labor would have avoided or reduced the impunity of the many crimes which have gone without punishment, saving many lives, [and] avoiding exile, disappearances, torture, and other suffering" (Oliva 1986).

In response to such criticism, which only increased in subsequent months, members of the Supreme Court offered explanations grounded in formalist reasoning. They argued that "we apply the law, which is written reason." If there exists any "silence, obscurity, contradiction, or insufficiency in the law, it falls to other sources to decide and respond." The Civil Code "establishes that when the meaning of the law is clear, [the judge] will not ignore its literal meaning on the pretext of consulting its spirit." Thus, they claimed, it would appear that "some people believe that the fulfillment of a legal mandate merits censure" (*El Mercurio*, July 8, 1987: 1).

The Supreme Court, for its part, had its own ideas about what merited censure. In August 1986, Santiago Appeals Court judge Carlos Cerda Fernández concluded his tenacious and thorough investigation of the 1976 disappearance of ten Communist leaders and indicted forty people. Among those he charged were thirty-two members of the armed forces, including the former head of the air force, Gustavo Leigh. Having reached this point in the investigation, some expected Cerda either to apply amnesty to close the case or to hand it over to the military courts. However, Cerda announced that he would do neither. He grounded his decision on the view that amnesty was a "social pardon" that could not be applied until the truth about the crime had been established and the guilt of the perpetrators declared (Vicaría de la Solidaridad 1986 [August]: 21–22; Verdugo 1991). Cerda emphasized that neither of these criteria had been met.

On appeal, the Supreme Court rejected this argument, overturning the indictments and ordering Cerda to apply the amnesty law to close the case. Cerda responded that to do so at that moment was "evidently contrary to law [*derecho*]" and that thus, according to Article 226 of the Penal Code, he had the right to refuse the order of his superiors. This act outraged the members of the Court, and, in an extraordinary plenary session, they suspended Cerda from the judiciary for two months with only half pay (Vicaría de la Solidaridad 1986 [October]: 55–59).

Two years later, the Supreme Court twice censured another judge, René García Villegas, for expressing disrespect for the military justice system and for "getting involved in politics." García, the judge of the twenty-first criminal court of Santiago, had taken on the investigation of more than forty cases of torture committed in his jurisdiction between 1985 and 1989. In interviews with journalists in 1987 and 1988, García made statements condemning the practice of torture in Chile, while in a 1988 judicial resolution he declared that the transfer of cases involving crimes presumably committed by security agents to the military justice system "resulted in impunity for those incriminated" (*La Época*,

November 15, 1987: 17–18; Vicaría de la Solidaridad 1988 [March]:
78–81). In annual evaluations for both 1988 and 1989, the Supreme
Court thus ranked García in list three for "incompetent performance,"
forcing his resignation from the bench on January 25, 1990 (García Villegas 1990). Thus, even as the country transitioned to democracy, the
conservative Court kept the rest of the judicial ranks in line.

THE JUDICIAL ROLE IN THE NEW DEMOCRACY, 1990–1994

On March 11, 1990, General Augusto Pinochet transferred the presidential sash to Patricio Aylwin Azócar, thereby bringing military rule to
a formal end. Aylwin was elected as the candidate of the Concertación
de Partidos para la Democracia (Concertation of Parties for Democracy),
which had formed out of the Concertación por el No (Concertation for
the "No" Vote) organized for the 1988 plebiscite. Upon coming to
power, the Concertación's top priority was to "reconstruct and consolidate democracy to ensure that the rule of law would be secured" (Oppenheim 1993: 206). As one Chilean author observes, "During the years
of resistance to the dictatorship, the concepts of democracy and human
rights had been forged into a single, indivisible ideal" (Otano 1995:
161). Important sectors of the population held that "to do justice is to
build democracy."[30] The judiciary was thus to be a central focus of the
continuing transition to democracy.

Consistent in its political orientation, however, the judiciary proved to
be an obstacle to the deepening of democracy during the Aylwin presidency. From 1990 to 1994, the Chilean judiciary, led by the Supreme
Court, generally endorsed the legal edifice constructed by the leaders of
the authoritarian regime and left largely unchallenged the principles and
values embodied therein. As in the past, those judges who attempted to
break publicly from this pattern were reprimanded by their superiors in
the Supreme Court. In short, rather than model, defend, and promote the
liberal principles and practices that support democracy, after 1990 the
Chilean judiciary continued to throw its symbolic weight behind illiberal
political principles and authoritarian institutions.[31]

In the first highly anticipated ruling after the transition, delivered on
August 24, 1990, the Supreme Court ruled *unanimously* that the application of amnesty was constitutional in disappearance cases, validating
the practice of applying amnesty before the facts of the case had been
clarified (RDJ 87 [1990] 2.4: 64–86).[32] The petition for *inaplicabilidad*
had been filed for a case involving the disappearance of seventy people

between 1973 and 1974, the evidence for which pointed to the guilt of (retired) General Manuel Contreras and other Dirección de Inteligencia Nacional (National Directorate of Intelligence; DINA) agents. The party that filed the *recurso* had argued that the amnesty law (Decree Law 2,191) was unconstitutional on three grounds. First, it violated the human rights guaranteed by both the constitution and the international treaties and covenants that had been incorporated into Chilean law via the reform to Article 5 of the constitution. Second, the law denied the judiciary its constitutional right and duty to investigate crimes and to identify the culprits. And third, the law violated the principle of equality of the law by granting amnesty only to those who had not yet been prosecuted for political crimes committed during the period in question (Etcheberry 1990).

In the decision, the Supreme Court offered a detailed defense of the amnesty law. The justices argued that the amnesty was "essentially general and equal in regard to the punishable facts" that it covered, and that it had been issued by a legitimate legislative power in the general interest of society. The law was neither arbitrary nor contrary to the constitutional order, since Article 60, Number 16, of the constitution expressly permitted legislation of this nature as part of the "legitimate exercise of sovereignty." The Court thus not only justified the amnesty law, but reasserted the legitimacy of the military regime.

Equally important, the Court offered a long analysis of the juridical concept of amnesty and explicitly established that "once it is verified that the facts in question are covered by the amnesty law, judges must declare amnesty...[and] are not bound by Article 413 of the Penal Procedure Code which requires the completion of the investigation in order to permanently close a case."

In regard to the place of international law, the Court argued that the convention for the Prevention and Sanction of the Crime of Genocide, although part of Chilean law since 1953, did not apply because "no specific sanctions had been established in the national legislation to punish such a crime." The International Pact on Civil and Political Rights, for its part, did not apply because the decree incorporating it into Chilean law had not been issued until April 29, 1989; that is, it could not have retroactive effects.

Finally, and perhaps most controversially, the Court said that although Chile had been bound by the terms of the Geneva Conventions since 1951, they were not applicable in this case since there had been no internal armed conflict in Chile. "Although [the criminal facts under investigation in this case] took place during the state of siege period covered by the amnesty law, they do not appear to be the consequence...of a state of internal conflict bearing the characteristics [defined by the convention]." This argument blatantly contradicted both the legal facts and the Court's previous criteria. Decree Law 5 had explicitly declared that the state of siege should be understood as a "state of war," as established in Article 418 of the Military Justice Code. Article 418 of the Military Justice Code, for its part, established that war is either declared via a law or via the decree of a state of siege. Moreover, the Court had repeatedly recognized the existence of a state of internal war in its decisions, even going so far as to renounce its power to review the decisions of war tribunals.

Although this particular ruling was, "technically speaking...binding only to the case under review, the message to the judiciary [regarding interpretation of the amnesty law] was clear" (Brett 1992: 200). Moreover, subsequent decisions reinforced the Court's position. For example, in June 1992 the Supreme Court overturned a decision of the Puerto Montt Appeals Court and granted *amparo* to a military officer arrested for a 1973 political murder. The Supreme Court stated that since it had been established that the crime had occurred on September 16, 1973, and since the suspect had not been on trial or convicted at the time the amnesty law was issued, he was clearly a beneficiary of amnesty and had to be released immediately (*Gaceta Jurídica* 1992 [June]: 82–85). Similarly, in September 1993, the plenary of the Supreme Court denied requests for information filed by lower-court judges on four cases closed by virtue of the amnesty law, arguing that since they had occurred in the period covered by the amnesty law, and since the statute of limitations had also expired, there was no justification for reviving them (*Fallos del Mes* 418: 768–69).[33]

It was not only through the appeals process that the Supreme Court exercised its control over the judicial hierarchy. As in the past, the Supreme Court also sanctioned district-level and appellate court judges who challenged the Court's stance on human-rights cases. Among those censured were Judge Nelson Muñoz, who participated in the uncovering of a secret grave of human-rights victims at Pisagua early in 1990; Judge Carlos Cerda Fernández, who again challenged the Supreme Court's definitive application of the amnesty law to the case of the disappeared Communist leaders; and Judge Gloria Olivares, whom the Court accused of "excessive protagonism" in her investigation of the 1974 disappearance of a young leftist activist, Alfonso Chanfreau (Rojas 1990; Brett

1992; Hidalgo 1992). Muñoz, anticipating dismissal, resigned in October 1990, while Cerda was formally dismissed but successfully supplicated for his return in 1991.

Many judges interviewed for this study affirmed the negative effect of this tight control of the Supreme Court over all other judges. "In Chile, the obsequious judge is rewarded, not the best trained or the most intelligent.... Everyone prefers to take the comfortable position: avoid compromising oneself. And why? Because everyone wants to be promoted!" (interview with author, June 13, 1996; all interviews cited were conducted in Santiago). "All that a mediocre judicial employee has to do to be favorably evaluated is be very friendly with the Supreme Court and accept any kind of request that the Court makes," complained another. "In contrast, a judge who is very independent of such influence will surely not receive the same [positive] evaluation" (interview with author, May 9, 1996). In sum, as a third judge observed,

> The structure of our judiciary is very outdated, Napoleonic. It works to transform a given personality, to produce a judge with a certain profile, one who tries to resolve always in accordance with what the Supreme Court says.... The judge from day one is sent messages that tell him, "Look, you need always to go along with your hierarchical superior." This is something quite negative, I think, and something which is always somewhat present,... for when the training of the judge causes him to identify with something other than the constitution, [such as the view of his superiors], he loses his independence. (interview with author, May 9, 1996)

RECENT REFORMS AIMED AT CHANGING THE JUDICIAL ROLE

Both President Aylwin and his successor, Eduardo Frei Ruiz-Tagle, recognized the built-in conservatism and conformity of the judiciary, and both were able to pass institutional reforms that may succeed, at long last, in liberalizing the judicial vocation. Aylwin made judicial reform a major policy priority. However, his reform package met with significant resistance, not least from the Supreme Court itself. He was thus forced to withdraw proposals for a National Judicial Council to take over planning, administration, and budgetary control of the judiciary, including judicial nominations, and for the creation of the office of ombudsman (defensor del pueblo) to provide an additional mechanism against abuses by public officials. He succeeded, however, in gaining legislative approval for the establishment of the Academia Judicial (Judicial School) to improve the caliber of incoming judges, to promote continuing education as they climb the hierarchy, and generally to improve the prestige of the judicial profession.[34] The Academia began functioning in April 1996, after twenty of one hundred applicants were accepted.

With the (largely failed) experience of the Aylwin government in mind, the Frei administration took a subtler and more gradual approach to judicial reform (Correa Sutil 1999b). With support from nongovernmental organizations associated with both the Concertación and the opposition, Frei's Ministry of Justice centered its efforts on a piece of Aylwin's package that had also been tabled: criminal procedure reform. This reform, which was finally approved by Congress in 1997, called for a transition of the criminal justice system from a written and inquisitory system to an oral and accusatory one. In other words, judges in criminal cases were no longer to have both prosecutorial (investigatory) and judicial functions, but would reach a decision based on the evidence and arguments presented by public prosecutors and defense lawyers. Moreover, criminal trials were to be conducted orally and publicly, introducing new procedural guarantees for defendants that were absent under the closed written system. Judges once again reacted negatively to the reform initiatives, but after a sustained effort on the part of the government to bring the judiciary on board, a majority of the Supreme Court did finally vote in favor of the reform.

In 1997, the Frei government was also able to capitalize on an alleged corruption scandal, involving members of the Supreme Court, to push a major reform of the Supreme Court through Congress.[35] Claiming that it wanted to address the root of the problem, the government seized the moment to propose fundamental structural changes to the Supreme Court. With support from the leading opposition party, Renovación Nacional (National Renovation), the Frei administration proposed a new nomination system for Supreme Court justices, reserving five posts on the Court for lawyers from outside the judiciary and requiring ratification of any appointee by two-thirds of the Senate. The bill also expanded Supreme Court membership from seventeen to twenty-one, provided for the comfortable retirement of all judges over the age of seventy-five, and shortened the term of Supreme Court president from three to two years. Although, or perhaps because, all of the Supreme Court justices in question survived impeachment attempts,[36] the judicial reform effort gathered momentum. Even the far Right party, the Unión Democrática Independiente, expressed support for most aspects of the reform package.

Despite opposition from the judiciary, the reforms prospered and the year 1998 brought eleven new faces to the Supreme Court, including five lawyers from outside the judicial hierarchy. Since then, the Supreme Court has taken a new liberal stance in key human-rights cases. On September 9, 1998, the criminal chamber of the Supreme Court, composed of one prereform justice, two of the new "external" appointees, and two substitute judges *(abogados integrantes)*, decided to reopen a 1974 disappearance case that had been previously closed by a military court.[37] For the first time, the Court embraced the argument that, as a signatory to the Geneva Conventions, Chile was bound by international humanitarian law and that amnesty thus could not apply to the case.[38] On December 29, 1998, in another disappearance case, the Supreme Court ruled that the judicial investigation must continue until the individuals responsible for the crime are identified.[39] Departing from past rulings, the Court thus insisted that amnesty applies to individuals, not to events (ChIP News, January 4, 1999).

Perhaps emboldened by these rulings, in 1999, a Santiago Appeals Court judge, Juan Guzmán Tapia, indicted the five army officials who led the so-called Caravan of Death operation in the weeks immediately following the 1973 military coup.[40] The operation resulted in the deaths of some seventy-five individuals, nineteen of whom had yet to be located. Guzmán thus charged the (now retired) officers with "aggravated kidnapping," a crime considered to be a continuing event, extending beyond the period covered by the 1978 amnesty law. Although recognizing and applying amnesty for the confirmed deaths of political prisoners, Judge Guzmán maintained the "aggravated kidnapping" charges against the leaders of the Caravan of Death, retired General Sergio Arellano Stark, retired Brigadier Pedro Espinoza, and retired Colonels Marcelo Moren Brito, Sergio Arrendono González, and Patricio Díaz Araneda (ChIP News, June 9, 1999).

During his investigation, Guzmán came under fire from the Supreme Court for making public statements on the case and for claiming in a newspaper interview after his ruling that judges "were not slaves to the law" and "maintained the authority to interpret legislation." Despite this, both the Santiago Appeals Court and the Supreme Court, in turn, upheld Guzmán's indictments of the Caravan of Death leaders (ChIP News, July 6 and July 21, 1999). In June and August 2000, these same courts voted to revoke General Pinochet's senatorial immunity, opening the way for his indictment, in January 2001, for his role in the Caravan of Death.[41]

CONCLUSIONS

Chile has often been held out as an "exception" in Latin America, more like England or France in its political and social characteristics than like Argentina, Brazil, or Peru. One might thus be led to think that, in the quest to institutionalize greater liberalism in the political system, Chileans have greater historical resources upon which to draw than do their counterparts in other Latin American countries. Indeed, based on past characterizations, it would not be unreasonable to assume that Chile's judiciary is among its enviably strong and nonpoliticized state institutions, in need of no more than a simple purge to rid its ranks of Pinochetistas. With recent developments in some major human-rights cases in Chile, some might even conclude that whatever damage the judiciary suffered under the authoritarian regime has been repaired and that Chile is well on its way to reestablishing itself as a liberal democracy.

This chapter is meant to correct these possible misconceptions about the historical role of the Chilean judiciary, and thereby to temper, though certainly not extinguish, the current enthusiasm regarding the development of political liberalism in Chile. Through the analysis of judicial behavior under democratic and authoritarian regimes, as well as interviews with numerous judges, I have sought to show that Chile has, in many ways, as far to go in establishing the judiciary as a check on other branches of government as do other Latin American countries. Chile may have been more democratic than her neighbors, in the sense of having gradually achieved a high level of inclusiveness and participation in the system, and may have been more rule-bound, orderly, and politically stable than other societies in the region. However, much like her neighboring countries, Chile has always had a tradition of constitutions without constitutionalism (Borón 1993). Chilean constitutions were designed to offer a "tool for governing society," not to set limits on government power (Frühling 1993). Thus, Chilean leaders constructed the judiciary to serve more as "ballast for the executive" than as a defense against the abuse of citizens' rights (Adelman 1999: 292), and Chilean judges have generally been true to this role.

Specifically, as I have attempted to demonstrate, the institutional characteristics of the judiciary did not encourage the development of a constitutionalist orientation among Chilean judges. To begin, the hierarchical structure of the judiciary under the tight control of the Supreme Court provided incentives for judges to look to their superiors, not the constitution, for cues on how to decide cases. Judges learned that to suc-

ceed professionally, the best strategy was to eschew independent or innovative interpretation in favor of safe, traditional rulings that would
please the high-court justices. This incentive structure operated within
the context of a system dominated by a rigid positivist legal ideology.
Judges were trained and socialized to believe that their professional integrity required them to eschew all involvement in politics, limiting themselves to the strict application of the law. In this tradition, appeals to the
constitution to question, challenge, or check the activities of the explicitly political branches of government (the executive or legislature) were
considered, in general, to be outside the professional purview of judges.
Judges deemed to have violated this professional code risked punishment
by the Supreme Court, which could in turn jeopardize their career ambitions. Thus, the institutional structure and ideology of the Chilean judiciary together created professional understandings and incentives that
tended to dissuade judges from taking stands in defense of constitutionalist principles. Consequently, and as revealed in my above discussion of
judicial decisions, Chilean courts might be better described as historically deferential than as "vigilant."

This does not mean, however, that the courts were "neutral" or apolitical. The institutional structure and ideology of the judiciary not only
fostered conformity among judges, but also reproduced conservatism.
Their bias in favor of conservative values and interests was evident in
their targeted assertion of judicial power and inconsistent appeal to
rights under the Frei and Allende governments, as well as in their continuous legitimation of authoritarian policies under military rule and
even after the transition to civilian government. This bias was also clear
in the Supreme Court's record of disciplinary action, which was taken repeatedly against judges who took stands at odds with the Court's own
conservative line.

In sum, then, I contend that the institutional setting of the judiciary
in Chile systematically inhibited the expression of liberal, but not conservative, judicial preferences. On the one hand, the Supreme Court's
vertical control of the judicial hierarchy and the institution's hegemonic
positivist ideology discouraged judges from exercising liberal qualities
of mind: openness, independence, creativity, and a sense of "humane
skepticism" (Shklar 1986). Indeed, the display of such characteristics
was considered "political" and hence unprofessional. On the other hand,
the judiciary's institutional features embodied and fostered conservative
values and attitudes: hierarchy and paternalism, an elitist disdain for politics, and a preference for uniformity and order over pluralism and tol-

eration. These characteristics were deemed timeless, natural, or necessary, and not "political." In a word, illiberal institutional dynamics account largely for illiberal judicial performance in Chile.

If one accepts this argument, then one must also recognize that the problem cannot be resolved overnight. "Institutional inertia" is a powerful force (Buscaglia, Dakolias, and Ratliff 1995). To the extent that there have been hopeful signs of liberal change in the Chilean judiciary in the late 1990s, then, it should be attributed to thoughtful, persistent, and thorough work on the part of Chilean reformers. Recognizing the institutional sources of judicial performance, a dedicated group of reformers has pursued a comprehensive reform strategy aimed at transforming the judiciary into an effective pillar of constitutional democracy (Correa Sutil 1999b). Here, perhaps, the Chilean political elite's experience with political bargaining and compromise (its democratic tradition), and its commitment to formal rule following (which others have termed a "rule of law" tradition), does give the country an advantage. First, consensus building on the issue of judicial reform has been easier and more successful than it has been in other Latin American countries (Prillaman 2000). Second, because Chilean political actors take seriously and respect formal institutional rules more than do their counterparts in neighboring countries, it is far more likely that the purposive construction of a more liberal political structure and culture will succeed. Thus, we may be cautiously optimistic about the development of a more liberal democracy in Chile.

However, it is also important to keep in mind that even a perfectly tuned liberal judiciary can't guarantee a "rights revolution." As several prominent U.S. judicial scholars have recently shown, progress in the area of rights seems to owe more to social and legal mobilization than to judicial leadership (Rosenberg 1991; Epp 1998). Thus, organizations in civil society need to establish and maintain mechanisms of support for and oversight of the judiciary, and of public officials in general (Jelin 1996; Smulovitz and Peruzzotti 2000). Neither judges nor any other authorities can be relied upon to respect and defend liberal democratic values and principles, "unless an alert public is constantly on the watch and ready, individually and collectively, to insist upon the enforcement of the rights it recognizes as expressing the community's values, interests, and beliefs" (Friedrich 1974: 80). Ultimately, then, the establishment of constitutionalism in Latin America (as elsewhere) will require far more than judicial reform.

NOTES

1. In this chapter, I follow Walter Murphy (1993) in defining constitutionalism as having an inherent liberal content, that is, an overriding concern with placing substantive limits on governmental authority. However, I recognize it is possible to conceive of constitutionalism more broadly and to consider liberal constitutionalism merely one type thereof (Jackson and Tushnet 1999: chap. 3). Relatedly, I believe there is a conceptual distinction between the rule of law, constitutionalism, and political liberalism (see esp. Shklar 1986), though many scholars tend to blur this distinction.

2. For one prominent exception to this view, see Waldron 1999.

3. Weissert (2000) cites Rachel Neild of the Washington Office on Latin America as saying, "The rule of law does seem like it could rise above political obstacles for the first time" in Latin America.

4. I use the term *liberal* to refer to attitudes and practices grounded in the concept of equal individual rights and the principle of limited government, and *illiberal* to refer to attitudes and practices at odds with these commitments. I use the term *conservative* (below) not simply to refer to resistance to change, but (in the Chilean context) to a perspective that accepts hierarchy as "natural" in the social order, and which thus tends to favor paternalistic government over liberal democracy (or order and discipline over liberty and equality). Chilean conservatism, as I define it here, is thus inherently illiberal.

5. This argument owes much to those of Jorge Correa Sutil (1993) and Hugo Frühling (1980), whose claims my own research confirmed. However, my work both expands upon and differs from theirs in important ways (see esp. Hilbink 1999a: 62–63 and 462–64).

6. The primary data for the three middle sections consist of all judicial decisions in civil- and political-rights cases published in Chile's three main jurisprudential journals between 1964 and 1994, judicial speeches and acts from the same thirty-year period, and field interviews conducted with nearly one hundred judges, lawyers, and former ministers of justice in 1995–96. The larger work on which this chapter is based gives at least brief mention to every case found in the journals, concentrating on those that received the greatest public attention and comment. In the interest of space, I include only the most salient and representative examples here, and I refer those interested in greater detail to Hilbink 1999a, which is now a book manuscript, entitled "The Politics of (In)Justice in Chile, 1964–2000."

7. However, as Frühling (1984) notes, this did not establish much of a check on executive power, since the president managed to get his will echoed in Congress via permanent practices of electoral intervention.

8. Legal positivism asserts that there is no necessary connection between legal validity and moral defensibility. A valid (and hence binding) law is one enacted consistently with the society's rule of recognition, that is, with the settled practice determining the procedures by which norms become laws. Rule application, that is, judging, should respect ordinary linguistic practice and legislative history. Formalism, a particularly strong version of positivism, refers to the

judicial inclination to apply canonical rules in a mechanical fashion, irrespective of the purposes and policies underlying them. It thus denies the possibility of judicial discretion.

9. Note that Chile remained under military rule until 1932, after which the 1925 constitution remained in effect.

10. By *professionalization* I mean the creation of a merit-based bureaucracy, in which members move up the ranks of a hierarchy based on some combination of seniority and performance, and who are thus (ostensibly) less beholden and/or vulnerable to the whims of governing politicians. On the politics of this transitional period, see Stanton 1997.

11. In this sense, they followed the logic of Andrés Bello, who believed that if citizens could see that laws were applied neutrally, they would respect legality and work within the system to resolve conflicts.

12. The constitution specified that two individuals on the lists of five and one on the lists of three had to be chosen on the basis of seniority. The others were to be chosen on "merit," the meaning of which was left to the discretion of the superior-court justices.

13. This review became annual in 1971.

14. I use the term *democratic* here simply to mean elected by a majority of eligible voters, though I share the view that meaningful democracy requires much more than this.

15. For more on the social background of Chilean judges, see Garth and Dezalay n.d.; and Hilbink 1999a.

16. It should be noted that these authors do not focus on habeas corpus cases in ordinary criminal arrests, but rather only in cases involving alleged political crimes. I hope to gather data on the former in a future research trip to Chile.

17. In Chile, presidential decrees are automatically reviewed for legality and constitutionality by the comptroller general. However, the "decree of insistence" was a widely accepted and frequently exercised instrument used to overrule the comptroller in the country's strongly presidential system (Silva Cimma 1977).

18. RDJ refers to the *Revista de Derecho y Jurisprudencia.* (All translations in this book are by chapter authors unless otherwise indicated.)

19. Indeed, in January 1967 the Frei administration had succeeded in getting a constitutional amendment passed that changed the article guaranteeing the right to property to allow government expropriation in the interest of society with less rigid terms of indemnification.

20. The citation is from the Supreme Court's decision in the writ of habeas corpus ruling in favor of the defendants *García Garzena, Víctor, y otros (recurso de amparo),* printed in RDJ 64 (1967) 2.4: 266–72. A similar conclusion was reached in the ruling on the substance of the case, appearing in RDJ 65 (1968) 2.4: 95–99. The emphases in the citations are mine.

21. In an official letter sent to President Allende to request authorization for a national radio and television station, Otero had made a statement implying that Allende's decisions were subordinated to instructions from a Cuban diplomat, an implication which, in the view of the government, constituted a public libel and an attack on public order.

22. The paper had published copies of documents that it claimed showed the involvement of the congressmen in the "campaign of terror" to prevent Allende from assuming the presidency, including the assassination of constitutionalist General René Schneider in 1970. It should be noted that the articles in question all appeared between July and December 1970, and that one of the congressmen, Raúl Morales Adriazola, had been under official suspicion of involvement in the assassination until the Supreme Court, in a highly controversial ruling, dismissed charges against him on January 4, 1971. The paper had also targeted one of the men for alleged marital and sexual improprieties.

23. See the speeches printed in the opening pages of RDJ 67 (1970) and 68 (1971).

24. Note that by this time, a "close fifty-fifty" split had emerged in the National Association of Magistrates between those supporting Allende and those opposed (author interview with retired judge, Santiago, June 11, 1996).

25. Among the denouncers were Senator Raúl Morales Adriazola (mentioned above in note 22) and lawyer Pablo Rodríguez Grez, both notorious members of the far Right.

26. Although after the coup, the Supreme Court expelled him from the judiciary.

27. National-security doctrine generally refers to the ideology with which the United States trained Latin American militaries during the Cold War, broadening the military mission to maintaining internal social order (i.e., counterinsurgency) and security from external threats. However, such a mission was not simply an import from abroad, as a number of works suggest. Indeed, the idea of the military as the guardian of the national interest and essence has a much longer history in Latin America. (See particularly Frühling, Portales, and Varas 1982; and Loveman and Davies 1989.)

28. See his speeches from 1975 and 1983, reprinted in Loveman and Davies 1989: 240–49. Note that the military regime introduced a new constitution in 1980, which was reformed as part of the transition to civilian rule in 1989 and remains in effect today.

29. Note that no court in Chile accepted a habeas corpus petition for an adult until 1977.

30. From the title of an article in a prodemocracy magazine (Badilla 1990).

31. This is not to dismiss the important investigations, and later convictions, in the Letelier-Moffitt assassination case and the *degollados* case. However, the former case was unique in that it was explicitly excepted from the amnesty law and drew important pressure from the U.S. government. The latter case involved crimes committed in 1985, and thus postdated the amnesty. Both cases are treated in more detail in Hilbink 1999a.

32. The case was *Iván Sergio Insunza Bascuñán (recurso de inaplicabilidad)*.

33. It should be noted that even in rights cases that postdated the transition, judges showed little proclivity to defend and promote liberal principles and practices. See Hilbink 1999b; and Couso and Hilbink 2000.

34. In the interest of space, other more technical reforms passed under Aylwin's tenure are not discussed here. Interested readers should refer to Hilbink 1999a and Prillaman 2000.

35. The scandal arose out of the case against accused drug dealer and money launderer Mario Silva Leiva, or "Cabro Carrera," who was allegedly protected for years by a network of government officials and public employees. Representatives from the opposition party Unión Democrática Independiente took advantage of the political uproar over the case to file impeachment charges against Supreme Court president Servando Jordán for undue intervention or interference in the Cabro Carrera case and in the case of another suspected drug dealer, Rita Romero. Not to be outdone, members of the Concertación filed a separate accusation against four justices, including Jordán, for misconduct in the 1991 case of convicted Colombian drug dealer Luis Correa Ramirez. Correa Ramirez had been convicted and imprisoned after smuggling a half ton of cocaine into Chile in 1989, and on April 17, 1991, the Third Chamber of the Supreme Court denied him parole. One month later, however, the justices unanimously and inexplicably paroled him on a bond of about eleven hundred U.S. dollars, after he had served only one-quarter of his sentence. Correa Ramirez then fled the country. (See ChIP News, July 1, 1997.)

36. For the charges brought by the Unión Democrática Independiente, Servando Jordán narrowly escaped impeachment: the July 25 vote in the Chamber of Deputies was fifty-two to fifty-two. In the other case, in which charges were brought against Jordán and three others, only twenty-four deputies voted to impeach the judges, while forty-nine voted to absolve.

37. The case was that of activist Pedro Enrique Poblete Córdova, who disappeared in 1974 after his arrest by DINA secret police operatives. Investigations into Poblete Córdova's disappearance had previously been impeded by legal rulings that did not recognize the binding nature of the Geneva Conventions.

38. "Por primera vez suprema aplicó Convenios de Ginebra," *La Tercera*, September 11, 1998 (web site, http://www.latercera.cl). Note that this predated Pinochet's arrest in London.

39. The case was that of Álvaro Miguel Barrios, abducted by the DINA in August 1974.

40. Judge Guzmán was investigating some three hundred charges of human-rights violations against General Pinochet.

41. Six months later, however, the Santiago Appeals Court ruled that Pinochet was mentally unfit to stand trial. In July 2002, the Supreme Court upheld that ruling, effectively bringing the effort to prosecute Pinochet for human-rights abuses to a close.

REFERENCES

Adelman, Jeremy. 1999. *Republic of Capital: Buenos Aires and the Legal Transformation of the Atlantic World.* Stanford, Calif.: Stanford University Press.

Arriagada, Genaro. 1974. *De la "Vía Chilena" a la "Vía Insurrecional."* Santiago: Editorial del Pacífico.

Athey, Lois Edwards. 1978. "Government and Opposition in Chile during the Allende Years: 1970–1973." Ph.D. diss., Columbia University.

Aylwin, Mariana, Carlos Bascuñán, Sofía Correa, Cristián Gazmuri, Sol Serrano, and Matías Tagle. 1996. *Chile en el siglo XX.* Santiago: Editorial Planeta.

Badilla, Iván. 1990. "Hacer justicia es hacer democracia." *ANÁLISIS* (January 15): 9–11.

Bauer, Carl. 1995. "The Contradictory Role of the Judiciary in Chile's Neoliberal Economic Model." Paper presented at the First Congress of the Latin American and Caribbean Association of Law and Economics, Mexico City, February 2–3.

Becker, David. 1997. "The Rule of Law in Latin America: A Framework for Analysis." Paper presented at the Annual Meeting of the American Political Science Association, Sheraton Washington Hotel, Washington, D.C., August 28–31.

Bertelsen Repetto, Raúl. 1969. *Control de constitucionalidad de la ley.* Santiago: Editorial Jurídica.

Bollen, Kenneth. 1980. "Issues in the Comparative Measurement of Political Democracy." *American Sociological Review* 45, no. 3 (June): 370–90.

Borón, Atilio A. 1993. "Latin America: Constitutionalism and the Political Traditions of Liberalism and Socialism." In *Constitutionalism and Democracy: Transitions in the Contemporary World,* ed. Douglas Greenberg, Stanley N. Katz, Melanie Beth Oliviero, and Steven C. Wheatley, pp. 339–53. New York: Oxford University Press.

Bravo Lira, Bernardino. 1991. "Bello y la judicatura: La reforma judicial." *Revista de Derecho y Jurisprudencia* 88, pt. 1: 49–58.

Brett, Sebastian. 1992. *Chile: A Time of Reckoning.* Geneva: International Commission of Jurists.

Buscaglia, Edgardo, Maria Dakolias, and William Ratliff. 1995. *Judicial Reform in Latin America: A Framework for National Development.* Stanford, Calif.: Hoover Institution.

Caffarena de Jiles, Elena. 1957. *El recurso de amparo frente a los regímenes de emergencia.* Santiago: Editorial Jurídica.

Cavallo Castro, Ascanio, Manuel Salazar Salvo, and Oscar Sepúlveda Pacheco. 1989. *La historia oculta del régimen militar.* Santiago: Antártica.

Cea, José Luis. 1978. "Law and Socialism in Chile, 1970–1973." Ph.D. diss., University of Wisconsin, Madison.

———. 1987. "Rasgos de la experiencia democrática y constitucional de Chile." *Revista Chilena de Derecho* 14, no. 1: 25–35.

ChIP (Chile Information Project) News, daily Internet newsletter. Web site, http://www.chip.cl.

Collier, Simon. 1967. *Ideas and Politics of Chilean Independence: 1808–1833.* New York: Cambridge University Press.

Collier, Simon, and William F. Slater. 1996. *A History of Chile: 1808–1994.* New York: Cambridge University Press.

Correa Sutil, Jorge. 1993. "The Judiciary and the Political System in Chile." In *Transition to Democracy in Latin America: The Role of the Judiciary,* ed. Irwin P. Stotsky, pp. 89–106. Boulder, Colo.: Westview Press.

———. 1999a. "Judicial Reform in Latin America: Good News for the Underprivileged?" In *The (Un)Rule of Law and the Underprivileged in Latin America,* ed. Juan E. Méndez, Guillermo O'Donnell, and Paulo Sérgio Pinheiro, pp. 255–77. Notre Dame, Ind.: University of Notre Dame Press.

———. 1999b. "Cenicienta se queda en la fiesta: El poder judicial chileno en la década de los 90." In *El modelo chileno: Democracia y desarrollo en los noventa,* ed. Paul Drake and Iván Jaksić, pp. 281–315. Santiago: LOM.

Couso, Javier, and Lisa Hilbink. 2000. "The Writ of Protection, Judicial Review, and Governance in Chile." Paper presented at the Annual Meeting of the American Political Science Association, Marriott Wardman Park, Washington, D.C., August 31–September 3.

Cumplido, Francisco, and Hugo Frühling. 1980. "Problemas jurídico-políticos del tránsito hacia la democracia: Chile, 1924–1932." *Estudios Sociales* 21: 71–113.

Dahl, Robert. 1971. *Polyarchy: Participation and Opposition.* New Haven, Conn.: Yale University Press.

De Ramón, Armando. 1989. "La justicia chilena entre 1875 y 1924." *Cuadernos de Análisis Jurídico,* Monograph 12 (October).

DeVylder, Stefan. 1974. *The Political Economy of the Rise and Fall of the Unidad Popular.* New York: Cambridge University Press.

Drake, Paul W. 1978. *Socialism and Populism in Chile, 1932–52.* Urbana: University of Illinois Press.

Echeverría, Andrés, and Luis Frei, eds. 1974. *1970–1973: La lucha por la juridicidad en Chile.* Santiago: Editorial Jurídica.

Ehrmann, Henry. 1976. *Comparative Legal Cultures.* Englewood Cliffs, N.J.: Prentice-Hall.

Epp, Charles R. 1998. *The Rights Revolution: Lawyers, Activists, and Supreme Courts in Comparative Perspective.* Chicago: University of Chicago Press.

Etcheberry, Alfredo. 1990. "Amnistía, derecho, y justicia." *Mensaje* 393 (October): 369–72.

Fallos del Mes. Santiago.

Figueroa, Gonzalo, ed. 1978. *Derecho y sociedad.* Santiago: Corporación de Promoción Universitaria.

Friedrich, Carl. 1974. *Limited Government: A Comparison.* Englewood Cliffs, N.J.: Prentice-Hall.

Frühling, Hugo. 1980. "Poder judicial y política en Chile." In *La administración de justicia en America Latina,* ed. Javier de Belaúnde L. de R., pp. 85–104. Lima: Consejo Latinoamericano de Derecho y Desarrollo.

———. 1984. "Law in Society: Social Transformation and the Crisis of Law in Chile, 1830–1970." Ph.D. diss., Harvard University School of Law.

———. 1993. "Human Rights in Constitutional Order and in Political Practice in Latin America." In *Constitutionalism and Democracy: Transitions in the Contemporary World,* ed. Douglas Greenberg, Stanley N. Katz, Melanie Beth Oliviero, and Steven C. Wheatley, pp. 85–104. New York: Oxford University Press.

———. 1998. "Judicial Reform and Democratization in Latin America." In *Fault Lines of Democracy in Post-Transition Latin America,* ed. Felipe Agüero and Jeffrey Stark, pp. 237–62. Miami: North-South Center Press of the University of Miami.

Frühling, Hugo, Carlos Portales, and Augusto Varas. 1982. *Estado y fuerzas armadas.* Santiago: Stichting Rechtshulp Chili and FLACSO.

Gaceta Jurídica. Santiago.

Garcés, Joan. 1973. *El estado y problemas tácticos en el gobierno de Allende.* Buenos Aires: Siglo XXI Editores.

García Villegas, René. 1990. *Soy testigo.* Santiago: Editorial Amerinda.

Gardner, James. 1980. *Legal Imperialism: American Lawyers and Foreign Aid in Latin America.* Madison: University of Wisconsin Press.

Garretón, Roberto. 1987. "El poder judicial en la dictadura." In *Encuentro internacional de magistrados, "Poder judicial y derechos humanos,"* ed. Comisión Chilena de Derechos Humanos. Santiago: Comisión Chilena de Derechos Humanos.

——. 1989. "El poder judicial chileno y la violación de los derechos humanos." Documento de Trabajo 28–29. Santiago: Corporación de Promoción Universitaria.

Garth, Bryant, and Yves Dezalay. n.d. "Chile: Law and the Legitimation of Transitions." American Bar Foundation. Photocopy.

Gil, Federico. 1966. *The Political System of Chile.* Boston: Houghton Mifflin.

González M., Felipe. 1989. "Modelos legislativos de seguridad interior, 1925–1989." *Revista Chilena de Derechos Humanos* 11 (November): 18–24.

Greenberg, Douglas, Stanley N. Katz, Melanie Beth Oliviero, and Steven C. Wheatley, eds. 1993. *Constitutionalism and Democracy: Transitions in the Contemporary World.* New York: Oxford University Press.

Hammergren, Linn. 1998. *The Politics of Justice and Justice Reform in Latin America: The Peruvian Case in Comparative Perspective.* Boulder, Colo.: Westview Press.

Harnecker, Marta, and Víctor Vaccaro. 1973. "Oscar Álvarez (Magistrado): 'La Justicia Es Necesariamente Clasista.'" *Chile HOY* 1, no. 36 (February 16): 29–32.

Hidalgo, Guillermo. 1992. "Ministra locuaz." *Qué Pasa* (October 12): 16–17.

Hilbink, Elisabeth C. 1999a. "Legalism against Democracy: The Political Role of the Judiciary in Chile, 1964–1994." Ph.D. diss., Department of Political Science, University of California, San Diego.

——. 1999b. "Un estado de derecho no liberal: La actuación del poder judicial en los años 90." In *El modelo chileno: Democracia y desarrollo en los noventa,* ed. Paul Drake and Iván Jaksić, pp. 317–37. Santiago: LOM.

Jackson, Vicki C., and Mark Tushnet. 1999. *Comparative Constitutional Law.* New York: Foundation Press.

Jaksić, Iván. 1997a. "Constitutionalism and the Rule of Law in Chile: The Role of Andrés Bello." Paper presented at the Twentieth International Congress of the Latin American Studies Association, Guadalajara, Mexico, April 17–19.

——, ed. 1997b. *Selected Writings of Andrés Bello.* New York: Oxford University Press.

Jelin, Elizabeth. 1996. "Citizenship Revisited: Solidarity, Responsibility, and Rights." In *Constructing Democracy: Human Rights, Citizenship, and Society in Latin America,* ed. Elizabeth Jelin and Eric Herschberg, pp. 101–19. Boulder, Colo.: Westview Press.

Jelin, Elizabeth, and Eric Hershberg. 1996. "Human Rights and the Construction of Democracy." Introduction to *Constructing Democracy: Human*

Rights, Citizenship, and Society in Latin America, ed. Elizabeth Jelin and Eric Hershberg, pp. 1–10. Boulder, Colo.: Westview Press.

Kaufman, Edy. 1988. *Crisis in Allende's Chile*. New York: Praeger.

Kinsbrunner, Jay. 1967. *Diego Portales: Interpretive Essays on the Man and Times*. The Hague: Martinus Nijhoff.

Linz, Juan, and Alfred Stepan. 1996. *Problems of Democratic Transition and Consolidation: Southern Europe, South America, and Post-Communist Europe*. Baltimore: Johns Hopkins University Press.

López Dawson, Carlos. 1986. *Justicia y derechos humanos*. Santiago: Editorial Documentas.

Loveman, Brian. 1988. *Chile: The Legacy of Hispanic Capitalism*. New York: Oxford University Press.

———. 1993. *The Constitution of Tyranny*. Pittsburgh: University of Pittsburgh Press.

Loveman, Brian, and Thomas M. Davies, Jr., eds. 1989. *The Politics of Anti-Politics*. 2d ed. Lincoln: University of Nebraska Press.

Mainwaring, Scott. 1992. "Transitions to Democracy and Democratic Consolidation: Theoretical and Comparative Issues." In *Issues in Democratic Consolidation*, ed. Scott Mainwaring, Guillermo O'Donnell, and J. Samuel Valenzuela, pp. 294–341. Notre Dame, Ind.: University of Notre Dame Press.

Matus Acuña, Alejandra. 1999. *El libro negro de la justicia chilena*. Santiago: Editorial Planeta.

Mera F., Jorge, Felipe González M., and Juan Enrique Vargas V. 1987. "Función judicial, seguridad interior del estado y orden público: El caso de la 'Ley de defensa de la democracia.'" Santiago: Academia de Humanismo Cristiano, Programa de Derechos Humanos, Cuaderno de Trabajo No. 5.

Murphy, Walter F. 1993. "Constitutions, Constitutionalism, and Democracy." In *Constitutionalism and Democracy: Transitions in the Contemporary World*, ed. Douglas Greenberg, Stanley N. Katz, Melanie Beth Oliviero, and Steven C. Wheatley, pp. 3–25. New York: Oxford University Press.

Navarro Beltrán, Enrique. 1988. *La judicatura chilena del absolutismo ilustrado al estado constitucional*. Santiago: Universidad de Chile, Facultad de Derecho.

Novoa Monreal, Eduardo. 1964. "La crisis del sistema legal chileno." *Mensaje* 13: 559–66.

O'Donnell, Guillermo. 1999. "Polyarchies and the (Un)Rule of Law in Latin America." In *The (Un)Rule of Law and the Underprivileged in Latin America*, ed. Juan E. Méndez, Guillermo O'Donnell, and Paulo Sérgio Pinheiro, pp. 303–37. Notre Dame, Ind.: University of Notre Dame Press.

Oliva, Alicia. 1986. "Nadie está obligado a obedecer leyes injustas." *ANÁLISIS* (August 29): 16–17.

Oppenheim, Lois Hecht. 1993. *Politics in Chile: Democracy, Authoritarianism, and the Search for Development*. Boulder, Colo.: Westview Press.

Otano, Rafael. 1995. *Crónica de la transición*. Santiago: Editorial Planeta.

Peña González, Carlos. 1994. "América Latina: ¿Una justicia emergente?" *Boletín de la Comisión Andina de Juristas* 41 (June): 9–17.

Prillaman, William C. 2000. *The Judiciary and Democratic Decay in Latin America: Declining Confidence in the Rule of Law*. Westport, Conn.: Praeger.

Przeworski, Adam. 1995. *Sustainable Democracy*. New York: Cambridge University Press.

Revista de Derecho y Jurisprudencia (RDJ). Santiago.

Rojas, Juanita. 1990. "Los escándalos del poder judicial." *ANÁLISIS* (April 15): 14–16.

Rosenberg, Gerald N. 1991. *The Hollow Hope: Can Courts Bring About Social Change?* Chicago: University of Chicago Press.

Schedler, Andreas, Larry Diamond, and Marc F. Plattner, eds. 1999. *The Self-Restraining State: Power and Accountability in New Democracies*. Boulder, Colo.: Lynne Rienner.

Schmitter, Philippe, and Terry Karl. 1991. "What Democracy Is...and Is Not." *Journal of Democracy* 2, no. 3 (July): 75–88.

Shklar, Judith. 1986. *Legalism: Law, Morals, and Political Trials*. Cambridge, Mass.: Harvard University Press.

Sigmund, Paul. 1977. *The Overthrow of Allende and the Politics of Chile, 1964–1973*. Pittsburgh: University of Pittsburgh Press.

Silva Cimma, Enrique. 1977. *El tribunal constitucional de Chile (1971–1973)*. Caracas: Editorial Jurídica Venezolana.

Smulovitz, Catalina, and Enrique Peruzzotti. 2000. "Societal Accountability in Latin America." *Journal of Democracy* 11, no. 4 (October): 147–58.

Stanton, Kimberly. 1997. "The Transformation of a Political Regime: Chile's 1925 Constitution." Paper presented at meeting of the Latin American Studies Association, Guadalajara, Mexico, April 17–19.

Tavolari, Raúl. 1995. *Habeas corpus: Recurso de amparo*. Santiago: Editorial Jurídica.

Valenzuela, Arturo. 1978. *The Breakdown of Democratic Regimes: Chile*. Baltimore: Johns Hopkins University Press.

———. 1989. "Chile." In *Democracy in Developing Countries: Latin America*, ed. Larry Diamond, Juan J. Linz, and Seymour Martin Lipset, pp. 159–206. Boulder, Colo.: Lynne Rienner.

———. 1995. "The Military in Power: The Consolidation of One-Man Rule." In *The Struggle for Democracy in Chile*, ed. Paul W. Drake and Iván Jaksić, pp. 21–72. Rev. ed. Lincoln: University of Nebraska Press.

Velasco, Eugenio. 1989. "El rol de los abogados." In *Cómo hacer justicia en democracia*, pp. 58–62. Santiago: Comisión Chilena de Derechos Humanos.

Verdugo, Patricia. 1991. "Hubo una acción planificada del alto mando." *Apsi* (February 25): 10–12.

Verdugo Marinkovic, Mario, ed. 1989. *La experiencia constitucional norteamericana y chilena sobre separación de poderes*. Santiago: Ediar Conosur.

Vicaría de la Solidaridad. Monthly reports. Santiago.

Waldron, Jeremy. 1999. *The Dignity of Legislation*. Cambridge: Cambridge University Press.

Weissert, Will. 2000. "Courts Gain Power in Latin America." *Boston Globe* (September 7), p. 9.

Whittington, Keith. 2003. "Constitutional Theory and the Faces of Power." In *Alexander Bickel and Contemporary Constitutional Theory*, ed. Kenneth Ward. Albany: State University of New York Press, forthcoming.

CHAPTER FOUR

Presidential Crises and Democratic Accountability in Latin America, 1990–1999

ANÍBAL PÉREZ-LIÑÁN

Despite the wave of democratization that has transformed Latin America since the 1980s, the region showed major signs of political instability during the 1990s in the form of confrontations between the executive and legislative branches. Between 1990 and 1999, two presidents attempted *autogolpes* (self-coups), in one case successfully, and five presidents were impeached. In previous decades, most constitutional crises were solved through military coups—imposing either short-term, moderating interventions (Stepan 1971) or long-term, bureaucratic authoritarian regimes (Collier 1979; O'Donnell 1988). In the 1990s, this pattern changed and crises were resolved through self-coups (in which the executive forced the dissolution of the legislature) or impeachment.

The new patterns of executive-legislative confrontation still need to be explored. Although self-coups have attracted much scholarly attention (e.g., Ferrero Costa 1993; McClintock 1993; Villagrán de León 1993; Cameron 1994, 1997; Kenney 1996, 1998), impeachment crises have been more or less ignored. Impeachment crises take place when an adverse legislative coalition asks for the resignation of the president and seeks the legal dissolution of an elected government. In parliamentary systems this would be achieved through a vote of no confidence, but in presidential regimes it typically involves a major constitutional crisis.[1] The crisis emerges in the form of public statements of congressional leaders calling for the ousting of the president, in the formation of special oversight committees, and in the treatment of declarations against the executive on the floor of the legislature.

In this chapter I trace the common origins of impeachment crises in the 1990s. The 1990s represented a critical decade for Latin American politics. On one hand, the process of democratization that took place during the 1980s had bred political elites more conscious of the perils of military intervention and less willing to use unconstitutional mechanisms to oust corrupt or ineffective presidents. On the other hand, the exhaustion of old models of development and the debt crisis of the 1980s exerted enormous pressures on newly elected governments to implement economic reform programs for the privatization of public companies and the deregulation of domestic markets and foreign trade. These policies were usually costly in terms of social inequality and unemployment. In this context, public opinion became particularly sensitive to corruption scandals that involved the president and congressional leaders became more willing to find a constitutional way to hold the chief executive accountable.

The first five sections of this chapter provide an overview of the crises in Brazil (1992), Venezuela (1993), Colombia (1996), Ecuador (1997), and Paraguay (1999).[2] A comparison of these cases shows that these impeachment crises have shared common features in media scandals, public outrage against the government, and weak legislative support for the president. The chapter's final section describes the broader historical context of these crises, emphasizing how the pressures of economic reform and inequality fostered public outrage against ineffective presidents. In the conclusion I briefly explore the significance of impeachments for democracy and accountability in Latin America.

BRAZIL: WEAK INSTITUTIONS
AND AN ISOLATED PRESIDENT

In 1989 the youngest president in Brazilian history, Fernando Collor de Mello, won the first direct presidential election Brazil had seen in twenty-nine years. Governor of the poor state of Alagoas, Collor was backed by a small party, the Partido da Reconstrução Nacional (Party of the National Reconstruction; PRN). Running on an antipolitical establishment platform, supported by the largest national TV network, and perceived by many as the only alternative to the leftist Partido dos Trabalhadores (Workers' Party; PT) candidate, Luiz Inácio "Lula" da Silva, Collor obtained 30.5 percent of the vote in the first round and 53 percent of the vote in the runoff election.

Collor inherited an economy on the brink of hyperinflation: at the time he was sworn into office, in March 1990, the consumer price index increased by 84 percent. Immediately after taking office, the government introduced the first "Collor plan." In order to reduce liquidity, the plan changed the currency and froze around 80 percent of the country's savings (Bresser Pereira 1991: 18). Unable to control inflation, the plan moved into more orthodox policies in May, and was finally replaced, in January 1991, by the "Collor II plan." Still lacking visible success, the minister of the economy resigned five months later. Failure of economic policy created popular dissatisfaction and weakened the position of the president in the following months.

On May 13, 1992, the president's brother, Pedro, accused Collor's campaign manager, Paulo César Farias, of funneling corruption money into ghost companies established in foreign countries.[3] Two weeks later, Pedro told the journal *Veja* that Farias was managing a corruption network for the president. Fernando Collor denied the accusations, while the police started to investigate Farias's business. In early June, Congress created a bicameral committee to examine the accusations. With just 8 percent of the seats in the lower chamber and less than 4 percent of the seats in the Senate, Collor's party was unable to control the investigative process. Soon, the committee realized that Farias had routed six and a half million dollars to Collor's (and his cronies') bank accounts. On August 11, 1992, the Cabinet virtually withdrew its support for the president. By the end of August, the congressional committee finished its report, while mass demonstrations in Brasília, São Paulo, and other major cities called for the resignation of the president. At that point, civil-society leaders formally requested Collor's impeachment. On September 29, the Chamber of Deputies approved with a 441–38 vote the impeachment by the Senate and suspended Collor from office for a period of six months (Lins da Silva 1993: 126). Three months later, the Senate voted 73–8 to oust Collor and authorized his prosecution on twenty-two charges of corruption. The president, anticipating the decision, submitted his resignation.

Why was a president who had been backed by thirty-five million votes so easily impeached? Analysts of Brazilian politics have been puzzled by this fact, but their explanations for it have been mostly based on the subtleties and nuances of the case. After holding several interviews with Brazilian politicians in the critical months of 1992, Flynn (1993) concluded that the Brazilian crisis resulted from three conditions: presidential lack of congressional support, an electorate deceived and disillusioned by a populist campaign, and the Collor administration's explosive mixture of betrayal and inefficiency. Weyland (1993) claimed that the very factors that led Collor to the presidency ultimately sealed his fate. Collor came to power as a young, anti-establishment politician with no commitment to any significant political party. In power, he tried to rule independently. His strategy created an exclusive niche for corruption. Traditional lobbying channels became ineffective, and interest groups were forced to deal with Farias. In the process, Collor prevented the formation of a dominant Center-Right coalition. The effects of political isolation combined with a changing political culture at the mass level. Brazilians had come to reject the idea that the president could be above the law. On the eve of the 1992 municipal elections—in which more than 15 percent of the national deputies ran as candidates for mayor in different cities—popular demonstrations against Collor encouraged politicians to impeach the president (Weyland 1993: 20–25).

VENEZUELA: THE COLLAPSE OF THE PARTYARCHY

Carlos Andrés Pérez won the 1988 Venezuelan presidential elections with 53 percent of the vote. An experienced leader of the powerful Acción Democrática (Democratic Action; AD) party, Pérez had been president between 1974 and 1979. During his first term in office, the oil boom had helped raise living standards in Venezuela, and the Pérez administration had followed a populist model by nationalizing the production of iron and oil, expanding the role of the public sector, and denouncing multinational corporations and international financial institutions. Pérez's program for his second term, however, was radically different: immediately after taking office in February 1989, he announced an economic reform package known as El Gran Viraje (the Great Turnaround). The "honeymoon" period didn't last long: on February 27, riots over an increase in the prices of public transportation and the scarcity of basic foodstuffs erupted in the city of Caracas and spread throughout the country, causing more than three hundred deaths.

Three years later, in February 1992, a group of young army officers attempted a coup d'etat. After the situation was controlled, the former president (and respected founder of the Copei Party) Rafael Caldera gave a speech in Congress condemning the military action but also blaming Pérez for his unpopular policies. A second coup attempt was carried out by navy and air force officers in November of that year. The coup failed again, but the Pérez administration was definitively under siege: although Pérez initially controlled 48 percent of the lower chamber of Congress and 45 percent of the Senate, partisan support for the president began to vanish as political leaders explored alternative institutional ways to dethrone the chief executive (Rey 1993: 101–12; Rodríguez-Valdés 1993). Politicians asked for a constitutional reform or a referendum in order to shorten the presidential term (Kornblith 1998). An influential group of intellectuals—known as Los Notables—insisted on the resignation of the president.

In November 1992, nineteen days before the second coup attempt, the press began to publish stories about the unknown destiny of more than 17 million dollars that had been earmarked as "secret security funds" by the Ministry of Interior. According to the reports, the money (equivalent to 250 million bolivares) had been converted to dollars using the Preferential Exchange Regime (Recadi) and routed to the president's office. The administration, in the name of "national security," refused to provide any information, and the Oversight Committee (Comisión de Contraloría) of the lower chamber created a special subcommittee to investigate the case. On March 11, 1993, the prosecutor-general asked the Supreme Court to evaluate the case in order to prosecute the president. On May 20, the court declared that the case merited further investigation, clearing the way for impeachment proceedings. The next day the Senate suspended Pérez from office and authorized the judiciary to prosecute the president. In late August, a joint session of Congress removed Pérez from office and named Ramón J. Velásquez to fill in the presidency for the rest of the term.

Explanations of the Venezuelan crisis typically focus on the collapse of the "petro-state," the resulting decline in living standards, and the dissolution of the old system of two-party dominance and elite conciliation (e.g., McCoy and Smith 1995). In such accounts, the ousting of Carlos Andrés Pérez appears as a mere episode—although a critical one—in a complex historical process. In an early attempt to understand the Venezuelan crisis, Rey (1993: 12) presented institutional conflict as the manifestation of a deeper "legitimacy crisis of the social and political order in Venezuela." From this perspective, voters had supported Pérez's candidacy because they had seen him as an alternative to the neoliberal program sponsored by the Copei candidate; he had represented for them the good old days of prosperity. But the Pérez administration—having inherited a deteriorated economy involving a scarcity of basic products, widespread price controls, and pending commitments to foreign creditors—imposed a strict adjustment program. Collapsing living conditions and presidential betrayal were compounded by institutional failure. The president's party failed to provide an alternative to his unpopular program, but it also failed to mobilize mass support for it. In this sense, Rey claims, the AD politicians—and to some extent all congressional parties—"abdicated" their political responsibilities.

According to Coppedge (1994), the ousting of President Pérez was an indicator of the ongoing collapse of the Venezuelan governability formula. Since the late 1960s, the political regime was organized as a *party-archy*. This formula assigned a central role to two major parties, Acción Democrática and Copei, led by a political establishment that managed to sustain inclusive patterns of representation and electoral competition, strong party discipline, consensus policymaking, and wide relationships between parties and interest groups.

In the 1980s, however, this formula began to crumble under the pressure of economic decline. In a context of increasing corruption, ossified political structures with dated platforms were unable to meet the new challenges. The sequence leading to impeachment, according to this view, was the ultimate manifestation of the inability of Venezuelan institutions to adapt. Against popular expectations, Pérez imposed harsh economic measures that compromised his mass support. This weakness paved the way for the later coup attempts in 1992 and created a vacuum that ultimately triggered his impeachment. From this perspective, impeachment was the first stage in the search for a democratic alternative for the old governability formula (Coppedge 1994: 51).

COLOMBIA: THE CONSPIRACY OF THE REFORMISTS?

Liberal candidate Ernesto Samper narrowly defeated his Conservative opponent, Andrés Pastrana, with 50.6 percent of the vote in the runoff election of June 19, 1994. Immediately after the election, Pastrana and the Conservative press disclosed a number of tapes with telephone conversations linking Samper's campaign treasurer, Santiago Medina, to the Cali drug cartel. The origin of the tapes was unknown, although most people believed that the U.S. Drug Enforcement Administration (DEA) had released them to put pressure on the Colombian government (on the origins of the tapes, see Vargas, Lesmes, and Téllez 1996: 22–26). Later that year, Prosecutor-General Alfonso Valdivieso collected further evidence implicating Samper's campaign treasurer.

On July 26, 1995, Santiago Medina was arrested, and he confessed that he had received campaign contributions from the drug lords (Medina Serna 1997: 170–81). The prosecutor asked the Supreme Court to investigate the minister of defense and former campaign manager, Fernando Botero. In a preemptive move, Samper himself requested Congress to investigate the accusations. Minister Botero resigned in the first week of August and was later prosecuted, while some journalists and political leaders claimed that Samper should be investigated too. On December 14, 1995, the congressional Comisión de Investigación y Acusaciones (Committee of Investigation and Accusations of the House of Representatives) that investigated the case presented a seventy-four-page report stating that the evidence presented by Medina was inconclusive. The committee, packed with members of Samper's Liberal Party, recommended that the investigation be dropped. Polls showed that most people believed Samper to be guilty but did not consider the scandal outrageous enough to justify an impeachment (*Economist,* September 2, 1995: 38).

A major shake-up came in January, when Fernando Botero gave a TV interview from prison and declared that Samper had known about the campaign funds. If any money had been taken from the drug lords, Samper insisted, it was without his knowledge. Opposition politicians and dissident Liberals pressured for Samper's resignation, and the administration claimed that the country was undergoing a "governability crisis." In a televised speech in late March, the president discussed alternative solutions to the crisis: a referendum, a government of national unity, holding presidential elections in advance. In May, however, the congressional oversight committee voted 10–3 in favor of clearing Samper. Despite the protests of some legislators (Betancourt Pulecio 1996; Victoria 1997) and of important civil-society leaders (Comisión Ciudadana 1996), the president had built an important shield in Congress. On June 12, 1996, the House of Representatives voted 111–43 in favor of clearing the president.

According to López Caballero (1997), the crisis in Colombia was the result of a latent conflict between two social coalitions, one opposing the emergent neoliberal model and another one pushing for neoliberal economic (and social) reform. López Caballero presented this as an ongoing battle between the "real" country and the proponents of a "New Colombia." In his view, the crusades for the New Colombia were typically well-educated citizens (often technocrats educated in foreign universities) who defended neoliberal policies, disdained traditional politics as clientelistic and corrupt, disregarded parties and institutions (they understood politics purely as a matter of spin control), and held a "pragmatic" approach to politics that justified any action in order to put an end to the "Old Colombia." This group had supported President Gaviria's (1990–94) economic policy and the constitutional reform of 1991, and had seen in Samper an obstacle for the consolidation of the new socioeconomic model. With the support of powerful media (including *Semana* and *El Tiempo*) and the U.S. intelligence, they had pushed the scandal in order to force an impeachment. The plan, however, failed due to the lack of direct proof against Samper. In López Caballero's account, the crisis was the result of a deeper social struggle: "what has truly motivated and triggered the trials and scandals is not a desire for correcting the [political] system or purifying it from its failures, but a desire to take it back over" (López Caballero 1997: 155).

John Dugas (2001) has correctly pointed out that "López Caballero's conspiracy theory lacks substance." But his interpretation is particularly important because it closely reflects the administration's version of the events. To the extent that many Colombians saw Samper as a Liberal president threatened by powerful elites and the U.S. government, they were less inclined to interpret the campaign finance scandal as a violation of the public trust and more willing to see it as the excuse for impeachment invoked by the president's enemies.

ECUADOR: THE POPULIST LEGACY

In July 1996, the candidate of the Partido Roldosista Ecuatoriano (Roldosist Ecuadorian Party; PRE), Abdalá Bucaram, won the majority runoff presidential election with 54.5 percent of the vote. Two months earlier, the Partido Social Cristiano (Social Christian Party; PSC) candidate, Jaime Nebot, had narrowly defeated Bucaram in the first round, with 27.4 percent of the vote against Bucaram's 25.5. Nebot's defeat was one of the few known examples in a majority runoff electoral system in which the winner of the first round (who would be the elected president under a plurality system) was defeated in the second round. A similar situation had taken place in Ecuador in 1984, when Rodrigo Borja narrowly defeated León Febres Cordero in the first round (28.7 to 27.2 percent) but was overpowered by Febres in the runoff election. Because congressional elections are concurrent with the first round of the presidential election, an inversion of the original outcome usually creates a bad prospect in terms of executive-legislative relations.[4]

Despite the populist overtones of Bucaram's campaign, which included strong invectives against the "oligarchy," he soon proposed a neoliberal economic plan, designed by former economic minister of Argentina Domingo Cavallo. Cavallo, who had devised a "convertibility"
plan to stop hyperinflation in Argentina—pegging the Argentine peso to
the U.S. dollar—endorsed a similar reform policy for Ecuador. In the
meantime, the press from Quito denounced the flamboyant style of the
president and the widespread corruption in his administration.

In response to the economic measures, ordinary citizens began to
protest in January. They first protested transportation and natural gas
price increases. Then a trade union/social movement alliance (involving
the Frente Patriótico, Patriotic Front) called for a general strike. Beginning already in mid-January, notable politicians and former presidents
such as Rodrigo Borja and Osvaldo Hurtado began to call for the resignation of the president (Carrión 1997: 139). With other civic organizations announcing that they would join the strike, on January 29 the
U.S. ambassador, Leslie Alexander, denounced the "rampant corruption"
in the customs service. The demonstrations of February 5 ended with a
mobilization in front of Congress that demanded the impeachment of
the president. After some negotiations, the legislature decided to declare
Bucaram "insane" and to name the Speaker, Fabián Alarcón, as temporary president. Unable to control the legislative process—his party only
held 23 percent of the seats in the assembly—Bucaram rejected the decision as a coup, while the vice president, Rosalía Arteaga, insisted that
she was the legal successor of Bucaram in case of impeachment. After
some mediation of the military, Arteaga—who also lacked legislative
support and was perceived as too close to the president—agreed to remain in power for two days and then allowed Congress to name Alarcón as the new president, while Bucaram flew into exile in Panama.

Interpretations of Ecuador's crisis typically have been framed in terms
of the populist tradition in the country. As Carlos de la Torre, a keen observer of Ecuadorian politics, pointed out, "Undoubtedly, populism has
been the most important political phenomenon in contemporary
Ecuadorian history" (de la Torre 1997: 12). According to de la Torre,
the populist tradition, inaugurated by the five-time president José María
Velasco Ibarra in the 1930s, has permeated much of the political life of
the country. In his ethnographic study of the "electoral rituals and char-
acters" of the Ecuadorian runoff election of 1996, de la Torre (1996)
shows that Bucaram clearly invoked a populist rhetoric and style of mobilization. This campaign would have two important consequences for

the emergence of the crisis. The first one was that Bucaram came to power with a vulgar political style and discourse against the oligarchy that terrorized traditional elites (de la Torre 1996, 1997). His candidacy was supported by an emergent segment of the Guayaquil bourgeoisie that, despite its rising economic power, had not achieved social recognition among traditional families and was viewed with suspicion by the old bourgeoisie (de la Torre 1996; Paredes 1997). Second, popular support for Bucaram was provided by "volatile" followers: Bucaram relied on clientelistic networks more than on loyal partisan voters and received support from low-class sectors that saw him mainly as a weapon to defeat the elite incarnated in Jaime Nebot (de la Torre 1996: 58–59, 72). This "negative" support (against the other candidates) was amplified by the majority runoff presidential system that encouraged voters to vote against the PSC candidate in the second round (Pachano 1997).

These two attributes (isolation from the elite and volatile support) were rooted in Bucaram's populist style and were the ultimate cause of his fall. Despite Bucaram's neoliberal agenda, the *patricios*—members of the aristocracy—feared that the privatization program would be manipulated to advance the interests of the new elite (in many cases, immigrants of Lebanese origin) that had supported Bucaram during the campaign (Pachano 1997; Paredes 1997). For most voters, on the other hand, the economic policy clashed with the populist overtones of the campaign. The reduction of subsidies to consumption threatened to erode real income in the short run and alienated much popular support (Acosta 1997; Luna Tamayo 1997). This dual isolation of Bucaram was deepened, observers insist, by a flamboyant and nepotistic style of government. In this context, the mobilization of early February emerged as a unique opportunity to terminate the Bucaram administration. Elites and masses supported the move, creating strong incentives for legislators to remove the president from office.

PARAGUAY: THE END OF THE TRANSITION

Paraguay also experienced an impeachment crisis, in early 1999. The origin of this crisis, however, dates back to 1996. In 1996 President Carlos Wasmosy, the head of the army, removed General Lino Oviedo from office. Angered, Oviedo conspired a coup d'etat. Although the coup effort failed, Oviedo built up his own political faction within the ruling Partido Colorado (Red Party). It was so forceful that he defeated party leader Luis M. Argaña in the primaries for the 1998 presidential elec-

tion. In the meantime, a martial court judged Oviedo on charges of sedi-
tion and he was sentenced to ten years in prison. The Supreme Court
confirmed the sentence in April 1998, twenty days before the general
election took place. With Oviedo in prison, his running mate, Raúl
Cubas Grau, became the official candidate. In accordance with the electoral law, Argaña, leader of the contending faction, became the vice-
presidential candidate for the national election. Despite this "unity"
ticket, confrontations among Colorado factions remained in place, as
Cubas ran his campaign under the promise that Oviedo would be freed
if he was elected president (Turner 1999).

Cubas won the 1998 election with 55 percent of the vote. The party
won 56 percent of the seats in the lower chamber of Congress and 53
percent of the Senate—although most seats were not controlled by the
president's faction. Immediately after taking office in August, the president granted a pardon to General Oviedo, triggering the outrage of the
opposition and the other Colorado groups in Congress. Congressional
leaders threatened impeachment and asked the Supreme Court to rule
on the constitutionality of the pardon. The court ruled against the decree
and urged the executive to arrest Oviedo. In response, Cubas stated that
"the president does not receive orders from any other branch of government."

After a period of impasse, in January 1999 Chief Justice Wildo Rienzi
decided to give the executive seventy-two hours to capture Oviedo and
stated in Congress that Cubas had "violated the rule of law" and could
be impeached. The opposition debated a declaration stating that the government was "illegal," and rumors of a self-coup ensued. Finally, in early
March the Constitutional Affairs Committee of the Chamber of Deputies
approved the initiation of impeachment proceedings by seven to one. The
president was charged with violating the Supreme Court ruling in the
Oviedo case. Vice President Argaña—who led the rebel Colorado faction
in Congress—would take office if Cubas was removed from office.

On the morning of March 23, however, a squad of men in military
uniforms intercepted Argaña's car and killed the vice president and his
bodyguard. Paraguayans were shocked. In a public statement, the board
of the Partido Colorado openly accused the president "and the political
movement that supports him" of the crime. Congressional leaders of all
blocs—with the exception of the Oviedista faction—released a commu-
niqué that blamed "President Raúl Cubas, in conspiracy with the runaway Lino Oviedo," for the "terrorist plan." The opposition warned
that "the National Congress will adopt all necessary measures to reestab-

lish the rule of law" (*ABC Color,* March 24, 1999). Next day, the Chamber of Deputies voted the impeachment by forty-nine to twenty-four (seven absent) and the trial moved to the Senate (Turner 1999).

People began to take the streets to demand the resignation of the president. A peasant demonstration evolved into a march for impeachment (Abente-Brun 1999: 97). On March 26, violent demonstrations against the president ended up tragically when paramilitary groups shot the mob, leaving six students dead. Facing the escalation of conflict, secret negotiations between the government, the opposition, the Church, and foreign ministers began to seek a "honorable solution" for the crisis. President Cubas resigned two days later and sought refuge at the Brazilian embassy—Brazil granted him asylum and dispatched an air force jet to Asunción. Constitutionally in line to become president, Luis González Macchi, the speaker of the Senate and a member of the Argañista faction, took office and formed a "national unity" cabinet with members of the parties Colorado, Liberal Radical Auténtico (Authentic Radical Liberal), and Encuentro Nacional (National Encounter). In the meantime, General Oviedo escaped to Argentina, where he was detained.

In an early analysis of the events, Diego Abente-Brun (1999) interpreted the crisis of March 1999 as the culmination of the Paraguayan transition to democracy. The transition had begun ten years earlier, when General Andrés Rodríguez deposed thirty-five-year dictator Alfredo Stroessner and under domestic and international pressure began to liberalize the regime (see Abente-Brun 1993; Lambert 1997). According to Abente-Brun, the politics of the transition remained under control of the Colorado elite but were marked by intense factionalism within the party. Confrontations between President Wasmosy (who promoted greater liberalization of the regime and the economy) and Argaña (a more traditional breed of Colorado) dominated the landscape until 1996, when General Oviedo launched his own faction and defeated them in the 1997 primaries.

Oviedo's popularity grew because the people were tired of traditional politicians and poor economic performance, but it was never grounded in strong leadership or solid ideological reasons. Public support for the general and for his ally, President Cubas, faded with the escalation of violence that led to Argaña's assassination. In Abente-Brun's terms, a "strong citizenry"—formerly unknown in Paraguayan politics—took the streets to demand the impeachment of the president (Abente-Brun 1999: 100). The press, particularly radio and television, provided live coverage of the events, igniting public outrage and encouraging mobilization. The events of May showed that public opinion had became an important force in Paraguay and that political outcomes would not be just the product of factional disputes anymore. The Cubas administration fell after seven months in office, and after fifty-two years of Colorado hegemony the opposition parties were incorporated into a broad government of national unity.

PROXIMATE CAUSES OF IMPEACHMENT CRISES

The previous pages delineated important differences but also interesting similarities between impeachment crises in Latin America. These crises have shared a common background of media scandals, the pressures of economic adjustment, and presidents striving to control hostile legislatures. Historical interpretations that deal with each crisis in its national context present very dissimilar narratives leading to very similar outcomes. We may be tempted to conclude, as Michael Coppedge has sharply pointed out, that "every country *is* unique, history never repeats itself *exactly,* and every event is the product of a long and densely tangled chain of causation stretching back to the beginning of time" (Coppedge 1997: 3). The question, however, is whether dissimilar historical paths may *converge into* similar causal configurations.

What specific case studies have overlooked is a common pattern underlying all impeachment crises in the 1990s. To some extent, all crises have been shaped by three common elements. First, the press has questioned the moral authority of the president and his or her administration to rule the country. Second, a social coalition typically involving both elites and masses has made charges against the president, eroding his or her survival capacity. The third element has been the inability of the president's office to prevent the formation of a hostile coalition in Congress.

Scandals

By *scandal* I refer to a process by which citizens learn (and deliberate) about questionable acts carried out by the president or his/her close collaborators (see Waisbord 1994: 21). Weyland (1998a) has claimed that "neopopulist" leaders (like Presidents Collor, Bucaram, and, to a lesser extent, Pérez) attempted to bypass traditional parties and interest groups in order to reach "the people" directly through television. The high costs of television campaigns encouraged widespread corruption, while the isolation of these leaders from traditional structures favored their impeachment once the scandals exploded.

Political scandal is a necessary component of impeachment crises because it allows Congress to investigate the president and eventually to call for his or her resignation. Typically, investigations begin with remote collaborators of the president and move up the ladder of power when these prosecuted, low-rank officials start to implicate their bosses and ultimately involve the president.

In Brazil, the scandal broke when Pedro, the president's brother, denounced to the journal *Veja* that a broad corruption network was commanded by Collor's former campaign manager. Because Pedro spoke on the record, the story was highly credible from the start. Additional evidence was disclosed when a car driver who worked for Collor's secretary declared that he had been asked to transport checks to make suspicious deposits in different bank accounts. The work of the attorney general and the Comissão Parlamentar de Inquerito (Parliamentary Investigative Committee) unveiled additional proof in later months.

In Venezuela, the scandal began in November 1992, when journalists Andrés Galdo and José Vicente Rangel disclosed that the Pérez administration had withdrawn funds from a secret account in the Ministry of Interior and multiplied the money using a preferential exchange rate. The case gained spin when the Chamber of Deputies formed a special oversight committee and officials from the Interior Ministry and Miraflores (the president's office) began to involve higher-rank politicians (Chitty La Roche 1993). In January 1993, former attorney general *(procurador general)* Nelson Socorro linked President Pérez to the story and was followed a few weeks later by the former interior minister, Alejandro Izaguirre, who admitted that the president had commanded the operation. The prosecutor-general, Jorge Escovar Salom, completed the investigation and asked the Supreme Court to initiate the impeachment process.

In Colombia, accusations against Samper were published early in his administration, but it was not until Prosecutor-General Alfonso Valdivieso arrested Samper's former campaign treasurer that the scandal took off. The confession of Santiago Medina involving high-rank officials, and the later statements of former minister Fernando Botero about Samper put the president against the ropes.

The situation was slightly different in the Ecuadorian case. Close collaborators of President Bucaram became involved in scandals, but Congress failed to investigate the connection of these to the president's office.

Instead of being affected by one highly investigated event, the Bucaram administration was permanently eroded by minor scandals involving the president, his family, and his closest associates. The administration was accused of stealing secret funds of the presidency (Carrión 1997: 127). Business people complained that public officials requested a "party tax" to release any bureaucratic authorization or service (Rodríguez Vicéns 1997: 40, 47, 67), and customs was depicted as highly corrupt. Suspected of influence peddling in the customs system, Bucaram's teenage son soon hosted a boisterous party to celebrate his first million dollars. The minister of education, Sandra Correa, was charged of plagiarizing her doctoral dissertation. In addition, Bucaram and some of his close collaborators showed a pattern of behavior that many politicians and opinion leaders considered overtly outrageous. Angry at his critics, the president would call them "donkeys" or use vulgar language to refer to his adversaries, and ministers and advisers would threaten to "crush" respected journalists or would call them "lunatics" (Carrión 1997). In Ecuador, the formal investigation carried out by state institutions (judiciary, prosecutors, or oversight committees) was not what proved the president's undoing, but rather a constant background noise of scandals investigated by the press. It was the *number* of scandals, rather than the *burden of proof,* that supported the crisis.

The component of scandal was even more complex in the Paraguayan case. President Cubas defied the political elite—including the dominant faction of his party—when he decided to release General Oviedo from prison. His rejection of the Supreme Court decision declaring his decree unconstitutional created a stronger justification for impeachment and a deeper sense that the president was acting as if he was above the law. This situation was aggravated by Oviedo's own attitudes: the general threatened to "bury" justices who had voted against him and mobilized paramilitary followers to intimidate his opponents (Abente-Brun 1999). But it was the assassination of Vice President Argaña on March 23 that ultimately triggered a widespread wave of indignation against Cubas and Oviedo. Suspected of plotting the crime, both leaders were challenged by popular mobilization. Outrageous behavior in this case had gone far beyond any "normal" form of corruption.

Thus, scandal was present in every impeachment crisis, but its role was different in each case. In the cases of Collor, Samper, and Cubas, scandals triggered the crisis and were at the core of the confrontation with Congress that ultimately led to impeachment. In the other two cases

(Pérez and Bucaram), scandals served as an excuse, a legal justification to oust an already weak president from power, despite the fact that the executive-legislative confrontation had deeper roots.

Public Outrage

A second component of the impeachment crises was popular mobilization against the president. Public outrage is particularly important because it signals to the elite that media scandals are having (or may have) substantive political consequences. Without it, political scandal is nothing but media entertainment. Civic reaction backs the stand of legislators in the opposition and creates incentives for defection among legislators in the president's camp.

For this reason, several accounts of presidential crises have depicted a mobilized civil society taking to the streets and virtually ousting the corrupt president. In the case of Ecuador, an observer pointed out that "without the massive and sustained protests demanding Bucaram's removal, it is unlikely Congress would have impeached him given the questionable constitutionality of its actions" (Selverston 1997: 12). The historical record tends to support this view. In January 1997, a group of major trade unions and social movements formed the Frente Patriótico and called for a general strike against Bucaram's economic policy in February. During late January, civic associations began to support the strike and public response "snowballed" (Luna Tamayo 1997: 202). Rumors spread that the demonstrations would seek the ousting of the president, inspiring support among the middle class. On February 5 and 6, more than two million people joined the "civic strike" and demanded the resignation of Bucaram. Rocío Rosero Jácome has depicted these demonstrations as the action of a cohesive "Ecuadorian social being" in a fight against corruption (Rosero Jácome 1997: 176).

According to Margaret Keck (1992: 6), in Brazil "the size of the demonstrations influenced wavering politicians. Municipal elections were only a month away, and close identification with Collor began to look like political suicide." Demonstrations for the ousting of Collor were the largest ones since the mass mobilization in support of direct presidential elections in 1984. In the conclusion to his memoirs Pedro Collor de Mello (1993: 282–83) asserted that "it was not I who debunked President Fernando Collor de Mello. It was Brazilian society, Congress, the judiciary, businessmen, workers, students, professionals, housewives. The country decided to say 'enough,' to put a stop. It was a lesson in political maturity never seen in any other place—especially in a country just emerging from an authoritarian regime."

The very same year Pedro published his book, another "lesson in political maturity" took place in Venezuela. Ellner (1993: 13–14) noted, describing the events, "What has brought the [corruption] issue to such prominence, however, has been the continuous expression of public discontent in local elections, demonstrations, spontaneous unruly protests, and even quiet support for the two abortive coups, whose banner was opposition to corruption in the government and the armed forces." In the case of Pérez, mobilization against the president long predated the emergence of the specific scandal. Soon after taking office, Pérez faced the riots of February 27 and 28, 1989 (Kornblith 1998: chap. 1). After two coup attempts, in 1992 and early 1993, people in Caracas, Mérida, and other cities carried out *cacerolazos* (beating on pots and pans) against the government, and strikes and other forms of popular protest became common (López Maya 1999: 230–31).

President Samper faced an important movement demanding his resignation and saw a significant decline in his levels of popularity (from 76 percent in January to 46 percent in December 1995) as a consequence of the accusations (Vargas, Lesmes, and Téllez 1996: 321, 401). During 1996, the government had to confront massive peasant demonstrations, especially of coca growers, that sometimes were violently repressed (Chernick 1997: 22; Medina 1999: 126–27). However, the intensity of popular protest was probably lower in Colombia than in the other cases. Describing the situation while the crisis was going on, the *Economist* pointed out that "Colombians do not take to the streets readily, as do their neighbors in Venezuela and Brazil. They are tiring of this scandal" (*Economist,* June 1, 1996: 41).

Public outrage erupted during the last week of the crisis, after the assassination of the vice president. Popular support for the impeachment grew (Abente-Brun 1999: 97). People poured into the plazas surrounding Congress, preventing Oviedo's supporters from attacking the legislature. A large demonstration of peasants protesting for debt relief from official banks under the circumstances took a political turn. The peasants decided to join forces with the students and others of the middle class demanding President Cubas's removal from office. Peasants ultimately received partial debt relief in return for lending their support, but the protest ended violently. Pro-Oviedo snipers attacked the crowd, killing six students and leaving two hundred others wounded.

Legislative Support

A president may prevent a media scandal from fueling impeachment if he (or she) has congressional support, if legislators are also implicated in the scandal so that they oppose a congressional investigation, and if the president's party has a congressional majority able to block parties favoring an impeachment inquiry. In the absence of these conditions, a president is not shielded from impeachment proceedings.

Because the neoliberal reforms governments were pressured to implement were politically unpopular, presidents privileged technocratic decision making. While useful for initiating the reforms, in the process they isolated themselves from Congress as well as their own political party. In reference to Carlos Andrés Pérez, Rey (1993: 82) noted that "more than a merit, being a member of the ruling party appeared to be an obstacle for achieving a post in the economy cabinet." Bucaram was accused of forming a government of cronies and of centralizing decision making (Luna Tamayo 1997: 211). Fernando Collor never built a strong Center-Right coalition in the legislature, and "especially in the beginning...[he] deliberately refrained from nominating powerful, able ministers who might have challenged his dominant position" (Weyland 1993: 10). In Paraguay, the Oviedistas dominated the Cubas cabinet, while the other Colorado factions were excluded by the president (Brian Turner, personal communication, 1999).

In addition, a president is more shielded when congressional leaders are also implicated in the scandal. While personal corruption is likely to trigger impeachment proceedings, institutionalized patronage is not. Legislators have low incentives to unleash a presidential crisis when the investigation may harm their own careers, but they have greater incentives to terminate an administration sustaining a corruption pattern that does not benefit them (see Weyland 1998a). In the latter situation they will seek to distinguish themselves from corrupt politicians in order to profit from public outrage. Calling for impeachment will emerge as a dominant strategy.

The evidence indeed suggests that impeachment crises are more prone to emerge when revelations of corruption are limited to the executive branch. The events affecting Bucaram, Collor, and Pérez did not involve congressional leaders. In the case of Samper, in contrast, the investigation carried out by the prosecutor-general involved the president and legislators of both parties. At least four representatives and five senators were convicted on charges similar to Samper's (see Victoria 1997: 149, 233–34).

Isolated forms of policymaking and executive-centered patterns of corruption are not, however, the only obstacles to building a legislative shield. The third factor is the size of the president's party in Congress—and the loyalty of those legislators to the chief executive. I am referring here to what Mainwaring and Shugart (1997) have called "partisan powers" of the president. The issue of partisan powers deserves careful consideration because not only presidents with very small legislative parties, like Collor or Bucaram, but also presidents with large parties, like Pérez or Cubas (or Samper, even if he survived), faced an impeachment. After the 1990 legislative election, Collor's party controlled just 8 percent of the lower chamber of Congress and Bucaram's Partido Roldosista Ecuatoriano held 23 percent of the seats in the unicameral legislature. Pérez's Acción Democrática, in contrast, had 48 percent of the lower chamber, while Samper controlled 54 percent. Cubas's Partido Colorado held 56 percent of the Chamber of Deputies, but intense factionalism within the party considerably weakened his control of the legislature.

Although weak partisan powers may not in themselves spark the onset of an impeachment crisis, we should expect that, other things being equal, a president with greater partisan powers will be more able to prevent the formation of a hostile coalition if scandal takes place. Table 4.1 presents information about all Latin American presidents between 1990 and 1999, classified according to their level of legislative support.[5] I selected 30 percent of the lower chamber as an arbitrary cutoff point distinguishing presidents with clearly weak partisan powers. Whenever presidents were supported by a coalition that helped to elect them and preserved a unified legislative label after the election (e.g., Aylwin and Frei in Chile, Paz Zamora in Bolivia, Chamorro in Nicaragua, Endara and Pérez Balladares in Panama), I took the size of the coalition as the measure of legislative support. Otherwise, I considered the size of the president's party.

If the degree of legislative support for the administration changed during the term because of midterm elections, I divided the administration into several observations.[6] I followed the same procedure when coalitions broke down or were reshaped, as in Panama after 1991 or Nicaragua after 1992 (McConnell 1993: 23). Thus, the units of analysis for this test are sixty-three *congressional terms*, defined as the time period in which a given administration and a given Congress overlap. The dependent variable is the emergence of an impeachment crisis during the

TABLE 4.1   PROBABILITY OF IMPEACHMENT
CRISIS (PIC) IN LATIN AMERICA,
BY LEGISLATIVE SUPPORT FOR THE PRESIDENT
(1990–99)[a]

Percentage of Seats Controlled by the President's Party in the Lower Chamber	Crises[b]	No Crisis[c]	PIC
30% or more	3	46	.06
Less than 30%	3	11	.21[d]
TOTAL	6	57	.09

SOURCE: Author's data.

[a] Units of analysis are executive-congressional terms (periods in which a given administration and a given congress coexist). Fifteen of the forty-seven administrations under study confronted midterm elections or saw their initial coalitions collapse during the term. Since the percentage of seats controlled by the president changed over time, they are counted as more than one case.

[b] Impeachment crises are Brazil (1992), Venezuela (1993), Colombia (1996), Ecuador (1997), Paraguay (1999), and a minor crisis in Peru (1991).

[c] Countries included in the analysis are Argentina, Bolivia, Brazil, Chile, Colombia, Costa Rica, Dominican Republic, Ecuador, El Salvador, Guatemala, Honduras, Mexico, Nicaragua, Panama, Paraguay, Peru, Uruguay, and Venezuela.

[d] Fisher exact test (.099) mid p-value significant at .07 level (one-sided). P-value significant at .12 level.

term. Although the number of crises is very small, the test suggests that the probability of facing an impeachment crisis was greater for presidents who lacked congressional support.

Preliminary Hypotheses

In order to understand the emergence of impeachment crises in the 1990s we must focus on three variables: the scandal revelations that serve as a reason-excuse to call for the resignation of the president, public anger against the government, and the president's control over Congress. Table 4.2 summarizes the information about the administrations described in this chapter. The evidence suggests that media scandals are a necessary condition for the emergence of an impeachment crisis. No matter how different in other respects, the administrations of Bucaram, Collor, Cubas, Pérez, and Samper were all touched by scandal. But media exposés are nevertheless not alone sufficient to trigger a crisis. The administration of Carlos Menem in Argentina, for instance, was harmed by scandal, but the president avoided any serious confrontation with Congress (Waisbord 1994).

Two other elements must be present. The first one is public outrage: Bucaram, Cubas, Collor, and Pérez—and to a lesser extent Samper—

TABLE 4.2   IMPEACHMENT CRISES IN
COMPARATIVE PERSPECTIVE
(1990–99)

Administration (Country/Year)	Scandal	Public Outrage	Legislative Support	Outcome
Collor de Mello (Brazil, 1992)	Yes	Yes	No	Impeachment President resigned
Pérez (Venezuela, 1993)	Yes	Yes	No	Impeachment President ousted
Samper (Colombia, 1996)	Yes	Yes	Yes	President avoided impeachment
Bucaram (Ecuador, 1997)	Yes	Yes	No	President declared insane and ousted
Cubas Grau (Paraguay, 1999)	Yes	Yes	No	Impeachment President resigned

confronted broad social coalitions that questioned their right to rule. According to table 4.2, the interaction of scandal *and* public outrage is sufficient to trigger an impeachment crisis.[7] The second factor is the president's capacity to control Congress. In contrast to the other presidents, Samper enjoyed powerful legislative allies that "shielded" him. Pérez had a large legislative party, but the party was reluctant to support his policies. In contrast to his predecessor, Jaime Lusinchi, Pérez never made the party a central partner of his government. By the end of his term, after two coup attempts and a corruption scandal, partisan support had vanished and many members of his party were prone to defect; his legislative shield had weakened considerably. Cubas faced strong opposition within his own party, and Presidents Bucaram and Collor lacked strong legislative machines. The historical cases discussed above suggest a concluding hypothesis: impeachment crises emerge when presidents face scandal *combined with* public outrage *and/or* weak legislative support.

This hypothesis does not account for the ousting of the president, but rather for crises leading to a congressional *attempt* to oust the president. The effective ousting of the chief executive seems to require the presence of all three factors: scandal, public outrage, *and* a weak "legislative shield." Because this explanation is based on the study of only five crises, it needs to be tested against a larger number of cases to prove its explanatory power.

PRESIDENTIAL CRISES IN PERSPECTIVE: DEMOCRACY, FREE EXPRESSION, AND ECONOMIC ADJUSTMENT

The emergence of several impeachment crises in the 1990s suggests that we are witnessing a new phenomenon in Latin American politics. In previous decades, political elites in the opposition typically engineered military coups in order to oust undesirable presidents. After the third wave of democratization, in contrast, the harsh memories of the bureaucratic authoritarian regimes, the end of the Cold War, and an international climate generally favorable to democracy have fostered political learning in favor of democratic rule. In this context, opposition leaders have turned to constitutional mechanisms like impeachment to confront presidents who are perceived as corrupt or unable to rule.

Two other factors contributed to the multiplication of impeachment crises during the 1990s: changes in the press and the pressures of economic adjustment. Over the last thirty years, the Latin American press underwent major transformations that facilitated the coverage of political scandals. Political democratization meant more freedom of the press in the region. Economic reform deprived governments of regulatory tools traditionally used to control the press. Last, but not least, journalists became "more professional and less emotional," in the words of a Brazilian journalist (Chagas 1998). Alves (1997) noticed the emergence of a "vanguard press" in Latin America, a new generation of newspapers with more aggressive coverage of politics and greater professionalism and independence. This trend fostered new journalistic values and expectations about the role of the press in the new Latin American democracies (Waisbord 1996; see also Conaghan 1996).

On the other hand, the pressures of neoliberal reform created a fertile ground for the eruption of public outrage against the executive. After a "lost decade" of economic crisis and declining living standards, the people in many Latin American countries reluctantly accepted harsh economic adjustment programs in hope of achieving economic stability and resuming growth. But they were less willing to pay the high costs of adjustment when they perceived their governments as corrupt and ineffective. The explosion of scandals and the inability of governments to deliver successful policies interacted in each country with deeply rooted frustrations, and hence civil society mobilized in search of accountability and greater social justice.

Some of the examples discussed above illustrate this factor. Presidents Collor, Pérez, and Bucaram attempted to reform the economy but were unable to claim success. President Collor inherited an inflation rate of 1,322 percent in 1989. Inflation rose to 2,562 percent in 1990, declined the next year, and bounced back to around 1,000 percent in 1992 (Sola 1994: 150, 165). In this context, public opinion was critical of economic adjustment, sensitive to scandal, and impatient with the chief executive. In Margaret Keck's (1992: 7) terms,

> This is not to say that Collorgate was not about corruption or about equal treatment. But more than these, I think it was about repeatedly raised expectations and about repeated failure and disappointment. Collor presented himself as the proverbial savior, the man on a white horse, who would clean out the corrupt politicians and speak for the marginalized poor. He did none of those things, and worse still, he alienated the middle class, whose standard of living has fallen precipitously over the last few years, by confiscating their savings accounts for 18 months without bringing down inflation.... Not only was the government incompetent, it lacked dignity, and people cared.

The *magnitude* of the inflationary threat was different in Brazil and Venezuela, but the political sense of *failure* was similar. During the first year of the Pérez administration, inflation rose from 35.5 to 81.0 percent. By 1991, the economy was showing important signs of recovery, but people remained concerned about the effects of neoliberal reform on their personal well-being (Weyland 1998b: 352). Two coup attempts in 1992 put an end to public expectations of policy success. An opinion poll conducted by *Consultores 21* in March 1992—after the first coup attempt—showed that 64 percent of respondents believed that the government had already failed;[8] six months later the percentage jumped 8 more points. The inflation rate was 32 percent, similar to the rate when Pérez began his term of office (Naím 1993: 78). According to Kurt Weyland (1998b: 356), the declining "support for neoliberalism affected presidential popularity substantially." In a context of frustration, the riots of early 1989 inaugurated a "protest cycle" (López Maya 1999) against neoliberal reform and political corruption that extended beyond the resignation of President Pérez.

At the time of the crisis, Bucaram was also perceived as a case of "failure," since he was reducing subsidies to consumption and authorizing increases in the price of basic services—what ultimately raised the cost of living. His short tenure in office makes it difficult to anticipate what the ultimate outcome of his policy would have been. In any case, the president had to face a highly mobilized society. The dismantling of rural state programs since the 1980s, together with contested development projects in the Amazon, had encouraged the formation of a strong indigenous movement that, acting through a national confederation—the Confederación de Nacionalidades Indígenas (Confederation of Indigenous Nationalities; CONAIE)—by 1996 was ready to enter the electoral arena as an independent political actor (Yashar 1998: 25). Together with the powerful energy unions, the CONAIE confronted the economic reform policies of the Durán Ballén administration (1992–96) and rapidly reacted against Bucaram's economic program. The Frente Patriótico of February 1997 unified indigenous peoples and other social movements, traditional unions (the Frente Unitario de Trabajadores [United Workers' Front; FUT]), and other forces of civil society against the austerity measures (Luna Tamayo 1997; Selverston 1997).

In contrast, President Samper of Colombia was seen by many as moderating the pace of neoliberal reform imposed by the Gaviria administration (1990–94). Samper took office with an inflation of 22.6 percent in 1994, and the country preserved this relatively low rate throughout his period: 19.5 in 1995, 21.6 in 1996, and 17.7 in 1997 (Banco de la República 1997). The administration, however, was not able to implement effective negotiations with the guerrillas, and violence kept rising. In 1996, almost twenty-seven thousand people were killed in Colombia, more than three thousand of them for political reasons (see Chernick 1997). Although the police arrested the leaders of the Cali cartel (reducing the credibility of the scandal), the U.S. government decertified Colombia two years in a row. Thus, it is hard to claim that the administration enjoyed great policy success. However, Samper was perceived by many Liberals as the alternative to crude structural adjustment. In this context, public opinion became divided as whether to demand the resignation of the president.

A deep sense of frustration was also part of the Paraguayan landscape. Ten years of democratization and slow neoliberal reform under Colorado rule had been unable to solve major social problems and widespread government corruption. According to Lambert (1997: 209–10), "Progress in the areas of civil and political liberties and electoral politics contrasted sharply with failings in the social and economic fields....A decline in the value of wages, plus unemployment, lack of access to health care and one of the most unequal distributions of land in Latin America were all vital issues that remained unaddressed during the political transition." Free of the traditional constraints imposed by the Colorado machine (see Arditi 1993: 166–68), civil society (peasants, students, unions, local movements) began to organize against these problems during the 1990s, showing unexpected strength during the 1999 presidential crisis.

To sum up, since the late 1980s a more independent and professional Latin American press has been willing to disclose scandals and investigate the executive. In this context, the inability of governments to manage the economy and improve the living conditions of vast sectors of the population encouraged public outrage and triggered mass mobilization. Aware of the perils of old-fashioned military intervention, members of Congress found in impeachment a constitutional solution for presidential crises. In this sense, impeachment crises proved true landmarks in Latin American politics. Yet, as the new trend predicts stronger forms of presidential accountability for the future, it may also anticipate a new "standard procedure" for ousting presidents in Latin America.

IMPEACHMENT AND THE QUALITY OF DEMOCRACY: A NOTE OF CAUTION

Besides the historical, sociological, and institutional causes of impeachment crises, it is important to examine their consequences. Impeachment crises are not unique to Latin America—as the examples of Presidents Andrew Johnson, Nixon, and Clinton illustrate in the U.S. context—and most observers saw the crises of the 1990s as a positive trend against corrupt administrations. This is a sensible argument, yet it overlooks the fact that crises always involve a tradeoff between greater accountability and government instability.

On one hand, impeachment crises may be an indicator that legislators are becoming more responsive to public outrage against corrupt executives. In this sense, they may be seen as a mature sign of growing accountability.[9] On the other, impeachment crises have costs in terms of governability and political stability. As in the case of Venezuela, important policies may be delayed or abandoned because of the dissolution of the government.

This difficult tradeoff between presidential accountability and government stability can lead legislators to push for impeachment either *too early* or *too late* during the course of a crisis. When impeachment takes place too early, legislators responding to popular pressures find a "fast track" to remove the president from office. Political actors learn from this experience that the stability of the government can be put at risk overnight. When, in contrast, impeachment takes place too late, Congress simply acts to legalize a de facto resolution of the political crisis.

The first problem is illustrated by the popular uprising leading to the ousting of the Ecuadorian president in January 2000. After the rapid congressional action that ended with the Bucaram administration in 1997, important political leaders concluded that public outrage was *sufficient* to remove an unpopular president from office. A new political crisis three years later showed how dangerous this conclusion could be for democracy. In the midst of an economic crash, which included a collapse of the exchange rate, the freezing of bank accounts, and a moratorium on foreign debt, President Jamil Mahuad proposed a "dollarization" plan that resembled Bucaram's convertibility program. As in 1997, the CONAIE opposed the measures and led a popular uprising. But this time the social coalition against the executive was narrower and the legislative conditions for impeachment were uncertain. Indigenous leaders overcame this obstacle through an alliance with middle-rank military officers. On January 21, 2000, a rebel group took over the Congress building and overthrew the president. Ecuador narrowly avoided the establishment of a military junta only because the joint command refused to take over and handed power to the vice president—who ultimately imposed the dollarization program.

The moral of the Ecuadorian experience is that any impeachment process must be transparent and solidly grounded in constitutional law. Even if the procedure is technically legal, in the absence of a transparent process observers (and protagonists) may be left with the impression that they attended a legislative coup d'etat. Once impeachment is seen as a functional equivalent for a coup, the expectation of government instability will hurt all democratic politicians—including those who initially benefited from the process.

In contrast, the end of the Fujimori era in Peru illustrates the futility of impeachment procedures that take place too late. Alberto Fujimori took office for the third time in late July 2000, after "winning" a runoff election in which the opposition candidate refused to participate because he anticipated electoral fraud. The administration confronted international criticism and increasing popular protest against the fraud, and this situation was aggravated a few weeks later when a TV station aired a video showing the head of the intelligence service and a strongman of the regime, Vladimiro Montesinos, bribing an opposition congressman.

Under internal and international pressure, Fujimori understood the need to organize a negotiated exit from power. On September 16, the

president announced the dissolution of the intelligence service and a plan
to call for new elections within a year. As important sectors of the military resisted this move, it became clear that Montesinos—who controlled
important information about the administration's corruption and
human-rights abuses—would not accept the role of a passive scapegoat.
Fujimori demanded an amnesty law from Congress that would guarantee impunity for the leaders of the regime after the transition.

Sensing the weakness of the administration, politicians began to re-
align. Vice President Francisco Tudela resigned in opposition to the proposed amnesty law, and at least ten members of Peru 2000, Fujimori's
legislative coalition, switched parties to join the opposition camp. On
November 16, the unicameral Congress appointed (in a sixty-four to
fifty-one vote) an opposition politician as president of the legislative
body. The president understood that his party was losing control of
Congress and that his legislative shield was now considerably weakened. In a context of media revelations, mounting public outrage, and
declining legislative support, Fujimori opted for a fast exit. On November 17, 2000, he flew to Tokyo and announced his resignation from
there. Five days later, the stunned Peruvian Congress decided to reject
his resignation (by sixty-two to nine) and to impeach the runaway president on the grounds of "moral incapacity." In the meantime, the Jap-
anese government granted Fujimori citizen status and political protection from extradition.

The moral of the Peruvian case is that congressional oversight must
be exercised continuously if legislators want to preserve their credibility.
If Congress reacts too late, impeachment becomes little more than a
farce. The cases of Ecuador and Peru in 2000 illustrate two sides of the
same coin: impeachment can be used as a mere tool to legalize the forced
departure of the president, rather than as a democratic institution promoting presidential accountability. The tradeoff between accountability
and stability suggests that impeachment is a complex institution with
important consequences for democracy that should be studied more
carefully in the future.

NOTES

I am indebted to Susan Eckstein, Robert Fishman, Carlos Guevara Mann, Naoko
Kada, Scott Mainwaring, Andrés Mejía Acosta, Martha Merrit, and Brian
Turner for their valuable comments. Research for this paper was supported by

the Social Science Research Council (SSRC) and by a Seed Money Grant from the Helen Kellogg Institute for International Studies.

1. In parliamentary systems, the prime minister is supported by a legislative majority, and a vote of no-confidence is a "normal" political event whenever the head of the executive loses the majority in the parliament. In presidential systems, in contrast, the president is independently elected, and an impeachment process typically requires proof of "high crimes and misdemeanors."

2. Another impeachment crisis took place in Peru in late 1991, prior to the 1992 self-coup, when the Senate threatened to declare the presidency "vacant"— but the motion was killed in the lower chamber. The magnitude of this crisis was not comparable to the other five discussed here. Unfortunately, reasons of space prevent me from exploring the case here. See Cameron (1997) and Kenney (1996, 1998).

3. Pedro, who managed the family business—a local media conglomerate in the state of Alagoas—had decided to "go public" after a long battle with Farias over the control of the local media market. He was afraid that with the capital obtained from government corruption, Farias (backed by the president) would build a stronger conglomerate and gain control of newspaper and TV operations in Alagoas (see Collor de Mello 1993).

4. Until 1997, the other cases of outcome inversion in Latin America had been the election of Presidents Fujimori of Peru in 1990, Serrano of Guatemala in 1991, and Fernández of the Dominican Republic in 1996. With the exception of the latter, all others confronted major constitutional crises during their terms.

5. The sample included all presidents ruling in Latin America who left office after 1989 or took office before 1999. Presidents appointed to complete a term after an impeachment process were excluded from the analysis.

6. Countries with midterm elections are Argentina, Chile, Ecuador, and Mexico. Some countries, such as Brazil prior to 1994 or El Salvador, had electoral cycles that created midterm elections. Although Colombia has, technically speaking, nonconcurrent elections, I took it as a case of concurrency because both the president and deputies have four-year terms, and deputies are elected just two months in advance of the presidential election.

7. I do not claim that these are *necessary* conditions for a crisis. Some confrontations between the president and Congress may take place in the absence of public outrage against the government—provided that the president has low legislative support. In Peru, for instance, the Fujimori administration faced a minor impeachment crisis in December 1991, when the president accused Congress of being under the influence of drug-related money laundering. At that point, the popularity of the president was high and legislators were unable to oust him. See Kenney (1996, 1998) and Cameron (1997).

8. I am indebted to Luis Christiansen, of *Consultores 21* (Caracas, July 1998), for sharing this information.

9. For a discussion of the role of media scandals, public debate, and political accountability in a Latin American context, see Conaghan (1996).

REFERENCES

Abente-Brun, Diego. 1993. "Las etapas de la transición y el camino por recorrer." In *Paraguay en transición,* ed. Diego Abente-Brun, pp. 147–60. Caracas: Editorial Nueva Sociedad.

———. 1999. " 'People Power' in Paraguay." *Journal of Democracy* 10, no. 3 (July): 93–100.

Acosta, Alberto. 1997. "El Bucarmismo en el poder." In *¿Y ahora qué? Una contribución al análisis político-histórico actual,* pp. 47–90. Quito: Eskeletra Editorial.

Alves, Rosental Calmon. 1997. "Democracy's Vanguard Newspapers in Latin America." Paper presented at the annual conference of the International Communication Association, May 22–26, Montreal, Quebec, Canada.

Arditi, Benjamín. 1993. "Del granito al archipiélago: El Partido Colorado sin Stroessner." In *Paraguay en transición,* ed. Diego Abente-Brun, pp. 161–72. Caracas: Editorial Nueva Sociedad.

Banco de la República. 1997. "Indice de precios al consumidor: Inflación total y 'Básica.' " *Revista del Banco de la República (Bogotá, Colombia)* 70: 255.

Betancourt Pulecio, Ingrid. 1996. *Sí Sabía: Viaje a través del expediente de Ernesto Samper.* Santafé de Bogotá: Ediciones Temas de Hoy.

Bresser Pereira, Luiz Carlos. 1991. *Os tempos heróicos de Collor e Zélia: Aventuras da modernidade e desventuras da ortodoxia.* São Paulo: Nobel.

Cameron, Maxwell. 1994. *Democracy and Authoritarianism in Peru: Political Coalitions and Social Change.* New York: St. Martin's Press.

———. 1997. "The *Eighteenth Brumaire* of Alberto Fujimori." In *The Peruvian Labyrinth: Polity, Society, Economy,* ed. Maxwell A. Cameron and Philip Mauceri, pp. 37–69. University Park: Pennsylvania State University Press.

Carrión, Andrés. 1997. "Y llegó el comandante y mandó a parar." In *¿Y ahora qué? Una contribución al análisis político-histórico actual,* pp. 117–44. Quito: Eskeletra Editorial.

Chagas, Carlos. 1998. Interview with author. TV Manchete, Brasília, August 7.

Chernick, Marc. 1997. "The Crisis of Human Rights in Colombia: It's Time to Internationalize the Peace Process." *LASA Forum* 28, no. 3: 20–23.

Chitty La Roche, Nelson. 1993. *Doscientos cincuenta millones: La historia secreta.* Caracas: Pomaire.

Collier, David, ed. 1979. *The New Authoritarianism in Latin America.* Princeton, N.J.: Princeton University Press.

Collor de Mello, Pedro. 1993. *Passando a limpo: A trajetória de um farsante.* Rio de Janeiro: Record.

Comisión Ciudadana de Seguimiento. 1996. *Poder, justicia, e indignidad: El juicio al Presidente de la República Ernesto Samper Pizano.* Santafé de Bogotá: Utópica Ediciones.

Conaghan, Catherine. 1996. "Public Life in the Time of Alberto Fujimori." Working paper 219. Woodrow Wilson International Center for Scholars, Washington, D.C.

Coppedge, Michael. 1994. "Prospects for Democratic Governability in Venezuela." *Journal of Interamerican Studies and World Affairs* 36, no. 2 (Summer): 39–64.

———. 1997. "How the Large N Could Complement the Small in Democratization Research." Paper presented at the annual meeting of the American Political Science Association, August 28–31, Washington, D.C.

De la Torre, Carlos. 1996. *Un solo toque: Populismo y cultura política en Ecuador.* Quito: Centro Andino de Acción Popular.

———. 1997. "Populism and Democracy: Political Discourses and Cultures in Contemporary Ecuador." *Latin American Perspectives* 24, no. 3 (May): 12–24.

Dugas, John. 2001. "Drugs, Lies, and Audiotape: The Samper Crisis in Colombia." *Latin American Research Review* 32, no. 2: 157–74.

Ellner, Steve. 1993. "A Tolerance Worn Thin: Corruption in the Age of Austerity." *NACLA Report on the Americas* 27, no. 3 (November–December): 13–16.

Ferrero Costa, Eduardo. 1993. "Perú's Presidential Coup." *Journal of Democracy* 4, no. 1 (January): 28–40.

Flynn, Peter. 1993. "Collor, Corruption and Crisis: Time for Reflection." *Journal of Latin American Studies* 25 (May): 351–71.

Keck, Margaret. 1992. "Brazil: Impeachment!" *NACLA Report on the Americas* 26, no. 3 (December): 4–7.

Kenney, Charles. 1996. "¿Por qué el autogolpe? Fujimori y el Congreso, 1990–1992." In *Los enigmas del poder: Fujimori, 1990–1996,* ed. Fernando Tuesta Soldevilla, pp. 75–104. Lima: Fundación Friedrich Ebert.

———. 1998. "Institutionalized Instability? Lessons for Democracy from Peru (1980–1993)." Ph.D. diss., Department of Government and International Studies, University of Notre Dame, Notre Dame, Ind.

Kornblith, Miriam. 1998. *Venezuela en los '90: Las crisis de la democracia.* Caracas: Ediciones IESA.

Lambert, Peter. 1997. "Assessing the Transition." In *The Transition to Democracy in Paraguay,* ed. Peter Lambert and Andrew Nickson, pp. 200–13. New York: St. Martin's Press.

Lins da Silva, Carlos Eduardo. 1993. "Brazil's Struggle with Democracy." *Current History* 92, no. 572 (March): 126–29.

López Caballero, Juan Manuel. 1997. *La conspiración: El libro blanco del juicio al Presidente Samper.* Santafé de Bogotá: Planeta.

López Maya, Margarita. 1999. "La protesta popular venezolana entre 1989 y 1993 (en el umbral del neoliberalismo)." In *Lucha popular, democracia, neoliberalismo: Protesta popular en América Latina en los años de ajuste,* ed. Margarita López Maya, pp. 211–38. Caracas: Nueva Sociedad.

Luna Tamayo, Milton. 1997. "Bucaram, Fuera!! La voz de los movimientos profundos." In *¿Y ahora qué? Una contribución al análisis político-histórico actual,* pp. 197–228. Quito: Eskeletra Editorial.

Mainwaring, Scott, and Matthew Soberg Shugart. 1997. "Presidentialism and the Party System." In *Presidentialism and Democracy in Latin America,* ed.

Scott Mainwaring and Matthew Soberg Shugart, pp. 394–439. Cambridge: Cambridge University Press.

McClintock, Cynthia. 1993. "Peru's Fujimori: A Caudillo Derails Democracy." *Current History* 95, no. 572 (March): 112–19.

McConnell, Shelley. 1993. "Rules of the Game: Nicaragua's Contentious Constitutional Debate." *NACLA Report on the Americas* 27, no. 2 (September–October): 20–25.

McCoy, Jennifer, and William Smith. 1995. "From Deconsolidation to Reequilibration? Prospects for Democratic Renewal in Venezuela." In *Venezuelan Democracy Under Stress,* ed. J. McCoy, A. Sebin, W. C. Smith, and A. Stambouli, pp. 237–83. Miami: North-South Center Press of the University of Miami.

Medina, Medófilo. 1999. "El neoliberalismo en Colombia y las alternativas de las luchas sociales, 1975–1998." In *Lucha popular, democracia, neoliberalismo: Protesta popular en América Latina en los años de ajuste,* ed. Margarita López Maya, pp. 111–28. Caracas: Nueva Sociedad.

Medina Serna, Santiago. 1997. *La verdad sobre las mentiras.* Santafé de Bogotá: Planeta.

Naím, Moisés. 1993. *Paper Tigers and Minotaurs: The Politics of Venezuela's Economic Reforms.* Washington, D.C.: Carnegie Endowment for International Peace.

Nickson, Andrew. 1997. "The Wasmosy Government." In *The Transition to Democracy in Paraguay,* ed. Peter Lambert and Andrew Nickson, pp. 185–99. New York: St. Martin's Press.

O'Donnell, Guillermo. 1988. *Bureaucratic Authoritarianism: Argentina, 1966–1973, in Comparative Perspective.* Berkeley: University of California Press.

Pachano, Simón. 1997. "Bucaram, Fuera! Bucaram, ¿Fuera?" In *¿Y ahora qué? Una contribución al análisis político-histórico actual,* pp. 229–64. Quito: Eskeletra Editorial.

Paredes, Willington. 1997. "Guayaquil, Ciudad-Puerto, y Bahía." In *¿Y ahora qué? Una contribución al análisis político-histórico actual,* pp. 145–72. Quito: Eskeletra Editorial.

Rey, Juan Carlos. 1993. "La crisis de legitimidad en Venezuela y el enjuiciamiento y remoción de Carlos Andrés Pérez de la presidencia de la república." *Boletín Electoral Latinoamericano* 9: 67–112.

Rodríguez-Valdés, Angel. 1993. *La otra muerte de CAP.* Caracas: Alfadil Ediciones.

Rodríguez Vicéns, Antonio. 1997. *La Patria Boba: Artículos sobre el gobierno de A. Bucaram.* Quito: Artes Gráficas Señal.

Rosero Jácome, Rocío. 1997. "El despertar del ser social hacia la identidad ecuatoriana." In *¿Y ahora qué? Una contribución al análisis político-histórico actual,* pp. 173–96. Quito: Eskeletra Editorial.

Selverston, Melina. 1997. "The Unraveling of a Presidency." *NACLA Report on the Americas* 30, no. 6 (May–June): 11–12.

Sola, Lourdes. 1994. "The State, Structural Reform, and Democratization in Brazil." In *Democracy, Markets, and Structural Reform in Latin America,* ed.

W. C. Smith, C.H. Acuña, and E.A. Gamarra, pp. 151–82. Miami: North-South Center Press of the University of Miami.

Stepan, Alfred. 1971. *The Military in Politics: Changing Patterns in Brazil.* Princeton, N.J.: Princeton University Press.

Turner, Brian. 1999. "The 1998 Elections in Paraguay." Paper presented at the Twentieth Conference of the Middle Atlantic Council of Latin American Studies, March 26–27, Ursinus College, Collegeville, Pennsylvania.

Vargas, Mauricio, Jorge Lesmes, and Edgar Téllez. 1996. *El presidente que se iba a caer: Diario secreto de tres periodistas sobre el 8.000.* Santafé de Bogotá: Planeta.

Victoria, Pablo. 1997. *Yo acuso: Un documentado pliego de cargos contra el Presidente Samper.* Santafé de Bogotá: Ediciones Temas de Hoy.

Villagrán de León, Francisco. 1993. "Thwarting the Guatemalan Coup." *Journal of Democracy* 4, no. 4 (October): 117–24.

Waisbord, Silvio. 1994. "Knocking on Newsroom Doors: Press and Political Scandals in Argentina." *Political Communication* 11, no. 1 (January): 19–33.

———. 1996. "Investigative Journalism and Political Accountability in South American Democracies." *Critical Studies in Mass Communication* 13: 343–63.

Weyland, Kurt. 1993. "The Rise and Fall of President Collor and Its Impact on Brazilian Democracy." *Journal of Interamerican Studies and World Affairs* 35 (Spring): 1–37.

———. 1998a. "The Politics of Corruption in Latin America." *Journal of Democracy* 9, no. 2 (April): 108–21.

———. 1998b. "Peasants or Bankers in Venezuela? Presidential Popularity and Economic Reform Approval, 1989–1993." *Political Research Quarterly* 51: 341–62.

Yashar, Deborah. 1998. "Contesting Citizenship: Indigenous Movements and Democracy in Latin America." *Comparative Politics* 31, no. 1 (October): 23–42.

PART TWO

The Polity, the Social Contract, and Injustice

CHAPTER FIVE

The Vicious Cycle of Inequality in Latin America

TERRY LYNN KARL

Latin America is the region in the world with the greatest inequities. The acute disparities, affecting virtually all aspects of economic, social, and political life, are fundamental to understanding why the results of the past two decades of development have been so disappointing there. Economic growth has been surprisingly low despite the region having embraced neoliberal restructuring, which cut inflation to single-digit levels, reduced budget deficits, and generally lowered country public external debt. As of the early years of the new century the quality of services remained poor, unemployment high, and widespread crime and violence threatened daily life. Moreover, more than a third of the people in the region lived in poverty, nearly eighty million in extreme poverty, with incomes of less than one (U.S.) dollar a day. When asked their opinions about social issues, Latin Americans consistently stated that poverty seemed higher than ever before, their quality of life lower, and their political institutions unsatisfactory. They also expressed anxiety about the future. Not surprisingly, in a region characterized by the most unequal distribution of income and assets in the world, most continued to believe their societies to be fundamentally unjust (Lora 2000).

Addressing acute inequality is imperative if Latin American democracies are to endure and deepen and if their economies are to thrive—a reality that some social scientists have been remarkably slow to recognize. In part, this inattentiveness to inequality can be explained by the overwhelming predominance of the neoliberal paradigm (or what some call the "Washington Consensus")[1] by the turn of the century, which prioritized the promotion of production for export, the retrenchment of the state's role in the economy, and the opening of the economy to foreign trade and investment (Williamson 1990). In this list of policies and preferences, equity concerns were either ignored altogether or relegated to secondary importance. This was due in part to long-standing economic beliefs that growth and the reduction of inequality were not compatible at some stages of development (Kuznets 1955), that any redistribution would deter growth by lowering savings and investment (Kaldor 1957), and that growth alone, therefore, should be the mechanism for reducing poverty and inequality. Economists believed, quite wrongly in the Latin American case, that policies aimed at extending and enhancing markets would generate sustained growth at an acceptable rate, which in turn would reduce poverty and inequality. These beliefs did not necessarily disregard distributive effects; instead, they endorsed a set of empirical assumptions about how to achieve better distribution through sustained growth that identified market efficiency as the immediate priority and saw equity goals as a long-term consequence of policy reform.

But there were also strong political interests and value-laden assumptions behind the beliefs that led scholars to defend above all else efficiency and the maximization of total personal utility, regardless of how resources were distributed throughout society. The U.S. Treasury, the International Monetary Fund, the World Bank, and all other important multilateral funding agencies—as well as many leading businesses in the region—fully embraced neoliberal approaches (often drowning out dissenting voices). Both Washington and multilateral agencies explicitly privileged market efficiency over direct measures to improve distribution and rejected greater social expenditures (the traditional approach for improving distribution) as inflationary and inconsistent with neoliberal policy choices. This encouraged the avoidance of judgments based on the social justice of different patterns of economic reform and wealth distribution. As John Williamson (1997), who first listed the key tenets of the Washington Consensus, later wrote: "I deliberately excluded from the list anything that was primarily redistributive, as opposed to having equitable consequences as a byproduct of seeking efficiency objectives, because I felt the Washington of the 1980s to be a city that was essentially contemptuous of equity concerns."

Neoliberals ignored the political context of their reforms in areas where their prescriptions were bound to have adverse consequences for inequality. Thus, while it may be the case that Latin American countries would have had even greater poverty without the macroeconomic adjustments that tamed inflation, there is accumulating evidence that the accentuation of inequality and the failure to reduce poverty is partially the consequence of the types of reforms enacted, and not merely the result of an economic crisis that plagued the region in the 1980s. For example, in their enthusiasm to liberalize financial markets very rapidly, there was little attempt to ensure that regulatory mechanisms aimed at minimizing the risk of financial crises were in place prior to liberalization—even though any resulting economic downturn would disproportionately affect the poor. Nor did they heed constant warnings that privatizations—when implemented in the context of huge wealth disparities, weak judiciaries, and rent-seeking politicians—were very likely to further concentrate wealth, often through the very corruption they sought to correct. Nor were policies designed to stave off the consequences of dismantling labor institutions or to address the growing discontent of the middle strata (civil servants, unionized workers, pensioners, etc.), whose proximity to blatant increases in wealth helped to create an especially corrosive sense of injustice. To the contrary, in a number of cases specific policies unnecessarily increased poverty and further skewed the distribution of income. Subsidies given to Chilean banks in 1983, for example, amounted to ten times the annual cost of the Pinochet regime's emergency employment program.

But such positions are becoming increasingly difficult to sustain in the face of Latin America's record in the struggle against poverty and inequality. A combination of factors—the end of the Cold War, with the demise of the egalitarianism that had long been associated with socialism; growing concerns about globalization's impact on volatility and wages; and sharp critiques coming from Latin Americans themselves, sometimes in the form of armed movements—has contributed to a mounting consensus: that more egalitarian development is both economically and morally desirable in the Americas.[2] Economists now argue that Latin America's highly unequal access to land, education, and other assets are not merely untouched by the benefits of growth; they directly contribute to low growth rates and therefore the perpetuation of poverty (Birdsall and Londoño 1997, 1998; Deininger and Olinto 1999). In effect, a vicious cycle exists in which poverty and high levels of inequality impede growth, and growth rates are subsequently too low to adequately address the problems of poverty and inequality.[3] Thus, if Latin American countries are to reach the more impressive development records of their Asian counterparts, tackling inequality is essential.

However welcome this new attention to poverty and inequality, an analysis of Latin America's vicious cycle is still incomplete if it is confined solely to economic understandings. While some economists have presciently pointed out the links between growth, poverty, and inequality,[4] the problem is not merely economic. Where virtuous cycles of development occur, there is a complementarity between equity and economic growth, on the one hand, and democracy and social justice, on the other. Where cycles are vicious, economic problems often originate at the political level, and they are often perpetuated or exacerbated through the normal functioning (or nonfunctioning) of political institutions. As I have argued elsewhere (Karl 1997), economic patterns of development shape the structures of the state, the prospects for collective action, and sometimes even the rhythms of stability and instability, and this in turn sets the contours of economic policy. Thus this newly emerging economic consensus needs to better incorporate the notion of power into its argument if it is to succeed in challenging Latin America's record of low growth, high inequality, and persistent poverty.

This chapter argues the following: if inequality is based on differences in initial endowments of wealth or family connections, as is surely the case in Latin America, these inequalities will not only affect the prospects for growth, but they will also shape social and political life. High inequalities bias the political rules of the game and mold polities in favor of the wealthy and privileged, and they do so (to different degrees) whether regimes are authoritarian or democratic. Exceptionally high inequalities of wealth and income are the basis for exceptionally inequitable distributions of political power and representation, even in the continent's young democracies, and these power arrangements are subsequently unlikely to address the basic problem of high inequality. This means that Latin American public policies cannot be understood as the product or equilibrium outcome of democratic voting among rational individuals, as models based on the "median voter" claim, because such models assume that the distribution of political power is relatively egalitarian. As scholars of comparative politics have repeatedly shown, politics in Latin America works only in limited ways through the democratic process, and then votes are often "delivered," especially in rural areas. Instead, economic and social policy operates largely through the exercise of private influence and the skewed functioning of politicized bureaucracies that favor large economic *grupos,* groups.[5] The unequal power distributions they both reflect and reproduce, in turn, help to se-

cure economic privileges, undermine competition and efficiency, encourage corruption, undermine productive growth, and in the end subvert democracy. Transforming this vicious cycle into a virtuous cycle will
not be easy because, as we shall see, this inevitably involves both asset
redistribution and the reordering of political priorities—no easy task in
Latin America.

A DISTURBING DEVELOPMENT RECORD

Evidence about Latin America's economic performance in the past two
decades is disturbing. Despite significant monetary and fiscal discipline,
an enormous surge in private capital inflows into the region, and an expansion of export and investment volumes, real GDP growth was just 3
percent a year for the decade of the 1990s, and just 1.5 percent per
capita. As Birdsall, de la Torre, and Menezes (2001: 7) note, this is not
much better than the 2 percent rate during the "lost decade of the 1980s,
and it is well below the rates of 5 percent or more during the import substitution decades of the 1960s and 1970s."

Inequality measures reveal an even more distressing trend. Latin America not only has the dubious distinction of being the region in the world
with the most unequal distribution of wealth, as already noted, but equality indicators have sharply deteriorated over time. A quarter of all national income is received by a mere 5 percent of the population, and the
top 10 percent own 40 percent of the wealth—a level of inequality that
can be found only in a few African countries, whose per capita income
levels are half that of Latin America! To underline the magnitude of these
inequalities and the concentration of wealth and power they represent,
suffice it to note that in the developed countries (no bastions of equality
themselves) the wealthiest 5 percent receive on average only 13 percent
of all national income—about half the Latin American norm (Karl 2000).
Income distribution, which had become more equal during the 1970s,
worsened considerably in the 1980s and remained stagnant in the 1990s,
despite positive growth rates throughout the decade. When examined
over a two-decade period beginning in 1980, almost all of Latin America showed deterioration, especially Venezuela, Guatemala, the Dominican Republic, Panama, Chile, and Brazil. Only Costa Rica, Peru, and possibly Colombia showed slight improvement (World Bank 2000: 13).

This record is powerful evidence of a new round in Latin America's
vicious cycle of development, which has taken place during the past two

decades of neoliberal economic policies. In 1970, the richest 1 percent of the population earned 363 times more than the poorest 1 percent; by 1995, this had risen to a whopping 417 times. Inequality in Latin America is not only the steepest in the world in absolute terms; it is also much greater than would "normally" accompany this level of development, with an especially acute concentration of wealth toward the top. Such a skewed distributional profile means that the poor face greater barriers to escaping their deprivation, because, first, extreme inequalities reduce growth and, second, the alleviation of poverty becomes less responsive to the growth that does occur. Thus, although Latin America's per capita GDP grew by almost 6 percent in real terms between 1990 and 1995, the years of highest growth over the past two decades, the number of extremely and moderately poor actually *increased* by 1.5 and 5 million people, respectively, over the same period. No other region in the world shows this pattern. If income and wealth had been distributed more equitably, poverty would have been reduced dramatically. Indeed, Juan Luis Londoño and Miguel Szekely (1997) estimate that poverty would be practically eliminated if Latin America had the same distribution observed in either Eastern Europe or South Asia, and it would be the lowest in the developing world if inequality patterns were similar to those of the Middle East, North Africa, or Central Asia.

This dismal record is neither inevitable nor necessary, as comparisons between East Asia and Latin America demonstrate. In general, the Latin American pattern is one of low growth and low equality with persistent poverty, while Asia displays the opposite characteristics: high growth and the reduction of inequalities.[6] While Latin America's real GNP per capita was barely growing at all throughout the 1980s, East Asia and the Pacific showed an amazing 27.2 percent increase in real GNP per capita over the same period. In Latin America, the richest 20 percent of the population captured, on average over the period 1965–92, about 16 times the income of the poorest, whereas in East Asia the difference is 7.9 times (Stallings, Birdsall, and Clugage 2000: 103). In effect, while poverty and inequalities increased just about everywhere in Latin America, the trends in East and Southeast Asia were completely different: between 1975 and 1995, the absolute number of poor was reduced by half, an achievement the World Bank claims is unprecedented in history.[7] Indeed, South Korea, Taiwan, Hong Kong, Singapore, and to a lesser extent Malaysia and Thailand virtually eliminated the problem of absolute poverty during this period—a far cry from the Latin American picture.

THE ORIGINS OF THE VICIOUS CYCLE

Why is Latin America so different from other regions? Elsewhere (Karl 1997), I have argued that Latin America's poverty and inequality is linked paradoxically to the asset distribution of its natural wealth, especially its mineral riches. Most certainly a key explanation for the difference between East Asian and U.S. patterns of development, on the one hand, and Latin America, on the other, lies in the difference in the nature of their "natural capital" or assets and the manner in which these assets were initially divided. In Latin America, from the very beginning mineral and agricultural riches were a mixed blessing; in the context of a specific form of colonial rule they produced concentrated rents that centralized economic and political power and established the region's patterns of inequality. This initial asset inequality not only had a significant negative impact on long-term growth, but it also established stable patterns of skewed distributions of political and economic power that persist to this day.

The concentration of political and economic power in Latin America is a legacy of colonialism. The colonizers who arrived from Spain and Portugal encountered highly developed and complex indigenous societies; the population of the Americas in 1492 was probably greater than that of all of Europe. The goal of these colonizers was ownership of Latin America's rich endowment of natural resources, and conquest was the means to that end. Granted control over huge tracts of land and huge concentrations of minerals, these settlers superimposed themselves by force at the top of existing social structures. Initially through the *encomienda* system, which "granted" huge numbers of Indians to the conquerors as laborers, and later through the slave trade, which aimed at guaranteeing a labor supply after the indigenous communities had been decimated, colonizers were able to cultivate vast expanses of land and work the mines. In contrast to the northern United States—where colonizers sought to expel natives from their lands, rather than using their labor—this labor-intensive mode gave rise to a very unequal distribution of income and assets.

This is the past that has its claws in the present. Colonizers captured concentrated rents by establishing hierarchical political structures based on arbitrary executive dominance, an extremely weak rule of law, and excessive militarism—patterns that persist to this day. In order to guarantee its rents, the Crown built an elaborate bureaucracy and military structure, overseen by viceroys who had broad authority to collect taxes, administer justice, and defend property. Thus, from the beginning, the colonial state was highly centralized and intricately tied to the extraction of rents. Both the mining and the *hacienda* or plantation system, reinforced by laws of descent founded on the right of primogeniture, were closely linked to the state, whose very raison d'etre was the redirection of tribute into the colonizers' hands. This fortified the link between family, centralized power, and wealth that has formed the basis for aristocracy everywhere.

By all accounts, political institutions were simultaneously strong and weak. On the one hand, they had tremendous capacity to control labor and enforce laws that were in the interests of landowners and miners, usually through the exercise of brute force. On the other hand, they had few mechanisms for authoritative or legitimate allocation and were highly exclusionary. Efficiency in the extraction of rents was bought through the utilization of power and influence; it came at the cost of a substantial share in the rents that were given by the Crown to miners, landowners, and provincial authorities in order to sustain their cooperation (Bakewell 1997). These are the earliest roots of centralized but weak states that are permeated by the private interests and clientelism that manage to capture the overwhelming share of the surplus.

Contrast this centralization of political and economic power with events in the north.[8] In the United States, an exceptionally egalitarian social and economic structure, based on small landholdings, established certain patterns of material equality, producing egalitarian sentiments, which in turn formed the basis for the principle of equal citizenship—the mutually recognized right of individuals to participate equally in the making of binding political decisions. Since people's economic circumstances, educational backgrounds, and everyday experiences were so similar, they were able to reach and sustain collective choices through majority rule. Politics in the United States became the province of the "common man" rather than the stronghold of an aristocracy deriving its position from superior education, status, or wealth. Furthermore, because all men (though not women or slaves) were created equal, they were equally eligible to hold government positions. Thus the institutional bulwarks of elitism could be removed. Property restrictions on suffrage were lifted, terms of office were limited, and many qualifications for office were removed.

The structure of property was the principal factor that made these developments possible. Because cheap labor was available rather belatedly and then only in the less dominant South, and because production was insufficient to support both owners and tenant farmers, land was broken up into small parcels, thereby destroying the basis for a new landed elite that *haciendas* provided in Latin America. The colonizers of New England, who initially sought religious freedom rather than riches, were exceptionally well educated, and thus were given the unique right to form themselves into a political society and to govern themselves under the protection of England. They established schools in every township and taxed inhabitants to support them, so primary instruction was accessible to everyone at a very early stage. The replacement of primogeniture with new laws of inheritance, the last major step in this egalitarian progression, brought about a virtual revolution in notions of property. By destroying the intimate connection between families and the preservation of landed estates, such laws helped to "divide, distribute and disperse both property and power" (Tocqueville 1990: 1: 48), while creating the basis for the subsequent growth of democratic manners and customs.

The difference is striking. In most of Latin America, the historical dispersal of economic resources that is the precursor to a plurality of political power never occurred. Thus there was no institutional balance of power from the start and there was no conception of the state (or any branch of it) as an independent adjudicator of interests. If democracy advances as asset ownership expands, as Tocqueville claims, then Latin America's point of departure did not bode well for its inclusiveness. Only Costa Rica, Uruguay, and to some extent Chile, where indigenous labor was so scarce that land was divided more evenly, initially managed to escape this hyperconcentrated pattern. Not surprisingly, two of these countries, Costa Rica and Uruguay, still have the strongest nonpresidential political institutions and the least inequality today.

THE PERSISTENCE OF THE VICIOUS CYCLE

Patterns persist, especially if designers of economies and polities do not choose or are not forced to change them. Independence may have rearranged property ownership and the terms of trade, but it did not change the emphasis on commodity exports or the distribution of property. Throughout the nineteenth century, the great agrarian transformations brought about by the export of cacao and, later, coffee, sugar, cotton, and other products, as well as the modes of development fostered by mineral exports, perpetuated the marked concentration of political and economic power. Wherever landed aristocracies were in command, they set up labor-repressive agriculture as the dominant mode of production and established authoritarian regimes to control the workers—a reality best exemplified by the difference between the development trajectories of Guatemala, El Salvador, and Nicaragua, on the one hand, and yeoman-farmer-based Costa Rica, on the other. Where the dominant class arose primarily from mining and its associated commercial and industrial interests, its need for considerable physical capital and relatively few workers left the majority of people in a difficult situation by lowering real wages and worsening the distribution of income. The confiscation of more lands and the tightening of coercive labor systems in turn reinforced the bias toward exports because the number of beneficiaries was far too few to develop stronger domestic markets. Because the region's exports were subject to strong external shocks, which contributed to a highly volatile macroeconomic environment, the rate of long-term growth was contained and the distribution of income worsened.

Such exclusion paved the way for elite control of political power. Despite having similar levels of per capita GDP as the British colonies in the Americas at the beginning of the nineteenth century, Latin America soon fell far behind the United States and Canada, experiencing no per capita GDP growth; during the same time, the U.S. GDP per capita grew between four- and sixfold (Atack and Pasell 1994). Evidence suggests that at least part of this poor performance was due to the region's exceptionally high inequality. The extent of this inequality is hard to convey; Bakewell (1997: 424) shows that a few families, "who inhabited four square blocks of central Santiago," controlled Chile. The structure of property gave dominant economic interests the political power necessary to control labor, prevent taxation of their wealth, and limit any fiscal or economic reforms that might have established a permanent and stable revenue base for the state (Graham 1990). Dominant classes, whose interests were based on labor repression, had no motivation to build up human capital, which could threaten their power. The regimes they built and influenced largely reflected these priorities. Even in the rare cases that governments sought reform, without a tax base they could not fund sufficient investments in education or health; thus they could provide neither the public goods nor the human capital accumulation that are the keys to sustainable development. Nowhere is this more apparent than in Central America.

The polities, including political institutions, built in this context were, in turn, simultaneously strong and weak. On the one hand, the concentration of political power, in part for the purposes of complementing, sustaining, and bargaining with economic power, gave the impression of great force. *Caudillismo*, and the heritage of personalism and presidentialism it produced, was a response to the persistent need for strong central authority. Presidents stood at the top of networks formed by their cronies, regional political bosses and armies, and they were the main contact points for foreign investors and domestic elites. The constitutions that replaced the colonial system contained provisions for turning this arrangement into a lasting legacy; they institutionalized especially strong executives and ultrapresidentialism. These presidents sat atop states that ever expanded their jurisdictions (since late development tended to exacerbate the tendency toward intervention), but the appearance of strength was deceptive. Because power was so concentrated, Latin American states, to varying degrees, developed no separation of powers and a very weak rule of law (Karst and Rosenn 1975; Rosenn 1990; Nino 1996). Moreover, because dominant economic interests blocked taxation, states could never develop their own extractive capacities vis-a-vis their own populations. This in turn circumscribed the growth of administrative capabilities (Karl 1997: 44–70).

By the beginning of the twentieth century, all Latin American states had "hitched their economic star to a dominant commodity," but the fruits of these commodities were not widely shared. Economic development models, especially the free-trade experiments of the 1920s, perpetuated the concentration of income among elites and sustained these patterns of social exclusion. Designed in the interests of ruling families, who were concentrated in export activities and who therefore benefited from economic openness, these models did manage to achieve a growth in exports as a response to increasing demand, especially from Europe and the Americas (Bulmer-Thomas 1994). But they also were the economic basis for an exclusionary political alliance between export elites, foreign investors, and the state, best exemplified by Juan Vicente Gómez in Venezuela, Gerardo Machado in Cuba, and Porfirio Díaz in Mexico. Such regimes were kept in place largely by force, and by the 1920s military institutions became fundamental political actors, possessing the capacity to topple governments and create new ones (Rouquie and Suffern 1994). Not surprisingly, political regimes with this social base never challenged the concentration of asset distribution—except its distribution among themselves—and they never questioned the overall benefits of free trade in a highly oligopolistic setting.

Indeed, they used its benefits to strengthen both the political and economic concentration of power.

Throughout most of the twentieth century, these gross material inequalities provided the social basis for exclusionary authoritarian regimes, which, in turn, promoted economic models that disproportionately benefited the rich and powerful. Political power was concentrated through ultrapresidentialism that lacked any meaningful form of accountability. To different degrees in different countries, both foreign governments and multinational companies were able to bend political decision making to serve their interests, usually by bargaining directly with powerful presidents and their representatives; influence of the giant, diversified, domestic, family-based economic groups, known as *grupos,* also distorted decision-making processes. In effect, Latin American countries were ruled by a "triple alliance" of foreign and domestic entrepreneurs and state officials, which retarded the region's democratic maturation. To some extent this pattern was altered with the fall in world demand for Latin American products during World War I, which catalyzed the rise of industrialists, urban labor unions, and the formation of political parties, and it was more thoroughly changed with import substitution industrialization, state-backed production for the domestic market, which generated solid economic growth between 1925 and the late 1970s.

Only countries that managed to build strong party systems and very influential labor unions—and hence a tradition of social-welfare policies—followed somewhat different trajectories. Not surprisingly, these were countries where property was distributed more equitably from the start (Uruguay and Costa Rica), where agrarian oligarchs were divided and competed with mining and other interests (Chile, Peru, and Venezuela), or where there was no peasantry at all (Argentina). Whatever democratization and redistribution did occur took place in the context of an interventionist state, economic protectionism, and organized mass pressures from below—a decidedly "illiberal," non-free-market model. Under these conditions, which prevailed in the democracies of the 1960s, the incomes of the poor and middle classes slowly expanded at the expense of the richest 20 percent of the population (Londoño and Szekely 1997). But in South America these developments were terminated by a wave of authoritarian regimes that put a brutal end to political democracy and further concentrated wealth; and in Central America (with the exception of Costa Rica), these developments never took place at all.

HOW INEQUALITY IS REINFORCED

What is especially disturbing about Latin America's economic and political development patterns is that they remain largely self-reinforcing. This is not unique to Latin America. Considerable evidence exists that inequality varies far more between countries at a given time than over time within a single country. In other words, the inequality rankings of countries are highly stable over decades, and past inequality may be the most important predictor of current inequality (Bruno, Ravallion, and Squire 2000: 47).

Reinforcement mechanisms lie in the nature of the economic model, not only in its contemporary neoliberal form but also in its past forms. What I have elsewhere called "the paradox of plenty" (Karl 1997) is, in part, the surprising finding that extensive natural wealth may reduce economic growth in the long run—at least under certain conditions. Countries with bountiful arable land per capita and various types of natural wealth (oil, minerals, and numerous agricultural products) grow more slowly than countries with fairly limited natural wealth. Indeed, Auty (1998) argues that from 1970 to 1993 countries with fairly limited natural wealth grew more than four times as rapidly as their resource-rich counterparts. There are several reasons for this. Resource-rich countries in the developing world suffer from a host of economic problems associated with dependence on mineral or agricultural wealth for exports, including vulnerability to heavy price volatility owing to global market conditions beyond their control. These problems translate into low domestic investment rates in comparison to world standards, and even the region's success in attracting foreign direct investment is insufficient compensation. This may be the basic difference between the growth performance of resource-rich Latin America and resource-poor East Asia. As the World Bank notes (1999), between 1960 and 1997 Latin America's investment rate was 2 percentage points below the world average and a full 7 percentage points below less well-endowed East Asian countries (World Bank 1999)! Latin America's resource-rich countries simply do not grow fast enough to address inequalities or the reduction of poverty, and they are not likely to do so in the near future.

Other inequality effects exacerbate these growth problems. A number of analytical models have demonstrated the importance of the initial distribution of endowments by showing how changes in more equitable directions potentially yield large increases in social welfare. These findings are verified by the experiences of Japan, Taiwan, and Korea, where high growth followed externally imposed land reform. The more inequitable the initial distribution, the more severe the constraints on growth. Deininger and Squire (1996) demonstrate significant adverse effects of higher land inequality on inequality of incomes, showing how especially inequitable distribution of land is associated with lower capital accumulation and growth, a finding that has been confirmed by others (Persson and Tabellini 1994). Such inequality in asset distribution is also at the root of many models that relate inflation to inequalities in the distribution of income. In effect, inflation taxes both rich and poor, but the access of the former to foreign currency and capital flight allows them to shift the burden of inflation to the poor. Credit constraints preventing the poor from making productive investments also reinforce the high inequality/low-growth cycle.

Even very modest changes in overall inequality can bring about sizable changes in the incidence of poverty, but social exclusion makes such reforms very difficult. The clear result of Latin America's history of high inequality, low growth, and concentrated political power has been dualistic development, the coexistence of two distinct but linked worlds within the same national territory: the rich (along with portions of the middle class and some workers) and the poor. What distinguishes these two groups, besides a huge disparity in wealth, is the enormous *social* distance between them despite their close proximity. The wealthy have their own schools, attend their own churches, and segregate themselves in walled neighborhoods. The poor have had either no schools or poor schools, especially in rural areas. They also attend separate religious institutions; have virtually no social services; and live in urban shantytowns that are physically proximate to wealthy neighborhoods but worlds apart in every other way.

Social exclusion does more than perpetuate inequality; it retards the accumulation of human capital that is so crucial for reducing human misery. Recent studies have found significant correlations between initial educational inequality (especially for women and girls) and both slow economic growth and poverty (Birdsall and Londoño 1997; Ravallion and Datt 1999). In this sense, the educational system is a key reinforcement mechanism in the region's vicious cycle. Average years of study has advanced more slowly in Latin America than in any other area of the world. By the early 1990s the average did not reach even five years. The low average reflected regime class and race/ethnic biases.

Contrary to what is often believed, the region's poor average educational performance is not due to exceptionally low levels of public spending, except in some countries in Central America. The region's comparative performance is good in this respect, spending more on education than more broadly schooled East Asia.

The patterns of Latin American spending, however, are skewed decidedly toward higher-income groups and, accordingly, toward higher over primary education. The figures are startling. The top 10 percent of income earners in Latin America have an average of 11.3 years of education (somewhat less than the time necessary to complete secondary school in the United States), a full seven years more than the poorest 30 percent of the population. There is a dramatic difference in secondary-school completion rates between the poorest 10 percent and the richest 10 percent of Latin Americans. One World Bank study (2000: 56) showed that of the fourteen countries examined, twelve demonstrated a difference of over 50 percent between the percentage of the richest and poorest children who finished secondary school! In Brazil and Panama in 1995 and in Greater Buenos Aires in 1996, the gap in completion rates topped 70 percent. In human terms, this means that profound stratification of education fortifies the enormous social distance between rich and poor in Latin America, and it guarantees that the poor, and the children of the poor, are unlikely to be able to escape their plight. And access to education is even correlated with life and death. In Bolivia, for example, the inability of parents to speak Spanish is associated with higher mortality rates for children under two years old (World Bank 2000: 63).

Public-education investment patterns reflect power arrangements and the manner in which political institutions function—another set of reinforcement mechanisms. In effect, when it comes to expenditures on public services the wealthy win the alliance of middle classes at the expense of the poor. While in principle fiscal policy could provide the necessary tools to protect the poor and redistribute income toward the disadvantaged, over the past twenty-five years the outcome in Latin America has been otherwise. Instead, the budget has been a key mechanism through which urban middle classes, directly or through government jobs, have captured benefits for themselves while preventing significant changes in income distribution. As growth rates stopped entirely or slowed in the 1980s and 1990s, the impact of total social expenditures in health, education, social security, public housing, water, and housing was either neutral or regressive for the poorest 20 percent in many Latin American

countries. In effect, the region with the highest levels of income inequality in the world is also characterized by low government spending
on the poor.

This bias of the political system is best exemplified by the fact that
taxation of private assets has never been a major part of government
revenue in Latin America. Indeed, governments of the region have done
everything possible to avoid taxation. They have turned to overvalued
exchange rates on primary exports to avoid asking elites to pay taxes
on land or other property (Hirschman 1971). When this has been
insufficient, they have used foreign borrowing as a substitute for taxation (Karl 1997). When tax reform does occur, it takes the form of consumption taxes, mainly the VAT, rather than taxes on income or assets
(Majon 1997). Consumption taxes are regressive. They impose propor-
tionally less of a burden on the rich.

Extreme income inequality has an insidious impact on the way democratic institutions actually operate in other ways. Observers as diverse
as Human Rights Watch, Freedom House, Transparency International,
and the Inter-American Dialogue have pointed out the ways in which
powerful economic and political elites have bent laws to their bidding,
enfeebled courts, violated rights, corrupted politicians, and run
roughshod over constitutions and contracts. In countries where mineral
and agricultural exports produce concentrated rents and thus disproportionate access and influence over politicians, greater wealth buys
greater influence. Exceptionally high inequality makes the state especially susceptible to influence-trafficking by producing the incentives and
the resources for greater rent-seeking; money contributions and job
promises are exchanged for political favors, affecting the direction of the
most important economic decisions. Thus, in Transparency International's turn-of-the-century surveys, most countries in the region end up
in the bottom half of the ninety-nine countries in their corruption rank-
ing—with Argentina fifty-second, Ecuador seventy-fourth, Venezuela
seventy-fifth, and Honduras ninety-fourth (Transparency International
2000). Such poor rankings capture behavior that impedes any type of
strategy designed to overcome inequities and to encourage competition,
and accordingly to increase prospects of small-business success. The situation, in turn, undermines confidence in government.

But if the rich have the political advantage through exceptional access to power, in general the poor are simply too weak economically
and politically to demand policies in their own favor. As the so-called
informal sector, where workers enjoy no guaranteed minimum wage,

health or unemployment insurance, or other benefits, has grown as a basis of employment and family incomes within the sector have fallen, the prospect of the poor, especially poor women, organizing collectively for better work-related conditions does not look promising. Nor are memories of the recent authoritarian past, where laborers were the greatest victims of repression, conducive to mobilizations to protect their interests. When compared to the rich, the poor are significantly more reluctant to engage in political action (MORI International 1998). In surveys conducted in Chile, Mexico, and Costa Rica, the lowest-income sector would never sign a letter of protest (41 percent, compared to 27 percent of the highest-income sector) or attend a demonstration (52 percent, compared to 37 percent). Especially high crime rates in poor *barrios* also explain this participation bias. Where crime lords rule, they destroy local bases of governance, including nongovernmental organizations that seek to promote antipoverty goals, and substitute new patterns of clientelism based on force and fear. This skews incentives for legal economic gains and removes state revenues that could be more productively and equitably invested in human-resource development.[9] Finally, the poor report feeling disempowered and humiliated by their governing institutions; they distrust their effectiveness and relevance and believe they are excluded from participation. With such negative assessments, they tend to vote less, thereby not fully utilizing the potential benefits of democracy to improve their lot (Narayan et al. 2000: 197). Indeed, unlike the rich, surveys find only a small majority of the poor hold governments accountable for their actions (57 percent, compared to 74 percent [Narayan et al. 2000: 197]).

Social scientists are often preoccupied with showing how this type of skewed polity may lead excluded actors to pursue their objectives outside normal channels—by means of violent political movements, riots, and protests. But they often fail to note that such actions are most often in response to the refusal of elites to operate through normal democratic channels. Even when dominant interests do not circumvent political institutions and choose to work within them, these institutions were originally built by them to protect their interests; thus they are still biased in favor of dominant interests despite the principle of "one person, one vote." For example, Snyder and Samuels (2001: 147–59) convincingly show that Latin America has the most malapportioned legislatures in the world, which, in turn, causes negative consequences for democracy that are relatively hidden from public view. Rural interests are overrepresented, producing a distinct rural and conservative bias in the polity (especially in Argentina, Bolivia, Brazil, Chile, Colombia, and Ecuador).

The failure of democratic institutions both to address economic problems and to function properly weakens their legitimacy in the eyes of all their citizens, rich as well as poor. Compare, for example, the 81 percent of Spaniards who claim that "democracy is preferable to any other form of government" with the 63 percent ten-nation average of Latin Americans. Where income inequality is greatest, people are more willing to accept authoritarian rule, less likely to be satisfied with the way democracy works, less trusting of their political institutions, and more willing to violate human rights. Thus, the two historically most equitable countries in Latin America—Costa Rica and Uruguay—show levels of support for democracy and trust in their democratic institutions that are comparable to the stable democracies of Western Europe, while the other fourteen countries surveyed by Latinobarometro demonstrate more ambivalent attitudes. Some countries, such as Brazil, Paraguay, Venezuela, and Colombia, even exhibit what Lagos (2001: 137) has called "a crisis in public attitudes towards democracy."

The comparison between attitudes in Uruguay, perhaps the region's most equitable country, to those of Brazil, one of the most inequitable, is striking. While Uruguayans favor democracy, as "the most preferable form of government," over authoritarian rule by 84 percent to 9 percent, the comparable figures in Brazil are 39 percent to 24 percent (Lagos 2001: 139). Moreover, in Uruguay an impressive majority (69 percent) is satisfied with the performance of democracy, while in Brazil the proportion is less than a quarter. Most of Latin America is much closer to the Brazilian pattern; only 37 percent of the public are satisfied with the way democracy works (compared with 57 percent, for example, in the newer democracies of Southern Europe). Levels of trust in institutions are especially low.

INEQUALITY AND DEMOCRACY

The combination of what the philosopher Rawls (1971) has called the "birth lottery" with what is sometimes referred to as Latin America's "commodity lottery" is the fundamental basis for the vicious cycle of unequal development in the region. This winner-loser setup is a self-reinforcing economic and political dynamic based on the concentration of both assets and power, the institutionalized bias this creates in political structures, and the permanent exclusion of large segments of the population. This means that in Latin America mitigating asset and income inequities is the principal task facing policymakers.

The reasons for addressing inequality are clear from the development record. Latin America has simply not grown fast enough to reduce human misery in the region, in large part because badly needed macroeconomic policies are not implemented at all, have been implemented too late, or have been reversed. But the reluctance to administer such policies has its roots in the way that inequalities in political power, based on highly distorted patterns of property, permit the capture of gains—first from the policies that exist prior to reform and later from the reform process itself. When majorities understand that the brunt of stabilization will be borne most by them, they in turn resist economic reform—even when it might ultimately benefit them. This is logical behavior when social safety nets have been inadequate, corruption flourishes, the rule of law is weak, and government institutions are not accessible to them. But the social conflict that is engendered from unequal income and asset distribution is especially destructive for both macroeconomic and political stability. The net result of this vicious cycle is other cyclical behavior. Thus the countries of Latin America are characterized by marked swings in their fiscal and macroeconomic policies, contributing to high inflation rates and the inability of governments to stabilize their budgets. Most dramatically, they move between democracy and authoritarianism, in part because macroeconomic instability helps to produce political systems characterized by frequent regime changes, party fragmentation, and political exclusion.

Can the latest round of democracy in Latin America reverse the region's historic pattern? In some respects, the prognosis is not good. What is most striking when examining the approaches taken to economic reform over the past two decades is that no government or multilateral agency was prepared or able to protect the poor from aspects of newly instituted neoliberal so-called structural adjustment policies (such as privatizations, the removal of barriers to trade, and ceilings on prices of basic consumer goods, including basic food) that adversely affect them, and most did not even try until some time after the distributive consequences of the reforms became painfully clear. Inattention to the negative effect on the middle as well as working and lower classes fueled urban riots in Venezuela and Argentina, the Chiapas partially indigenous uprising in Mexico (see chapter 11, by June Nash), the election of populist former coup leaders in Venezuela and Bolivia, the inability to consolidate any type of governance in Ecuador, the assassination of political leaders in Paraguay, and spreading warfare in Colombia (see chapter 7, by Marc Chernick). Such dramatic events demonstrate how difficult it is for democratic institutions to function correctly or to be maintained in a polity sharply divided by income and wealth, and they illustrate the limits to what a universal franchise can deliver, especially against the current backdrop of fiscally slimmed-down neoliberal states, highly mobile capital intent on minimizing tax burdens, and unorganized majorities. Because the globalization of economies in this context can erode the social consensus so tentatively forged in new democracies, especially where inequalities are so stark, the basis for demagogic populist solutions is being reproduced in a number of countries. Unless this is counteracted by socially just redistributive policies that consciously do not replicate the unstable spending policies of the past, protectionist pressures are likely to soar in the longer term, economic progress will be jeopardized, and democratic stability will be threatened. This seems to be the likely fate of much of the Andes.

But there are more hopeful signs as well. Most democracies, especially those with strong party systems, show a greater commitment to gradually changing deeply entrenched patterns of inequality, and there are new opportunities that may help to redress the political imbalances wrought in the past. First, despite the paucity of real debate in the past over development policy, debate is becoming more common, as is the knowledge about what permits development and democracy to coexist. There is a newly emerging consensus that free trade, combined with effective regulation and social protection—for example, support for primary education, income transfers to the poor to improve nutrition, better access to social infrastructure, preferential credits for low-income housing, and improved health care—can simultaneously raise labor productivity, reduce poverty, and create more capable citizens. Most important, there is a new effort to distinguish between extensive state-financed populist economic policies and badly needed redistributive policies (e.g., through progressive taxation), which are not the same thing and do not lead to the same results. Multilateral lending and development agencies need to shift the conditionality of their loans. Until now they have called for ending price controls and holding down wages. Instead, they should insist on more progressive taxation and transparent budgetary processes, and they should target spending on the poor.

Second, just as markets have become more globalized, so too have democratic processes. Powerful new opportunities for transnational progressive coalitions have come to improve the quality of polities. In effect, as capital and labor have become more nomadic, so too have sites for democratic struggle. Reformers, hoping to win support for their policies, no longer must depend merely on appeals to the enlightened self-interest of elites or obfuscation in presenting their programs. Reformists seeking to broaden the social base of their new democracies through such measures as lowering barriers to entry into the electoral system, the opening of political parties to new constituencies, and the creation of new sources of municipal power have come to have new allies. With survey data consistently showing women are more likely than men to support environmental regulation, controls over business, programs that assure the survival of society's weakest members, and a general softening of the harshest aspects of markets in virtually every polity, appeals to the women's vote have become an effective means of building new coalitions for change.[10] The aggressive recruitment of women leaders, the leap in women's representation due to gender-based quotas in countries like Argentina and Brazil, and the expression of explicitly female voices in politics largely reflects the impact of a now globalized women's movement, whose efforts at combating discrimination lend weight to the battle against inequality. But it is also the product of some economists who want to build human capital as a means of achieving better development performance. Thus, reformers have acquired political allies powerful enough to promote equity.

Democracies seem to endure for decades when they are capable of generating moderate levels of economic growth along with moderate to low levels of inflation (Przeworski et al. 1996), when they improve the distribution of wealth (c.f. Muller 1988), and when they respect the political rights of their citizenry. Formal democratization aside, of the countries in the region with populations over one million, almost half have experienced a significant decline in their levels of freedom over the past decade. In Latin America, the economy and the polity go hand in hand. To the extent that both are reformed to benefit those in society who are worst off, Latin America's vicious cycle can be stopped. (The Workers' Party [PT] in Brazil, elected to power in 2002, aims to do just that.) The alternative is not pretty.

NOTES

A portion of this chapter appeared previously in Terry Lynn Karl, "Economic Inequality and Democratic Instability," *Journal of Democracy* 11, no. 1 (January 2000): 149–56.

1. More specifically, *neoliberalism* refers to a broad set of policies that are designed to promote free markets, including the liberalization of rules concerning

foreign direct investment, the reduction of tariffs and quantitative restrictions on imports, the elimination of export and import licenses, the privatization of state enterprises, the reduction or elimination of subsidies, the removal of price controls, cutbacks in public spending, the deregulation of financial markets, and the devaluation of currencies. This paradigm has been dubbed the Washington Consensus because the International Monetary Fund, the World Bank, and the U.S. Treasury, all with offices in the U.S. capital, support it.

2. Evidence for this newly emerging consensus can be seen in the decision of the World Bank and the Inter-American Development Bank to make poverty reduction the overriding objective of their corporate mission, the move toward debt relief for the world's poorest countries, the awarding of the Nobel Prize to Amartya Sen in 1998, and the statements of heads of state of the Americas in the 1998 summit.

3. As far as I can tell, this term was first used by economists in Birdsall, Pinckney, and Sabot (1996).

4. See especially works of Nancy Birdsall and colleagues (e.g., Birdsall and de la Torre, with Menezes [2001], Birdsall and Londoño [1997], and Birdsall, Pinckney, and Sabot [1996]).

5. Case studies of the exercise of power repeatedly show this pattern, as do larger comparative studies. See, for example, Leff (1968); Cardoso and Faletto (1969); Cavarozzi and Petras (1974); Collier (1976); Evans (1979, 1995); Handelman (1979); O'Donnell (1994); Weyland (1996); and Karl (1997).

6. The exception is the Philippines, which follows the Latin American pattern.

7. The number of people in poverty dropped from 716.8 million to 345.7 million during these years, according to World Bank statistics cited in the *Wall Street Journal* (August 22, 1997), p. A8.

8. The rest of this section is taken from Karl (2000).

9. André de Mello e Souza (2001) describes this dynamic by examining violence in the shantytowns of Rio de Janeiro, showing how crime, while distributing resources differently, also gives rise to a greater militarization of both army and police forces.

10. This is not to argue that women are more progressive voters or replicate the gender gap in advanced industrialized societies. In most cases, where data are still available, women tend to vote more conservatively than men in Latin America.

REFERENCES

Atack, Jeremy, and Peter Passell, 1994. *A New Economic View of American History.* New York: W. W. Norton.

Auty, Richard M. 1998. "Resource Abundance and Economic Development: Improving the Performance of Resource-Rich Countries." UNU (United Nations University)-WIDER Working paper. Helsinki.

Bakewell, Peter. 1997. *A History of Latin America.* Oxford: Blackwell Publishers.

Birdsall, Nancy, and Augusto de la Torre, with Rachel Menezes. 2001. *Washington Contentious: Economic Policies for Social Equity in Latin America.*

Washington, D.C.: Carnegie Endowment for International Peace and the InterAmerican Dialogue.

Birdsall, N., and J. L. Londoño. 1997. "Asset Inequality Matters: An Assessment of the World Bank's Approach to Poverty Reduction." *American Economic Review* 87, no. 2 (May): 32–37.

———. 1998. "No Tradeoff: Efficient Growth via More Equal Human Capital in Latin America." In *Beyond Tradeoffs: Market Reforms and Equitable Growth in Latin America*, ed. Nancy Birdsall, Carol Graham, and Richard Sabot. Washington, D.C.: Brookings Institution Press and Inter-American Development Bank.

Birdsall, Nancy, Thomas Pinckney, and Richard Sabot. 1996. "Why Low Inequality Spurs Growth." Inter-American Development Bank Working Paper. Washington, D.C.

Bruno, Michael, Martin Ravallion, and Lyn Squire. 2000. "Equity and Growth in Developing Countries." In *Distributive Justice and Economic Development: The Case of Chile and Developing Countries*, ed. Andrés Solimano, Eduardo Aninat, and Nancy Birdsall, pp. 37–65. Ann Arbor: University of Michigan Press.

Bulmer-Thomas, Victor. 1994. *The Economic History of Latin America since Independence*. Cambridge: Cambridge University Press.

Cardoso, Fernando Henrique, and Enzo Faletto. 1969. *Dependencia y desarrollo en América Latina*. Mexico City: Siglo XXI Editores.

Cavarozzi, Marcelo J., and James F. Petras. 1974. "Chile." In *Latin America: The Struggle with Dependency and Beyond*, ed. Ronald Chilcote and Joel Edelstein, pp. 495–578. Cambridge: Schenkman.

Collier, David. 1976. *Squatters and Oligarchs: Authoritarian Rule and Policy Change in Peru*. Baltimore: Johns Hopkins University Press.

Deininger, K. [Klaus], and P. Olinto. 1999. "Is Broad Asset Growth Good for Growth? Panel Evidence from 62 Countries." Washington, D.C.: World Bank.

Deininger, Klaus, and Lyn Squire. 1996. "A New Data Set Measuring Income Inequality." *World Bank Economic Review* 10, no. 3 (September): 565–91.

de Mello e Souza, André. 2001. "The Perils of Exclusion: Politics and Violence in the Shantytowns of Rio de Janeiro." Field paper. Stanford University Department of Political Science, Stanford, Calif.

Evans, Peter. 1979. *Dependent Development: The Alliance of Multinational, State, and Local Capital in Brazil*. Princeton, N.J.: Princeton University Press.

———. 1995. *Embedded Autonomy: States and Industrial Transformation*. Princeton, N.J.: Princeton University Press.

Graham, Richard. 1990. *Patronage and Politics in Nineteenth-Century Brazil*. Stanford, Calif.: Stanford University Press.

Handelman, Howard. 1979. "Economic Policy and Elite Pressures in Uruguay." American Universities Field Staff Reports, South America Series 27. Hanover, N.H.

Hirschman, Albert. 1971. "The Political Economy of Import-Substituting Industrialization in Latin America." Chap. 4 in *A Bias for Hope: Essays on Development in Latin America*, by Albert Hirschman. New Haven, Conn.: Yale University Press.

Kaldor, N. 1957. "A Model of Economic Growth." *Economic Journal* 67 (December): 591–624.

Karl, Terry Lynn. 1997. *The Paradox of Plenty: Oil Booms and Petro-States.* Berkeley: University of California Press.

———. 2000. "Economic Inequality and Democratic Instability." *Journal of Democracy* 11, no. 1 (January): 149–56.

Karst, Kenneth, and Keith Rosenn. 1975. *Law and Development: A Case Book.* Berkeley: University of California Press.

Kuznets, Simon. 1955. "Economic Growth and Income Inequality." *American Economic Review* 45, no. 1 (March): 1–28.

Lagos, Marta. 1997. "Latin America's Smiling Mask." *Journal of Democracy* 8, no. 3 (July): 125–38.

———. 2001. "Between Stability and Crisis in Latin America." *Journal of Democracy* 12, no. 1 (January): 137–45.

Leff, Nathaniel. 1968. *Economic Policy Making and Development in Brazil, 1947–1964.* New York: John Wiley and Sons.

Londoño, J. L., and M. Szekely. 1997. "Distributional Surprises after a Decade of Reforms: Latin America in the Nineties." In *Latin America after a Decade of Reforms: What Comes Next?,* ed. R. Hausman and E. Lora. Washington, D.C.: Inter-American Development Bank.

Lora, E. 2000. "Development Challenges for Latin America in the 21st Century." Photocopy. Washington, D.C.: Inter-American Development Bank.

Majon, James E. 1997. "Tax Reform and Its Determinants in Latin America, 1977–1994." Paper presented at the Twentieth International Congress of the Latin American Studies Association, Guadalajara, Mexico, April 17–19.

MORI Internacional. 1998. "Vision latinoamericana de la democracia: Encuestas de opinión pública en México, Chile, y Costa Rica." Hewlett Foundation, Palo Alto, Calif.

Muller, Edward N. 1988. "Democracy, Economic Development, and Income Inequality." *American Sociological Review* 53, no. 1 (February): 50–68.

Narayan, Deepa, Robert Chambers, Meera K. Shah, and Patti Petesch. 2000. *Voices of the Poor: Crying Out for Change.* New York: Oxford University Press.

Nino, Carlos Santiago. 1996. "Hyperpresidentialism and Constitutional Reform in Argentina." In *Institutional Design in New Democracies: Eastern Europe and Latin America,* ed. Arend Lijphart and Carlos H. Waisman, pp. 161–74. Boulder, Colo.: Westview Press.

O'Donnell, Guillermo. 1994. "Delegative Democracy." *Journal of Democracy* 5, no. 1 (January): 55–69.

Persson, Torsten, and Guido Tabellini. 1994. "Is Inequality Harmful for Growth?" *American Economic Review* 84, no. 3 (June): 600–21.

Przeworski, Adam, Michael Alvarez, José Antonio Cheibub, and Fernando Limongi. 1996. "What Makes Democracies Endure?" *Journal of Democracy* 7, no. 1 (January): 39–55.

Ravallion, Martin, and Gaurav Datt. 1999. "When Is Growth Pro-Poor? Evidence from the Diverse Experience of India's States." Working paper. World Bank, Washington, D.C.

Rawls, John. 1971. *A Theory of Justice*. Cambridge, Mass.: Harvard University Press.

Rosenn, Keith. 1990. "The Success of Constitutionalism in the United States and Its Failure in Latin America: An Explanation." *University of Miami Inter-American Law Review* 22, no. 1.

Rouquie, Alain, and Stephen Suffern. 1994. "The Military in Latin American Politics since 1930." Chap. 4 in *The Cambridge History of Latin America*, vol. 6, *Latin America since 1930*, pt. 2, "Politics and Society," ed. Leslie Bethell. Cambridge: Cambridge University Press.

Snyder, Richard, and David Samuels. 2001. "Devaluing the Vote in Latin America." *Journal of Democracy* 12, no. 1 (January): 146–59.

Solimano, Andrés, Eduardo Aninat, and Nancy Birdsall, eds. 2000. *Distributive Justice and Economic Development: The Case of Chile and Developing Countries*. Ann Arbor: University of Michigan Press.

Stallings, Barbara, Nancy Birdsall, and Julie Clugage. 2000. "Growth and Inequality: Do Regional Patterns Redeem Kuznets?" In *Distributive Justice and Economic Development: The Case of Chile and Developing Countries*, ed. Andrés Solimano, Eduardo Aninat, and Nancy Birdsall, pp. 98–118. Ann Arbor: University of Michigan Press.

Tocqueville, Alexis de. 1990. *Democracy in America*. New York: Vintage Classics.

Transparency International. 2000. *Annual Report 2000*. Berlin: Transparency International.

Weyland, Kurt G. 1996. *Democracy without Equity: Failures of Reform in Brazil*. Pittsburgh: University of Pittsburgh Press.

Williamson, John. 1990. "What Washington Means by Policy Reform." In *Latin American Adjustment: How Much Has Happened?* ed. John Williamson, pp. 5–20. Washington, D.C.: Institute for International Economics.

———. 1997. "The Washington Consensus Revisited." In *Economic and Social Development into the XXI Century*, ed. Louis Emmerji, pp. 48–69. Washington, D.C.: Inter-American Development Bank.

World Bank. 1999. *World Development Report, 1998–1999*. Oxford and Washington, D.C.: Oxford University Press.

———. 2000. *The Quality of Growth*. Oxford and New York: Oxford University Press.

CHAPTER SIX

Perpetrators' Confessions

*Truth, Reconciliation, and Justice
in Argentina*

LEIGH A. PAYNE

Truth-telling has become a widespread practice in settling accounts with past repressive regimes in Latin America. It has also assumed a variety of forms: from government-mandated truth commissions, to non-governmental-organization-sponsored historical memory projects, to individual testimonials.[1] In nearly all of these instances, victims of repression have seized an opportunity to break the silence imposed on them by authoritarian regimes, or, as Ariel Dorfman writes, to "rebel against the false and immaculate tranquility of the official versions" of the past (1991: 189). The recent debate over Rigoberta Menchú's testimonial illustrates the complications inherent in establishing new truths through victims' accounts. But this chapter examines an even thornier sort of truth-telling: perpetrators' confessions.

This chapter begins with a discussion of the potential value of perpetrators' confessions to truth and reconciliation in countries emerging from authoritarian rule. The second section then tests this potential by examining four Argentine confessions. Drawing on the case studies, the chapter concludes with a discussion of the conditions under which confessions advance the process of truth, justice, and reconciliation.

TRUTH AND RECONCILIATION

The literature on truth and reconciliation suggests four overlapping roles that perpetrators' confessions might play: establishing *truth; acknowl-*

edging victims' stories to promote individual and societal healing; bringing *justice;* and creating collective *memory* to avoid repeating the past.[2] Perpetrators' confessions, like victims' testimonies, defy official silence and denial by recounting the violence used by the authoritarian regime. Perpetrators' admissions, therefore, contribute to an authoritative and truthful version of past state violence. Moreover, they reveal previously censored information—for example, the whereabouts of victims' bodies and the cause and circumstances of deaths—that helps the families of victims to reach closure regarding their losses.

Most therapists working with victims of torture concur that a crucial component of healing is acknowledgment of the offense. While silence perpetuates self-blame, confusion, and rage that prevent healing, confirmation of human rights violations allows victims to reconstruct pasts erased by the regime's silence (Flanigan 1992: 106). Victims' healing depends on knowing who harmed them. Perpetrators' confessions both confirm victims' accounts and acknowledge individuals' responsibility for committing violent acts, thus advancing the healing process.[3]

Perpetrators' confessions contribute to justice by providing the evidence needed to investigate, prosecute, and convict perpetrators. Even where amnesty, immunity, and pardons inhibit retributive justice, confessions contribute to restorative justice, that is, restoring wholeness to the lives and relationships of victims of criminal offenses (Dickey 1998: 107–8). By exposing the truth through perpetrators' confessions, governments publicly acknowledge past wrongs, and sometimes even accept responsibility for crimes committed by past regimes. In addition, perpetrators' confessions may provide the only conclusive evidence that makes it possible for governments to issue legal death certificates and to expunge criminal records fabricated by past authoritarian regimes. With the death certificates, families can perform important burial and grieving rituals that allow them to move on in their lives. Erving Goffman, remarking on the potential power of restorative justice, concludes, "Remorse, apologies, asking forgiveness, and generally, making symbolic amends are a more vital element in almost any process of domination than punishment itself" (cited in Scott 1990: 57).

The acknowledgment of past wrongs also allows for collective remembrance: ceremonies, rituals, and memorials that help prevent "forgetting," and therefore repeating, the past. By disclosing the truth about state terrorism, confessions put "still potent events into the more distant category of 'history'" (Popkin and Roht-Arriaza 1995: 93). The role of memory is crucial to both individual and societal healing. On the individual level, Flanigan (1992: 5) argues that "without remembrance, no wound can be transcended." Silence, says Laub (1992: 64), "swallows up" personal histories so that it becomes impossible for individuals to come to terms with their own past.[4] The function of memory on the societal level is slightly different. Jean Baudrillard, quoted by Young (1993: 1), hints that without memory the authoritarian regime becomes the victor: "Forgetting the extermination is part of the extermination itself." Social scientists further conclude that the denial of past violence, the failure to establish truth, healing, justice, and memory, perpetuates violence since society itself has failed to claim it or put a stop to it (Milburn and Conrad 1996: 167). With public admission of torture, official history can be rewritten to condemn past political violence.

The above are powerful arguments in favor of the idea that confessional texts (truth, acknowledgment) and the official responses to them (acknowledgment, justice, collective memory) pave the way to truth and reconciliation. The following examples from Argentina, however, will show that the reality falls short of these lofty goals.

ARGENTINE CONFESSIONS

Beginning in 1994, Argentine perpetrators confessed to their involvement in the military regime's "war against subversion" (1976–83), referred to as the Dirty War because of the regime's particularly brutal repressive tactics, including an estimated thirty thousand murders and disappearances. Those who confessed did so voluntarily and with immunity from prosecution. President Raúl Alfonsín, the first democratic government (1983–89) after military rule, issued a Due Obedience Law that protected lower-ranking officers from prosecution for their human rights violations. His successor, President Carlos Saúl Menem (1989–99), extended the amnesty provisions by granting pardon to the military junta leaders and other top officials serving time for ordering human rights violations.

The four Argentine confessions that are examined in this chapter represent different, but overlapping, types of texts, settings, and audience responses. Consistent with the common understanding of the term *confession,* one case involves admission of guilt and expression of remorse. In contrast, the others involve less commonly recognized forms of confession: "a simple declaration" or statements of "fact."[5] Most perpetrators, at least in public, do not repent, but rather justify, or even glorify, their acts of violence. Personal redemption, therefore, is only one motivation behind perpetrators' confessions, along with defense of the armed forces, material gain, and individual social advancement. Settings influence the language used by perpetrators, and therefore the types of confessions they make. Television, print media, and formal legal institutional confessions vary in content and style. Confessional settings and texts, moreover, produce diverse reactions among victims, fellow perpetrators, and government authorities. Audience responses to confessions can even subvert the meaning that perpetrators, the media, and official institutions intended. This chapter contends, therefore, that audience responses to the confessions, rather than the confessional text and setting alone, have a profound impact on truth-telling, acknowledgment, justice, and collective memory.

Scilingo and the Remorseful Confession

I entered the Naval School as a sailor and I left an assassin.
                Adolfo Scilingo (Blixen 1996)

Adolfo Scilingo approached leftist journalist Horacio Verbitsky in the Buenos Aires subway one day in 1995 and told him that he needed to talk to him about his experiences in the Escuela Mecánica de la Armada (Navy School of Mechanics; ESMA). No doubt because of Scilingo's tortured look, Verbitsky mistook him for a victim in that infamous torture camp, an impression Scilingo corrected over the next several months as he recounted the murders he had committed as a navy captain. Scilingo eventually told his story on television, and in newspapers in Argentina and abroad, transforming it into one of the most well-known cases of perpetrators' confessions.[6]

Scilingo accepted personal responsibility for the murder of thirty of the so-called disappeared. As head of the Automotive Division of ESMA, he participated in two of the weekly "death flights," in which tortured and clandestine prisoners were drugged, stripped, shackled, and pushed to their death from a hole in a plane.

Scilingo's confession shocked Argentina and the world, but not because it revealed new information: an official report, academic studies, numerous human rights agencies' records, and countless testimonies and testimonial novels written by prison survivors had previously documented the numbers and names of the tortured, torture techniques, and torture centers.[7] Even the ESMA "death flights" formed part of the official accounts of the Dirty War. The shocking part of Scilingo's story was that by telling it he had broken the military's "conspiracy of silence" about the Dirty War. He was the first military officer to admit his responsibility in the military regime's repressive apparatus. In addition, Scilingo showed that the repressor was human, not an abstract system. Decades earlier, Hannah Arendt had described Nazi war criminals as "neither perverted nor sadistic, that they were, and still are, terribly and terrifyingly normal," that "this normality [the "banality of evil," in Arendt's phrase] was much more terrifying than all of the atrocities put together" (Arendt 1963: 276). Likewise, the frightening aspect of Scilingo's avuncular look was that it demonstrated that seemingly normal people could commit mass murder.[8]

Scilingo's confession recounts his transformation from sailor to assassin. A confirmed anti-Communist, he believed in the war against subversion. He even accepted, at least in the abstract, the need to engage in illegal activities to eliminate subversion. His patriotism and sense of military duty convinced him that the war was just and necessary. But this sympathy with the objectives of the war made the silence around the violence unbearable. It undid him.

And so he sought solace in religious confession. But the priests Scilingo encountered rejected his act of contrition. Instead, they reassured him that his acts were Christian, recounting the biblical parable of separating the wheat from the chaff and arguing in favor of painless and peaceful deaths. These reassurances only increased Scilingo's unraveling; he wondered if he was alone in his revulsion against the military's tactics and brought a new officer into the concentration camp to register his reaction to the inhuman conditions. Scilingo expressed relief that the officer was profoundly horrified at the prisoners' conditions. Scilingo tried to explain to his superiors his unease with the "death flights" and torture, but this cost him promotion within the navy. Scilingo retired early, but leaving the navy did not end his nightmares. He was nonfunctional in civilian life. He withdrew from his family. Having lost his moral compass, he participated in shady business schemes. He lost all of his money and his wife's inheritance. And he anesthetized his emotional pain with alcoholic binges and tranquilizers. The ghosts continued to haunt him, forcing him to confront the source of his insanity.

But political events, and not nightmares, eventually prompted Scilingo's confession. The Senate denied promotion to two of Scilingo's colleagues because of their involvement in the Dirty War. Scilingo viewed this event as betrayal by the military high command, who kept silent about the systematic use of torture and murder and blamed "excesses" on renegade officers, thereby forcing loyal officers to take the fall for the Dirty War.

Scilingo initially came forward, not to express remorse, but to criticize the high command. His confession initially included only the facts about the death flights. He explained events from the perspective of a loyal soldier fighting a heroic war against subversion. In his view the military high command's denial of the methods used in that war constituted a betrayal of the soldiers. He maintained his loyalty to the armed forces by controlling what he confessed to and how he confessed it. He rejected the label "traitor" used in the past against individuals like Lieutenant Jorge Alberto Devoto, who had "disappeared" in a death flight after objecting to the military regime's use of repression.

Scilingo used euphemism and avoidance to control the confession. When Verbitsky pressed for details, for example, Scilingo withdrew. He turned off the tape recorder when he needed to reestablish his control; denied knowing certain facts and failed to recall others; claimed to recollect events only vaguely; changed the subject to return to issues he wanted to reinforce; and put off talking about certain themes, stating that he might be willing to discuss them later. Despite these tactics, Scilingo still lost control over the confession. Feeling trapped, as if held against his will, he pleaded: "I don't want to talk about it. Let me go" (Verbitsky 1996: 49).

Reluctance to admit murder is hardly surprising. Trauma induces us to shut out information as a means of defense. The process of filtering and selecting facts, seeing only what it is convenient to see, and knowing but refusing to acknowledge the implications of that information, is part of creating the myths or "vital lies" that keep our images of ourselves and our actions intact (Goleman 1985; Cohen 1993).

But Scilingo had less trouble admitting to his role in the death flights than in discussing relatively minor aspects of his military service. He could not recall, for example, how the vehicles under his control were acquired or even his own code name. Psychologists might describe this as "doubling," whereby Scilingo separated his good, professional-soldier image from the side of himself who was a criminal who murders (Lifton 1986). Yet even when discussing his criminal self, Scilingo avoided discussing his acts as criminal. He corrected Verbitsky's use of terms, employing euphemism to disguise brutality and attempting to put Verbitsky in the loyal soldier's frame of mind. Here is one example:

No Navy officer participated in kidnapping, torture, and clandestine elimi-
nations. The entire Navy participated in detentions, interrogations, and the
elimination of the subversives, which could have been done by various
methods. (Verbitsky 1996: 35–36)

Scilingo even tried out on Verbitsky some of the rationalizations that he
had accepted to justify the death flights: "Shooting someone is immoral
too. Or is it better? Who suffers more, the one who knows he is going to
be shot or the one who dies by our method?" (Verbitsky 1996: 31). He
knew that his acts were immoral, and that prevented him from coming to
an understanding of how he could do it. He tried to find explanations for
it in the regime's official discourse, but these explanations had failed him
in the past and continued to fail him during his confession.

Scilingo's use of military rationale may also have resulted from his
need to deflect Verbitsky's harsh criticism. Verbitsky exhibited no empathy, but only revulsion for Scilingo and his acts. He called Scilingo a
sick coward. Scilingo could not have expected any other attitude from
Verbitsky, whose political views could have put him on one of ESMA's
death flights.

And yet Scilingo chose Verbitsky as his confessor. Why? In part it was
happenstance: they ran into each other in a Buenos Aires subway. But
happenstance does not explain why Scilingo would follow through with
Verbitsky rather than tell his story to a more sympathetic ear. It doesn't
explain why Scilingo repeatedly subjected himself to Verbitsky's hostile
questions. Perhaps Scilingo sought an antagonist because those on his
side repeatedly ignored him. While he was on active duty, none of his
superiors listened to his concerns. After he retired, he wrote to former
junta leader General Videla, the navy chief of staff, and President
Menem, but no one answered him (Blixen 1996). Perhaps serendipity
brought Verbitsky and Scilingo together in the subway, but their later
meetings confirmed Scilingo's need to have his story heard and acknowledged as true. Scilingo must have known that only a handful of
journalists possessed the political will and readership to help him achieve
his goals.

Despite his confession to Verbitsky, Scilingo still faced attempts to silence him. One "friend" in the navy offered Scilingo money in exchange
for silence. One of his superiors urged him to remain silent to maintain
his family's health insurance. Scilingo describes one occasion in which
his friend's wife railed against him for ignoring the consequences of his
acts. He responded, "That's fine, but what do I do with my thirty dead
ones?" (Blixen 1996). To avoid opening old wounds, Menem tried to si-

lence Scilingo. He impugned Scilingo's motives, calling him a mythoma-
niac, a criminal, and a scoundrel. He stripped Scilingo of his retired military status and jailed him for fraud.[9] Thus, Menem sent an implicit
warning through the armed forces that military officers considering confession should understand the price they eventually would pay in terms
of their personal reputation.[10] Other key national figures followed suit
in silencing Scilingo. The minister of foreign affairs, Guido DiTella, dismissed the confession as internally inconsistent and therefore unreliable
(Blixen 1996). Navy admiral and former junta member Emilio Massera
simply denied the death flights, and Monsignor Emilio Bianchi de Car-
cano categorically rejected Scilingo's claim that the Church knew about
or justified them.[11] Despite all these denials, Scilingo's confession certainly threatened some groups. In September 1997, two years after his
initial confession, unknown assailants kidnapped Scilingo and carved
the initials of three journalists into his face, warning him that if he continued to speak, he and the journalists would die.

Rather than silencing Scilingo, however, these responses made him
bolder. He felt a sense of relief, which he modestly described in this way:
"Though it may be a little egotistical to say so, my public confession has
brought me a certain relief. Before, I had a secret I couldn't talk about
to anyone. Now I can talk to everyone. But the problem still exists." He
left behind euphemisms and avoidance of the past in favor of direct accusations:

> The Navy is guilty. What is it trying to hide? Those who criticize me say
> that what happened during the Dirty War was a patriotic defense to save
> the country from falling into Communist hands. Fine, if they are so proud
> of this why do they hide the issue of the disappeared? What is the problem?
> This is inconsistent: I feel proud of my participation in the War against
> Subversion, but at the same time I continue hiding the truth. So, it's clear:
> we are ashamed, they are ashamed to say what we did. (Blixen 1996)

Through the confessional process, Scilingo began to remember, both
in the sense of publicly recalling specific events and finding a unitary
foundation for his previously fractured self. Scilingo tried to identify individuals on his death flights, provided information on deaths in which
he was not directly involved, testified in cases about kidnappings of babies born in torture centers to political prisoners, and collaborated with
efforts to discover the lists of "disappeared." This recall is consistent
with Scilingo's heroic self-image: his identity has been transferred from
the loyal soldier who fought a heroic War against Subversion to the
moral soldier who spoke out against the war's atrocities. Scilingo justifies

his confession as loyalty to the armed forces and future soldiers, not to the military regime. He is committed to telling the truth to prevent the armed forces from committing immoral and illegal acts in the future:

> We could offer up a true, permanent *mea culpa* and pay our debt. And the most important effect of that would be on those who remained in the institution, people who are new or who didn't get their hands dirty. It would help them to reflect, as a reminder of what they must not do. The president should order the chief of staff of the Navy to inform the country of everything that happened during those years, to give out the list of the disappeared. It did me good to speak, it would also do the society good, and it would do the Navy good. Especially the new generations of the military, so they don't continue to bear the stigma of ESMA. Otherwise we can't be sure these things won't happen again some time. (Verbitsky 1996: 153)

Scilingo also accepted that their must be punishment for his acts. He claimed that contrition is too easy, that it isn't equal to the seriousness of the crimes committed. As he states, "I am not a repentant, the facts are too out of the ordinary; it's too easy to say 'I'm sorry' and everything is OK" (Blixen 1996). But he also appeared willing to accept punishment for his past: "It seems to me that all of us who committed those barbaric acts should be in prison" (Verbitsky 1996: 153). His willingness was tested in early 1998, when Scilingo submitted voluntarily, without immunity, to questioning by Spanish judge Baltasar Garzón.[12] Using international law to prosecute Argentine and Chilean human rights violators in Madrid, Garzón first jailed Scilingo and later released him to house arrest.

Scilingo's confession has served important functions in the process of truth and reconciliation. It broke a silence imposed on the armed forces. Other officers followed Scilingo's lead by providing truths about specific acts of violence and the systematic use of violence.[13] Scilingo's confession also encouraged institutional soul-searching and apologies. The commander and chief of the army, General Martín Balza, confirmed that the military used illegal methods during the war and condemned the act of obeying immoral orders. Some members of the Argentine Catholic Church hierarchy have apologized for their complicity. And the confession has opened up the possibility of revisiting the laws that protected perpetrators. Congress voted to force the navy to construct the list of detained individuals, even though this vote lost in a second round. Efforts are afoot to annul the amnesty provisions that prevented the possibility of indicting perpetrators. And former junta leaders Videla and Massera were placed under house arrest (while others were jailed) for kidnapping and trafficking babies of former prisoners, one of the only crimes not covered by the blanket pardons and amnesties. Similarly, some of the most notorious perpetrators, like retired General Antonio Domingo Bussi, governor of Tucumán province, faced embezzlement charges resulting from investigation of his Swiss bank accounts (Izaguirre 1998). Lastly, Scilingo's confession to the death flights has played an important role in collective memory. The flights have become cultural symbols of the Dirty War that are expressed in protest songs, poems, and novels.

Because of its positive contribution to reconciliation, Scilingo's confession must be examined for what it can teach us about situations of this kind. Remorse is central, but how did Scilingo escape the socialization within the military that silenced other perpetrators? His feeling of having been betrayed may explain an initial rupture with the military regime, but the confessional process also played a crucial role: Scilingo broke with the military version only after the confession had begun. While he initially concealed his guilt through euphemism and avoidance, the act of confession allowed him to confront that guilt. Borrowing from analyses of testimonies of victims, the very act of confessing forced him to "know" the event: to speak the unspeakable and inscribe the event for the first time, by breaking with the official version and the silence imposed on him. By explaining to those "outside" the repressive apparatus exactly what took place, he began to see himself and his acts without the protective shield of official discourse (Laub 1992: 59–63; Beverley 1996: 276).

The unique features of Scilingo's confession point to some limitations of the remorseful confession. First, such confessions are scarce. Even where immunity from prosecution exists, as in the Scilingo case, perpetrators close ranks. They may want to confess aspects of the past, but they live in an insecure environment, unable to know what recriminations, personal or institutional, they may face.[14] Moreover, they can justify silence as a virtue: a way to protect family, colleagues, the armed forces, and their country's political stability. Finally, perpetrators learn to live with their secrets, adopting official justifications as adequate to exonerate them from criminal acts. Scilingo's confession illustrates the difficulty perpetrators have in letting go of the authoritarian regime's discourse on state-sanctioned violence (Crelinsten 1994).

Second, despite the remorse expressed in these confessions, they employ rhetorical devices intended to shield perpetrators from criticism. All of us are familiar with such devices. When we recount our own unflattering past behavior, we often exclude certain details, until we eventually forget them ourselves. We gloss over the parts of the story that are inconsistent with our own construction of events and image. We phrase the story in a way that projects a particular, flattering image. We deflect criticism by identifying ourselves as well intentioned, betrayed, or misled (by our superiors). These are not lies; they are stories and partial truths. They suggest that full disclosure, when it involves self-recrimination, is nearly impossible.[15]

These rhetorical devices tend to inhibit truth in the confessions of perpetrators. Perpetrators confess with the hope of receiving forgiveness, empathy, or comprehension, and they withhold certain information that might subvert that end. Too many gruesome details will cast them in the glaring light of the torture chamber, undeserving of pity or forgiveness. Perpetrators, thus, have to conceal details; they search for the means to distance themselves from the violence. Expressing fear is an effective device in this process. Perpetrators portray themselves as victims of the same repressive system: their refusal to torture or kill would transform them into victims of repression. Perpetrators also justify their acts as a duty to obey their superiors. They contend that they now know right from wrong, but that in the context of fear and war they could not question orders. Avoidance, amnesia, selective memory, euphemisms, and self-identification as the victim are rhetorical techniques, used to reduce perpetrators' culpability, that block the truth.

Third, these confessions may hinder reconciliation because of the audience's mixed reactions. Fellow perpetrators may interpret the confession as a way to come forward with an admission of their own guilt, or they may attempt to silence those colleagues who confess. Governments also react in contradictory ways. President Menem aggressively silenced Scilingo, questioning why he wanted to rub salt in old wounds. This silencing seemed intended not only for Scilingo, but also for other perpetrators considering public confessions. Among victims and their loved ones are those who know that the reconstruction of events depends on confessions of perpetrators. But perpetrators will not confess without immunity from prosecution. How do societies reconcile the need for truth with the need for justice?

Remorseful confessions, in short, involve a tangle of contradictions that impede the truth and reconciliation process. The perpetrator's fractured identity tends toward contradictory motives, from self-flagellation to denial. The multiple functions of the confession and its mixed audience produce veiled confessions. And these limitations leave audiences uncertain that they can, or should, put the past behind them.

Astiz and the Heroic Confession

I wasn't a torturer; I did intelligence.

> Alfredo Astiz
> (Feitlowitz 1998: 227)

In confessional terms, naval captain Alfredo Astiz is the antithesis of Scilingo. Although, like Scilingo, he is implicated in the ESMA tortures and murders, Astiz's confession constitutes denial of his own personal involvement in torture while simultaneously justifying the Dirty War. His confession thus provides an example of heroic confessions and the constraints they place on truth, acknowledgment, justice, and memory.

Astiz is best known for his infiltration of the Madres de Plaza de Mayo. Posing as a young man looking for his "disappeared" brother, Astiz quickly won the affection of the Madres. They called him the Blond Angel in honor of his good looks and pleasant disposition. Eventually they would come to call him the Angel of Death, referring to his role in the December 8, 1977, kidnapping and "disappearance" of two Madres, two French nuns, and other human rights activists, from the Santa Cruz Church in Buenos Aires, who were later murdered in ESMA's death flights. By kissing particular women, Astiz signaled to an onlooking soldier which of them to kidnap from the church. Astiz also has the murder of Swedish-Argentine teenager Dagmar Hagelin on his hands. Mistaking her for another blond teenager he had been waiting to seize, Astiz shot Hagelin in the back as she fled from capture.

Protected by the Due Obedience Law, Astiz cannot face charges for these human rights abuses. His image within the military is untarnished. A 1997 investigation revealed that Astiz had been working for naval intelligence since the end of the military regime. The navy chief, Admiral Molina Pico, praised Astiz's military service and supported him in his bid for promotion, referring to him as a "good soldier." A group of officers protested when Astiz was denied his promotion. He is widely viewed within the armed forces as a "gentleman sailor," free of petty scandals.

But Astiz has not avoided recriminations outside the armed forces. Despite strong support within the military high command, Astiz did not get his promotion. In fact, he was forced into early retirement in 1996. French courts, moreover, tried Astiz in absentia, imposing on him a life sentence for the murder of the two French nuns. Astiz has also faced social repercussions for his acts. A frequent guest in Buenos Aires discotheques, he was the object of a smear campaign by the Madres de Plaza de Mayo, who plastered discotheque walls with posters that exposed Astiz and his murderous past and that urged young women to avoid him. Astiz also suffered spontaneous retributions. On an Argentine ski slope in 1995, a former concentration-camp victim assailed Astiz as a "son of a bitch" and a "murderer of teenagers" and then punched him in the nose. In another encounter in Buenos Aires, two university students, apparently recognizing Astiz, pulled him out of his car and severely beat him, while a passenger on a passing bus shouted, "Good boys! Kill him!" (Feitlowitz 1998: 246).

Despite the severe hostility toward him, or maybe because of it, Astiz has not remained silent. In January 1998, Astiz made his confession to *Revista Trespuntos:*

> I never tortured anyone. It wasn't my job. But would I have tortured if I was told to? Yes, of course. The armed forces taught me to destroy, not to build; to plant mines and set off bombs; to infiltrate and destroy an organization; to kill. I know how to do all of this well. I am the best-prepared man in Argentina to kill a politician or a journalist.[16]

Astiz made this declaration-style confession voluntarily. He admitted to his training, preparation, and capacity. Devoid of remorse, Astiz's confession glorifies the heroism in torture: the manliness, expertise, and danger. While he denied his own use of torture, he confessed to a willingness to use it. Boasting about his qualifications to murder, he issued a thinly veiled warning that the Dirty War was not over.

The Menem government acted quickly, charging Astiz with "provocation with dangerous social and political intent." The government sentenced him, stripped him of his military rank and status, and put him in jail.[17] Astiz, like Scilingo before him, serves time in prison not for murder, but for his confession.

Astiz employed an exaggerated set of the same rhetorical devices Scilingo used. He justified the war in terms of enemy threat. Astiz constructed his acts as a personal sacrifice to the nation, characterizing the enemy as demonic, capable of undermining the country. According to Astiz, the enemy's clandestine and extensive networks throughout the country demanded interrogation under torture and death. Heroic confessions, in short, reassert the authoritarian regime's justification for violence and blame the victims for the violence, thereby resilencing victims' accounts of repression.

A second rhetorical device is contradiction. Heroic confessions simultaneously deny and glorify violence. These confessions generally deny personal involvement in torture, the practice of systematic torture, and the extent or brutality of violence. These confessions sometimes even blame cases of extreme violence on "excesses" and "the bad egg" within the armed forces that cannot be controlled. At the same time, heroic confessions openly support violence, consider it heroic and justified; they minimize the extent and the nature of torture, shrouding it in the patriotic and heroic language of personal sacrifice to the nation. These confessions bury the facts with contradictions.

The motivations behind heroic confessions differ from remorseful confessions. As one scholar of memory politics states, "Memory is never shaped in a vacuum; the motives of memory are never pure" (Young 1993: 2). Heroic confessions are intended to restore dignity to the individual and the security forces. The confessors and their associates want to clear their names and their actions, not through repentance, but by rewriting the past from their own perspective. They want to reclaim history from the victims. They want to transform the image of the perpetrator (and the authoritarian regime) from pathological and brutal to heroic and patriotic. Heroic confessions, in other words, constitute what James Scott (1990: 45) calls "enactments of power" that employ "affirmation, concealment, euphemization and stigmatization, and finally, the appearance of unanimity" to sustain the official and dominant version. This is especially true since the "audience" for these confessions are not only victims, but also colleagues who may need to be reminded of the official line. Scott states that "elites are also consumers of their own performance" (Scott 1990: 49). Heroic confessions provide the means to reinforce, maintain, and adjust the official story to maintain its dominance (Scott 1990: 45).

Astiz's confession could also be viewed as constituting part of a "spiral of denial," a variation on Scilingo's spiral of remorse (Cohen 1993: 102–3). The spiral begins with outright denial that violations happened. This is certainly what the authoritarian regime in Argentina claimed, even if, in the face of testimonies, investigations, and evidence, that denial became untenable. Thus, the second part of the spiral acknowledges violence, but claims that it was different than the way it has been portrayed. Violence is reconstructed in a more positive light, with euphemisms that shroud torture and murder. The junta leaders in their trials denied systematic torture and assassinations and blamed them on "excesses" by middle- and lower-ranking officers. The third part of the spiral is justification. Astiz admitted that torture occurred, but justified it as necessary to protect the nation from subversives immune to conventional military strategies. Scilingo continued along this spiral to feel remorse for the harm he and the rest of the military had caused. Astiz stopped short at justification.

Heroic confessions, as illustrated by Astiz, appear to undermine truth and reconciliation. After all, Astiz's "truth" not only denied his own involvement (despite ample evidence to the contrary), but also justified violence. Instead of acknowledging atrocities, moreover, Astiz accused victims of unleashing the violence that justified the war. He silenced victims' versions and reasserted the military regime's official version of the Dirty War. It is true that Astiz served time in jail for his confession—a sentence intended to silence him, as was the case with Scilingo's sentence in Argentina. But in Astiz's case the Menem government had silenced a perpetrator who had been attempting to justify and glorify torture as national and heroic virtue. This official reaction is unlikely to change the views of those who share the heroic image of torture and who, no doubt, consider Astiz a martyr. But Menem's silencing of Astiz prevented the reversal of victims' accounts that had begun to shape collective memory of the Dirty War. Thereby, it reassured victims and critics of torture that the nation's history would not be written in the perpetrators' words. The eventual justice and its impact on collective memory, therefore, shows that even heroic confessions can play a role in advancing truth and reconciliation.

Julián the Turk and the Exchange Confession

What I did I did for my Fatherland, my faith, and my religion. Of course I would do it again....I am not repentant. I'm no crybaby like that sorry Scilingo....This was a war to save the Nation from the terrorist hordes.
Look, torture is eternal. It has always existed and always will. It is an essential part of the human being.

> Julián the Turk (Feitlowitz 1998: 2)

This confession submitted by Julio Simón, alias Julián the Turk, has many of the characteristics of the heroic confession analyzed above. Simón initiated the television interview in which he made this confession. He showed absolutely no remorse; on the contrary, he considered torture a natural part of life with the virtue that it protects the nation.

But Simón's confession is distinct from Astiz's in two important ways. First, Simón admits to engaging in torture, albeit "on very few occasions" (Feitlowitz 1998: 210). What Simón means by "very few" is obscured by Simón's own statement: "The norm was to kill everyone and anyone kidnapped was tortured" (Feitlowitz 1998: 210). The audience of his confession can interpret this ambiguity in a number of ways. Simón may intend the statement to reflect that, while torture is widespread, he participated in very little torture. Do perpetrators have a threshold of respectability that they may cross if they engage in too many torture sessions or too much brutality? But the ambiguity presents other interpretations. Perhaps Simón felt that he would have liked to engage in more torture sessions. Maybe he feels that the military regime did not kidnap enough "subversives," who, he suspects, run the government today. But when Simón's statement that "torture didn't always work, it left people too destroyed" is added to his other comments, one suspects that he is trying to show that torture served a function, to fight subversion (Feitlowitz 1998: 210), and that it was used only in that noble fight. Simón, then, like Astiz, considers torture heroic in the struggle for national defense.

The second difference between Simón's confession and Astiz's is that Simón submitted his confession in exchange for payment. Unlike Astiz, Simón was not employed by navy intelligence after the military regime's demise. To make ends meet, the destitute Simón searched for a buyer for his testimony and for his personal "archives" from the war (Feitlowitz 1998: 213).

The trend of confession-peddling began shortly after Scilingo's confession, it seems, when unconfirmed rumors circulated that Hollywood had given him a million-dollar deal. After Simón had made money from his confession, even more perpetrators came forward with their story, no doubt in search of lucrative deals.[18] These bought confessions have tended to resemble the heroic kind, like Astiz's, rather than Scilingo's remorseful confession.

Exchange confessions, as the above implies, possess the limitations already observed in heroic confessions, while also introducing other limitations that are inherent in the exchange relationship. Such confessions, for example, produce information that will secure reward. They generate partial truths, therefore, since perpetrators need only confess the minimum needed for the reward. But they also produce fictions, inventing confessions of torture, for which they have immunity, to reduce sentences for robbery and other criminal charges, for which they do not have im-

munity. A human rights activist involved in the Argentine truth commission, CONADEP, describes perpetrators' fictions in this way:

> Lying was a trait they had in common, also a need to be in the limelight,
> and to get revenge on the institution they felt betrayed them. Virtually all
> of these men had separated from their force, in fact most of them were in
> jail for stealing more than their "fair share" of the war booty. They were so
> intent on peddling testimony (in exchange for immunity from prosecution
> or leniency in sentencing) that they'd get together in their cells and concoct
> stories, taking an element from this one's experience, another detail from
> someone else. It was hair-raising. They were profoundly, essentially crimi-
> nal. (quote from Graciela Fernández Meijide, in Feitlowitz 1998: 208–9)

The Scilingo, Astiz, and Simón cases suggest that it is unlikely that
perpetrators will confess without the "exchange" of immunity. In order
to convince individuals to come forward with their stories, they will need
protection from retribution. Otherwise, the incentives are too low and
the costs are too high. In this light, nearly all confessions involve some
kind of exchange relationship.[19]

These cases demonstrate, however, the limitations of the exchange relationship, particularly in relationship to immunity from prosecution. In
all three cases the perpetrators went to jail after making confessions. The
government used detentions to silence Scilingo and Astiz. In addition,
Scilingo served time in jail in Spain. Simón was tried and sentenced in Argentina for kidnapping babies born in captivity to political prisoners.
These perpetrators would have probably escaped prosecution and imprisonment had they remained silent about their past.

Pernías and Rolón Deposed

I tried to do things as humanely as possible...but it's
difficult for anyone who wasn't there to understand that.
    Captain Antonio Pernías (Verbitsky 1995: 168)

All officers rotated into the task forces that were
formed to carry out what was called the anti-subversive
struggle.
    Captain Juan Carlos Rolón (Verbitsky 1995: 180)

Captains Antonio Pernías and Juan Carlos Rolón provided the catalyst
for Scilingo's confession. They both lived in Scilingo's neighborhood and
Scilingo counted Rolón among his friends. More importantly, these
officers symbolized for Scilingo the military high command's treachery

of silence. Scilingo indicted the high command for failing to defend the war and its tactics that had led to the condemnation, shattered careers, and broken lives of loyal officers.

The Argentine Senate in 1994 called Pernías and Rolón to testify in public hearings to consider their promotions. Their testimonies admitted, for the first time in an official hearing, to officers' use of torture. Pernías, known for using prisoners to test poison darts developed to facilitate the apprehension of "subversives," for his participation in the Santa Cruz Church attack, and for his infiltration of exile organizations abroad, admitted that torture was "the hidden weapon in a war without rules." He confessed, "I did my part just like many others" (Verbitsky 1995: 158). Rolón also admitted to inflicting torture on prisoners, claiming that such practices involved nearly everyone in the navy (Verbitsky 1995: 176).

There is little doubt about the power of such testimonies and the admissions made under oath. Neither Pernías nor Rolón would have confessed without the hearings. Surprisingly, their confession and the repercussions for their promotions evoked a chain reaction of confessions, beginning with Scilingo. Yet their admissions hardly involved remorse, repentance, or even regret. The closest Pernías came to such emotions is his statement, "What bothers me is the death of innocent people." But when he cites examples of those "innocent people," he mentions "Lieutenant Mayol, petty officers, and also civilians" (Verbitsky 1995: 167). The closest Rolón comes to accepting guilt for his actions is in stating that he would never become involved in such activities again, that he now knows they were wrong, but that he could not make that judgment at the time.

Rather than repentance, these two formal and institutional confessions involved defensiveness, a justification of actions on a variety of grounds. The perpetrators had a duty, for example, to follow orders and not question them. As good and loyal officers they would carry out an order equally whether it were issued under an authoritarian or a democratic regime. Rolón rhetorically and cynically questioned whether he should have disobeyed the orders of commanding officers appointed by the Senate, the same body he was testifying to for his promotion. Both Pernías and Rolón also claimed that they had no alternative; they would have had to retire if they hadn't carried out orders.

The second defense in these confessions involved the nature of the war. Pernías, avoiding the "Dirty War" moniker, referred to it as an unconventional war that required unconventional methods. Rolón defended the violence by demonizing the enemy; he falsely labeled it "the largest urban guerrilla movement in the history of the world" (Feitlowitz 1998: 203). Both officers admitted that the armed forces were unprepared for antisubversive war, being trained, rather, for conventional war. "This was really unprecedented and we were unprepared," stated Rolón. "We received very little training and then we were sent off to participate in these urban operations" (Verbitsky 1995: 173). He added that no one liked the "traumatic methods required to resolve the traumatic events, least of all those of us who had to carry them out. [But] these were historical circumstances" (Verbitsky 1995: 170–71). But while admitting to their involvement in the Dirty War, these two officials also tried to plead their innocence. Pernías, for example, argued that the navy had dismissed from its ranks any of the officers who had used excessive force in the antisubversion war. While he refused to "name names" of purged officers, Pernías emphasized that he had remained on active duty, attesting to his own good record.

Third, these officers justified their involvement in the Dirty War in terms of their goals to defend democracy and the country. Pernías claimed that he was motivated by the desire to end the war as soon as possible to avoid "unnecessary deaths" (Verbitsky 1995: 168). Rolón described his involvement as "service . . . to reestablish a democratic style of life in Argentina." They both confessed that they subsequently knew better than to use torture, but more accurately, they felt that circumstances had changed so dramatically that they would not be called upon to use that kind of force again. In Rolón's own words: "I believe that this was an unprecedented experience and that the situation will never occur again" (Verbitsky 1995: 163).

Pernías and Rolón's testimony contributes to the argument that perpetrators' confessions bury the truth behind lies and misperceptions, heroic justifications, euphemisms, and denials—and that this can happen even in formal institutional proceedings. Even where the perpetrator receives amnesty for confession, as in the South African Truth and Reconciliation Commission on the apartheid era, these confessions tend to include the rhetorical devices employed in heroic confessions. Facing prosecution, perpetrators will attack the forum as a "kangaroo court" or a show trial. If they confess at all, they admit to nothing—claiming amnesia, using avoidance tactics, minimizing their involvement, or pleading innocence. Alternatively, they justify their acts as duty, thereby blaming higher authorities, or they rationalize the act in terms of historical circumstances and national threats.

Yet despite such limitations in uncovering truths, the Argentine case suggests that confessions in public hearings have the greatest potential of achieving justice. These confessions put torture and torturers into the official record, thereby bearing witness to victims' claims, even where the perpetrators themselves do not admit to specific acts and justify violence. The stigma shifts as perpetrators, once protected from public scrutiny, face their charges, while victims, stigmatized by past violence, are vindicated. With immunity from prosecution, these perpetrators cannot be brought to justice for murder or torture. But public hearings can advance restorative justice. By denying Pernías and Rolón their promotion, the Senate imposed a sanction on them spared on officers not asked to confess. The public hearings, while not a court of law, symbolize an official recognition of human rights protections. Ironically, then, confessions in public hearings may mask truths, even as they provide acknowledgment, partial justice, and collective memory.

CONCLUSIONS

Argentina provides an ideal case for analyzing public confessions, since so many perpetrators have come forward to tell their stories for different reasons and in diverse contexts. The cases examined in this chapter represent the kinds of confessions that emerged in other countries transitioning from authoritarian rule.[20] This chapter, then, provides insights into the relationship of perpetrators' confessions to truth and reconciliation.

The chapter suggests that perpetrators' confessions play a very limited role in the process of truth and reconciliation, since none of the Argentine confessions advanced truth, acknowledgment, justice, *and* collective memory. But viewed from a different vantage point, the Argentine case identifies when and under what conditions perpetrators' confessions do advance this process. The Argentine confessions contributed the most to truth-gathering, as reflected in the summary provided in table 6.1. Although no confession provided full disclosure of events, they all confirmed the fact of torture, and in some cases they even provided specific information about it.

Confessions proved more limited in advancing acknowledgment, justice, and collective memory. The Scilingo confession went the farthest by providing specific information about the repressive apparatus, acknowledging the crimes, sending him to jail in Spain, creating the powerful symbol of the death flights in collective memory, and reopening the question of immunity from prosecution. But few remorseful confessions

TABLE 6.1   SUMMARY OF ARGENTINE CASES

Perpetrator	Truth	Acknowledgment	Justice	Collective Memory
Scilingo	Yes, specifics	Yes, remorse	Partial	Yes, death flights
Astiz	Partial admission	No, heroic war	Partial	Yes, silencing
Simón	Partial admission	No, heroic war	Partial	No
Pernías, Rolón	Partial admission	Partial and tempered	Partial	Yes, public hearing

emerge because of perpetrators' socialization in the repressive apparatus, self-protection, trauma, fear of retribution, and use of rhetorical devices.

Moreover, Scilingo's confession evolved in a setting difficult to reproduce. Although Scilingo's confession initially resembled the heroic confession, the antagonistic Verbitsky drew out Scilingo's remorse. Scilingo's sense of betrayal by the military high command further aided that process, releasing him from his loyalty to the military regime. Scilingo's confession, in short, demonstrated that remorseful confessions are rare, and are nearly impossible to institutionalize, but that when they occur they have a powerful impact on truth, acknowledgment, and collective memory.

The Argentine case also identifies an irreconcilable trade-off between two pillars of reconciliation: truth and justice. It is extremely unlikely that any one of these perpetrators would have come forward with their "truths" without immunity from prosecution. Yet granting immunity involves a Faustian bargain: immunity facilitates truth while it precludes justice. Victims of human rights abuses and their families might finally understand who did what, when, and why to them, but they cannot bring the perpetrators of those crimes to justice.

When responses to the confessions enter into the analysis, however, the trade-off appears overblown. The Senate hearing, for example, provided some justice (promotion denial) without violating amnesty provisions. Similarly, Scilingo and others have gone to jail and produced confessions that have promoted investigation into crimes for which officers do not have immunity, thereby circumventing amnesty laws. Charges and imprisonment for fraud, embezzlement, and kidnapping children have ensnared perpetrators otherwise protected under the Due Obedience Law. Certainly none of these "punishments" match the enormity of the crimes. They do, however, serve at least some role in creating restorative justice that shifts the stigma from the victim of violence to the perpetrators. They also contribute to public acknowledgment of victims' experiences and check the "culture of impunity" rampant in Latin America.

Responses are even more crucial with regard to heroic confessions that attempt to reassert the military regime's official version of the past. Astiz's heroic confession undermined victims' accounts, but the government's response to it brought justice and created collective memory by landing one of the most notorious perpetrators of state violence in jail (albeit *not* for his human rights violations). Similarly, while one television station seemed to endorse Simón's heroic confession by dressing him up in a respectable sartorial guise, another countered that image with a more accurate portrayal of a desperate man peddling his confession for material gain.

Indeed, the absence of collective outrage to perpetrators' confessions may harm the truth and reconciliation process. An Argentine with whom I spoke criticized the Jerry Springer–style programs that bring victims together with their perpetrators on split screens. Tragically, she remarked that Argentines "have become accustomed to living with their torturers." The Argentine case demonstrates that the degree to which confessions contribute to collective memory, amnesia, or "normalcy" depends as much on the confessional text as on the responses to it.

In sum, perpetrators' confessions are crucial to the truth and reconciliation process. Confessions by perpetrators break the authoritarian regime's silence about violence in a way that no other group can—from the inside. But this chapter has suggested that the role of the confessional text should not be exaggerated. Against the claim that "once again, essential questions of public life are being settled by an Army chief and that, in a country like Argentina, is serious,"[21] this chapter concludes that audience responses may undermine the confessional text and reverse its deleterious impact on truth and reconciliation; it shows that government, citizen, and media responses to even heroic confessions can promote truth-telling, acknowledgment, symbolic justice, and collective memory of atrocities. Such responses can roll back the authoritarian regime's official story and minimize the trade-off between immunity from prosecution and the truth and reconciliation process.

NOTES

1. For a review of official truth commissions, see Hayner (1994). The Catholic Church has sponsored a number of projects to disclose the truth: for example, *Brasil* (1985) and Proyecto (1998). The proliferation of testimonials have constituted a genre analyzed by literary critics. See, for example, "Voices" (1991) and Harlow (1987).

2. One source of scholarly work on the value of truth for reconciliation is Margaret Popkin and Naomi Roht-Arriaza (1995). The South African Truth and Reconciliation Commission is designed to establish truth by providing those involved in human rights violations immunity from prosecution in exchange for their confessions. It is premised on the four assumptions described in this chapter. For more information on this commission and its work, see its web site: http://www.doj.gov.za/trc.

3. As Joanna North states, "Forgiveness does not remove the fact or event of wrongdoing but instead *relies* upon the recognition of wrong having been committed in order for the process of forgiveness to be made possible" (North 1998: 17, her emphasis). While some therapists consider forgiveness a critical step in the healing process, I believe that such a process may be nearly impossible and puts an unreasonable burden on the victim of violence. Even "forgiveness scholars" question whether this is always possible. North (1998: 27), for example, claims that unforgivable acts include torture and murder of children, genocide, and mass extermination. Flanigan (1998: 98) contends that injuries that assault our belief system are the most difficult to forgive.

4. Milburn and Conrad (1996: 167) make a key contribution in showing how the same justifications used to promote support for war make it nearly impossible to accept blame for atrocities in that war. They emphasize the importance of healing not only the victims but also the perpetrators whose lives are fractured as a result of the war.

5. See *The Oxford Dictionary of English Etymology* (Oxford: Clarendon Press, 1992) and *The New Shorter Oxford English Dictionary* (Oxford: Clarendon Press, 1993). For a different taxonomy of confessions, but one from which I have drawn insights, see Huggins (2000).

6. Verbitsky first played excerpts from the confession during the popular Argentine television news program *Hora Clave* on March 2, 1995. The following day, Verbitsky published Scilingo's confession in his article "The Final Solution," in the newspaper *Página 12*, and subsequently in a book entitled *El vuelo* (Verbitsky 1995, 1996). Scilingo's story was widely published and televised in Europe and in the United States, including his appearance on the CBS program *60 Minutes* in a segment entitled "Tales from the Dirty War" (April 2, 1995).

7. For the government report, see Comisión Nacional sobre la Desaparición de Personas (1992). A wide range of academic studies include Acuña and Smulovitz (1991); Brysk (1994); and Graziano (1992). Americas Watch and Amnesty International published their reports based largely on archives collected by Argentine human rights groups, such as Centro de Estudios Legales y Sociales (CELS) and the Madres de Plaza de Mayo. Testimonies such as those by Timer-

man (1982) and Partnoy (1986), and testimonial novels such as Valenzuela's (1983), sold widely in Argentina and abroad.

8. Emilio Mignone, cofounder of CELS, described the shock around Scilingo in this way: "In our day and age people need to see faces. It's the only way for them to realize that nice-looking, well-dressed, articulate Mr. Scilingo, that gentleman who could be your next-door neighbor, is the very embodiment of the Process, the very horror itself, and here he is addressing you in your living room night after night" (Feitlowitz 1998: 195).

9. Scilingo and his partners were accused of writing bad checks, opening bank accounts under false names, and defrauding suppliers. After spending a year in jail, Scilingo proved that the charges lacked substantiation.

10. Scilingo described this warning in an interview with Blixen (1996). This idea is also reflected in an interview with Martín Abregú, director of CELS, in Calvin Sims, "In Exposing Abuses, Argentine Earns Hate," *New York Times* News Service, web site, http://www.latinolink.com/arg1028.html (October 28, 1995).

11. Jason Webb, Reuters, http://www.mosquitonet.com/~prewett/reutmar 95.html (March 8, 1995).

12. Two Spanish judges—Manuel García Castellón and Baltasar Garzón—initiated investigations of military officers in Chile and Argentina. Garzón charged 110 former as well as active police and military chiefs with illegal detention and murder of 320 Spanish citizens during the Dirty War. He also issued eleven arrest warrants (Marlise Simons, "Madrid Throws Cold Water into Latin Atrocities," *New York Times* [January 4, 1998], p. 5). This is the same judge who in 1998 filed for the extradition from England to Spain of General Augusto Pinochet, former Chilean dictator, to stand trial for human rights abuses.

13. I draw extensively on the discussion of these confessions and their political context in Feitlowitz (1998: 193–255). In addition to the confessions I examine in this chapter, she includes those by Victor Ibañez, Dr. Jorge Antonio Bergés, Federico Talavera, Pedro Caraballo, Juan Antonio del Cerro, and Osvaldo Etchecolatz.

14. Summarizing the paralyzing effect of fear of recrimination, Luis Muñoz, a former conscript who confessed to hand-delivering lists of kidnapped prisoners to the military command, said that he had not come forward sooner because "I was afraid they would make me disappear" (Feitlowitz 1998: 226). Scilingo's own kidnapping and assault point to the insecurity perpetrators face in recounting events.

15. As Flanigan (1992: 84) states: "Offenders try to manipulate those they injure into believing their renditions of injuries. They try to expunge themselves of blame, their main objective being to manage the other person's impressions. People try to get others to think well of them even if they have lied, betrayed, or broken promises."

16. *Revista Trespuntos* (January 15, 1998). See also Izaguirre (1998: 34).

17. "Finalización del sumario militar al Capitán de Fragata (re) Astiz," http://www.ara.mil.ar/informacion/sumario.htm (September 4, 1998).

18. Not everyone succeeded in these endeavors, however. Despite running the notorious La Perla concentration camp, Captain Héctor Vergez could not find a buyer for his story, which he valued at thirty thousand U.S. dollars. He did, however, get a job investigating the 1994 bombing of the Jewish Cultural Center. According to Feitlowitz, Vergez approached the federal intelligence services, who hired him to investigate the bombing of the Asociación Mutual Israelita Argentina (AMIA), in which eighty-six people were killed and two hundred wounded. By his own admission, he received two million dollars to build a case against an early suspect. Vergez, she notes, is a reputed anti-Semite, having participated in the Comando Libertador de América, known for its pro-Nazi views. Trafficking in human misery has proved lucrative for Vergez, who during the dictatorship held political prisoners for ransom and sold the furnishings and utensils stolen from their houses (Feitlowitz 1998: 213–15).

19. The South African Truth and Reconciliation Commission is set up to provide amnesty only to those who confess the truth. It is probably the best case of an exchange confession.

20. For a discussion of some of these cases, including Argentina, Brazil, Chile, Rwanda, South Africa, and Yugoslavia, see Payne (forthcoming).

21. Martín Abregú, quoted in *Página 12* (March 18, 1995): 2, and reprinted in Feitlowitz (1998: 224).

REFERENCES

Acuña, Carlos H., and Catarina Smulovitz. 1991. "Ni olvido, ni perdón: Derechos humanos y tensiones cívico-militares en la transición Argentina." Documento CEDES 69.

Arendt, Hannah. 1963. *Eichmann in Jerusalem: A Report on the Banality of Evil.* New York: Viking Press.

Beverley, John. 1996. "The Real Thing." In *The Real Thing: Testimonial Discourse and Latin America,* ed. Georg M. Gugelberger, pp. 266–86. Durham, N.C.: Duke University Press.

Blixen, Samuel. 1996. "Para que no haya mas Scilingos." *Semanario Brecha* (Montevideo, Uruguay) web site, http://www.brecha.com.uy/numeros/n549/tapa.html (June 7).

Brasil: Nunca Mais. 1985. Petrópolis: Vozes.

Brysk, Alison. 1994. *The Politics of Human Rights in Argentina: Protest, Change, and Democratization.* Stanford, Calif.: Stanford University Press.

Cohen, Stanley. 1993. "Human Rights and Crimes of the State: The Culture of Denial." *Australian and New Zealand Journal of Criminology* 26: 98–106.

Comisión Nacional sobre la Desaparición de Personas (CONADEP). 1992. *Nunca Más.* Buenos Aires: Editorial Universitaria de Buenos Aires.

Crelinsten, Ronald D. 1994. "In Their Own Words: The World of the Torturer." In *The Politics of Pain: Torturers and Their Masters,* ed. Ronald D. Crelinsten and Alex P. Schmid, pp. 35–64. Boulder, Colo.: Westview Press.

Dickey, Walter J. 1998. "Forgiveness and Crime: The Possibilities of Restorative Justice." In *Exploring Forgiveness,* ed. Robert D. Enright and Joanna North, pp. 106–20. Madison: University of Wisconsin Press.

Dorfman, Ariel. 1991. *Some Write to the Future: Essays on Contemporary Latin American Fiction.* Trans. George Shivers, with the author. Durham, N.C.: Duke University Press.

Feitlowitz, Marguerite. 1998. *A Lexicon of Terror: Argentina and the Legacies of Torture.* New York: Oxford University Press.

Flanigan, Beverly. 1992. *Forgiving the Unforgivable.* New York: Macmillan.

———. 1998. "Forgivers and the Unforgivable." In *Exploring Forgiveness,* ed. Robert D. Enright and Joanna North, pp. 95–105. Madison: University of Wisconsin Press.

Goleman, Daniel. 1985. *Vital Lies, Simple Truths: On the Psychology of Self-Deception.* New York: Simon and Schuster.

Graziano, Frank. 1992. *Divine Violence: Spectacle, Psychosexuality, and Radical Christianity in the Argentine "Dirty War."* Boulder, Colo.: Westview Press.

Harlow, Barbara. 1987. *Resistance Literature.* New York: Methuen.

Hayner, Priscilla B. 1994. "Fifteen Truth Commissions—1974–1994: A Comparative Study." *Human Rights Quarterly* 16: 597–655.

Huggins, Martha K. 2000. "Legacies of Authoritarianism: Brazilian Torturers' and Murderers' Reformulation of Memory." *Latin American Perspectives* 27, no. 2 (March): 57–79.

Izaguirre, Inés. 1998. "Recapturing the Memory of Politics." *NACLA: Report on the Americas* 31, no. 6 (May–June): 28–34.

Laub, Dori. 1992. "Bearing Witness or the Vicissitudes of Listening." In *Testimony: Crises of Witnessing in Literature, Psychoanalysis, and History,* ed. Shoshana Felman and Dori Laub, pp. 57–74. New York: Routledge.

Lifton, Robert Jay. 1986. *The Nazi Doctors: Medical Killing and the Psychology of Genocide.* New York: Basic Books.

Milburn, Michael A., and Sheree D. Conrad. 1996. *The Politics of Denial.* Cambridge, Mass.: MIT Press.

North, Joanna. 1998. "The 'Ideal' of Forgiveness: A Philosopher's Exploration." In *Exploring Forgiveness,* ed. Robert D. Enright and Joanna North, pp. 15–34. Madison: University of Wisconsin Press.

Partnoy, Alicia. 1986. *The Little School: Tales of Disappearance and Survival in Argentina.* Pittsburgh: Cleis Press, 1986.

Payne, Leigh A. Forthcoming. *Unsettling Accounts: The Political Uses of Confessions by Perpetrators of State Violence.*

Popkin, Margaret, and Naomi Roht-Arriaza. 1995. "Truth as Justice: Investigatory Commissions in Latin America." *Law and Social Inquiry* 20, no. 1 (Winter): 79–116.

Proyecto Interdiocesano de Recuperación de la Memoria Histórica. 1998. *Guatemala: Nunca más.* Guatemala City: ODHAG.

Scott, James C. 1990. *Domination and the Arts of Resistance: Hidden Transcripts.* New Haven, Conn.: Yale University Press.

Timerman, Jacobo. 1982. *Prisoner without a Name, Cell without a Number*. Trans. Toby Talbot. New York: Vintage Books.

Valenzuela, Luisa. 1983. *Cambio de armas*. Mexico City: M. Casillas.

Verbitsky, Horacio. 1995. *El vuelo*. Buenos Aires: Planeta.

———. 1996. *The Flight: Confessions of an Argentine Dirty Warrior*. Trans. Esther Allen. New York: New Press.

"Voices of the Voiceless in Testimonial Literature." 1991. *Latin American Perspectives* 18, no. 3, pt. 1 (Summer): 3–14.

Young, James E. 1993. *The Texture of Memory: Holocaust Memorials and Meaning*. New Haven, Conn.: Yale University Press.

CHAPTER SEVEN

Colombia

Does Injustice Cause Violence?

MARC W. CHERNICK

By the year 2000, the rule of law in Colombia was being degraded every day by state agents who perpetrated illegal violence and by nonstate actors who used illegal violence to advance and protect their own interests. Justice was further crippled by a formal legal system that was inoperative throughout much of the national territory and by legislators and judicial leaders who were unable and unwilling to prosecute state officials and their proxies that operated outside the law.

Colombia's tortured descent into lawlessness was the direct result of more than fifty years of internal armed conflict. The nation plunged into a civil war between the Liberal and Conservative parties from 1946 to 1958, in a period that came to be known simply as La Violencia. What had begun as one of the bloodiest wars in the history of the western hemisphere was then transformed in the 1960s and 1970s into a relatively low-intensity guerrilla insurgency, as peasants, students, intellectuals, Communists, and former Liberal guerrillas took up arms against a closed and fundamentally undemocratic regime that had emerged with the ending of the first phase of violence. By the 1980s and 1990s, the violence had again escalated and evolved into a multipolar war with left-wing guerrillas, right-wing paramilitaries, and a weak and fragmented state competing for control across the political divisions of the national territory.

Most studies have analyzed Colombia's periods of violence as distinct and unrelated events, with fundamentally different protagonists, issues, and cleavages.[1] Yet despite the changing narrative of conflict—Liberals against Conservatives in the 1940s and '50s; guerrillas against the state in the '60s and '70s; multiple actors, including guerrillas, paramilitaries, and drug traffickers in the '80s and '90s—there has been remarkable continuity in the geographic zones of the violence, in the actors in conflict, in the illegal use of state and para-state violence, and in the regional and social causes of violence.

If armed conflict and state violence constituted one pole that shaped Colombian politics, the other pole comprised peacemaking and amnesty. Liberals and Conservatives negotiated a power-sharing agreement in 1957. From 1982 to 2001, five Colombian presidents initiated some form of negotiations and peace processes with the armed guerrilla movements (Chernick 1999). During these peace processes, some guerrilla movements negotiated their reincorporation into legal political life and were granted pardons or amnesties. Amnesties were offered in 1953 (to military officers), 1954 (to Liberal guerrillas), 1958 (to Liberals and Conservatives in specific regions), and 1982, 1990, and 1994 (to leftist guerrillas and urban militias associated with the guerrillas). The amnesties, while addressing the individual juridical situation of certain armed combatants, left the illegal state and para-state institutions intact and permitted serious human-rights violators to escape justice.

Colombia's protracted violence and failed amnesties exposed a state that was unable to protect its citizenry or to consolidate a binding and legitimate legal order throughout its national territory. O'Donnell (1999: 331) calls the "part of the state that is embodied in a legal system" the "legal state," and argues that the legal dimension of state authority is critical for consolidating democratic governance.[2] In Colombia, the absence of the legal state in many regions of the country had far-reaching consequences. Throughout Colombia's long history of conflict, the legal state was reduced to an inoperable core of ineffective judicial institutions with limited reach and with little authority over other state actors.

In this chapter, I argue that the degradation of justice and the absence of a functioning legal system helped fuel more than fifty years of war during the second half of the twentieth century and was a major obstacle to consolidating effective peace processes. The chapter examines the origins, causes, and duration of violence at the national and local levels, finding that the most violent regions in the country were (1) those areas where authority had been delegated to or usurped by illegal, private, armed actors; and (2) those areas where state institutions and officials had overstepped the bounds of the legal use of force. Moreover, this chapter concludes that the regular granting of amnesties, without regard to larger questions of justice or historical accountability, had little effect in promoting national reconciliation. Such amnesties, divorced from the larger needs of constructing a legal state, helped institutionalize illegal and unjust forms of political authority that further perpetuated the violence.

NATIONAL DYNAMICS OF VIOLENCE

The persistent violence of the second half of the twentieth century was precipitated by the 1946 presidential election. In the 1930s, the Liberals had emerged as the majority party, and populist leader Jorge Eliécer Gaitán attempted to transform the Liberal Party, one of Colombia's two traditional parties, into a multiclass, mass, populist party, similar to those emerging throughout Latin America in this period. Gaitán faced strong resistance from his own party. In the 1946 elections, the Liberals eventually ran two candidates and forfeited the presidency to the Conservatives, ending sixteen years of Liberal Party hegemony.

The removal of Liberals from political power incited major violence throughout the country. Conservatives forcefully replaced their opponents at all levels of what was still a highly centralized government that was in charge of appointing regional and local officials. The figures in table 7.1 reveal that the violence began to escalate dramatically in 1947–48. By then, Gaitán had consolidated his position as the undisputed leader of the party and was poised to win back the presidency for the Liberals in 1950. His mission was cut short when he was assassinated on the streets of Bogotá on April 9, 1948, a murder that led to days of looting and rioting in Bogotá and sparked urban uprisings throughout the country. The urban riots were quickly repressed. However, the escalation of rural violence following the assassination endured throughout the next decade, and, in many areas, it persisted throughout the next fifty years.

The most violent years were 1948 to 1953. Over 144,000 people were killed in this period. After 1953, the violence temporarily declined following the coup d'etat of General Gustavo Rojas Pinilla, which was essentially a *golpe de opinión,* or opinion coup. The leaders of the principal factions of the two elite parties were concerned that the violence was creating its own dynamic beyond their control; they were frightened that the spreading violence would foment a social revolution and so placed the military in power to pacify the country. Among Rojas Pinilla's first acts was an amnesty for the military, followed by an amnesty for Liberal guerrillas.

TABLE 7.1 PHASES OF THE VIOLENCE IN COLOMBIA

Violence	Organized Actors in Conflict	Number of Deaths	Annual Number of Deaths per 100,000	Most Violent *Departamento* (in Descending Order— All Above National Average)
Period 1 La Violencia (1946–57)	Liberal-Conservative Communist self-defense groups	1947: 13,968	—	Antiguo Caldas (Caldas, Quindío, Risaralda)
		1948: 43,557	404	Tolima
		1949: 18,519	168	Antioquia
		1950: 50,253	447	Norte de Santander
		1951: 10,319	90	Santander
		1952: 13,250	113	Valle
		1953: 8,650	71	Meta
		1954: 900	7	Huila
		1955: 1,013	8	Cundinamarca
		1956: 11,136	86	
		1957: 2,877	22	
Period 2 Low-intensity conflict (1964–84)	Guerrillas-state	1958–62: 19,449	32	Tolima
		1963–67: 18,827	31	Santander
		1968–72: 21,691	32	Cundinamarca
		1973–77: 29,117	37	Norte de Santander, Meta
		1978: 6,601	37	Risaralda
		1979: 7,503	37	Quindío
		1980: 8,569	36	Boyacá
		1981: 10,194	36	Caquetá
		1982: 9,959	35	Antioquia
		1983: 8,951	—	Bolívar
		1984: 9,912	—	Cauca

Period 3
Escalating
multipolar
violence
(1985–)

Guerrillas, state, paramilitaries		
1985: 11,919	Antioquia	—
1986: 14,315	Cundinamarca	—
1987: 16,535	Valle	59
1988: 21,509	Santander	73
1989: 23,441	Risaralda	74
1990: 24,279	Caldas	75
1991: 28,260	Norte de Santander	86
1992: 28,141	Tolima	84
1993: 28,021	Meta	82
1994: 26,826	Boyacá	77
1995: 25,398	Cesar	72
1996: 26,643	Santander	74
1997: 25,379	Magdalena	63
1998: 23,133	Atlántico	62
1999: 24,358	Cauca	62.5
2000: 26,522	Cordoba	63.5
	Quindío	

SOURCE FOR PERIOD 1: Doctor Carlos Lemoine, Compañia Colombiana de Datos, cited in Oquist 1978: 16, 59.

SOURCES FOR PERIOD 2: Policía Nacional Dijin, cited in Consejería para los Derechos Humanos 1991: 14; and Policía Nacional, cited in Departamento Nacional de Planeación 1998: 8.

SOURCE FOR PERIOD 3: Policía Nacional, cited in Echandía Castilla 1999: 45–63, 132–33.

SOURCE FOR 1999 AND 2000: Policía Nacional, cited in Observatorio de los Derechos Humanos web site, http://www.derechos humanos.gov.co/observ.

As the initial period of violence evolved into the next phase, the armed actors were transformed. Liberal guerrillas, particularly those from the eastern plains, or Los Llanos Orientales, handed in their arms in 1954 and accepted amnesties in 1954 and 1958. The Liberal and Conservative parties ousted Rojas Pinilla from power in 1957 and signed a long-term power-sharing agreement, the Frente Nacional (National Front), which was ratified in a constitutional plebiscite.[3] However, a significant faction of the Liberal guerrillas—most notably those in the coffee-growing regions of the Andes—were not covered by or refused these amnesties. They kept their arms and made alliances with the self-defense groups linked to the Colombian Communist Party that had been established throughout the coffee zones following the assassination of Gaitán (Chernick and Jiménez 1993).

The National Front reduced the violence but was unable to consolidate the peace. Following failed efforts to negotiate with the remaining armed groups, the National Front leaders unleashed a series of bombing campaigns against the major Liberal-Communist self-defense communities. One prominent Conservative senator declared that the communities constituted communist "independent republics" that were unlawfully established on Colombian soil (Alape 1985: 248–49).[4] The 1964 bombing of the first community, Marquetalia (in Tolima), became part of the iconography of the subsequent guerrilla insurgency. According to Manuel Marulanda Vélez, then military leader of the self-defense communities, he and a small fighting force withstood the onslaught of a combined force of sixteen thousand troops from the Colombian Army and Air Force (Marulanda 1973: 79–80). Marulanda escaped the assault and went on to found a more modern guerrilla force, the Fuerzas Armadas Revolucionarias de Colombia (Revolutionary Armed Forces of Colombia; FARC). The renewed military campaign was fully supported by the United States and placed Colombia's conflict squarely within the international Cold War context.

However, the aerial assaults proved to be a fatal miscalculation. They converted what had been armed self-defense communities into a mobile guerrilla force. The FARC initially maintained strong ties to the Colombian Communist Party and spent the next four decades developing a sizeable army and political machine under Marulanda's leadership.

In the second phase, then, the vertical cleavage between the followers of the two elite-dominated, multiclass parties, the Liberals and the Conservatives, gave way to a horizontal cleavage between the state, now dominated by the power-sharing arrangement between Liberals and

Conservatives, and those who believed they were excluded from the new regime. The latter included the new Liberal-Communist self-defense groups converted into a mobile guerrilla force, the FARC, and also newer groups founded in this period, particularly the Ejército de Liberación Nacional (National Liberation Army; ELN) and the Ejército Popular de Liberación (Popular Liberation Army; EPL). The ELN was founded by Colombian students in Havana who had been inspired by the example of the Cuban Revolution, which had triumphed less then six months after the inauguration of the National Front. The EPL was a Maoist group also founded by Colombian students caught up in the ideological reverberations of the breakup of the Sino-Soviet alliance. Unlike other South American countries, where revolutionary movements modeled on the experience of the Cuban or Chinese revolutions were quickly defeated, in Colombia these movements were able to successfully insert themselves into communities with recent experiences of rebellion against the state.

The old and new guerrilla insurgencies were echoed in social protests, labor strikes, peasant marches, *paros cívicos* (community strikes), and a wealth of unconventional forms of protest and opposition. The state's response was to criminalize most forms of protest, viewing them as subversive. Successive presidential administrations extended the authority of the military. During the Julio Turbay administration (1978–82), a national-security statute was decreed that gave the armed forces broad powers to search, arrest, imprison, and try civilians in military courts. The increased repressive capacity of the state reflected the growing weakness and reduced legitimacy of the regime. One study revealed that between 1971 and 1980, 44 percent of *paros cívicos* had ended with military interventions (Giraldo and Camargo 1984: 12). Most *paros cívicos* centered on grievances relating to public services, such as inadequate electricity, water, sewerage, or roads.

The act of criminalizing social protest had an effect opposite to the one intended. By closing off channels of legitimate participation, support shifted to the guerrillas. As Charles Tilly (1975, 1978) has noted, the line between armed insurrection and legitimate protest is porous and is easily crossed—in both directions—depending on the perceived and real opportunities for participation, access, and change.

By the mid-1980s, as the authority of the National Front regime eroded, a third and distinct phase of violence began. Multiple armed actors, including guerrillas, paramilitaries, and the government's armed forces, regularly clashed even though none was able to achieve military dominance. A second generation of guerrilla groups appeared in the 1970s and early 1980s, reflecting the limited space for political participation. Most notable was the Movimiento 19 de Abril (April 19th Movement; M-19), founded in the wake of the fraudulent elections of 1970,[5] and the Movimiento Revolucionario Quintín Lame (Quintín Lame Revolutionary Movement; MRQL), which represented an indigenous movement in the Cauca region. These newer groups gained significant public support. In 1990, after negotiating peace and handing over its arms to an international commission, the M-19 won 27 percent of the vote for seats in a constituent assembly (Chernick 1999). The MRQL also negotiated its reentry into legal political life and gained significant rights for indigenous peoples as participants in the assembly.

But even as these partial peace processes advanced, the violence escalated significantly and once again the armed conflict was transformed. Several factors converged to spark the spread of the war. First, the peace processes of the 1980s coincided with the insertion of the Andean region, and particularly Colombia, into the global economy as a major exporter of illicit narcotics. This growing drug trade altered the parameters of Colombia's conflict. It provided significant resources to all the armed actors and diminished and corrupted already weak state institutions, particularly in the judicial and legislative branches of government.

Second, the drug trade led to the vast expansion of right-wing paramilitary groups. Drug traffickers invested a considerable portion of their illicit earnings in rural landholdings, which led to a vast turnover in farm ownership throughout Colombia (Reyes 1997). These new narco-elites invested in private armies to protect themselves and their investments from the guerrillas, thereby significantly changing the dynamics of the war. The new paramilitary groups, some founded with the assistance of the armed forces, were created expressly to confront the guerrillas. They did so by attacking the social bases of the guerrillas, killing thousands of innocent civilians and displacing hundreds of thousands of peasants from their homes (Codhes and Unicef Colombia 1999: 16).

Third, the FARC, the largest guerrilla movement, significantly expanded its military capacity in the late 1980s and 1990s. It had participated in the early peace processes of the 1980s and had founded a political party, the Unión Patriótica (Patriotic Union; UP), in 1985. Yet after its founding, thousands of UP leaders and members were assassinated. The FARC withdrew from the ceasefire agreements and concentrated its efforts on creating a more effective fighting force and expanding its territorial presence. The FARC financed its military buildup by aggressively engaging in kidnapping, extortion, and "revolutionary taxes" on the drug trade and other commercial activities.

Fourth, the ELN, too, in this period augmented its military capacity and resource base. For them, the key factor was the petroleum boom of the late 1980s and 1990s. They "taxed" the multinational oil and construction companies in Arauca, Santander, and Casanare and increased their involvement in kidnapping. Ideologically and socially, they rebuilt their support bases around the image of the slain Colombian revolutionary priest Camilo Torres[6] and advocated a Christian-Marxist approach to politics, based on the Catholic notion of a "preferential option for the poor" (Medina Gallego 1996; Hernández 1998).

Fifth, the armed forces openly opposed negotiations with the guerrillas and began a policy of creating and supporting paramilitary forces to stop the growth of the guerrillas and to obstruct the peace process. Although the armed forces initially had a legal right to arm civilians, their involvement with narco-landowners and in mounting human-rights violations placed their actions outside the law (Medina Gallego 1990). In 1989, the laws granting the authority to arm civilians were overturned, yet the military did not sever their involvement with these groups. By the turn of the century, the paramilitaries had become a national force, responsible for over three-fourths of the extrajudicial killings and massacres in the country (Comisión Colombiana de Juristas 2000).

The confluence of these five developments fueled a dramatic escalation of the conflict. Violence tripled between 1980 and 2000 (see table 7.1). Yet now the internal war had evolved into an atomized and multipolar conflict. No side was able to defeat the other; no side gained sufficient leverage to dictate terms of peace.

This periodization of the conflict, covering over fifty years, from the mid-1940s to the early years of the twenty-first century, underscores an inescapable but often neglected truth: the violence in Colombia antedated the drug-export boom, which actually emerged only in the most recent period of violence. The drug trade fueled and transformed an already existing conflict. It thrived in the absence of a legitimate state presence and the application of the rule of law throughout the national territory. It funneled new resources—both financial and military—to old adversaries. It created new social sectors, particularly the drug-entrepreneurial nouveau riche, who invested heavily in the Colombian countryside and directly financed right-wing paramilitaries. It corrupted state officials and undermined the already limited reach of the legal state. In certain urban areas, particularly Medellín, it led to the creation of youth gangs and teenage killers known as *sicarios* (Salazar 1990). The drug trade deepened and broadened the violence and severely degraded the conflict.

The drug traffickers themselves, however, were not significant actors in the armed conflict, except during one limited period from 1989 to 1991. In this period, the Medellín cartel directly challenged the state over the issue of extradition to the United States and waged a terrorist campaign in urban areas. Urban terrorism had heretofore been limited in Colombia, so the advent of the Medellín cartel as another armed actor seemed to augur a new phase of the violence. However, the Medellín drug traffickers soon negotiated lenient prison terms in Colombia in exchange for a cessation of the terrorism. When Medellín cartel leader Pablo Escobar and others subsequently escaped from prison, they were hunted by special police units and gunned down. That experience crippled the Medellín cartel. Their successors from other Colombian cities, most notably the Cali cartel, considerably reduced their reliance on violence to influence the state, turning more to bribery and other forms of corruption (Salazar and Jaramillo 1992; Cañón 1994).

The roots of late-twentieth-century violence, then, were much deeper than the drug-export boom, which merely tapped into social and political conflicts whose resolution had been deferred for decades. Further, the protracted political violence was built on a foundation of regional conflicts that transcended but continually ignited the armed conflict at the national level.

REGIONAL SOURCES OF VIOLENCE

Colombia's violence was intensely regional in scope, a fact that reflected the limited reach of the legal state and its substitution by a mosaic of local and regional networks of private power. These networks consisted of *gamonales* (political bosses) associated with one of the traditional parties that maintained strong ties to the armed forces, landowners, local businessmen, and paramilitary groups. They also included areas dominated by the guerrillas, as well as those effectively controlled by narcolandholders and more autonomous paramilitary groups. In each area, justice and authority were exercised predominantly by extrajudicial and illegal means. State actors either served as witting accomplices or they were completely absent or marginalized from the exercise of power. As table 7.1 reveals, the same *departamentos* appeared as the epicenters of the violence in each historical period.[7] Individuals, groups, and communities who took up arms in the 1940s were still key protagonists a half century later.[8] Regional cleavages and local conflict fueled unrest and rebellion. Violence at the local level was related to social and economic cleavages that remained unresolved or worsened during the latter half of the twentieth century. They included conflicts over land and labor, unequal access to political power and to state resources and services, social marginalization, repression, and control of natural resources and the cultivation of agricultural products—including illicit crops (Echandía Castilla 1999: 131–47).

Although Colombia, like most of Latin America, became a predominantly urban society, the most violent areas of the country continued to be overwhelmingly rural. In the 1990s, 93 percent of the most violent municipalities in the country were rural in structure, while 7 percent were urban (Echandía Castilla 1999: 132). Yet violence did not correlate with the poorest regions of Colombia. Rather, conflict was most closely associated with areas of natural-resource extraction or commercial agricultural production (legal and illegal), where the state, social justice, and the rule of law had a minimal presence, and where private justice prevailed.

The coffee regions continued to be among the most violent areas of the country in the 1990s, just as they had been in the 1950s. Newer colonization zones, particularly the coca-growing regions, also emerged as primary sites of violence. The contrast between the Andean coffee regions and the lowland coca regions east of the Andes reflects the great diversity of violent zones throughout the country. The former are incorporated into the legal economy with some form of state presence; the latter are incorporated into the illegal economy and are most characterized by the absence of the state or of the traditional parties.

In both types of zones, one or more of the country's armed actors—guerrillas or paramilitaries—emerged as a significant or dominant political actor. In many traditional coffee and cattle zones, paramilitaries were integrated into the structure of local power relations and repressed most forms of social activism or protest through terror, assassination, and forced displacement (Medina Gallego and Téllez Ardila 1994: 32–102). In zones where guerrillas dominated, particularly in the coca-growing regions where state authority was absent, they often performed such ordinary state functions as maintaining order, adjudicating conflicts, building and servicing roads and bridge, and taxing and regulating illegal commerce (Molano 1987; Jaramillo et al. 1986; Chernick 1991). In other parts of the country, where the guerrillas were present but less dominant, they channeled most forms of social protest into armed opposition and directly threatened local elites and power holders through kidnapping, extortion, and murder.

A brief look at some of the most violent *departamentos* and economic zones underscores the issues of private justice, illegal state violence, and the absence of a legal state. In Urabá (Antioquia), conflict centered around the consolidation of the banana-plantation economy, which had transformed the area into the world's third-largest banana exporter. Urabá is a colonization zone with only a limited state presence. The FARC and EPL guerrillas moved into the zones in the 1980s and founded the first labor unions of banana workers. The Virgilio Barco administration (1986–90), in yet another attempt to control public order through ceding authority to the military, passed new antiterrorism legislation that created special "public order jurisdictions" under the control of the military. The armed forces established such a jurisdiction in Urabá while at the same time they helped establish a strong paramilitary force with close ties to the plantation owners. The paramilitary–military–plantation-owner network unleashed a deadly campaign against the unions and the social bases of the guerrillas, and the region became one of the most violent in Colombia (Comisión Andina de Juristas 1990).

In Arauca, Santander, and Norte de Santander much of the conflict centered on the oil industry. The ELN (since the 1960s) and the FARC (in the 1980s) consolidated certain bases of support among the local populations. Both groups extorted from the multinational oil companies and foreign construction firms. The ELN, in particular, directed its war against foreign oil companies and the state-run oil concern Ecopetrol; it repeatedly dynamited the oil pipeline that was built in the late 1980s to carry oil from Arauca to the Atlantic coast. The region has a long history of rebellion, closely associated with Gaitán and the Liberal guerrillas in the 1950s; the oil workers and their unions maintained a conflictive but close relationship with the ELN since its founding in 1966. In 2000 and 2001, the military and the paramilitaries began a campaign to eliminate guerrilla support in key urban centers, including Barrancabermeja (Santander), the region's largest city and the site of the nation's only oil refinery (Hernández 1998; Echandía Castilla 1999: 53–57).

Elsewhere, in parts of Boyacá, violence permeated the unregulated emerald trade and the emerald-mining industry. Paramilitary groups associated with the emerald traders and drug traffickers attempted to regulate the industry and to impose order and their version of justice (Guerrero 1991). In Cauca, large landowners clashed with a resurgent peasant and indigenous movement that laid claims to collective lands. Even after the disarmament of the indigenous guerrilla movement MRQL in 1990, the FARC continued to be active in these zones, though often in conflict with the indigenous communities that prefer their own authorities.

In the colonization zones of Guaviare, Caquetá, and Putumayo, large-scale migration into the rain forest was spurred by the coca/cocaine boom beginning in the 1980s. In these areas, the FARC was the dominant political and military actor, though their position was challenged in the late 1990s as drug traffickers and paramilitaries began to create large-scale coca plantations and to displace the first generation of small farmers (González Arias et al. 1998) The stepped-up war against the drug trade, by the Colombian and U.S. armed forces beginning in the 1990s, also intensified the conflict.

Finally, in the northern part of the country, particularly along the Atlantic coast, as well as in the mid–Magdalena Valley region, known as Magdalena Medio, and in the eastern plains *(llanos orientales),* drug traffickers invested heavily in large-scale cattle farms. These land purchases led to a further concentration of land tenure in Colombia, a country where land tenure was already among the most concentrated in the world (Puyana and Thorp 1998: 168). These narco-investments can best be described as an agrarian counter-reform that have overwhelmed Colombia's minimal efforts to implement a succession of limited agrarian reforms since the 1960s (Reyes 1997). Paramilitary groups were not only formed here to fight the guerrillas; they were also used to displace rural peasants and small-scale farmers from their lands in order to absorb the lands and create even larger estates.

It is estimated that, since 1985, one and a half million people have been forced to flee their homes and abandon their lands because of the armed conflict. Over a third of these displacements have been directly attributed to the paramilitaries and their sponsors. According to survey research sponsored by the United Nations, the principal methods used to displace people from their homes were threats (64 percent), assassinations (14 percent), forced disappearances (4 percent), attacks (3 percent), torture (1 percent), other (15 percent) (Codhes and Unicef Colombia 1999: 163).

Taken together, these regional patterns underscore a central element of Colombia's political evolution: the state developed with little control over large areas of its national territory. In the absence of state control, local power holders generally tied to the dominant economic activity of the various regions substituted their own authority and implemented their own forms of private justice. These areas were characterized by great concentrations of wealth and land, surrounded by impoverished populations with few rights. The presence of guerrilla movements channeled these conditions into armed rebellion. The presence of the military and wealthy landowners spurred the creation of paramilitary armies to fill the vacuum of the absent state and to further concentrate private wealth, privilege, and authority. Limited state presence, together with the exercise of private justice by armed elites or armed guerrillas, proved to be a recipe for chronic violence in Colombia.

DIRTY WAR, PARAMILITARISM, AND IMPUNITY

By the 1980s, Colombia's war was primarily a dirty war. The overwhelming number of victims came from the unarmed civilian population accused of cooperating with or belonging to an enemy group. Under the military regimes of the Southern Cone nations in the 1970s, dirty wars were equated with state-directed terrorism against political opponents and their perceived sympathizers or collaborators. In Colombia, on the other hand, the chief source of political violence by the late 1990s was the paramilitary groups. Even though some of these groups were directly tied to key sectors of Colombia's fractured state, others were rooted more in the nation's conflictive civil society (Chernick 1998).

There were three subgroups of paramilitaries, although the categories are not mutually exclusive: those founded directly by the armed forces; those organized by local officials, business interests, *gamonales,* and large landowners; and those founded by narco-landowners who invested drug profits in land purchases. In 1997, seven regional organizations of paramilitaries comprising each of these subgroups unified as the Autodefenses Unidas de Colombia (United Self-Defense Force of Colombia; AUC). The AUC continued to work directly with the armed forces in many regions; in others, they were permitted to operate in zones patrolled by the military.

The U.S. State Department accurately described the paramilitary's system of private justice in its 2000 Human Rights Report, though they continued to overemphasize the narcotics dimension of the problem:

> Throughout the country, paramilitary groups killed, tortured and
> threatened civilians suspected of sympathizing with guerrillas in an orchestrated campaign to terrorize them into fleeing their homes, thereby depriving guerrillas of civilian support and allowing paramilitary forces to

challenge the FARC and ELN for control of narcotics cultivations and strategically important territories. Paramilitary forces were responsible for an increasing number of massacres and other politically motivated killings. They also fought guerrillas for control of some lucrative coca-growing regions and engaged directly in narcotics production and trafficking. The AUC paramilitary umbrella, whose membership totaled approximately 8,150 armed combatants, exercised increasing influence during the year and fought to extend its presence through violence and intimidation into areas previously under guerrilla control while conducting selective killings of civilians it alleged collaborated with guerrillas.... Although some paramilitary groups reflect rural residents' desire to organize solely for self-defense, most are vigilante organizations, and still others are actually the paid private armies of narco-traffickers or large landowners. (U.S. Department of State 2001)

The paramilitaries did not always play such a dominant role in the conflict. In 1992, in cases of extrajudicial killings and massacres where a perpetrator could be determined, 56 percent were committed by the army and state security agents, 12 percent by paramilitary groups, and 25 percent by the guerrillas (Comisión Andina de Juristas 1993).

By 1999, over 75 percent of extrajudicial killings were being committed by paramilitary groups. The guerrillas were responsible for 21 percent of these crimes. State security forces directly involved in such grave human-rights violations had declined significantly to 3 percent (CINEP and Justicia y Paz 2002), only to be replaced by indirect involvement through their support of the paramilitaries. The military was thus able to "improve" its human-rights record by *illegally* supporting, overlooking, and delegating murderous authority to the paramilitaries. One human-rights investigator concluded: "The army tendency is to make this war increasingly clandestine and assign the dirty work to paramilitaries" (cited in Human Rights Watch 1998a: 17).

Colombia has a long history of paramilitarism. In the 1940s and 1950s, Conservative paramilitary groups known as *pájaros* and *chulavitos* unleashed terror against suspected Liberals in select regions of the country, particularly in Valle del Cauca, where their party controlled the government. Between 1965 and 1989, the government granted the Colombian military the right to arm civilians. In 1989, this practice was declared illegal by the Colombian Supreme Court, yet the attempts to dismantle the paramilitaries were inadequate and unsuccessful; over the next decade their numbers actually quadrupled (Republic of Colombia 2001: 10). After a thorough investigation, Human Rights Watch (2000) found that half of Colombia's eighteen brigade-level army units continued to maintain clear and documented links to paramilitary activity. The Colombia office of the U.N. high commissioner for human rights placed the responsibility squarely on the Colombian state:

> The Colombian state has an undeniable historic responsibility in the origins and development of paramilitarism, which were legally sanctioned from 1965 to 1989. Since then, although the so-called "self-defense groups" were declared unconstitutional, ten years have passed and they still have not been effectively dismantled. From this same historical perspective, the Armed Forces bear particular responsibility, because during the long-period when "self-defense groups" were legal, it was their responsibility to promote, select, organize, train, arm and give logistical support to these groups within the general framework of supporting the Armed Forces in their counter-insurgency fight. (Alto Comisionado 2000: 27)

The paramilitaries prospered for the simple reason that they were able to implement a successful counterinsurgency strategy in zones that had long been dominated by the guerrillas. They succeeded where the armed forces alone had failed. Moreover, through their ties to local power holders they gave new life to older rural elites who had been on the losing side of history in practically every other Latin American nation throughout the twentieth century. At the same time, they integrated newer narco-elites into these antiquated and concentrated structures of local power. And as the world began to focus on Colombia's internal conflict in the 1990s, they were able to act with fewer constraints than official state actors, particularly during times of peace negotiations or international attention to human-rights violations.

The paramilitarization of Colombia's conflict not only ensured that the war would continue unabated. The high levels of political violence also stimulated extraordinarily high rates of nonpolitical violent crime throughout the society (Echandía Castilla 1999; Moser 2000). Annual homicides tripled in number from 1980 to 2000. Compared with earlier levels of violence, the most violent year of the twentieth century was 1950; yet the 1990s became the most violent decade (see table 7.1).[9]

There is a distinction between political violence, on the one hand, and criminal and social violence, on the other. Assassinations and massacres for political reasons represented between 15 percent and 20 percent of the total homicides during the 1990s. In 1999, for example, of the 24,358 murders registered, over 82 percent were attributed to crime, delinquency, and social causes such as intrafamilial violence; only 17 percent to armed political actors—guerrillas, paramilitaries, or public security forces (Comisión Colombiana de Juristas 2000). The average citizen was more affected by the general rise in crime and social violence than by the escalating political violence.

The data suggest a causal relation between political violence and crime and other forms of violence. The unceasing political violence appears to have led to an increase in criminal and social violence by a vast array of political, nonpolitical, and criminal actors. Social violence includes intrafamilial violence and feuds, as well as violence against unwanted social sectors, including thieves, prostitutes, and homosexuals. The correlation between political violence and other forms of violence needs to be studied further.[10] The data reveal that the areas with the highest levels of political violence (extrajudicial killings and massacres) were also the areas with the highest levels of violence unrelated to the armed conflict (Echandía Castilla 1999: 130–64). Concomitantly, those areas that experienced low levels of political violence were also the areas with the lowest overall homicide rates (Echandía Castilla 1999: 138). The relationship between high rates of political violence and high rates of criminal and social violence is most evident in the traditional agricultural zones (coffee) and colonization zones (coca, bananas, cattle, petroleum).

The dramatic rise in nonpolitical violence in zones where the political violence was most intense was another cost of tolerating private justice and illegal state violence. Groups for private justice achieved some success against political enemies. In Magdalena Medio and along much of the Atlantic coast, paramilitary private justice and the Dirty War succeeded in reducing and eliminating much of the social base of the guerrillas. But the renewed Dirty War also opened the floodgates to a wave of social violence and crime, in many cases inflaming social conflicts that had festered since the first phase of violence in the 1950s.

The Dirty War was also facilitated by the common failure to bring criminals to justice. Impunity is a key indicator of the lack of cohesiveness, reach, and effectiveness of the legal state. In 1997, the National Planning Department released a study stating that impunity for all violent crimes was 97.5 percent.[11] Another study demonstrated that the probability that a murderer would be tried and sentenced fell from 11 percent in the 1970s to 4 percent in the 1990s (Rubio 1997). For high-profile political crimes such as the assassination of political leaders or activists or massacres in zones of conflicts, impunity rates were even higher. Of the more than two thousand killings of members of the UP political party from 1985 to 1995, only ten were fully investigated, brought to trial, and sentenced. Six ended in acquittals (Giraldo 1996: 69).

Undergirding the nearly absolute levels of impunity for political crimes was a legal system that separated military justice from ordinary justice. The armed forces repeatedly refused to prosecute their own members for direct involvement in human-rights violations or for illegally supporting paramilitary activity. Beginning in the 1980s, as some civilian officials attempted to confront the mounting epidemic of violence and impunity, great tensions emerged between the two spheres of justice. The independent attorney general's office *(procuraduría general),* which is charged with monitoring criminal conduct by state officials, began to confront the issue of human-rights violations by state actors but was repeatedly thwarted and intimidated by the armed forces. In 1983, in an unprecedented act, the attorney general accused over fifty military officers of involvement in the notorious paramilitary group Muerte a Secuestradores (Death to Kidnappers; MAS), associated with the Medellín cartel. The minister of defense publicly attacked the attorney general for his actions. One attorney general, Carlos Mauro Hoyos, moved to render all the paramilitary groups illegal and unconstitutional, overturning the law that gave the military the legal authority to arm civilians. He was assassinated while still in office in 1988 (Comisión Andina de Juristas 1990: 225–30). One year later, the Supreme Court followed Attorney General Mauro's lead and declared the paramilitaries unconstitutional, an action that led to an increase in illegal activity by state actors.

The issue of there being a separate sphere of justice for the military was debated extensively throughout the 1990s. Colombia signed and ratified several international treaties relating to international humanitarian law, including treaties on the conduct of internal war, forced disappearance, and genocide.[12] The contents of these international agreements were incorporated into Colombia's criminal code, and all violators, including the military, were to be subject to criminal proceedings in civilian courtrooms.

Additionally, several new judicial institutions were created in the 1991 constitution, including the Fiscalía General (Prosecutor-General's office), which created an independent state investigative capacity; and the Defensoría del Pueblo (Human Rights Ombudsman), including the Office of the Public Defender, which provided an adequate defense to those accused.[13] Over the next decade, special human-rights investigative units were created in both the newly created Fiscalía General and in the Procuraduría General. The latter were charged with investigating state abuses, including human-rights violations by the military, directly or by omission. However, these units were woefully underfunded, did not have adequate resources to send investigators into the field, and did not have the full cooperation or support of other branches of government.

In 1999, under great pressure from the United States in the run-up to a major increase in military aid, the Pastrana administration took the unprecedented steps of removing two senior generals from their posts due to ties to the paramilitaries. Over two years later, one of these generals was arrested when the special human-rights unit of the Fiscalía General opened an investigation into his collaboration with paramilitaries in Urabá when he was commander of the Eighteenth Brigade there (*El Espectador*, July 24, 2001: A1). One other general was similarly investigated by the Fiscalía, in 1999, for failing to stop a paramilitary massacre in Mapiripán (Meta) that took place in 1997. The civilian court system sent the case to the military court for trial. In 2001, the general was convicted and sentenced to forty years in prison. This action represented the first conviction of a general for human-rights violations (*El Espectador*, July 24, 2001: A1).

After a decade of minimal but important advances in laying the foundation for constructing a more legal state, the pendulum began to swing back during the final year of Pastrana's four-year term. In August 2001, in the face of declining support for the peace process and a steady increase in military actions and violations of international humanitarian law by all the armed actors, President Pastrana signed into law the Security and National Defense Bill. This "antiterrorist" measure was passed in part because of growing complaints by the armed forces and their allies that the new human-rights laws and institutions were hindering their ability to prosecute the law. The bill once again strengthened military justice and judicial autonomy and subordinated civilian officials within specific emergency zones that could be declared to confront terrorism. United Nations human-rights officials declared that several of the law's provisions were in direct violation of Colombia's international treaty commitments. Soon thereafter, Colombia's Constitutional Court declared the bill unconstitutional, a seeming victory for the rule of law.

However, by 2002 public opinion had turned against the government's approach to peace and war. In February 2002, the peace process with the FARC finally collapsed and President Pastrana ordered troops to retake the demilitarized zone that had been established three years earlier to facilitate negotiations. As the race to succeed Pastrana moved into full gear, the independent presidential candidate, Alvaro Uribe Vélez, who had consistently advocated a hard-line position against the insurgents, raced ahead in the polls. In the May balloting, Uribe won an unprecedented first-round victory and prepared to assume office in August of that year. Once in office, he immediately declared a "State of Internal Commotion," the emergency powers still available to the president under the 1991 constitution. With this special authority, Uribe once again authorized the armed forces to assume extraordinary powers, including the power to arrest, detain, and search without judicial authority or oversight, within specially designated "Zonas de Rehabilitación y Consolidación," or rehabilitation and consolidation zones. In these special zones, elected civilian officials would also be subordinate to the local military commander. By subsuming this authority within the constitutionally sanctioned "State of Internal Commotion," and by providing a detailed explanation outlining the need for emergency rules in these specially designated zones of violence, Uribe was able to circumvent most of the constitutional objections raised earlier by the Constitutional Court.

The first "rehabilitation zones" were established in the oil-producing *departamento* of Arauca, as well as in the most conflictive zones around the oil pipeline that connects the Arauca oil fields to ports on the Atlantic coast (see Resolución 129 sobre Zonas de Rehabilitación y Consolidación, on http://www.presidencia.gov.co/documentos/septiem/reso lucionzonas.htm). The series of events beginning with Pastrana's ill-fated Security and National Defense Bill and culminating in Uribe's Zonas de Rehabilitación y Consolidación follows a long-established pattern in Colombia's conflictive history of war making, civilian oversight, and the establishment of the rule of law: as violence mounts and state authority is challenged, the enfeebled political system delegates extraordinary powers to the military and undercuts the judicial authority of the state. Despite a decade of steadily incorporating international human rights and international humanitarian law protections into Colombian law, this pattern persisted as Colombia entered the twenty-first century.

AMNESTY, INJUSTICE, AND THE SEARCH FOR THE WAR'S END

While sectors of Colombia's fractious state and society made war, others attempted to search for a negotiated end to the armed conflict. Since 1953, the principal legal instrument to promote national reconciliation had been the granting of amnesty to combatants and pardons to those imprisoned for political reasons. The regular granting of amnesties was influenced by a particularly Catholic notion of *perdón y olvido* (pardon and forget) that firmly took root in Colombia. Amnesties effectively suspended and barred most investigations or prosecutions of human-rights violations and war crimes by state authorities, rebels, or paramilitary groups.

Despite the repeated use of amnesties in Colombia, they have not led to peace, but have proved instead to be a form of impunity granted to war criminals and human-rights violators. Despite talk of reforms at key historical junctures, each effort at national reconciliation has failed to address the institutional, social, and regional causes of violence. The result has been that amnesty has not contributed to national reconciliation, but has left unhealed scars of hatred and revenge. Each amnesty has left a palpable sense of injustice that has proved to be the midwife of the next phase of violence.

The first policies to reduce the violence at the height of the initial period known as La Violencia, in 1953, represented the beginning of a cycle that has lasted into the twenty-first century: insurgency, amnesty, nominal social investment in the zones of violence, assassination or political marginalization of former insurgents, renewed insurgency (Molano 1978). This pattern occurred following amnesties in 1954, 1958, 1982, 1990, and 1994 (see table 7.2). In each case, former insurgents were amnestied, leaders were subsequently assassinated, rehabilitation of zones proved inadequate, insurgencies reappeared.

Former guerrillas and other political actors were gunned down following each of the amnesties, creating a long list of secular martyrs who have been memorialized in plays, songs, and partisan memory.[14] Following the 1982 amnesty and pardons, for example, political leaders of both the M-19 and the EPL were assassinated. The amnesties had been granted at the outset of the peace process and were designed to pave the way for a ceasefire and political talks. The political assassinations torpedoed those talks and both groups soon resumed fighting. Most notoriously, when the FARC founded the UP political party in 1985 after signing a ceasefire agreement with the government a year earlier, over two thousand UP officials and followers were subsequently assassinated. These included two presidential candidates, three senators, three members of the House of Representatives, six departmental deputies, eighty-nine town councilmen, nine mayors, and many more local candidates.

In 1990, when the M-19 signed a definitive peace agreement with the government and laid down their arms, their amnestied leader, Carlos Pizarro, was assassinated while campaigning for president. In that same election, the UP's candidate, Bernardo Jaramillo Ossa, was also assassi-

TABLE 7.2   AMNESTIES AND PARDONS IN
COLOMBIA

Year	Instrument	President	Groups Receiving Pardon
1953	Amnesty and pardon	General Gustavo Rojas Pinilla	Armed forces
1954	Amnesty and pardon	General Gustavo Rojas Pinilla	Liberal guerrillas (principally from the Llanos Orientales)
1958	Suspension of judicial actions	Alberto Lleras Camargo (Liberal; first National Front president)	Liberal guerrillas, Conservative paramilitaries *(pájaros)*—limited to the *departamentos* of Caldas, Cauca, Huila, Tolima, and Valle del Cauca
1980	Amnesty	Julio César Turbay Ayala (Liberal)	Revolutionary guerrillas who had first surrendered to authorities. Very few guerrillas accepted this condition.
1982	Amnesty and pardon	Belisario Betancur (Conservative)	Revolutionary guerrillas: M-19, ADO (Autodefensa Obrera; Workers' Self-Defense Group), EPL, ELN, FARC
1990	Amnesty and pardon	Virgilio Barco (Liberal)	M-19, EPL, MRQL, PRT (Partido Revolucionario de Trabajadores; Workers' Revolutionary Party)
1994	Amnesty and pardon	César Gaviria (Liberal)	Corriente de Renovación Socialista of the ELN, urban militias of Medellín

SOURCE: Author's research.

nated, as was as the Liberal candidate, Luís Carlos Galán, who had only recently reentered the party after leading a dissident faction throughout the 1980s.

The EPL experienced a similar fate when its leaders signed a definitive peace accord with the government in 1990. After demobilizing, the guerrillas founded a new political party with the same EPL initials, standing for Esperanza, Paz, y Libertad (Hope, Peace, and Liberty). Yet as soon as they handed in their arms, they faced a campaign of extermination, particularly in the banana region on the northern coast of Urabá. While they had agreed to lay down their arms and participate in democratic politics, their enemies had not. Among their enemies were paramilitaries deeply linked to the region's landowners and the military, and also a small faction of the EPL guerrillas, now aligned with the FARC, that had refused to hand in their arms and that began targeting their former comrades-in-arms (Comisión de Superación de la Violencia 1992).

In 1998, President Pastrana (1998–2002) initiated another round of negotiations with the FARC. To facilitate the negotiations, Pastrana authorized a *zona de despeje,* or "demilitarized zone," under FARC control. The *despeje* covered five municipalities in Caquetá and Meta, equal in size to Switzerland. The two sides agreed that negotiations would take place without ending the hostilities outside the special zone; cease-fire and amnesty would be deferred to later stages in the process. The FARC also conditioned all talks on the government's willingness to combat the paramilitaries.

Between 1998 and 2001, the two sides agreed to a twelve-point negotiating agenda covering major political, economic, social, and institutional reforms. The issues of the judicial system and the role of the armed forces, as well as historical issues of agrarian reform and exploitation of natural resources, were part of the agenda. But as the 2002 election campaign heated up, it was clear that the two sides would not make headway on the agenda and much of civil society was clamoring for greater action to stem the violence.

In February 2002, the FARC hijacked a regional airliner and kidnapped and killed a prominent congressman. Under great pressure, Pastrana declared the peace process over and ordered the army to move into FARC-held zones, including the *despeje* zone. The dramatic collapse of the peace process reinforced the public's long-standing frustration with Pastrana's peace efforts and strengthened the presidential candidacy of the hard-line opposition candidate, Alvaro Uribe Vélez.

However, the premature end of the negotiations and the return to war only deferred a central question that had been ignored during the three years of the peace process: how would the actors in conflict be reincorporated into the political system if agreements were reached? Would war criminals be held accountable and would they be brought to justice? Both sides apparently assumed that the old model of pardon and amnesty would simply be implemented at the proper time.

Peace processes in other countries underscore the need for truth commissions, even if such commissions leave certain issues unresolved (see Payne, chapter 6 in this book). Priscilla Hayner, who studied truth commissions from a comparative and cross-regional perspective, wrote: "There are certain basic assumptions that are widely shared: that ending impunity requires justice in the courts, that establishing the truth about past abuses helps a society put the past behind it, that reconciliation—either individual or societal—is dependent on a full knowledge of atrocities committed on both sides" (Hayner 1999: 363).

In Colombia, the long history of granting amnesties as an instrument of peace demonstrated that the model of historical forgetting—*perdón y olvido*—was not viable. The armed antagonists did not forget, no one was held accountable, and the violence persisted.

The application of traditional Colombian models of amnesty is further complicated by the evolution of international human-rights and humanitarian law. Beginning with the Pinochet precedent in 1998, when a Spanish judge sought the extradition of the former Chilean dictator to stand trial in Spain, international courts began to rule that certain human-rights violations have universal jurisdiction and can be pursued in courtrooms in any country (Human Rights Watch 1998b). These norms apply to violations that rise to the level of crimes against humanity or that are covered by international treaties such as those on torture, genocide, or war crimes. Also in 1998, 160 nations signed a treaty creating an international criminal court that will formalize and codify such practices; the court began operating in July 2002. Colombia signed and ratified the treaty, though in a controversial move, the Pastrana administration elected to defer its application in Colombia for a period of seven years.

Throughout Latin America, earlier policies of amnesties are being called into question. Argentine courts ruled in 2002 that previous amnesties covering certain human-rights violations perpetrated by military officials during the brutal authoritarian government that ruled from 1976 to 1983 were not valid under international law. The Inter-American Court of Human Rights invalidated a similar amnesty granted in Peru.

In this new environment, amnesty will be much more problematic in Colombia than it was in the past. Colombia's armed political antagonists will need to address the issue of amnesty within a much broader context of accountability and justice. This new exigency, rather than making peace a more distant reality, may be the key ingredient to end the cycles of amnesty, rehabilitation, and war that have defined Colombian politics for more than fifty years.

NOTES

1. The first period gave rise to studies on La Violencia, producing a number of classic books. See Oquist 1978; and Guzmán Campos, Fals Borda, and Umaña

Luna 1980. In the second period, studies emerged on the National Front and vi-
olence: Leal 1984; Alape 1985; Lara 1986; and Hartlyn 1988. The final phase
gave rise to multiple, sometimes contradictory analyses. Human-rights groups
emphasized the critical situation of human rights: see, for example, Comisión
Andina de Juristas 1993; and Human Rights Watch 1993, 2000. Many North
American authors overemphasized the role of the drug trade. See Bagley and
Walker (1994) and Jordan (1999), or, from a policy perspective, Rabassa and
Chalk (2001).

2. O'Donnell describes the legal state as follows:

> Insofar as most of the formally enacted law existing in a territory is issued
> and backed by the state, and as state institutions themselves are supposed
> to act according to legal rules, we should recognize (as continental Euro-
> pean theorists have known and Anglo-Saxon ones ignored) that the
> legal system is a constitutive part of the state. As such, what I call the
> "legal state," i.e. the part of the state that is embodied in a legal system,
> penetrates and textures society, furnishing a basic element of stability to
> social relations. (O'Donnell 1999: 313)

O'Donnell goes on to say that in Latin America the "legal state" is generally limited or absent.

3. The National Front constitutionally divided power equally between the
Liberals and Conservatives throughout the executive, legislative, and judicial
branches of government at the national, regional, and local levels. The presidency was alternated between the two parties every four years for a period of sixteen years, beginning in 1958. The National Front prohibited third parties from
participating in electoral politics. After 1974, third parties were allowed to compete, although constitutional reforms gave preference to the two traditional parties, which continued to marginalize other parties. Although the National Front
was initially designed to be in place for twelve years, it was then extended to sixteen years and ultimately became the dominant framework for governance until
the 1991 constitution.

4. The principal "independent republics" were, besides Marquetalia: Rio
Chiquito (Cauca and Huila), El Pato (Caquetá), Guayabero (Meta), Alto Suma-
paz (Cundinamarca), Alto Ariari (Meta), and El Duda (Meta). For a detailed account of these zones, see the work of José Jairo González Arias (1992).

5. In 1970, former president Gustavo Rojas Pinilla launched a populist campaign for president, despite the prohibition on non–National Front candidates.
As votes were being tallied on election day, April 19, Rojas was leading the
official candidates. Radio and television broadcasts were soon suspended. When
they returned to the airwaves the following day, the official candidate, Misael
Pastrana, had won the election. The April 19th Movement, or M-19, was
founded by disaffected followers of Rojas Pinilla, together with dissident members of the FARC seeking to create a more urban movement.

6. Father Camilo Torres, a sociologist and priest, joined the ELN in 1965
but died in combat only months after joining the guerrillas in the mountains.

7. If levels of violence in each *departamento* are categorized by the number
of homicides per one hundred thousand, as opposed to absolute numbers, an
additional trend emerges in the regional distribution of violence: in the 1990s,

violence escalated in the newly colonized zones; in the areas mostly east of the Andes; or in the intermontane regions, known in Colombia as the agricultural frontier. Using this criterion, newer *departamentos* such as Guaviare, Casanare, and Putumayo join the list of the most violent. Guaviare and Putumayo are coca-growing areas. Casanare is an oil-producing zone.

8. The continuity of the Colombian violence is most poignantly underscored through the life of Manuel Marulanda Vélez, who in the year 2001 celebrated his seventy-first birthday, still leader of the nation's largest guerrilla movement, the FARC (see Alape 1989).

9. Such figures place Colombia among the most violent countries in the world, with a per capita homicide rate surpassed in 2000 only by El Salvador and South Africa, according to the World Health Organization (http://ww3.who .int/whosis/).

10. The causal relationship between political violence and crime can be observed in other countries as well. In South Africa and in El Salvador, violence actually increased after the peace settlements in the 1990s, because political violence had weakened the legal state. Crime rates and social violence soared in the postconflict period in both countries.

11. According to an interview with former Fiscal General (Prosecutor-General) Alfonso Gómez Méndez, this figure appeared to have improved somewhat by 2000. However, using his methodology that cites an increased reporting of crimes, the overall impunity rate would still hover at about 91 percent (Gómez Méndez 2000).

12. International treaties that were ratified and subsequent adjustments to Colombia's judicial system include:

- Geneva Conventions of 1949 and Additional Protocol II of 1977;
- Law 424 of 1998, which ratifies the authority of all international treaties signed by Colombia;
- reform of the Colombian military penal code, delineating areas of jurisdiction between military and ordinary justice;
- the finding of the Superior Judicial Council, Disciplinary Section (Consejo Superior de la Judicatura, Sala Jurisdiccional Disciplinaria), on July 21, 2000, which establishes civilian jurisdiction for human-rights violations and crimes committed by military and police outside of their legally sanctioned duties;
- reform of the Colombian penal code, which introduces the crimes of "forced disappearance," "forced displacement," "genocide," and "torture."

13. Other judicial institutions created in the 1991 constitution were the Constitutional Court, designed to resolve conflicts arising over basic rights, and the Superior Judicial Council, to oversee the court system. At the same time, the new constitution created the right of *tutela,* which made available an innovative mechanism whereby any citizen could petition any judge at any time if she or he believed that her or his constitutional rights were being violated. Despite these reforms, the redesigned system of justice was implemented unevenly and incompletely. Over the next ten years these reforms and new judicial institutions were unable to overcome the weak and fragmented legal state or to stanch the continued escalation of the armed conflict. Impunity for political crimes did not

decline and state actors that violated human rights were only minimally prosecuted or held accountable. Many of the pre-1991 problems that led to the reforms remained intractable, including limited access to justice, high rates of impunity for all crimes, extreme delays and congestion within the court system, excessive pretrial detention, inefficiency, and corruption (Corporación Excelencia en la Justicia 1998).

14. For example, one of Bogotá's most important political theater groups, the Teatro de la Candelaria, regularly performed *Guadelupe: Años sin cuenta,* a play written by Sergio García and Arturo Alape, which won the famous Cuban Casa de las Américas award for best play. The story is about the assassination of Liberal guerrilla Guadelupe Salcedo, the leader of the Liberal guerrillas of the eastern plains (Los Llanos Orientales) in 1954. Salcedo was assassinated after meeting with government leaders in Bogotá and after declaring his support for those Liberal guerrillas who did not hand in their arms. The flood of assassinations of amnestied guerrillas in the 1980s and 1990s followed a similar pattern.

REFERENCES

Alape, Arturo. 1985. *La paz, la violencia: Testigos de excepción.* Santafé de Bogotá: Planeta.
————. 1989. *Las vidas de Pedro Antonio Marín, Manuel Marulanda Vélez, Tirofijo.* Santafé de Bogotá: Planeta.
Alto Comisionado de las Naciones Unidas para los Derechos Humanos, Oficina en Colombia. 2000. *Informe de Actividades.* Santafé de Bogotá: Alto Comisionado de las Naciones Unidas para los Derechos Humanos (April).
Bagley, Bruce Michael, and William O. Walker, III, eds. 1994. *Drug Trafficking in the Americas.* New Brunswick, N.J.: Transaction Publishers.
Cañón M., Luis. 1994. *El patrón—vida y muerte de Pablo Escobar.* Santafé de Bogotá: Planeta.
Chernick, Marc W. 1991. "Insurgency and Negotiations: Defining the Boundaries of the Political Regime in Colombia." Ph.D. diss., Department of Political Science, Columbia University.
————. 1998. "The Paramilitarization of the War in Colombia." *NACLA Report on the Americas* 31, no. 5 (March–April): 28–33.
————. 1999. "Negotiating Peace amid Multiple Forms of Violence: The Protracted Search for a Settlement to the Armed Conflicts in Colombia." In Cynthia J. Arnson, ed., *Comparative Peace Processes in Latin America,* pp. 159–200. Washington, D.C., and Stanford, Calif.: Woodrow Wilson Center and Stanford University Press.
Chernick, Marc W., and Michael Jiménez. 1993. "Popular Liberalism, Radical Democracy, and Marxism: Leftist Politics in Contemporary Colombia." In *The Latin American Left,* ed. Barry Carr and Steve Ellner, pp. 61–81. Boulder, Colo.: Westview Press and the Latin American Bureau.
CINEP and Justicia y Paz, Banco de Datos de Violencia Política. 2002. *Noche y Niebla.* Santafé de Bogotá: CINEP and Justicia y Paz.

Cohdes (Consultoría para el Desplazamiento Forzado y los Derechos Humanos) and Unicef Colombia. 1999. *Un país que huye—Desplazamiento y violencia en una nación fragmentada.* Santafé de Bogotá.

Comisión Andina de Juristas, Seccional Colombiana. 1990. *Sistema judicial y derechos humanos en Colombia.* Santafé de Bogotá: Comisión Andina de Juristas.

———. 1993. *Autores de atentados contra la vida por razones políticas.* Santafé de Bogotá: Comisión Andina de Juristas. January–September.

Comisión de Superación de la Violencia. 1992. *Pacificar la paz.* Santafé de Bogotá: CINEP, Iepria, Comisión Andina de Juristas.

Consejería para los Derechos Humanos. Presidency of the Republic of Colombia. 1991. Santafé de Bogotá: Presidencia de la República de Colombia.

Corporación Excelencia en la Justicia. 1998. *Justicia para el nuevo siglo: Aportes a la agenda de Gobierno, 1998–2002.* Santafé de Bogotá: Corporación Excelencia en la Justicia.

Departamento Nacional de Planeación. 1998. "Los costos económicos de la criminalidad y la violencia en Colombia." *Archivos de Macroeconomía* (March 10).

Echandía Castilla, Camilo. 1999. *El conflicto armado y las manifestaciones de violencia en las regiones de Colombia.* Santafé de Bogotá: Presidencia de la República de Colombia, Oficina del Alto Comisionado para la Paz.

Giraldo, Javier. 1996. *Colombia: The Genocidal Democracy.* Monroe, Me.: Common Courage Press.

Giraldo, Javier, and Santiago Camargo. 1984. "Paros y movimientos cívicos en Colombia." Serie Controversia 128. Santafé de Bogotá: CINEP.

Gómez Méndez, Alfonso. 2000. "Estamos doblegando la impunidad." *Cambio* (Santafé de Bogotá), no. 373 (August 14–21): 26–27.

González Arias, José Jairo. 1992. *El estigma de las Repúblicas Independientes, 1955–1965.* Santafé de Bogotá: CINEP.

González Arias, José Jairo, et al. 1998. *Conflictos regionales Amazonía y Orinoquía.* Santafé de Bogotá: IEPRI y FESCOL.

Guerrero, Javier. 1991. *Los años del olvido: Boyacá y los orígenes de la Violencia.* Santafé de Bogotá: Tercer Mundo Editores y IEPRI.

Gúzman Campos, Germán, Orlando Fals Borda, and Eduardo Umaña Luna. 1980. *La Violencia en Colombia.* Vols. 1 and 2. Santafé de Bogotá: Carlos Valencia Editores.

Hartlyn, Jonathan. 1988. *The Politics of Coalition Rule in Colombia.* Cambridge: Cambridge University Press.

Hayner, Priscilla B. 1999. "In Pursuit of Justice and Reconciliation: Contributions of Truth Telling." In *Comparative Peace Processes in Latin America,* ed. Cynthia J. Arnson, pp. 363–84. Washington, D.C., and Stanford, Calif.: Woodrow Wilson Center and Stanford University Press.

Hernández, Milton.1998. *Rojo y negro: Aproximación a la historia del ELN.* Santafé de Bogotá: Nueva Colombia.

Human Rights Watch/Americas. 1993. *State of War: Political Violence and Counterinsurgency in Colombia.* New York: Human Rights Watch.

———. 1998a. *War without Quarter: Colombia and International Humanitarian Law.* New York: Human Rights Watch.

———. 1998b. *The Pinochet Precedent: How Victims Can Pursue Human Rights Criminals Abroad.* New York: Human Rights Watch.

———. 2000. "Colombia—the Ties That Bind: Colombia and Military-Paramilitary Links." Vol. 12, no. 1 (B) (February).

Jaramillo, Jaime Eduardo, Leónidas Mora, and Fernando Cubides. 1986. *Colonización, coca, y guerrilla.* Santafé de Bogotá: Universidad Nacional de Colombia.

Jordan, David C. 1999. *Drug Politics: Dirty Money and Democracies.* Norman: University of Oklahoma Press.

Lara, Patricia. 1986. *Siembra vientos y recogerás tempestades: La historia del M-19, sus protagonistas y sus destinos.* Santafé de Bogotá: Planeta.

Leal, Francisco. 1984. *Estado y política en Colombia.* Santafé de Bogotá: Siglo XXI Editores.

Lucio, Ramiro. 1989. "Anapo and Anapo socialista." In Gustavo Gallón Giraldo, comp., *Entre movimientos y caudillos: 50 años de bipartidismo, izquierda, y alternativas populares en Colombia,* pp. 91–97. Santafé de Bogotá: CINEP and CEREC.

Marulanda V., Manuel. 1973. *Cuadernos de campaña.* Santafé de Bogotá: Ediciones CEIS.

Medina Gallego, Carlos. 1990. *Autodefensas, paramilitares, y narcotráfico en Colombia: Orígen, desarrollo, y consolidación. El caso puerto Boyacá.* Santafé de Bogotá: Editorial Documentos Periodísticos.

———. 1996. *ELN: Una historia contada a dos voces.* Santafé de Bogotá: Rodriguéz Quito Editores.

Medina Gallego, Carlos, and Mireya Téllez Ardila. 1994. *La violencia parainstitucional y parapolicial en Colombia.* Santafé de Bogotá: Rodriguéz Quito Editores.

Molano, Alfredo. 1978. "Amnistía y violencia." *Controversia,* nos. 86–87. Santafé de Bogotá: CINEP.

———. 1987. *Selva adentro.* Santafé de Bogotá: El Áncora Editores.

Moser, Caroline. 2000. "Violence in Colombia: Building Sustainable Peace and Social Capital." In Andrés Solimano, ed., *Colombia: Essays on Conflict, Peace, and Development,* pp. 9–77. Washington, D.C.: World Bank.

O'Donnell, Guillermo. 1999. "Polyarchies and the (Un)Rule of Law in Latin America: A Partial Conclusion." In *The (Un)Rule of Law and the Underprivileged in Latin America,* ed. Juan E. Méndez, Guillermo O'Donnell, and Paulo Sérgio Pinheiro, pp. 303–37. Notre Dame, Ind.: Notre Dame University Press.

Oquist, Paul. 1978. *Violencia, conflicto, y política en Colombia.* Santafé de Bogotá: Instituto de Estudios Colombianos.

Puyana, Alicia, and Rosemary Thorp. 1998. *Colombia: Economía política de las expectativas petroleras.* Santafé de Bogotá: Tercer Mundo, FLACSO/Mexico, and IEPRI.

Rabassa, Angel, and Peter Chalk. 2001. *Colombian Labyrinth: The Synergy of Drugs and Insurgency and Its Implication for Regional Stability.* Santa Monica, Calif.: Rand Corporation.

Republic of Colombia. Ministry of National Defense. 2001. *Annual Human Rights and International Humanitarian Law Report, 2000.* Santafé de Bogotá: Ministry of National Defense.

Reyes, Alejandro. 1997. "Compra de tierra por narcotraficantes." In Francisco Thoumi et al., eds., *Drogas ilícitas en Colombia,* pp. 279–346. Santafé de Bogotá: Ariel, Naciones Unidas–PNUD, Ministerio de Justicia, Dirección Nacional de Estupefacientes.

Rubio, Mauricio. 1996. "Crimen sin sumario." Santafé de Bogotá: CEDE, Universidad de los Andes.

Salazar, Alonso. 1990. *No nacimos pa'semilla.* Santafé de Bogotá: CINEP.

Salazar, Alonso, and Ana María Jaramillo. 1992. *Medellín: Las subculturas del narcotráfico.* Santafé de Bogotá: CINEP.

Tilly, Charles. 1975. "Revolutions and Collective Violence." In Fred I. Greenstein and Nelson W. Polsby, eds., *Handbook of Political Science,* vol. 3, pp. 483–556. Reading, Mass.: Addison-Wesley.

———. 1978. *From Mobilization to Revolution.* New York: Random House.

U.S. Department of State. 2001. *Country Report on Human Rights Practices, 2000* (February).

PART THREE

Democratization

The Promise of Justice and Its Limitations

CHAPTER EIGHT

Progressive Pragmatism as a Governance Model

An In-Depth Look at Porto Alegre, Brazil, 1989–2000

SYBIL DELAINE RHODES

GOVERNANCE MODELS IN THE 1980S AND 1990S

Neoliberalism, Latin America's dominant governance model in the 1980s and 1990s, often failed to have significant positive effects on social justice; in fact, its overall impact was negative in many areas. In this chapter, I argue that a promising alternative to the perceived, and real, injustices of neoliberal governance emerged at the municipal level in Brazil and several other countries during the same two decades. I call this new model progressive pragmatism. This model is derived from the general theory of pragmatic liberalism, which argues that democratic process and efficiency outcomes are equally important to good governance (Anderson 1990).

The core of progressive pragmatism in Latin America is, I argue, the specific combination of popular participation in government decisions with prudent fiscal policies. The emphasis on participatory democracy was developed in answer to the worldwide discrediting of socialism and communism. As the noted leftist intellectual Jorge Castañeda argues, the demise of the old models brought about new opportunities for the Latin American Left to compete in democratic elections on its own terms rather than in terms of Cold War conflicts (Castañeda 1993). In many cases, newly elected leftists relied upon existing grassroots organizations for support. In other instances, leftist officials actually learned to mobilize and empower previously unorganized people in the popular sectors.

Several scholars have analyzed the Brazilian Workers' Party's (PT; Partido dos Trabalhadores) especially notable success at promoting popular participation in the city of Porto Alegre during the 1990s. (See, especially, Fedozzi 1997; Baierle 1998; and Abers 2000.) Each of these works analyzes the importance of the emphasis on the grassroots to the regrouping of the Latin American Left after the Cold War and also links the case of Porto Alegre to general theories of participatory democracy.

In this chapter, I build upon their contributions by constructing a governance model that incorporates both the participatory budget process and policies founded upon technocratic expertise. I contend that in the 1980s and 1990s the Left learned a lesson from some of its neoliberal opponents: participatory governance only works well when there is also a commitment to sound fiscal policy. The remainder of the chapter explores the factors that led to the emergence of this combination in Porto Alegre and discusses the extent to which progressive pragmatism is a genuine option for governance throughout Latin America.

The Successes and Failures of Neoliberalism

Latin American citizens accepted neoliberalism as the primary governance model in the aftermath of the 1980s debt crisis for one primary reason: neoliberal policies ended the hyperinflation that had disrupted the lives and livelihoods of many poor and middle-class families. Alberto Fujimori in Peru, Carlos Saúl Menem in Argentina, and Fernando Henrique Cardoso in Brazil are some of the most important examples of neoliberals who courted popular sectors with the argument that their mode of governing was the only alternative to economic chaos. It became clear that the traditional Left, including populists and socialists, had underestimated the negative impact of hyperinflation and other effects of loose monetary policy and overspending on the poorer sectors of society. Neoliberals seized the opportunity to accuse their opponents, especially the Left, of not understanding the importance of fiscal and macroeconomic soundness.

Once economies were stabilized, neoliberalism's weak point often was its failure to combat poverty further or to improve the management of social policy in significant ways. It was no secret that neoliberalism was the preferred model of multinational corporations, international financial institutions, and the United States, and that neoliberal leaders were often more answerable to those actors than to citizens and domestic political institutions. Thus, neoliberalism was associated with a high level of concentration in the executive branch and other undemocratic practices. Witness Fujimori's self-coup, Menem's reliance on rule by decree, and the various instances of unconstitutional attempts at reelection.

The Exhaustion of Traditional Leftist Models

In addition to the rise of neoliberalism, the collapse of the communist bloc and the exhaustion of the import substitution industrialization (ISI) development model in Latin America challenged the political Left to search for new governance models in the 1980s and 1990s. State ownership of industry, protectionist measures, and other highly centralized policies were discredited. Latin American communist and socialist parties, along with traditional populists, stood little chance of winning widespread public support for their state-centered development paradigm and opaque, bureaucratic style of internal governance.

GREATER POSSIBILITIES FOR LOCAL GOVERNMENT

Few leftists were in power at the national level in Latin America, in any case. The Left thus found itself in the position of having to build political capital at the subnational level. During the same period, the trend toward political decentralization in Latin American countries provided greater opportunities for subnational governments to play a more active role in policy. City officials from different countries began to meet to exchange experiences and even formed international bodies such as Mercociudades ("the cities of Mercosur"). International financial institutions offered direct assistance to city or county governments. Nongovernmental organizations increasingly targeted their programs at the local level. By the end of the 1990s, there was unprecedented variation of performance and models of subnational governance in the region, particularly at the local or municipal level, and especially in Brazil.

Innovation in Porto Alegre

The Brazilian state of Rio Grande do Sul and its capital, Porto Alegre, have a history of opposition to national governments. (That opposition was less likely when the state's native sons, who have often been successful national politicians and included the populist hero Getúlio Vargas and the 1970s reformist general Ernesto Geisel, among others, were ruling the country.) During the presidential terms of Fernando Collor, Itamar Franco, and Fernando Henrique Cardoso, who were all essentially neoliberals, Porto Alegre became a showcase local government for the Latin American political Left under the leadership of the PT. The city was commended for its Participatory Budget program at the United Nations Habitat Conference in 1992. Porto Alegre achieved a major increase in its fiscal capacity, substantial improvements in infrastructure, and increased confidence in government in the period after 1989. At the same time, many of its policies were directed toward improving the lot of the poor and promoting popular participation in government decisions. More telling than the international prize is the overwhelming electoral support with which the city's citizens reelected the PT in every subsequent election for the remainder of the century.

Four conditions made the innovation in Porto Alegre possible. First, the Left was traditionally strong there; second, the city already had a fairly vibrant civil society, including active neighborhood associations and social movements; third, the relatively high socioeconomic level of the region meant that the municipal government had greater than average resources among Brazilian cities; fourth, and most importantly, I argue, the elected officials from the PT were politically ambitious and seized an opportunity to build political capital by showing that they and their party could govern effectively in a way that was distinct from neoliberalism.

THE ELECTORAL EMERGENCE OF THE PT

The strongest political force in Rio Grande do Sul prior to the 1964 coup was the populist party created by Getúlio Vargas. When the military regime of 1964–85 abolished existing parties and restructured the system in an attempt to consolidate its rule, the opposition Movimento Democrático Brasileiro (Brazilian Democratic Movement; MDB) maintained a majority in the Porto Alegre City Council. After the reliberalization of the party system, most of the former Vargas supporters left the MDB to form the Partido Democrático do Trabalho (Democratic Work Party; PDT), under the leadership of Leonel Brizola, the brother-in-law of deposed president João Goulart. Mayoral elections were held in state capitals in 1985, and the PDT's Alceu Collares easily won the election in Porto Alegre.

The combination of national economic crisis and poor management resulted in economic and political disaster for the Collares administration, however. The municipality was in debt but did not have good enough record keeping to distinguish among its creditors (Cassel and Verle 1994). Almost all or possibly more than all of its resources were spent on personnel, leaving no funds for investment. Citizens were disgruntled because of the national and local economic problems. The conditions of the 1988 mayoral elections were therefore favorable to new political forces.

The PT was well placed to fill the political vacuum left by Collares's departure. The party had been created by the new union movement in the heavily industrialized region of São Paulo in the 1970s. It was modeled after European labor and socialist parties rather than traditional Latin American populism. In addition to unions, the party also developed strong ties with social movements, neighborhood associations, and human-rights organizations, among others (see Keck 1992).

Rio Grande do Sul was the first region outside of the southeastern states of São Paulo and Rio de Janeiro where the PT won a good deal of support. In 1982, this region elected one city council member in Porto Alegre. The south quickly became the PT's most significant support base after the southeast. Nonetheless, the party remained a minor force in Rio Grande until the mayoral elections of 1988 (Passos and Noll 1996). The PT candidate, Olívio Dutra, won the mayorship that year, and the PT also increased its representation on the city council. The PDT won eleven of the twenty-nine council seats, followed by the PT with nine, the PMDB (the successor of the MDB) with five, and the Partido Democrático Social (Social Democratic Party; PDS) with four. PT candidate Tarso Genro, the vice mayor of the Dutra administration, won the next mayoral race, in 1992. Genro's victory marked the first time in the city's history that the incumbent party had succeeded at electing its own candidate for mayor. The composition of the council remained roughly the same as in 1988. The mayor elected in 1996 was Raul Pont, who had been vice mayor under Genro. The PT thus had a dramatic increase in support between 1985 and 1988, and then retained the mayorship and shared dominance of the city council with the PDT through the elections of 1992, 1996, and 2000.

Several PT leaders benefited from the political capital constructed in Porto Alegre and used it to advance beyond the municipal level. The first PT mayor of Porto Alegre, Olívio Dutra, won the governorship of the state of Rio Grande do Sul in 1998. Tarso Genro, elected mayor in 1992 and 2000, became a national political figure in the late 1990s. An intellectual, he began to publish essays criticizing the national government, and his name began to be mentioned in speculations about future Brazilian presidents.

The PT won the mayoral election in 1988 because the financial crisis had created a political vacuum. Once in office the party suffered an internal dilemma over whether it would target its traditional base of support or try to cast a broader net. Centrist elements triumphed over the more radical leftists, and the party opted to attempt to build a broader constituency. It implemented many policies that appealed to the middle classes, such as the renovation of the historic downtown market, the improvement of important roads, and increased environmental protection for the Guaíba River. The most striking aspects of the PT's municipal program, however, were the ways it increased citizen participation in government and turned around city finances.

POPULAR PARTICIPATION

Beginning with its first mayoral administration (that of Dutra), the PT developed a mechanism for community participation in the municipal budget process, called the Orçamento Participativo, or Participatory Budget program. The Dutra administration viewed this program as a form of direct democracy, an alternative to the centrist, bureaucratic models espoused by the traditional Left. Members of the administration also viewed it as an alternative to what they perceived as the technocratic and undemocratic neoliberalism of the national government. Finally, the Participatory Budget was an alternative to the clientelistic budget processes of the past under both democratic and military national regimes (Augustin 1994; Fedozzi 1997).

The PT, which had almost no experience in government at that time, developed the Participatory Budget mostly by trial and error. The program originated in the platform for the mayoralty of Porto Alegre, approved by the PT convention that nominated Dutra as a mayoral candidate. This platform called for the creation of popular councils, which would introduce elements of direct democracy into the mayoral administration. The plan was not very specific as to how to promote greater inclusion, an ambiguity that, along with the party's inexperience and the poor economic situation, made the Participatory Budget a clear failure in Mayor Dutra's first year in office.

The immediate reason for the initial failure was that the PT did not coordinate its fiscal policy with the Participatory Budget process (Cassel and Verle 1994). In 1989, the newly elected administration organized two rounds of discussions with the city, which it had divided into microregions. Each microregion elected representatives to plan the 1990 budget jointly with the municipal Planning Ministry. The first version of the Participatory Budget proposed a great number of public works, almost none of which, because of the disastrous situation of municipal finances, were actually implemented. This situation led to a high degree of tension between different branches of the mayoral administration. The Planning Ministry, in particular, was frustrated at what it viewed as the Participatory Budget's obliviousness to the need for financial prudence and good bookkeeping.

Outside the Planning Ministry, PT leaders considered the tension a result of a contradiction between the technical concerns of the Planning Ministry and the democratic nature of the Participatory Budget. To alleviate this problem, Mayor Dutra transferred the program the following year from the Planning Ministry to the Mayoral Office (the mayor's closest advisors). Because of the previous year's disappointing performance, a smaller number of people showed up for the meetings. Those who did appear selected sanitation and paving as their top priorities, and this time the budget was carried out in its entirety by the administration. In the following years, community participation in the Participatory Budget increased, and the *prefeitura* (mayoral administration) and city council continued to respect the popularly planned budget.

The scope of the Participatory Budget increased over time. At first the program was highly regional or local in content. Its main effect was to provide basic services to needy areas. A weighting system, based on such criteria as percentage of extremely poor inhabitants and overall population (and some others, which varied over the years), determined which neighborhoods were the priority for investments.

In 1994, the Genro administration began to hold five yearly thematic meetings, in addition to the sixteen regional ones. The thematic sessions were formed for the following categories: transportation; education, leisure, and culture; health and social services; economic development and taxation; and city organization and urban development. Each session elected delegates to sit with the regional delegates on the Participatory Budget Council. The thematic sessions, while open to everyone, generally involved participation by groups, such as labor unions, business entrepreneurs, and professional organizations, who were less likely to participate in the regional meetings. A leftist faction within the government, led by then vice mayor Raul Pont, called for corporatist-style organic participation of labor unions in the thematic sessions, but more moderate elements defeated this proposal. The thematic sessions introduced some elements of specific expertise into the planning process, while retaining the popular participation aspect.

The basic structure of the Participatory Budget remained the same throughout the decade. Regional assembly meetings, in which city administrators and participants review the investment plans of the previous year, are held early in the year. Several months later, the administration makes a presentation about revenue collection and the funds that will be available for investment in the following year. The regional sessions also rank their investment priorities for the year and elect delegates to sit on the Participatory Budget Council. This body discusses the executive administration's budget and develops the next investment plan according to the weighting system and the rankings of the regional assemblies. In the second semester of the year, the Participatory Budget Council follows the progress of the bill in the city council and discusses the details of implementation of the investment plan with the municipal bureaucracy.

In the late 1990s, a faction of party members attempted to introduce participation in the city administration. Up until then, the Participatory Budget had been limited mainly to investment spending, which constitutes a small portion of the budget. As in most Brazilian cities, however, the largest chunk of Porto Alegre's budget went to pay the salaries of personnel. These personnel costs generated tension within the party, which faced trade-offs between different factions of its traditional base of support—syndicates, public employees, and popular movements. During the Dutra administration, however, the Participatory Budget began to include personnel nomination as part of its responsibilities (jointly with the Sindicato Municipal de Porto Alegre, or SIMPA, the municipal employees' syndicate), giving the community direct control over the creation of new positions in public administration. The Tripartite Commission, as this organ was called, had representatives from the Participatory Budget Council, the mayoral office, and SIMPA. The latter was somewhat reluctant about participating. It was difficult for a PT mayor's office to attempt to cut personnel costs at the same time that the party was fighting administrative reform at the national level. The Pont administration initiated a project called the Internal Participatory Budget, the aim of which was to "democratize" relations within the government, which presumably would alleviate the struggle over personnel costs. This plan included such measures as the election, rather than appointment, of some department leaders and managers (Lucena 1997).

In addition to irresponsible spending, Brazilian municipal governments have traditionally suffered from "incrementalism," meaning that the present year's budget is formulated on the basis of the previous year's (Fedozzi 1997). Following this pattern, the original Participatory Budget involved only short-run planning. The Pont administration initiated what it called the Pluriannual Plan in 1996. The purpose of this four-year investment plan was to expose long- as well as short-term planning to the Participatory Budget process (Lucena 1997). Prospects for the long-term institutionalization of the Participatory Budget appear mixed, however. Between 1989 and 1992 the total number of people who attended planning sessions increased tenfold, but participation leveled off and even decreased in later years.

The PT also never managed to reach an agreement regarding the institutional structure of the Participatory Budget. It is unclear what would happen to the program if the PT no longer controlled the *prefeitura*. The secretary of planning during the Dutra administration, Clóvis Ilgenfritz da Silva, who first organized the Participatory Budget in 1989, left the government because of conflict between the technical problem of solving the city's severe economic crisis and the investment-oriented direct democracy of the budget process (Fedozzi 1997; Ilgenfritz da Silva 1997). Ilgenfritz favored a more regulated environment for community participation. Beginning in 1991, by which time he was a member of the city council, Ilgenfritz da Silva presented a bill to institutionalize and regulate the Participatory Budget (with the support of the civil-society organizations mentioned earlier), but he was unable to pass the bill into law. Disagreement about the bill centered around its legal implications for the role of the legislature, and probably also the knowledge that thus far there was no serious electoral challenge in the city to the PT. Party members who opposed the bill characterized the budget as an autonomous, self-regulating entity, belonging to the public, nonstate sphere *(esfera pública não estatal)* that did not require official recognition (Porto Alegre n.d.). The bill's supporters claimed that regulation was necessary both to keep the program from being dismantled by future non-PT administrations and to ease the tension between technical and democratic issues. Problems also arose with preexisting urban popular movements, which had traditionally been an important base of political support for the PT. Some well-established representatives of *vila* ("slum") residents claimed that the budget process was reducing their autonomy. Some of the movement leaders, accustomed to private or clientelistic negotiation for local benefits, did not favor the more universalistic, public process of the budget (Fedozzi 1997).

FISCAL RESPONSIBILITY

During the 1980s, Porto Alegre experienced a decline in investments and in public salaries (due to the national economic crisis), a decline in municipal tax collection (due in part to greater federal funding but also to governmental incompetence), and an increase in the number of public employees (due to the new patronage opportunities that accompanied the transition to democracy). The first PT mayoral administration successfully cleaned up the city's catastrophic financial situation and maintained a prudent fiscal policy. Such a feat is not uncommon for the first two years of a municipal administration in Brazil, but the fact that the Dutra administration did not follow up its sanitation efforts with two years of irresponsible spending is unusual (Utzig 1996). Although the administration spent its first two years cleaning up city finances, a lack of resources prevented it from keeping its campaign promises of investments that would favor the poorer segments of society. Although the *prefeitura* promoted meetings to develop the Participatory Budget, none of the community's suggestions were actually implemented. By the third year in office, however, the municipality was able to make available considerably more money for investments (chosen by the Participatory Budget), without incurring further debt. The Dutra administration achieved the financial reform by cutting spending, improving relations with creditors, and implementing a tax reform and a partial administrative reform. The administrations that followed (Genro and Pont) continued the policy of responsible finances.

Upon assuming office in January 1989, the municipal secretary of finance, João Verle, found that there were practially no data showing the financial situation of the city (Cassel and Verle 1994). The room for financial maneuvering in 1989 was extremely limited, given that the previous administration had determined the budget and the fiscal structure could not be changed legally. The salaries of municipal employees constituted 98 percent of the budget.

The administration's first move was to negotiate with creditors and suppliers to establish a schedule for the payment of debts, and it improved its credibility with creditors and suppliers by making this schedule available for public inspection. The administration also took out some short-term loans, which it repaid by mid-1990. Additionally, it underwent an internal audit.

The most significant achievement in the area of fiscal policy was the improved city income. The administration submitted fifteen tax bills to the city council in 1989, of which fourteen were approved. The most successful reform involved the urban property tax, the Imposto Predial e Territorial Urbano (IPTU). The PT reform made this tax much more progressive, increasing the number of brackets for buildings and urban lots, and increasing the onus on the latter. It also improved collection of the Imposto sobre Serviços de Qualquer Natureza (ISSQN), a service tax. Of several other new taxes created, only one or two remained active for more than a year or so, but between 1989 and 1992 the percentage of the city's income due to local tax collection increased from 47.9 percent to 59.1 percent (Cassel and Verle 1994). As part of the strategy to persuade the public to accept the tax reform, the Dutra administration promised that income from the property tax would be used to fund investment rather than to pay for salaries or debt.

In addition to making tax collection more progressive and increasing the general tax rate, the PT also greatly reduced municipal tax evasion, which was previously a serious problem. In a new approach, the administration adopted the principle of no tax amnesty as one of its formal pledges, claiming that two previous amnesties by the Collares administration had only encouraged tax evasion. It published a list of debtors to the city in local newspapers to shame them publicly into paying what they owed (rather than threatening them, which would have been illegal).

Upon entering office, the PT encountered administrative difficulties that were as bad as or worse than the problems with tax collection. In December 1988, upon leaving office, the Collares administration had passed a law that increased municipal employees' salaries almost threefold and provided for bisemester readjustments. Although the economic crisis had resulted in lower salaries for public employees nationwide (the real salary of the lowest-paid municipal employees in December 1988 was 62.31 percent of what it had been in 1985), the municipality's budget was still overloaded by the demands of its payroll (Lucena 1997). In June 1990 the Dutra administration implemented a law that provided for bimonthly adjustment of salaries to keep up with inflation as long as expenditure on personnel did not exceed 75 percent of current account spending—an administrative reform that actually provided employees with an effective raise. The same basic policy on salaries was maintained by the Genro and Pont administrations. In the 1990s, almost no other Brazilian municipality provided a twice-monthly adjustment; some provided them monthly and others less regularly. All three administrations, however, experienced problems with the employees' union, SIMPA. The Pont administration had especially bad relations with SIMPA, which picketed city hall to complain about low salaries.

Albeit at the cost of poor relations with city employees, the PT achieved the best economic policy in Porto Alegre in at least fifty years, without having to cut the administrative apparatus. All three PT administrations managed to reduce the percentage of the budget devoted to salaries and to maintain this percentage close to the constitutional limit of 60 percent (officially imposed by the national Congress in 1997). This reduction was achieved mainly through increases in revenue rather than through spending cuts. There was no actual reduction of the size of the state.

The implementation of a progressive tax program, coupled with responsible spending, marked a real shift in the city of Porto Alegre's priorities. The middle class received tangible benefits (the brightly colored downtown market area and better transportation) for its tax monies, but that money also subsidized basic infrastructure in slums and peripheral areas. At the same time, the PT managed to direct more government spending toward the social arena. In 1985, the municipality spent 13 percent of its budget on education and health: by 1995, it spent 36 percent (Porto Alegre 1996). Another clear trend of the PT's administrative policy was that it increased attention to social services, especially health, relative to other kinds of government employment. Improved fiscal policies made redistribution possible and also improved overall governmental performance.

PORTO ALEGRE AS A "PROGRESSIVE PRAGMATIC" GOVERNANCE MODEL

Developing sound fiscal policy and promoting popular participation were the twin pillars of the PT's electoral success. The party attempted to draw attention to this success by choosing Porto Alegre as the meeting place for leaders of the Forum da Esquerda Latinoamericana (Forum of the Latin American Left) in the 1990s. Party members also used Porto Alegre's success to build political capital at the state and national level. In 1998 ex-mayor Dutra was elected governor of Rio Grande do Sul, and ex-mayor Genro became a serious contender for the PT presidential candidacy (although he lost to the party leader, Inácio "Lula" de Silva).

Most scholarly accounts, as well as the PT's own propaganda, emphasize the Participatory Budget more than the fiscal achievements of the three mayoral administrations (see, for example, Baierle 1998 and Abers 2000). Although greater participation characterizes many other municipal governments run by the PT, none of these have the same showcase quality. Again, the difference in Porto Alegre was the combination of a sustained fiscal turnaround and the emphasis on popular participation.

What made this combination possible in Porto Alegre, and not elsewhere in Brazil? The socioeconomic structure of the municipality was surely a contributing factor. Southern Brazil is generally much richer and has a more equal distribution of wealth than the northern and western parts of the country. In 1994, the state of Rio Grande do Sul's gross product ranked fifth in the country. The state's per capita income of nearly five thousand U.S. dollars was one thousand dollars over the national average. Porto Alegre is consistently cited as one of the most desirable Brazilian cities in which to live. The city's relative wealth contributed to the PT's successful fiscal reform, particularly with regard to the service tax. By definition, poorer municipalities with lower tax bases must be more dependent upon federal and state transfers.

While structural factors were more favorable to the success of progressive pragmatism in Porto Alegre than elsewhere, they were not the impetus for the idea. Porto Alegre was wealthier and more equitable than most of the rest of Brazil *prior* to the emergence of the PT. For most of the century, its major political tendency was caudillo-style populism. The key explanation of the development of progressive pragmatism as an alternative was the triumph of neoliberalism as the dominant political model in the country as a whole. Socialism and populism were no longer attractive options. New leftist leaders created progressive pragmatism as a way of showing they could govern more responsibly than neoliberals, without abandoning their ideals about social justice.

CYCLES OF GOVERNANCE IN LATIN AMERICA

We may distinguish generally among models of governance in Latin America by the importance they attach to two variables: degree of financial or fiscal responsibility and level of inclusion or participation of the masses. Clientelism is associated with low levels of fiscal responsibility and low levels of popular participation; populism with low levels of fiscal responsibility and high levels of popular participation; and liberalism

with high levels of fiscal responsibility and low levels of popular participation. The remaining combination of high levels of both fiscal responsibility and popular participation—which I refer to as progressive
pragmatism—does not correspond to any well-known model of governance in the region.

Surprisingly few other broad and systematic analyses of forms of governance exist in the political science literature about Latin America. Weyland (1995) develops a typology of models of democracy based upon the
degree to which the organization of citizens is predominantly bottom-up
or top-down and upon the degree of "special weight" given to social
movements or interest organizations. While this typology captures the
variations of participation with greater specificity than the one I propose,
it leaves out the dimension of fiscal policy. Mechanisms such as the Participatory Budget are true innovations in governance that may overcome
the democratic deficits in neoliberalism, and comprehensive frameworks
such as Weyland's may be quite helpful for understanding and implementing them. Yet economic policy and performance are so central to citizens' views of their governors, and so often the central focus of political
debate in Latin America, that including an economic dimension adds
much to the power of an analytic framework for studying governance.

The PT implemented participatory budget programs—with varying
levels of success—in other cities as it began to win more mayorships in
Brazil toward the end of the twentieth century. The PT was not the only
Brazilian political party, however, that responded to the challenge of neoliberalism with increased appeals to democratic participation. Other parties, including the centrist Partido da Social Democracia Brasileira (Party
of Brazilian Social Democracy; PSDB) and PMDB, started to copy the
participatory budget, with varying degrees of success. Political leaders
in the state of Ceará created another showcase example of governance
by increasing participation and technocratic expertise (see Tendler
1997)—a success that launched the national political career of 1998 and
2002 presidential contender Ciro Gomes.

During the heyday of neoliberalism, leftist parties all over Latin America searched for innovative ways to build political capital at the local
level. Mayoral administrations in the neighboring cities of Montevideo,
Uruguay, and Buenos Aires, Argentina, for example, when governed by
left-leaning parties in the mid-'90s, looked to Porto Alegre for guidance
in developing programs. And in other countries in the region, ranging
from Mexico and El Salvador to Peru and Chile, urban-based participatory programs were also introduced, with varying degrees of success.
Comparative in-depth studies could reveal conditions under which suc-

cessful participation programs are associated with improvements in fiscal capacity. Meanwhile, the election of the PT's "Lula" to the Brazilian presidency in 2002, based on a campaign stressing democratic participation along with prudent economic policy, may usher in changes at the national level as well that, if successfully implemented, will also serve as a source of inspiration elsewhere in Latin America.

NOTES

Research for this chapter was possible thanks to an International Pre-Dissertation Fellowship from the Social Science Research Council. I would also like to thank the Department of Political Science at the Universidade Federal do Rio Grande do Sul and the Fundação Estadual de Estatística in Porto Alegre for institutional support; and Susan Eckstein, Terry Karl, Philippe Schmitter, the Graduate Working Group on Latin American Politics at Stanford University, and a Latin American Studies Association panel for helpful comments on various drafts.

REFERENCES

Abers, Rebecca Neaera. 2000. *Inventing Local Democracy: Grassroots Politics in Brazil*. Boulder, Colo.: Lynne Rienner.

Anderson, Charles W. 1990. *Pragmatic Liberalism*. Chicago: University of Chicago Press.

Augustin F., Arno. 1994. "A experiência do Orçamento Participativo na administração popular da prefeitura municipal de Porto Alegre." In *Porto Alegre: O desafio da mudança*, ed. Carlos Henrique Horn, pp. 49–68. Porto Alegre: Ortiz.

———. 1997. Interview by the author. Secretario de Fazenda, Prefeitura de Porto Alegre, July 2.

Baierle, Sérgio Gregório. 1998. "The Explosion of Experience: The Emergence of a New Ethical-Political Principle in Popular Movements." In *Cultures of Politics/Politics of Cultures: Re-Visioning Latin American Social Movements*, ed. Sonia E. Alvarez, Evelina Dagnino, and Arturo Escobar, pp. 118–36. Boulder, Colo.: Westview Press.

Brasil, Assis. 1997. Interview by the author. Prefeitura de Porto Alegre, July 14.

Cassel, Guilherme, and João Verle. 1994. A política salarial dos servidores públicos de Porto Alegre no Governo de Olívio Dutra. In *Porto Alegre: O desafio da mudança*, ed. Carlos Henrique Horn, pp. 69–82. Porto Alegre: Ortiz.

Castañeda, Jorge G. 1993. *Utopia Unarmed: The Latin American Left after the Cold War*. New York: Vintage Books.

Fedozzi, Luciano. 1997. *Orçamento Participativo: Reflexões sobre a experiência de Porto Alegre*. Porto Alegre: FASE/IPPUR.

Ilgenfritz da Silva, Clóvis. 1997. Interview by the author. Presidente, Câmara de Vereadores, Porto Alegre, July 3.

Keck, Margaret E. 1992. *The Workers' Party and Democratization in Brazil*. New Haven, Conn.: Yale University Press.

Lucena, Teresa. 1997. Interview by the author. Asesora do Gabinete, Secretaria de Administração, Prefeitura de Porto Alegre, July 15.

Passos, Manoel. 1997 Eleicões municipais em Porto Alegre (1997). Porto Alegre: UFRGS.

Passos, Manoel, and Maria Isabel Noll. 1996. Eleicões municipais em Porto Alegre (1947–1992). Porto Alegre: UFRGS.

Porto Alegre, Prefeitura Municipal. 1993–97. Plano de investimentos.

———. n.d. "O Orçamento Participativo e a radicalização da democracia."

Tendler, Judith. 1997. Good Government in the Tropics. Baltimore: Johns Hopkins University Press.

Utzig, Luis Eduardo. 1996. "A gestão petista em Porto Alegre." Novos Estudos CEBRAP 45 (July): 209–24.

Verle, João, and Paulo Müzell. 1994. "Receita e capacidade de investimento da Prefeitura Municipal de Porto Alegre, 1973–92." In Porto Alegre: O desafio da mudança, ed. Carlos Henrique Horn, pp. 13–26. Porto Alegre: Ortiz.

Weyland, Kurt. 1995. "Latin America's Four Political Models." Journal of Democracy 6, no. 4 (October): 125–39.

CHAPTER NINE

Citizen Responses to Conflict and Political Crisis in Peru

Informal Politics in Ayacucho

DAVID SCOTT PALMER

The most dramatic political development in Latin America over the final two decades of the twentieth century was the restoration of democracy to many countries of the region.[1] Elections are now a routine part of the political landscape. Military coups, so recently a recourse of choice of opposition groups, have all but disappeared. Now, oppositions compete for votes and actually win elections more often than not (O'Donnell, Schmitter, and Whitehead 1986; Dominguez and Lowenthal 1996; Mainwaring and Shugart 1997). Making such a development all the more remarkable was its occurrence at a time of severe economic stress in most countries (Remmer 1993; Carrión 1998: 64). Given the authoritarian political history of the region and the tendency in many countries to gravitate toward political instability in times of social and economic crisis, the emergence of mass democracies almost everywhere took most Latin American specialists by surprise (Malloy 1977; Collier 1979).

However, most studies of this democracy phenomenon in Latin America focus on macropolitics, or activities at the national level and political center, rather than on micropolitics, or activities at the local level or political periphery (Greenstein and Polsby 1975). In addition, they tend to define and evaluate democracy in terms of how well it meets standards of free and fair elections, transparent electoral processes, separation of powers, and institutionalized parties (O'Donnell 1994; Mattiace and Camp 1996: 5). While such studies help to explain the tendency in many of the new or "Third Wave" democracies of the region to appeal directly to their citizenries (Huntington 1991), there is not very much emphasis on the nature or dynamics of citizen initiative or response.

To help rectify the present imbalance, this chapter explores politics at the base of society, rather than at its center, by examining the case of Peru, a significant example of "delegative democracy"[2] in the 1990s that has been characterized as an "authoritarian democracy" or "democratic dictatorship" (Balbi 1998: 1; Von Mettenheim and Malloy 1998: 18). It reviews the political dynamics of local-level governance in Peru, understood as policy implementation and interaction with civil society, in the south-central highland *departamento* Ayacucho. While recognizing the importance of the analytical distinction between government policy initiatives and the activities of entities within civil society, the present chapter also reflects the difficulty of distinguishing between "government-down" and "citizen-up" activities in concrete cases and their implications for local organization capacity (MacDonald 1997; Hammergren 1999: 193). This chapter also analyzes the proposition that micropolitics may be very different from macropolitics. It suggests that various combinations of factors have contributed to the emergence of an array of responses from local society that may be characterized as "informal politics."[3] These factors include increasing levels of literacy and education, internal migration, urbanization, and exposure to television and other media, as well as severe economic crises, dramatic alterations in central government capacity and activity, and political and/or social violence (Chalmers et al. 1997).

Ayacucho, as one of Peru's poorest departments and the one most affected by the country's widespread political violence in the 1980s and early 1990s, offers a particularly appropriate subject for exploring the hypothesis that local populations try to find their own solutions to meet basic needs and wants when government is unable or unwilling to do so. The specific cases in Ayacucho selected for closer study reflect representative local realities—rural communities and settlements (Sarhua and Tinte), small towns (Tambo), urban neighborhoods (Belén and Quinuapata), and evangelicals (Iglesia Israelita, or Israelite Church). While the findings are illustrative rather than definitive, and no claim as to their generalizability can be made, the analysis of concrete examples provides a greater understanding of local-level forces and dynamics. An additional qualification is that Ayacucho is not typical in some important ways. Over the years of extensive political violence, this region, as the birthplace of Sendero Luminoso (Shining Path) and the center of many of its activities, came to be identified with this guerrilla movement and also with the human suffering it inflicted. As a result, nongovernmental organizations (NGOs), beginning in the mid-

1980s, and the government, several years later, targeted the area for special attention. So Ayacucho has benefited from outside resources relatively more, in recent years, than other regions. Even so, the special circumstances of this area are revealing for our study because of the degree to which Ayacucho's local residents, whose lives had been so disrupted, put together new organizations to meet their multiple needs and wants or dramatically revised old ones, often with access to outside sources willing to help.

After the following review of aspects of national and local contexts that contributed to the emergence of informal politics in Ayacucho, the chapter will analyze five local cases to highlight some of the forms that informal politics has taken. The chapter concludes with an analysis of what these developments imply for the politics of Peru and Latin America more generally.

NATIONAL AND REGIONAL CONTEXTS

Of particular significance is the set of circumstances in Peru at both the national and regional levels that opened up spaces at the local level for citizen-led initiatives to meet pressing needs.[4] One was the progressive delegitimation of the country's most important political parties in the 1980s due to their failure to govern effectively or to their internal leadership and ideological divisions (Palmer 1990: 33; Rudolph 1992: 137–44). Their marginalization opened up opportunities for new organizations with national aspirations as well as for autonomous expression of concerns at the local level.

A second was the impact of the Shining Path guerrilla movement on national and local politics (Degregori 1990; Palmer 1994). Between 1980, when democracy was restored, and 1992, over 30,000 people had been killed and more than 650,000 displaced, a third of the totals in Ayacucho alone. Damages to the country's infrastructure came to some twenty-six billion U.S. dollars (Kirk 1991; Coronel 1998; Senado 1992). The presence of the state at the local level was severely eroded as a result, as was the capacity of formal political organizations to function (Palmer 1995).

A third circumstance was the administrations of President Alberto Fujimori Fujimori (1990–2000). As a candidate without party affiliation or political experience, Fujimori symbolized the electorate's disillusionment with traditional parties. While he succeeded in bringing Peru back from the brink of collapse through a series of draconian measures and had strong popular support in his 1992 *autogolpe* (self-coup) and 1995 reelection, democratic forms and procedures paid a very high price in the process (Cameron and Mauceri 1997). Political power became centralized in the office of the presidency, new political groups emerged to replace the traditional party system, and assured representation at the department level was eliminated by the creation of a single national electoral district (LASA 1995). Politics became more personalized and less democratic over time, increasingly manipulated after 1995 to ensure control by the president (Palmer 2000; Balbi and Palmer 2001).

The overall result was a national political scene that was quite inhospitable to democratic institutionalization through parties. Fujimori's populist style, combined with the maneuvers of key followers to undermine opposition forces and internal divisions within the opposition parties themselves, contributed to their further weakening (Tanaka 1998). Most analysts agree that such a dynamic does not favor democratic consolidation and is likely to lead at some future point to a severe political crisis (Mainwaring and Scully 1995). At the same time, however, such national political dynamics tended to open spaces at the local level for a variety of organized responses.

INFORMAL POLITICS: A USEFUL CONCEPT?

Given the erosion of political parties as channels for transmitting local needs and demands in the context of prolonged economic crisis and hyperinflation (1988–92), as well as a guerrilla war that focused disproportionately on the periphery of Peruvian society, much of the local population of the countryside was forced to develop its own mechanisms for protection, survival, and meeting basic wants and needs. While Peru may be an extreme case, the failure of the national political system to respond to concerns of local populations is repeated in a variety of ways throughout the region, even under democracy (Chalmers et al. 1997). In such circumstances, citizens organize to search for alternatives with or without outside support, official or otherwise, in what I call informal politics.

Such a search within the political arena is analogous, it may be argued, to a similar economic dynamic, termed the "informal economy" (Hart 1973; de Soto 1986; Portes, Castells, and Benton 1989). The informal economy includes a wide array of activities, from providing services to producing goods, that have not been officially sanctioned or legally registered even though they are not in and of themselves illegal.

Just as the informal economy emerges from the limitations of the formal economic system, informal politics develops from similar limitations in the formal political system. When the formal economy cannot or does not respond to basic economic needs and wants of some sectors of society, those affected search for alternatives to satisfy them and, if possible, to improve their economic situation. The informal economy fills the economic spaces that the formal economy either does not or cannot fill. Likewise, informal politics arises when the formal political system is in crisis and less capable over time of meeting citizens' political wants and needs, particularly in terms of access to the political system itself or for dealing with sets of local issues, such as security, governance, education, child care, health, and nutrition.

In Peru, a combination of factors—including the failure of established parties, generalized political violence, hyperinflation, and the virtual collapse of government—forced many citizens to seek out their own devices for resolving fundamental problems. Local citizen initiatives included the formation of self-defense committees to ward off Shining Path, mothers' clubs to help feed communities and care for children, and parents' organizations to support local schools. A variety of NGOs contributed to the citizens' initiatives and helped to strengthen them (del Pino 1998). As central government regained some of its lost capacity over the 1990s, it moved to support these organizations and regain influence over their activities. As with the proposals for incorporating the informal economy into its formal counterpart, such official initiatives interacted with the informal polity but also left spaces within which such local organizations retained much independence and autonomy.

The result was a modest reinforcing of civil society at the grassroots level, with substantial contributions by NGOs and government agencies. Overall, a complex mosaic of local organizations and activities emerged, some more independent of external actors than others. On balance, however, they produced a distinctive set of local dynamics in which citizens have a greater say and influence over outcomes affecting them than in the recent past.

Tocqueville (1960: vols. 1 and 2) makes a compelling case for the value of citizen associations, or civil society, in fostering, maintaining, and strengthening democracy. His reflections, although drawn from his observations of the American experience of the 1830s, resonate in the contemporary realities of Peruvian civil society, however differently it has developed. Peru was affected greatly by long-term centralized colonial government, which contributed to what became a deeply ingrained pattern of citizens looking to central authority to solve all problems (Palmer 1980: 14–15, 18–19). These patterns continued, with ebbs and flows, in postindependence national governments with institutions and legal mechanisms and procedures that kept official authority and resources concentrated in the center (Palmer 1980: 24–41). In practice, nevertheless, the capacity and reach of central authority was often less than total, leaving spaces for actors at the periphery to function and operate over the years.

Since the 1960s, furthermore, the multiple effects of ineffective governance by reformist military and civilian governments alike have transformed local political landscapes by upsetting prior patterns of local political activity and interaction as well as by changing the scope and range of central government initiatives, capacity, and control in the periphery (Cameron and Mauceri 1997). With the growing local role of evangelical churches, NGOs, new government agencies, and foreign government aid, a stronger and more pluralistic local base has emerged (Stokes 1995). The organizations of informal politics interact with the organizations of government, religious entities, and NGOs to meet basic needs in multiple ways. This has occurred even in the context of the restoration of central government authority under President Fujimori and the recentralization of power in the executive branch (Stern 1998).

In their wide-ranging study of new modalities of participation and representation in Latin America, Douglas Chalmers and his colleagues help to explain this paradox of emerging dynamism in civil society within the new democracies of the region even as greater power is being concentrated in central governments' executives. In what they call "the reinvention of popular politics," beyond parties, unions, and pluralist groups and the mechanisms associated with them—clientelism, populism, corporatism, or mass mobilization—they see an emerging model of popular representation that they call "associative networks" (Chalmers et al. 1997: 544, 545). This model reflects "bottom up qualities of making claims [which] are simultaneously channels for top down processes of securing compliance" (Chalmers et al. 1997: 544, n. 2). Especially significant in the development of associative networks, they conclude, is the "dispersion of decision-making activity away from the centralized state of an earlier era to a more polycentric state, with multiple centers of decision-making," around which the networks are constructed and whose development they further (Chalmers et al. 1997: 545).

What Chalmers and his colleagues are observing in various Latin American settings is an array of locally generated initiatives that effectively supplant, replace, or supplement political parties as vehicles for organizing and channeling citizen supports of and demands on the political system. It seems preferable to characterize such organized local initiatives of demands and supports as manifestations of informal politics, rather than as associative networks, in order to highlight the degree to which they are formed and operate on their own terms, with or without outside support. In this alternative formulation, associative networks are the connections between informal political entities and other, similar organizations or outside groups and agencies, both governmental and nongovernmental. Furthermore, the term *informal* politics makes explicit the parallels with the informal economy in reflecting popular responses to meet perceived needs that are unable to be fulfilled by the national system.

The new local involvements emerged after former mechanisms of popular incorporation broke down, and they built on efforts by ordinary people to seek their own solutions to pressing problems through grassroots organizing, inspired and assisted by NGOs. Chalmers and his collaborators (1997: 552) trace the new local dynamism to five significant developments not only in Peru but in other countries in the region. Each of the developments Chalmers et al. point to, listed below, arose in Ayacucho. Accordingly, the Ayacucho case reflects a broader regional phenomenon.

1. *Dispersion of decision-making activity toward multiple decision-making centers* (Chalmers et al. 1997: 555). In Ayacucho, over thirty NGOs, largely foreign-financed, have been operating since the mid- to late 1980s, with total budgets ranging from five million to twenty million U.S. dollars per year. The most important of these include CARE Peru, World Vision International, Rural Educational Services (Servicios Educativos Rurales; SER), the Center for Population Development and Promotion (the Centro de Promoción y Desarrollo Poblacional; CEPRODEP), the Institute for the Promotion of Development and Peace in Ayacucho (Instituto de Investigacación y Promoción del Desarrollo y Paz de Ayacucho; IPAZ), and FINCAPeru. Their reach into neighborhoods and communities of the department is remarkable, with contacts in over two-thirds of Ayacucho's estimated six hundred communities, and with about 260 organizations in urban neighborhoods of the two cities of Ayacucho and Huanta (del Pino 1998).

In addition, about a dozen government agencies have been carrying out a range of activities in the region, most of them beginning in the early 1990s, with total annual budgets of thirty to forty million U.S. dollars.

The most important include the Office of the Public Defender (La Defensoría del Pueblo), the Fund for Social Compensation and Development (Fondo de Compensación y Desarrollo Social; FONCODES), the Resettlement Support Program (Programa de Apoyo al Repoblamiento; PAR), the National Food Assistance Project (Proyecto Nacional de Asistencia Alimenticia; PRONAA), and the National Project for Water and Soil Conservation Management (Proyecto Nacional de Manejo de Cuencas Hidrográficas y Conservación de Suelos; PRONAMACHCS). Together they reach virtually every community in the Department of Ayacucho with a variety of small-scale projects ranging from school lunch programs and legal protection services to electrification, irrigation, reforestation, and road and trail building. Both FONCODES and PRONAMACHCS require the establishment of local, elected, project-oversight committees for implementation of their programs. Even though most are closely tied to the central government as agencies within the Ministry of the Presidency, they have in fact substantial autonomy in their local initiatives (Palmer 1999: 285–90).

2. *Availability of mass media and specialized communication* (Chalmers et al. 1997: 561). In Ayacucho, many new radio stations initiated operations. The number rose from two to eighteen over twenty years. Meanwhile, television became quite common in the capital and accessible in provincial capitals as well. Some districts, recently electrified, even installed satellite dishes for community televisions. Telephones were introduced in the late 1960s and now link Ayacucho to the rest of the country and to the department's provincial capital and to the majority of the district capitals. In addition, electronic communication via computer networks between local offices and their headquarters in Lima provides coordination and opportunities for greater flexibility in local adaptations of national policies. Literacy increased in the department from less than 20 percent in 1960 to almost 80 percent in the 1990s, so people have become more exposed to and aware of events and developments outside their communities and neighborhoods. Substantial migration to the coast, both temporary and longer-term, has further increased popular awareness and capacity at the local level in Ayacucho.

3. *More actors perceiving the need for "complex social coordination" to carry out decisions in settings of greatest concern, which produces "more diffuse participation focused around relatively specific purposes"* (Chalmers et al. 1997: 561, 562). One of the significant changes in the

communities and neighborhoods of Ayacucho in recent years is the proliferation of local groups and organizations to meet the multiple and pressing needs and wants precipitated by prolonged economic crisis and political violence. Among the most important are self-defense committees (over twelve hundred in 1998), mothers' clubs (about fifteen hundred in 1998), and community improvement groups. These groups tend to be led by individuals who have some education and experience outside their home communities. The demands put forward tend to be quite basic and specific, such as for security, schools and school lunches, community irrigation and potable water, electrification, and improved access roads or trails. Their goals are usually defined in terms of community protection, enhancement, and development, and collaboration among local organizations is often the norm.

This combination of demand initiation and response generation highlights the interactive nature of civil society, government, and NGOs, and the multiple loci as well as opportunities for access and resolution of problems of high priority to the citizenry. It also suggests how blurred the boundary between them may become in practice. Informal politics emerged in the spaces created by Peru's specific experiences, as local populations tried to cope with their multiple basic needs and wants. In Ayacucho these provide multiple reinforcing opportunities for which successful outcomes depend on citizens' ability to interact with others both within civil society and in governmental and nongovernmental agencies.

4. *New patterns of the internalization of Latin American politics, from "partisan and government influences [to] those of international organizations, foreign NGOs, and international corporations...and towards project oriented mobilization focused on delimited groups of people"* (Chalmers et al. 1997: 562). In Peru, these new patterns emerged due to the combination of party crisis, political violence, and governmental implosion, followed by a new set of government initiatives in a context of economic liberalization. Many international NGOs and foreign government programs stepped in to carry out an array of locally based initiatives. New Peruvian government agencies with regional offices and considerable de facto autonomy began to direct significant central government resources to the poorest districts of the country. In both cases, Ayacucho was a major beneficiary (Palmer 1999). While political parties themselves failed to serve as effective instruments of popular mobilization and channeling of popular demands, the government itself furthered party disarray by encourag-

ing the proliferation of new political groups, by undermining formal democracy, and by concentrating power in the executive (LASA 1995).

5. *"A complex learning process seems to have grown that may also contribute to nascent forms of popular representation"* (Chalmers et al. 1997: 562). Through a combination of factors—including the multiple crises of the 1980s and early 1990s, higher levels of literacy and education, extensive migrations to cities and return migrations, better communication and media access, and both government agency and NGO activity—local populations in Peru have turned to new forms of organization or have revamped old forms to meet perceived needs.

In Ayacucho, one notes a network of local leadership and local entities working in multiple ways to improve their communities and the people within them. Such experiences improve the skills of members in accomplishing their objectives; they are assisted further by a variety of local leadership training programs implemented by NGOs and government offices alike. Achieving modest success legitimates their role among the populace and stimulates further activity.

The five characteristics of the new forms of popular participation help focus attention on the activities of local populations and of governmental and nongovernmental agencies to articulate and respond to citizen needs and demands. They suggest the importance of such activities in serving to strengthen local networks within civil society and the role of outside actors in facilitating that process. In addition, they highlight the autonomous capacity of citizens in communities and neighborhoods to work together to solve perceived problems with whatever external resources they find available, in combination with whatever internal resources (usually limited to labor) they can muster.

By turning to several concrete cases in Ayacucho, it is possible to assess the degree to which these dynamics of informal politics, in conjunction with outside agency support, are actually meeting basic demands and serving to strengthen civil society in the process.

Tambo: Generating, Sustaining, and Expanding Local Capacity

Tambo, an important commercial and agricultural crossroads town of five thousand on the dirt highway from the sierra to the jungle, exemplifies an aware and proactive citizenry.[5] It organized itself to meet its security needs against the incursions of Shining Path, beginning in the mid-1980s, when the government was unable to assist. The residents themselves established self-defense committees, or *rondas campesinas,* in all thirty-eight communities of the district by 1990, with coordination into five zonal committees as well, backed by their commando force.

After 1991, when the Peruvian military changed its approach to combat the guerrillas, these preexisting *rondas* became part of the government's new counterinsurgency strategy but retained considerable autonomy. Once the main challenge posed by Shining Path had been overcome in 1993, they began to use the organizational experience they had achieved to carry out other kinds of activities for the benefit of the district's communities. This transition was led by a dynamic head of the *rondas* in Tambo, with assistance from the mayor and the committed and constructive leadership of local groups, particularly the mothers' clubs.

Subsequent activities include local development projects, from community parks to schools, youth nutrition, electrification, and irrigation, and are coordinated with other local groups in a committee that helps to coordinate initiatives to secure support from governmental and nongovernmental agencies. In some cases, they develop their own projects; in others they take advantage of government initiatives to meet their needs.

Tambo is an example of a local population that organized itself to face a major challenge to its continued existence and then used this experience to advance other needs, garnering resources from NGOs and government agencies as they became active. The routinization of informal politics in Tambo includes retention of strong local organizations within civil society that can interact with outside agencies on their own terms for the benefit of the community.

Tinte: The Challenge of Small Size in Building Civil Society

Tinte, a small farming settlement of about 225, is representative of the significant portion of the rural population of Ayacucho which lives in small clusters that lack numbers, infrastructure, and official recognition, making them vulnerable and dependent on forces largely beyond their control.[6] Unable to cope with Shining Path activities in the 1980s, citizens succumbed to their influence or migrated to urban centers. Only the army's sustained presence in the early 1990s restored a semblence of order, but at the price of bringing in members of outlying communities so that they could be protected, which further eroded community solidarity. As normalcy returned by the mid-1990s, local organizations were established, but largely at the initiative of associations of former residents in Ayacucho and Lima (who actually outnumber their local counterparts), government organizations like FONCODES, NGOs such as the Peru-Canada Fund, and the Parish of Santa Rosa in Ayacucho. The emerging civil society—active in the *ronda,* the community governing council, the mothers'club, and work teams for local infrastructure projects and rebuilding the local church—is largely dependent on outside actors.

Small size and the large number of temporary residents until recently have inhibited the development of an autonomous network of local organizations. Change has occurred, and projects are ongoing with the participation of local organizations. However, the sociopolitical dynamics are more clientelistic than autonomous, and may not become autonomous without the return of more families and the presence of a more dynamic local leadership.

Sarhua: Adaptation from Within

Although it is a long-standing autonomous community and district capital of about twelve hundred, renowned for its folk art, Sarhua suffers by being remote (some eight hours by road and trail from the city of Ayacucho) from the department's network of NGOs and government agencies.[7] The district is further handicapped by having been a community that accommodated itself to Shining Path's presence in the area for several years during the 1980s. Even though Sarhua is one of the poorest districts in the region (number 4 out of 109 in Ayacucho and Huancavelica), it has received much less support from outside agencies than similar communities closer to transportation (FONCODES 1998c). In addition, the elected local political leadership, known to include former Shining Path supporters, has initiated few specific requests for outside support. Even so, Sarhua has retained a strong sense of community.

These considerations influence the community's organizational dynamics. The civil-defense committees, originally initiated by the military rather than by the citizens themselves, play only a minor role in Sarhua. A mothers' club and a school parents' association are active, but the most dynamic organizations are the traditional *ayllus* (neighborhoods) of Inca empire origins (one is now Protestant, the other Catholic, a dramatic demonstration of adaptation to change), and the artisans' association. Material support for their local initiatives tends to come from associations of Sarhua natives now living in Ayacucho or Lima who travel back and forth frequently.

Sarhua is an example of a community that has tended to adapt to change by utilizing more traditional mechanisms of local origin to gain needed outside resources and to be affected less directly by the new set of

NGOs or government agencies now present in Ayacucho. The community has not developed an array of associative networks to enhance local capacity, although this could change with improved communications (members have recently completed a one-lane road into Sarhua) and new local leadership. What Sarhua does have is a set of local organizations that work together to assist in resolving residents' needs with the support of community members now living and working in urban centers.

Belén-Quinuapata: Urban Fragmentation and Uncertainty

The adjoining close-in Ayacucho urban neighborhoods of Belén and Quinuapata date from the city's colonial era but have become increasingly subject over time to outside pressures and influences over which residents have little control.[8] Local initiatives to improve their communities were undermined frequently by political infighting and a strong Shining Path presence during which key independent leaders were killed. Unable to become recognized as a district, they were dependent for funding from the municipality of Ayacucho, which seldom was forthcoming. A new generation of university-educated young neighborhood committee leaders attempted to overcome these problems. However, they were unable to secure outside support to address community needs, and they could not resolve internal divisions among committee members. In addition, many residents refused to support them, in part because they were young and inexperienced, and in part because the city's recent rapid growth and transformation had caused social fragmentation and disarticulation. The obstacles notwithstanding, the committee successfully initiated community improvements by coordinating efforts with other local groups, especially with mothers' clubs. They formed neighborhood-watch organizations and helped the local health center, school, and library expand their offerings.

This case illustrates the lack of locally generated resources, a general problem in a centralized political system, and the difficulties in accessing the array of outside organizations with the necessary resources. It also highlights the challenges of effective local leadership in channeling the complex dynamics of internal politics.

The Iglesia Israelita: Channeling Informal Politics into a National Party

This religious organization is one of many Protestant evangelical sects that have appeared and spread in Peru over the past thirty years and that are now estimated to include about 15 percent of the country's population of twenty-four million (Minaya 1995: 471).[9] These organizations, which tend to attract the least privileged sectors of society, try to deal with the problems of their members by meeting both spiritual and material needs. The evangelical religious identification creates a new sense of community and mutual obligation, and it expanded rapidly in the 1980s at least in part as an alternative to Shining Path, and because of the lack of priests to serve the religious needs of Ayacucho's population, which is overwhelmingly formally Catholic.[10]

At the local level, rather than seeking outside help for members, the Iglesia Israelita tries to generate resources on its own from within the agricultural communities that it has organized. The church's leaders believe that recourse to outside agencies cannot assure their future and that it is better to meet needs from within to enhance community capacity over time. The organization's presence in the four churches in the city of Ayacucho, as well as in a number of rural communities, such as Llamoqtachi, represents a manifestation of informal politics within civil society. The Iglesia Israelita's choice to work from within its communities to generate the new resources that they need is a significant challenge, given the limited resource base of the Ayacucho area and of the membership, but it is also a challenge that holds out the prospect of a stronger, more diversified, and pluralistic local civil society, to the degree that they are successful in building community at the grassroots level (*Somos* 1998).

Beyond meeting local community needs, however, the Iglesia Israelita chose to establish a political party, the Frente Popular Agrícola del Perú (Popular Farm Front of Peru; FREPAP), to compete in elections to spread its message of moral and spiritual regeneration. In this endeavor it has had only limited success (about fifty thousand votes and a seat in Congress). However, it does reflect one option for channeling informal politics into national formal political organization, and it reflects a modality that combines locally generated capacity with a national political agenda.

CONCLUSIONS

While Ayacucho is a special case in some important respects, it nevertheless reflects Peru's recent experience in the generation of multiple manifestations of informal politics, as local populations organize to meet needs and wants in the context of the collapse of political parties, the

economic crisis, and the generalized political violence. Such local organizations in Ayacucho interact with an array of associative networks,
that is, government agencies and NGOs, most of which are new to the
region over the past ten to fifteen years. The variety of specific interactions here is enormous, given the number of communities (over six hundred) and organizations (about forty) present. The cases observed in this
chapter reflect this variety.

Perhaps Tambo is the best example of the strength and depth of informal politics in the region in the late 1990s. With the failure in the
1980s of central government and political parties to cope with Shining
Path's violence, local residents had to organize resistance to guerrilla incursions themselves, and then used the skills thus developed to relate to
and gain benefits from outside organizations. By virtue of being a crossroads community with good communications, leadership, and resource
capacity, Tambo has effectively combined outside resources for specific
programs with an array of local organizations to meet needs and wants
and to enhance local civil society.

Tinte and Sarhua have benefited as well, but in different ways. Tinte—
smaller, closer to the city of Ayacucho, and more dependent on members
now resident in urban centers—has used some of the outside associative
networks in more traditional clientelistic fashion to garner resources to
benefit the community. However, the local set of informal political organizations is fairly weak and tentative. Sarhua, on the other hand, has
retained a strong sense of community in a more isolated location by
adapting traditional local organizations, such as the artisans' association, the residents' organizations in Ayacucho and Lima, and the *ayllus,*
to meet some of their needs with some, though limited, connections to
new associative networks.

The Iglesia Israelita is itself a response, through religious conversion,
to the chaos of political violence. In creating a new community for its
members that sustains itself by generating its own resources, it, too, en-
gages in informal politics. At the same time, the church attempts to be a
formal political actor by relating to the national system with a political
party organization. Belén-Quinuapata is the least successful of the cases
studied, in which informal political initiatives by the communities' youth
are limited by distrust, a loss of a sense of community, and a lack of successful access to outside resources.

As Ayacucho's recent experience indicates, a signal characteristic of
political dynamics in Peru in recent years is the proliferation of organizations at the local level over a period when the formal political system

was unable to meet citizen needs and wants. They have taken a variety of forms and vary in vitality. However, with the exception of the Iglesia Israelita, the organizations operate outside formal political party structures.

The variety of NGOs in the area in the late 1980s, and of new government agencies with considerable local autonomy as of the early 1990s, enabled many of these organized manifestations of informal politics to gain access to resources to meet local needs and wants through associative networks that serve to enhance their capacity at the local level. Decision-making activity is dispersed through multiple centers and is enhanced through improved communications and mass media. Some of the local actors have succeeded in coordinating efforts to significantly enhance local capacity, as the case of Tambo illustrates, organized largely around a set of specific projects of NGOs and government agencies. Others have been less successful, as in Tinte and Sarhua or in Belén-Quinuapata, but even in these localities a variety of initiatives have to some degree also fostered and strengthened local organizations and activities.

The distinction between government-down and citizen-up activities is less important than the overall effect, on balance, for the strengthening of local organizations and, through that process, of civil society. The recent experience in Ayacucho suggests that the political disarray of organized parties and other national institutions that has characterized Peru's macropolitics in recent years is not replicated in Peru's micropolitics, where a lively range of organizations works in multiple ways to solve local problems.

The two most significant factors affecting the quality of the political dynamic at the local level appear to be outside the parameters of the present chapter: the availability of local resources and the quality of local leadership. Tambo is the only case explored here that had both, a fact that helps to explain Tambo's success. Some local resource-generating capacity helps organizations in Tambo to be more autonomous, and good local leadership helps those organizations to take better advantage of the associative networks for the benefit of the community.

Without local financial resources, group activity rests on domestic or foreign NGO, government, or other assistance. But when dependent on outside resources, groups may lose de facto decision-making autonomy, in that access to resources and usages of funds are beyond their control. Even when faced with such resource constraints, though, groups typically benefit. Funders may foster the formation of new groups and strengthen preexisting groups. They also tend to apply more consistent and objective criteria for providing resources and thereby foster modern, rather than traditional, forms of clientelism. In addition, they enhance local organizations and their leadership by legitimating them in the eyes of community or neighborhood beneficiaries, thus strengthening civil society in the process.

In working with governmental entities, as most local organizations do, informal politics typically becomes, de facto, more formalized with time. Absence of systematic central government control, however, helps local groups to retain some independent scope of action, a certain level of informal politics, even as organization is routinized—again resulting in strengthened civil society. Even so, historic limitations in formal local political autonomy in Peru keep local governments and organizations there from manifesting the citizen-based local model of democracy that Tocqueville found in the United States in the 1840s. In the modern Peruvian variant, organizations may be less permanent, shifting and adapting to meet changing circumstances, in the combination of alliances that Chalmers and his colleagues noted as signaling new forms of citizen representation.

The challenge here, as in other Latin American cases, is to determine how these manifestations of informal politics can be supported in ways that enhance civil society as organizations become more formalized, and not be subjected to the manipulations of a short-sighted central government that tries to utilize them for partisan control purposes. In the case of Peru at the start of the twenty-first century, both tendencies are present. To the degree that the local political dynamics observed in Ayacucho represent trends elsewhere in Peru, however, the array of citizen initiatives in informal politics appears, on balance, to be aiding significantly the construction of a more viable local civil society. Over time, such activities can be expected to contribute to the strengthening of democratic processes and practices.

NOTES

1. This study is based on fieldwork carried out by the author in Ayacucho, Peru, between May and September 1998, under a Fulbright Senior Researcher/Lecturer Fellowship. Support for the field research was provided by student members of the research workshop codirected by the author and Professor Ponciano del Pino at the Universidad Nacional de San Cristóbal de Huamanga—most particularly Mariano Aronés Palomino, Karín Gamonal Rezza, Telésforo Huashuayo Ramos, Enver Quinteros Peralta, and Carlos Vega. Preliminary ver-

sions of the study (in Spanish) were presented at the annual meeting of the American Political Science Association in Boston on September 4, 1998; and at the International Congress of the Latin American Studies Association (LASA) in Chicago on September 26, 1998. The author is grateful for the careful review and comment provided by Shane Hunt, Martin Scurrah, Susan Eckstein, and Timothy Wickham-Crowley on these earlier versions, one of which was published (Palmer 1999). Errors of fact or interpretation that remain are, of course, the responsibility of the author.

2. Guillermo O'Donnell's (1994) useful concept enabling an assessment of the degree to which elected presidents and the executive bureaucracies they control appropriate powers of both legislative and judicial branches of government.

3. The term used by John C. Cross in his study of Mexico City street vendors to define "the individual and collective strategies of even the most 'powerless' groups of political actors in the analysis of political economy" (Cross 1998: 5).

4. This is not to imply that the emergence of local citizen initiatives at society's base is only a very recent phenomenon in Peru. See, for example, Dobyns and Doughty (1976) for a review of the multiplicity of local organizations and associations in the 1950s and 1960s and their impact. Clearly, local organization was also a feature of traditional Indian communities that occurred largely outside the purview of central government, as did the meticulously planned and executed urban land invasions (Collier 1976). However, the events of the 1980s and early 1990s gave rise over time to regional and national contexts that opened up new opportunities, along with new challenges, for organization at the local level.

5. This section of the chapter is based on field research carried out by Enver Quinteros Peralta, Ponciano del Pino, and the author as part of a research workshop at the University of Huamanga, Ayacucho, June–September 1998.

6. This section is based on field research conducted by Mariano Aronés Palomino, Ponciano del Pino, and Diane Nagel Palmer as part of the research workshop at the University of Huamanga, Ayacucho, June–September 1998.

7. This section is based on fieldwork carried out by Telésforo Huashuayo Ramos, Ponciano del Pino, Tom Marks, and the author as part of the research workshop at the University of Huamanga, Ayacucho, July–September 1998.

8. This section is based on field research carried out by Carlos Vega, Ponciano del Pino, and the author as part of the research workshop at the University of Huamanga, Ayacucho, June–September 1998.

9. This section is based on field research carried out by Karín Gamonal Rezza as part of the research workshop at the University of Huamanga, Ayacucho, June–September 1998.

10. In the entire *departamento* of Ayacucho, for example, with a population of about six hundred thousand, the local bishop in 1998 had only thirty priests available for all the parishes (Cipriani 1998).

REFERENCES

Balbi, Carmen Rosa. 1998. "Permanencia y cambios en la política social peruana en un contexto de democracia autoritaria." Paper presented at the International Congress of the Latin American Studies Association, Chicago, September 24–27.

Balbi, Carmen Rosa, and David Scott Palmer. 2001. " 'Reinventing' Democracy in Peru." *Current History* 100, no. 643 (February): 65–72.

Berrocal, Americano (coordinator of the Comité de Autodefensa Civil [Civil Self-Defense Committee; CAC] of Sarhua). 1998. Interview by the author. Field notes. Sarhua, Víctor Fajardo Province, Ayacucho Department, Peru, August 18.

Cameron, Maxwell A. 1997. "Political and Economic Origins of Regime Change in Peru: The *Eighteenth Brumaire* of Alberto Fujimori." In *The Peruvian Labyrinth: Polity, Society, Economy,* ed. Maxwell A. Cameron and Philip Mauceri, pp. 37–69. University Park: Pennsylvania State University Press.

Cameron, Maxwell A., and Philip Mauceri, eds. 1997. *The Peruvian Labyrinth: Polity, Society, Economy.* University Park: Pennsylvania State University Press.

Carrión, Julio F. 1998. "Partisan Decline and Presidential Popularity: The Politics and Economics of Representation in Peru." In *Deepening Democracy in Latin America,* ed. Kurt Von Mettenheim and James Malloy, pp. 55–70. Pittsburgh: University of Pittsburgh Press.

Chalmers, Douglas A., Carlos M. Vilas, Katherine Hite, Scott B. Martin, Kerianne Piester, and Monique Segarra. 1997. *The New Politics of Inequality in Latin America: Rethinking Participation and Representation.* New York: Oxford University Press.

Cipriani, Monseñor Juan Luis (bishop of Ayacucho). 1998. Interview by the author. Field notes. Ayacucho, Peru, August 28.

Collier, David. 1976. *Squatters and Oligarchs: Authoritarian Rule and Policy Change in Peru.* Baltimore: Johns Hopkins University Press.

———, ed. 1979. *The New Authoritarianism in Latin America.* Princeton, N.J.: Princeton University Press.

Coronel, José. 1998. "La movilidad de las poblaciones campesinas afectadas por la violencia política en Ayacucho, 1983–1992." Taller Internacional de Investigación y Estudios Comparativos sobre la Reconstrucción del Tejido Social en Perú, Guatemala, y África del Sur, Huancayo, Peru, March 22–23.

Cotler, Julio. 1968. "La mecánica de la dominación interna y del cambio social." In *Perú problema: Cinco ensayos,* ed. José Matos Mar, pp. 153–97. Lima: Instituto de Estudios Peruanos.

Cross, John C. 1998. *Informal Politics: Street Vendors and the State in Mexico City.* Stanford, Calif.: Stanford University Press.

Curahua, Néstor (mayor of the district of Tambillo). 1998. Interview by the author. Field notes. Tambillo, Huamanga Province, Ayacucho Department, Peru, August 23.

Defensoría del Pueblo. 1998a. "Partidos y elecciones municipales en Ayacucho." Ayacucho, Peru office.

———. 1998b. "Mapas de la violencia política en el Perú." Ayacucho, Peru office.

Degregori, Carlos Iván. 1990. *Ayacucho, 1969–1979: El surgimiento de Sendero Luminoso.* Lima: Instituto de Estudios Peruanos.

del Pino, Ponciano. 1998. "Actores de desarrollo en el Departamento de Ayacucho." Study prepared for the Servicio Holandés de Cooperación al Desarrollo (Dutch Development Cooperation Service; SNV). SNV, Amsterdam. May.

de Soto, Hernando. 1986. *El otro sendero: La revolución informal.* Lima: Instituto Libertad y Democracia.

Dobyns, Henry F., and Paul L. Doughty. 1976. *Peru: A Cultural History.* New York: Oxford University Press.

Dominguez, Jorge I., and Abraham F. Lowenthal, eds. 1996. *Constructing Democratic Governance: South America in the 1990s.* An Inter-American Dialogue Book. Baltimore: Johns Hopkins University Press.

Fondo Nacional de Cooperación y Desarrollo Social (FONCODES). 1998a. *Guía de orientación.* Lima. March.

———. 1998b. "Evolución de gasto, 1991–1997." Internal document.

———. 1998c. "Ejecución, 1991–1997: Departamento de Ayacucho a nivel distrital por ámbito de Oficina Zonal." Internal document.

———. 1998d. "Relación de convenios, 1992–1998, Distrito de Sarhua."

Greenstein, Fred I., and Nelson W. Polsby. 1975. *Handbook of Political Science.* Vol. 2, *Micropolitical Theory;* vol. 3, *Macropolitical Theory.* Reading, Mass.: Addison-Wesley.

Hammergren, Lynn. 1999. "The Development Wars: Analyzing Foreign Assistance Impact and Policy." *Latin American Research Review* 34, no. 2: 179–97.

Hart, J. Keith. 1973. "Informal Income Opportunities and Urban Employment in Ghana." *Journal of Modern African Studies* 11: 61–89.

Huarco, Vladimiro (regional representative, Ayacucho). 1998. Interview by the author. Field notes. Ayacucho, Peru office of the Defensoría del Pueblo, July 8.

Huntington, Samuel P. 1991. *The Third Wave: Democratization in the Late Twentieth Century.* Norman: University of Oklahoma Press.

Isbell, Billie Jean. 1994. "Shining Path and Peasant Responses in Rural Ayacucho." In *Shining Path of Peru,* 2d ed., ed. David Scott Palmer, pp. 77–100. New York: St. Martin's Press.

Kirk, Robin. 1991. *The Decade of Chaqwa: Peru's Internal Refugees.* Washington, D.C.: U.S. Committee for Refugees.

Latin American Studies Association (LASA). 1995. *The 1995 Electoral Process in Peru: A Delegation Report of the Latin American Studies Association.* Pittsburgh: LASA.

Macdonald, Laura. 1997. *Supporting Civil Society: The Political Role of Non-Governmental Organizations in Central America.* New York: St. Martin's Press.

Mainwaring, Scott, and Timothy Scully, eds. 1995. *Building Democratic Institutions: Party Systems in Latin America.* Stanford, Calif.: Stanford University Press.

Mainwaring, Scott, and Matthew Shugart, eds. 1997. *Presidentialism and Democracy in Latin America.* New York: Cambridge University Press.

Malloy, James M., ed. 1977. *Authoritarianism and Corporatism in Latin America.* Pittsburgh: University of Pittsburgh Press.

Marks, Tom A. 1998. "Mapa de bases de apoyo y comités populares de SL." Base Militar "Los Cabitos," Ayacucho, Peru. Ca. 1989.

Mattiace, Shannan, and Roderic Ai Camp. 1996. "Democracy and Development: An Overview." In *Democracy in Latin America: Patterns and Cycles,* ed. Roderic Ai Camp, pp. 3–19. Jaguar Books on Latin America 10. Wilmington, Del.: Scholarly Resources.

McClintock, Cynthia. 1993. "Peru's Fujimori: A Caudillo Derails Democracy." *Current History* 92, no. 572 (March): 112–19.

Millones, Luis. 1994. "Las tablas de Sarhua." In *Shining Path of Peru,* 2d ed, ed. David Scott Palmer, pp. vi–ix. New York: St. Martin's Press.

Minaya, Luis. 1995. "Is Peru Turning Protestant?" In *The Peru Reader,* ed. Orin Starn, Carlos Iván Degregori, and Robin Kirk, pp. 471–76. Durham, N.C.: Duke University Press.

Muñoz, Maximiliano (president of the Civil Defense Committee [CAC] of Pineo, Tambillo). 1998. Interview by the author. Field notes. Tambillo District, Huamanga Province, Ayacucho Department, Peru, August 23.

O'Donnell, Guillermo. 1994. "Delegative Democracy." *Journal of Democracy* 5, no. 1 (January): 55–69.

O'Donnell, Guillermo, Philippe Schmitter, and Laurence Whitehead, eds. 1986. *Transitions from Authoritarian Rule: Tentative Conclusions about Uncertain Democracies.* Baltimore: Johns Hopkins University Press.

Palmer, David Scott. 1973. *Revolution from Above: Military Government and Popular Participation in Peru, 1968–1972.* Ithaca, N.Y.: Latin American Studies Program, Cornell University.

———. 1980. *Peru: The Authoritarian Tradition.* New York: Praeger.

———. 1990. "Peru's Persistent Problems." *Current History* 89, no. 543 (January): 5–8, 31–34.

———, ed. 1994. *Shining Path of Peru.* 2d ed. New York: St. Martin's Press.

———. 1995. "The Revolutionary Terrorism of Peru's Shining Path." In *Terrorism in Context,* ed. Martha Crenshaw, pp. 249–308. University Park: Pennsylvania State University Press.

———. 1996. "'Fujipopulism' and Peru's Progress." *Current History* 95, no. 598 (February): 70–75.

———. 1999. "Soluciones ciudadanas y crisis política: El caso de Ayacucho." In *El juego político: Fujimori, la oposición, y las reglas,* ed. Fernando Tuesta Soldevilla, pp. 273–306. Lima: Fundación Friedrich Ebert.

———. 2000. "Democracy and Its Discontents in Fujimori's Peru." *Current History* 99, no. 634 (February): 60–65.

Portes, Alejandro, Manuel Castells, and Lauren A. Benton, eds. 1989. *The Informal Economy: Studies in Advanced and Less Developed Countries.* Baltimore: Johns Hopkins University Press.

Remmer, Karen. 1993. "The Political Economy of Elections in Latin America, 1980–1991." *American Political Science Review* 87, no. 4 (December): 393–407.

Rudolph, James D. 1992. *Peru: The Evolution of a Crisis.* Westport, Conn.: Praeger.

Senado de la República. 1992. *Violencia y pacificación en 1991*. Comisión Especial de Investigación y Estudio sobre la Violencia y Alternativas de Pacificación. Lima: Senado de la República del Perú.

Sevilla, Víctor (director of the Ayacucho Zonal Office of FONCODES). 1998a. Interview by the author. Field notes. Ayacucho, July 9.

————. 1998b. Interview by the author. Ayacucho, August 24.

Somos (weekly magazine of *El Comercio*, Lima). 1998. "La Iglesia Israelita y sus actividades" (July 18), pp. 19–22.

Starn, Orin. 1996. "Senderos inesperados: Las rondas campesinas de la sierra sur central." In *Las rondas campesinas y la derrota de Sendero Luminoso*, ed. Carlos Iván Degregori, José Coronel, Ponciano del Pino, and Orin Starn, pp. 227–69. Lima: Instituto de Estudios Peruanos.

Stern, Steve J., ed. 1998. *Shining and Other Paths: War and Society in Peru, 1980–1995*. Durham, N.C.: Duke University Press.

Stokes, Susan. 1995. *Cultures in Conflict: Social Movements and the State in Peru*. Berkeley: University of California Press.

Tanaka, Martín. 1998. *Los espejismos de la democracia: El colapso del sistema de los partidos en el Perú, 1980–1995, en perspectiva comparada*. Lima: Instituto de Estudios Peruanos.

Tapia, Carlos. 1997. *Las Fuerzas Armadas y Sendero Luminoso: Dos estrategias y un final*. Lima: Instituto de Estudios Peruanos.

Tocqueville, Alexis de. 1960. *Democracy in America*. Vols. 1 and 2. New York: Vintage Books.

Vásquez, Major Carlos (Peruvian Army coordinator for the Comité de Autodefensa Civil [Civil Self-Defense Committee; CAC] of Ayacucho and Huancavelica). 1998. Conversation with the author. Ayacucho, May 28.

Von Mettenheim, Kurt, and James Malloy, eds. 1998. *Deepening Democracy in Latin America*. Pittsburgh: University of Pittsburgh Press.

Webb, Richard. 1977. *Government Policy and the Distribution of Income in Peru*. Cambridge, Mass.: Harvard University Press.

Werlich, David P. 1991. "Fujimori and the 'Disaster' in Peru." *Current History* 90, no. 553 (February): 61–64, 81–83.

PART FOUR

Ethnic Responses to Injustices

CHAPTER TEN

Social Justice and the New Indigenous Politics

An Analysis of Guatemala, the Central Andes, and Chiapas

JOHN A. PEELER

Democratization in Latin America since the 1980s has included the emergence of indigenous peoples into the political arena, especially in the four countries where these peoples approach or exceed a majority of the population—Bolivia, Ecuador, Guatemala, and Peru (Warren 1993; Radcliffe and Westwood 1996; Díaz Polanco 1997; Yashar 1998)—and in Chiapas, Mexico (Harvey 1998; Womack 1999).[1] Indigenous peoples gained political power and cultural rights within these fragile new democracies either by emphasizing class and economic issues or by stressing cultural identity. This chapter will argue that the former emphasis constitutes a demand for social justice as equality among citizens, while the latter constitutes a demand for social justice as recognition of difference. Social and economic structures render the achievement of either model of social justice highly problematic.

Citizenship is, of course, central to democracy. While liberal approaches to democracy depict the citizens' role as consenting to rulers, radical approaches build on Rousseau and Marx to envision a more participatory citizenship. In either case, citizenship is crucial (López 1997; Peeler 1998). Both of these currents tend to treat citizenship as unitary and, in principle, equal. Whatever levels of inequality may persist between citizens are problematic.

The model of unitary citizenship does not allow space for difference, for distinct communities to coexist within one polity. Lijphart and others developed a theory of "consociational" democracy to account for the "politics of accommodation" that prevails for long periods between potentially hostile political communities whose rivalries could not immobilize the government or destabilize democracy. Advocates of this position argue that justice is to be found in the effective autonomy and self-determination of each of the communities within a plurinational or pluriethnic state. Lijphart focused principally on the European cases of the Netherlands, Belgium, Switzerland, and Austria. Peeler (1985: chap. 3) deals with this issue in the Latin American cases of Colombia, Costa Rica, and Venezuela. And increasingly, in Latin America and elsewhere, subaltern ethnic groups demand recognition as constituents of plurinational or pluriethnic states, rather than as individually equal citizens of nation-states. (On consociational democracy, see Lijphart 1984; on plurinational and pluriethnic states and democracy, see Young 1990.)

The indigenous peoples of the cases compared in this chapter have used an intriguing variety of struggles for equality and for autonomy. After an extensive review of the cases, the chapter will conclude with an analysis of what promise each strategy holds for bettering the lives of Latin America's indigenous peoples.

HISTORICAL OVERVIEW

At the time of the Spanish conquest, all of the territories under discussion in this chapter were densely populated by complex, sophisticated societies. (Useful sources on the history of indigenous peoples in these countries include Handy 1984; Stern 1987, 1993; Smith 1990; Quintero and Silva 1995; and López 1997.) These highly developed societies were conquered in the course of the early to mid-sixteenth centuries, though pockets of autonomy like Machu Picchu persisted. The populations were large enough to survive the depredations of disease, repression, and forced labor that ensued. The surviving indigenous populations came to be absolutely fundamental to the colonial economy. The colonial regimes and their republican successors, depending on the indigenous societies for labor, thus sought simultaneously to subjugate and to sustain them. The indigenous responses to the colonial regimes included submission (with a variety of insubordinate subterfuges), flight, and armed rebellion.

The main emphasis of the liberal regimes that emerged in the mid- to late nineteenth century was to open the region to trade. In promoting capitalist private property, liberalism frequently resulted in the dispossession of the indigenous peoples and their reduction to wage labor and debt peonage.[2] Many communities barely survived. Political liberalism showed no concern for community integrity, but considered indigenous individuals, in principle, as citizens. However, the exercise of citizenship was usually limited to those with either property or literacy, so the vast majority of the indigenous were politically marginalized. To the extent that there was indigenous political participation, it usually took the form of *gamonalismo,* or local clientelism, whereby a local *jefe* (chief, perhaps indigenous, perhaps *mestizo*) would buy and sell votes in return for favors.

By about 1930, then, all five cases considered here displayed a remarkably similar pattern: an indigenous majority that was politically marginalized, socially and culturally besieged, and economically exploited. The indigenous peoples were not part of the nation, but they were part of the economy.

Initial Political Mobilization

The dominant approach to indigenous affairs since the 1930s may be called *indigenismo,* a movement among white or *mestizo* intellectuals that affirms the indigenous heritage of Latin America while advocating the integration of the indigenous into the *mestizo* nation. This outlook was systematically formulated by Víctor Raúl Haya de la Torre, founder of Alianza Popular Revolucionaria Americana (American Popular Revolutionary Alliance; APRA) in Peru, and by his Marxist compatriot and founder of the Peruvian Communist Party, José Carlos Mariátegui.

In the Chaco War (1932–35), indigenous peoples were politically mobilized for the first time in Bolivia and Paraguay, but especially in Bolivia, where the mobilization led to their being treated, for the first time, as part of the nation. Subsequently, in the 1940s, the indigenous peasantry of the Bolivian highlands formed peasant *sindicatos* (unions), as part of the political effervescence that led to the great revolution of 1952. Indigenous communities compelled the new revolutionary government of the Movimiento Nacional Revolucionario (National Revolutionary Movement; MNR)[3] to recognize them and to institutionalize a massive land redistribution that vested the land in peasant communities and individual small landholders. In an important rhetorical shift, speakers of Aymara and Quechua insisted that they not be called *indios,* but rather *campesinos,* or peasants. The MNR shrewdly incorporated the peasantry as its principal mass political base. MNR governments were then able, in the late 1950s, to rely on their peasant base to effect a shift to a much more conservative stance that would attract aid from a U.S. government obsessed with communism and revolution. The indigenous peasantry could never again be ignored, but after the mid-1950s it was part of the MNR's clientelistic machine (Malloy 1970; Dunkerley 1984).

Also during this period, reformers and revolutionaries in Guatemala sought to mobilize the indigenous majority for the overthrow of the hated dictator, Jorge Ubico (in 1944), and the subsequent decade of radical reform under Presidents Juan José Arévalo and Jacobo Arbenz. The reformers (drawn from elite and middle-class urban sectors and allied with the small Guatemalan Communist Party and its working-class supporters in the cities and banana plantations) implemented an extensive agrarian reform. There was a substantial blossoming of peasant and indigenous-based unions supporting the reform, only to be repressed and driven underground with the CIA-sponsored coup of 1954 (Handy 1989).

In Peru, the political mobilization of indigenous peoples took place within the context of a long-standing national policy of legally recognizing indigenous peasant communities and permitting them access to the court system. The peasantry and the indigenous populations of the Andes were essentially conflated, which permitted indigenous communities considerable success in pursuing land disputes with nonindigenous landowners. Defining indigenous communities in terms of class promoted the organization of peasant *sindicatos* that borrowed organizational and mobilizational techniques from urban labor unions. By the early 1960s, in such areas as the La Convención Valley of the *departamento* of Cuzco, nonindigenous revolutionaries had made common cause with the peasants in armed resistance (Remy 1994).

In Ecuador, peasant *sindicatos,* allied with the national Communist Party, were organized as early as the 1920s, emphasizing economic demands in the context of a class analysis of society. Peasant land seizures and other uprisings became quite widespread in the late 1950s and early 1960s. The agrarian reforms of 1964 and 1973 finished the peasant unions by breaking down cohesion, creating divergent interests among those who benefited from reform and those who did not. Still, the tradition of an assertive, predominantly indigenous peasantry did not die. Rather, as we will see below, it transformed itself into an emerging national indigenous movement (Ibarra 1992; Selverston 1994; Quintero and Silva 1995: chap. 15).

Chiapas, like the rest of Mexico, was involved in the reforms of the Lázaro Cárdenas era, which involved the promotion of peasant organizations paternalistically integrated into the ruling party. The indigenous population was organized as part of the peasantry but was not permitted to act independently (Harvey 1998: chap. 2).

All of these cases had significant experience with political action by the indigenous, often in alliance with nonindigenous sectors. Most often, they demanded land and benefits from the state without explicit regard for ethnicity. Up to the 1960s, indigenous political activity was frequent, but it was framed more as class conflict than as ethnic conflict.

Repression and Counterinsurgency

The victory of the Cuban revolutionary movement of Fidel Castro in 1959 was a seminal event: in virtually every country of Latin America, leftist forces sought to analyze it for lessons that could be applied to their own national conditions. Pressure for revolutionary change was often reflected in the emergence of insurgent forces. In the places under discussion in this chapter, revolutionary movements sought to mobilize the indigenous majorities. Although none was very successful, their presence promoted new thinking among ruling elites about national security (Wickham-Crowley 1991, 1992).

The response of the authorities took two forms, reformist and repressive. The Peruvian military regime of Juan Velasco Alvarado, which took power in 1968 and ruled until 1975, is the prototype of the reformist response. Seeking to safeguard national security through a strategy of social justice, the Velasco regime carried out the most extensive agrarian reform in Peruvian history and promoted popular organizations, both rural and urban. Its insistence on maintaining corporatistic state control over these organizations, however, limited their effectiveness. Similar military regimes prevailed for shorter periods in both Ecuador (Guillermo Rodríguez Lara, from 1972 to 1976) and Bolivia (René Barrientos, Juan José Torres, and Alfredo Ovando, from 1966 to 1971). Guatemala saw only the faintest echo of this reformist pattern in the weak civilian presidency of Julio César Méndez Montenegro (1966 to 1970), whose main thrust was to preside not over reforms but rather over a brutal counterinsurgency campaign (Wickham-Crowley 1992: chap. 8).

Although the intent of the military reformers was to prevent revolution, their redistributive strategy usually provoked resistance from both national economic elites and from multinational corporations. This conservative resistance was generally supported by the United States, which after 1965 increasingly emphasized counterinsurgency and encouraged Latin American military establishments to see their national defense role in terms of combating internal subversion (Schoultz 1981, 1987).

The result was a series of reactionary military regimes during the 1970s that repressed popular movements, imposed rigorous controls on indigenous communities, and promoted the concentration of income and property at the expense of the poor and indigenous. In Guatemala, a series of repressive and corrupt military presidents ruled from 1970 until 1985, when they finally yielded to internal and external pressure for a transition to democracy. During the period over two hundred thousand Guatemalans, most of whom were noncombatant Mayans, died in the civil war. Many more thousands disappeared and about one million were forced into internal or external exile. Hundreds of Mayans joined the insurgents.

With Bolivia's indigenous peasantry clientelistically incorporated first by the MNR and then by the progressive military governments of Barrientos, Torres, and Ovando, that country did not develop a generalized national insurgency; thus there was less call for military savagery. Though not as brutal as the contemporaneous Guatemalan regime, the Bolivian military did nevertheless repress autonomous popular movements after 1971, breaking down the so-called Military-Peasant Pact that had been forged by General Barrientos (Malloy 1988).

In Peru, the more conservative regime led by General Francisco Morales Bermúdez (1975–80) ended many of the populist initiatives of Velasco Alvarado and implemented an orthodox policy of capitalist development. Repression was considerably less intense than in Bolivia and hardly bears comparison with what was happening in Guatemala. No national insurgency existed in Peru during the 1970s, but in the 1980s (see below) two major insurgencies, Sendero Luminoso (Shining Path) and Tupac Amaru, emerged (McClintock and Lowenthal 1983).

The conservative military reaction was briefest in Ecuador, where the reformist regime of General Rodríguez Lara was ousted by more conservative officers in 1976 and elections for a civilian president were held in 1978, after a new constitution had been drafted that year. Although reformist and redistributive policies were replaced by more orthodox approaches, repression was minimal in Ecuador as compared with the other three countries. There was no national insurgency in Ecuador during the 1970s (Martz 1987).

Mexico, with its highly institutionalized ruling party, did not experience an analogous cycle of reformist and conservative regimes, but the presidency of Luis Echeverría Álvarez (1970–76) was somewhat more reformist, while that of José López Portillo (1976–82) was more repressive—at least in terms of how these presidencies affected Chiapas (Harvey 1998: chaps. 2–3).

In sum, Guatemala appears distinguished both by the presence of a nationally significant insurgency during the 1970s and by a much higher level of repression. The insurgency showed increasing ability to appeal to the Mayan population. By contrast, the three Andean countries had only localized insurgencies and less repression. This is not to say that they were politically quiescent, only that mass political action was not channeled into insurgency in the Andean cases but was in Guatemala.

An important influence on the indigenous response to repression and counterinsurgency was the progressive sector of the Roman Catholic Church, which promoted the empowerment of the poor (including indigenous peoples) to act for themselves. Meanwhile, more traditional religious sectors were politically conservative and allied with the military authorities (Berryman 1987).

Conditions in all countries were profoundly shaped by external forces. The United States, trying to prevent the spread of the Cuban Revolution, expanded military aid and pushed military establishments to preempt or repress any potentially revolutionary movement. Interwoven with this counterinsurgency emphasis, the United States also pushed for human rights and for transitions to democracy as another means of preventing revolution. This emphasis on human rights and democracy was particularly evident in the early years of President Carter (1977–79), and reemerged in the later years of President Reagan (1985–89). The military rulers in all four countries would have had to swim against a strong current to retain control far into the 1980s. Even in Guatemala, where repression was strongest and the insurgency the most threatening, movement toward a transition began to emerge with the Ríos Montt coup of 1982, and was completed in 1985 with the inauguration of President Cerezo Arévalo (Schoultz 1998: 362–66).

Further, a deterioration in the economic climate in the early 1980s left all four countries with the need to resort to the International Monetary Fund and other sources of concessionary finance. This exposed them to intense pressure to adopt orthodox stabilization plans and neoliberal structural adjustment plans that concentrated adverse effects on the poor majority of the populations, including the indigenous (Haggard and Kaufman 1995). The prolonged economic crisis mobilized indigenous political movements, pushing people into the political arena to demand attention to their needs as well as getting them to work together in order to maximize their influence. The establishment of democratic regimes gave them space to act politically with much less fear of repression. The emergence of important indigenous movements in all five cases since the early 1980s is thus directly related to these global changes (Peeler 1998: chap. 3).

INDIGENOUS POLITICAL ACTION

Bolivia

Following the breakdown of the clientelistic Military-Peasant Pact in the mid-1970s, the energy of Bolivian peasants was increasingly directed toward autonomous organization. Leftists generally emphasized the class status of peasants and viewed ethnic appeals as divisive. However, as early as the 1960s, some parties and movements emphasized indigenous (especially Aymara) culture and tradition. The symbolic inspiration for most of these movements was the figure of Tupak Katari, indigenous rebel of 1781 in the colonial province of Upper Peru.

Katarismo was less a movement than a banner denoting the political and cultural assertion of Aymara identity. It was prone from its inception to fragmentation based on competing leadership ambitions and ideological perspectives. Nevertheless, Katarismo was notably more successful than class-based movements in gaining adherents among indigenous peasants of the altiplano. By the 1990s, at least six Katarista political parties were active on the national scene. Multiple divisions assured that none of the Katarista parties ever captured a large vote. One beneficiary of the political mobilization of indigenous people was the populist Conciencia de Patria (Patriotic Consciousness; CONDEPA) movement of La Paz radio commentator Carlos Palenque, who was elected mayor of La Paz three times on the basis of a broad cultural appeal to the poor cholos (i.e., mestizos) and indigenous people living in and around La Paz. Palenque, who died in 1997, also made serious runs for the presidency, gaining more than 10 percent of the vote in 1989 and 1993. By the 1990s most of the major parties and candidates were appealing to indigenous voters on the basis of themes originally raised by the Kataristas.

Katarismo wielded more power as a principal current in the organization of peasant unions. There, too, the conflict between class orientation and cultural orientation was generally present, posing a challenge to unity. However, after 1983, the Confederación Sindical Única de Trabajadores Campesinos de Bolivia (Single Union Confederation of Peasant Workers of Bolivia; CSUTCB) held together in spite of this strain. This confederation's founding document reaffirmed class struggle, but it also condemned ethnic discrimination and called for a plurinational state (Albó 1994: 61).

The diverse indigenous peoples from the tropical lands to the north, east, and southeast of the Andes emerged onto the national stage in 1991, when hundreds of individuals from the northern lowlands (Beni) marched for thirty-five days from the lowlands, over high passes of fourteen thousand feet, to La Paz, demanding recognition of their right to "territory and dignity." The lowland peoples organized the Confederación Indígena del Oriente, Chaco, y Amazonía de Bolivia (Indigenous Confederation of the Oriente, Chaco, and Amazonia of Bolivia; CIDOB). However, there is not yet (in contrast to Ecuador; see below) an organization that links indigenous peoples of highland and lowland.

Bolivia has a long tradition of class-oriented organization of its peasants, who are predominantly indigenous (Quechua and Aymara). Without losing that tradition, the emphasis shifted since the early 1980s to organization based on indigenous cultural interests. The two orientations are not totally incompatible in a society where the vast majority of peasants are indigenous and the vast majority of indigenous are peasants—and virtually all are poor. But it is not yet clear whether the increasing consciousness and organization of Bolivia's indigenous peoples will yield more than symbolic gains, such as the election of the Aymara Víctor Hugo Cárdenas as vice president in 1993 (Rivera Cusicanqui 1991; Ströbele-Gregor 1994; Ticona, Rojas, and Albó 1995; Albó 1996).

Ecuador

As in Bolivia, indigenous political organization in Ecuador has two distinct histories, one in the Sierra, another in Amazonia. Ecuador also saw an incipient indigenous movement in its Pacific coastal region (Selmeski 1992: 98). As distinct from Bolivia, however, in Ecuador movements from the different regions overcame their distinct origins and social bases to build a durable and powerful national movement.

The earliest modern indigenous organization in Ecuador, the Federación Ecuatoriana de Indígenas (Ecuadorian Federation of Indigenous Peoples; FEI), was founded in 1944 under the aegis of the Ecuadorian Communist Party and sought to organize indigenous people as workers and peasants. Progressive sectors of the Church sponsored the leading indigenous federation of the Sierra, Ecuador Runacunapac Riccharimui (Awakening of the Ecuadorian Indigenous People; ECUARUNARI), but after 1980 this federation increasingly became more leftist and class-oriented, without abandoning its indigenous identity (Selverston 1994: 138). In 1980, Confederación de Nacionalidades Indígenas de la Amazonía del Ecuador (Confederation of Indigenous Nationalities of the Amazonia of Ecuador; CONFENIAE) was founded to integrate all indigenous organizations from the Oriente, or Amazonia.

The separate indigenous communities in Ecuador succeeded as early as 1986 in forming the Confederación de Nacionalidades del Ecuador (or CONAIE), a national indigenous confederation that merged the ECUARUNARI, from the Sierra, and CONFENIAE (Pacari 1996: 24). CONAIE, moreover, became much more than a passive umbrella organization. It provided the principal organizational force behind the succession of indigenous demonstrations and strikes that marked Ecuadorian politics since 1990 (Pacari 1996).

In 1990, members of CONAIE occupied the Cathedral of Santo Domingo in Quito, while thousands of others closed roads and shut down commerce and transportation for over a week. The principal demand was for action by the government to expedite land claims in the Sierra and territorial claims of indigenous peoples in the Oriente. For the first time in the hemisphere, a unified, coherent coalition of indigenous peoples had forced their way onto the national stage, demanding attention to their needs, as defined by them (Almeida et al. 1991; Field 1991; Selverston 1994).

In 1992, Organización de Pueblos Indígenas de Pastaza (Organization of Indigenous Peoples of Pastaza; OPIP) organized a march from the lowland province of Pastaza to Quito, to demand the settlement of indigenous land claims in Pastaza (Collins 1992). In 1994, CONAIE (with two other organizations, the Federación Nacional de Organizaciones Campesinas-Indígenas [National Federation of Indigenous-Peasant Organizations; FENOC-I] and the Federación Evangélica de Indígenas Ecuatorianos [Evangelical Federation of Indigenous Ecuadorians; EFIE]) organized another mobilization that shut down the country for two weeks (Guerrero 1996). In 2000, an indigenous uprising in league with military reformers forced President Jamil Mahuad from power after he had attempted to implement neoliberal economic reforms, but the military high command, responding to pressure from the United States, prevented the consolidation of a reformist government.

CONAIE and other indigenous organizations placed indigenous concerns and perspectives on the Ecuadorian agenda. These groups are very far from controlling the state, but they have achieved recognition as a legitimate voice to be heard in national policymaking. An indigenous-oriented political party, Pacha Kutic, gained seats in Congress in the mid-1990s (Sánchez and Freidenberg 1999). Selverston (1994: 131) argues that the leaders of the indigenous movement created this political space by couching their demands in "cultural" terms. However, in spite of the tendency to organize along ethnic lines, basic economic issues were always a central part of the agenda of indigenous organizations. Class is a meaningful organizational principle, but it apparently needs to be mediated by ethnicity to engage indigenous people (León 1991; Ibarra 1992; Santana 1992; CONAIE 1994; Zamosc 1994).

Peru

For the Quechua and Aymara of the Peruvian Sierra, a key turning point was the decision of the Augusto Leguía y Salcedo government in the 1920s (reflecting *indigenista* thinking then current) to extend legal recognition to indigenous communities, thereby reversing the liberal policy of treating indigenous people purely as individual citizens. This shaped indigenous politics in Peru; first, by opening the courts to communities for restitution of lands, thereby reinforcing the economic integrity and political legitimacy of indigenous communities; and second, by cementing an equation between indigenous status and peasant class that still characterizes Peru today. The indigenous/peasant communities of the Andes characteristically make demands that focus on economic or class-based objectives, rather than cultural objectives, because the long-standing recognition of their communities permits them to take for granted the integrity of their cultural communities (Remy 1994: 111–13).

The Amazonian indigenous peoples of Peru had a distinct experience that set them apart from their Andean compatriots. Until the 1980s the state did not have a strong presence in Amazonia; it left administration of the region largely to Catholic missions and other private actors. The indigenous inhabitants were not seen as effective citizens with rights until they became "civilized." Finally, in the 1950s, the state organized the first reserves for Amazonian peoples (Ballón Aguirre 1987; Remy 1994: 117).

By the 1950s, the Peruvian Andes were characterized by a mix of peasant communities and *haciendas,* the latter having peasants as quasi-feudal laborers who were attached to the *hacienda* rather than to a community. Both sectors (communities and *haciendas*) were increasingly organized in *sindicatos* to defend their economic interests, and by the late 1950s these organizations were establishing links among themselves and organizing regional confederations such as the Federación Provincial de Campesinos de La Convención y Lares (Provincial Federation of Peasants of La Convención and Lares), in the *departamento* of Cuzco (Handelman 1975: 70–83; Remy 1994: 114–15).

During the 1960s, peasant organizations such as that of La Convención became more militant, supporting insurgent movements inspired by the Cuban Revolution. Under President Fernando Belaúnde Terry, the armed forces successfully put down the La Convención insurgency, then imposed an agrarian reform in the valley. The threat of peasant support for insurgency, and the direct experience of counterinsurgency, led the Peruvian armed forces in the direction of major social reforms for the purpose of immunizing Peru from the threat of revolution (McClintock 1981: chap. 3).

After the 1968 military coup, the military government of Velasco Alvarado sponsored the most sweeping agrarian reform in Peruvian history, as well as local and national peasant organizations. Both initiatives were part of an attempt to aid and mobilize the poorest sectors of society as a means of preventing a more radical and uncontrolled revolution. The reform destroyed the *haciendas* of the Sierra and constituted peasant cooperatives to replace them, thereby irreversibly changing the rural class structure in favor of the indigenous peasantry. The failure of the government to control all peasant organizations left a highly organized but fragmented peasantry that is tied to various parties but not under state control, and that continues to define its demands more in terms of class than of ethnicity (Handelman 1975; McClintock and Lowenthal 1983).

The military coup of 1968 opened new opportunities for Amazonian peoples. The new government recognized a new organizational form, the native community, which was to have a status quite distinct from that of peasant communities in the Andes. The native communities of the Amazon tended to be concerned with retaining or regaining territory, and with demanding bilingual education in order to maintain their cultures. These preoccupations certainly have an economic dimension, but they are principally aimed at preserving cultural integrity and autonomy in the face of economic and political pressures from outside. Since the 1970s, Amazonian indigenous populations have built ethnic and zonal federations, which have received strong backing from a variety of outside interests that have their own reasons for supporting indigenous organization in the region. In addition to the long-standing Catholic missions, Protestant groups such as the Summer Institute of Linguistics,[4] a variety of nongovernmental organizations such as Cultural Survival, and environmentalists and anthropologists working in the region—all have come to support (and guide) the organization of Amazonian peoples. Meanwhile, the populace seems to be learning from the outside groups how better to define and defend their societies and cultures.[5]

The most significant development of the 1980s in the Peruvian Sierra was the emergence of the Shining Path insurgency. The radical group experienced some early success in mobilizing the peasantry for revolutionary struggle. By 1990, the Peruvian state was seriously threatened. While the army initially overreacted to the threat by attacking peasant villages on the mere suspicion of complicity, indigenous peasant communities throughout the highlands and in much of Amazonia on their own had organized local self-defense squads *(rondas campesinas)* that kept the guerrillas from dominating many communities. These self-defense squads were at first resisted by the army, but were later encouraged (with support from President García and especially President Fujimori) as part of its counterinsurgency strategy. By the mid-1990s, the threat from Shining Path was largely blunted (NACLA 1990–91; Palmer 1992; Degregori 1997; McClintock 1998; also see chapter 9 of the present volume).

Indigenous peasant communities, with a tradition of autonomous organization and defense of their own interests, were in some cases initially receptive to Shining Path's appeals, which were designed to appeal to them as oppressed people. However, the ruthlessness of the guerrillas in eliminating even the most popular non–Shining Path local leaders eventually undermined their support. By the late 1980s, peasant communities increasingly resisted Shining Path's hegemony and even collaborated with the army. It may be that their willingness to do so was also a fruit of the army's agrarian reform and its promotion of peasant organizations after 1968. One result, argues Remy (1994: 127), was that the indigenous peasantry gained increased acceptance in urban circles as a legitimate and respected interlocutor in Peruvian national affairs. Paradoxically, this brutal revolutionary insurgency may have finally cemented a bond between the indigenous peasants and the *mestizo* nation (Degregori 1997; McClintock 1998).

Amazonian peoples were deeply affected by the confluence of insurgency, illegal cocaine trade, and government efforts (with U.S. support) to control and repress them, all of which led to displacement and exploitation. These conflicting forces led to intense battles in the Amazonian region, with Amazonian peoples often fighting each other, as well as the drug traffickers, the insurgents, and the army (Remy 1994: 126–27).

Indigenous peoples from both the Sierra and the Amazon emerged into important political roles in Peru, but the two sectors have yet to unite in a common cause.[6] The massive peasant population of Quechua and Aymara, from the highlands, along with their close relatives who, having fled poverty and violence in the altiplano, live in the nation's urban slums, are now indisputably the mass base of Peruvian politics, speaking through their own organizations as peasants and workers more than as indigenous people. In Peruvian consciousness it is still largely the case that to be a peasant is to be indigenous, and vice versa. One's indigenous status need not be defended in Peru, while one's interests as a peasant or worker must be. The minority Amazonian populations, in contrast, still see themselves principally as distinctive peoples who want to preserve their identity and autonomy even while demanding their rights as Peruvians.

Guatemala

The relations between Guatemala's indigenous Mayan population and the state have been more conflictual than in any of the Andean countries. The Guatemalan revolutionary insurgencies were more durable than those of Peru, probably affected a larger portion of the territory and population, and may have posed as serious a challenge to the state as did the Peruvian Shining Path. During the 1980s, the challenge from the Unión Revolucionaria Nacional de Guatemala (Revolutionary Union of Guatemala; URNG) to the Guatemalan state elicited a response from the army that was unprecedented in terms of the savagery of the repression inflicted upon the indigenous population.

Prior to the 1970s, the Guatemalan approach to indigenous peoples was rhetorically parallel to those of the Andean countries: there was some commitment, in constitution, law, and policy, to the special needs of indigenous communities. But Guatemalan governments did even less to bring these policies to fruition. When the insurgency began to gain indigenous support in the 1970s, the military response was harshly repressive. Guatemala's military had seen nothing like the reformist Peruvian junta of 1968–75. The last reformist push had been the civil-military coalition of 1944–54, and all military elements sympathetic to that regime were systematically purged after the 1954 CIA-backed coup. A thoroughly reactionary army dominated Guatemalan politics from 1954 to 1985 and continued thereafter to have autonomous control of the counterinsurgency effort, notwithstanding the election of civilian presidents after 1984 (Jonas 1991; Wickham-Crowley 1992).

The Mayan peoples contrived to survive in a repressive environment mostly by avoiding direct assertions of their rights or direct challenges to authority. But the escalating repression of the 1970s and 1980s forced them to forge new, more assertive organizations, including (1) community-level or grassroots movements; (2) popular organizations; and (3) Mayan cultural institutions (Adams 1994: 162; Fischer and Brown 1996; Warren 1998).

The army attacked indigenous communities as a basic aspect of counterinsurgency. Mayan communities throughout the country responded by fleeing into exile or into the forests of northern Guatemala, or by staying and organizing to resist (see chapter 12 in this volume, plus Menchú 1984; Montejo and Akab' 1992; Stoll 1993; Wilson 1995; Zur 1998). Communities that stayed were subjected to counterinsurgency tactics, to which they responded in various ways. Virtually all villages were required to set up Patrullas de Autodefensa Civil (Civil Self-Defense Patrols; PACs). In contrast to Peru, in Guatemala the patrols were seen as an imposition by the army on a population that perceived itself as caught "between two armies" (Stoll 1993). By the late 1980s, many communities had dismantled their PACs. In 1990, the community of Santiago Atitlán, outraged by the murder of community members at the hands of an army patrol, was successful in its demands that the army withdraw entirely from the village (Adams 1994: 167).[7]

Community organization led to national popular organizations with a strong indigenous thrust. For example, the Comité de Unidad Campesino (Committee of Campesino Unity; CUC), was organized in 1978 to unify indigenous and Ladino peasants in their struggles for land and labor rights. Although the CUC had indigenous leadership, its class-based orientation and alignment with the Left provoked some members to form the more explicitly ethnic Coordinadora Nacional de Pueblos Indígenas y Campesinos (National Coordinating Committee of Indigenous People and Campesinos; CONIC). The two principal human-rights organizations, the Grupo de Apoyo Mutuo (Mutual Support Group; GAM) and the Comité Nacional de Viudas Guatemaltecas (National Committee of Guatemalan Widows; CONAVIGUAs), both had majority indigenous memberships, and the latter had indigenous leadership. Resistance to PACs took on a national dimension with the organization of the Consejo de Comunidades Étnicas "Runujal Junam" (Council of Ethnic Communities "Runujal Junam"; CERJ) in the late 1980s. In 1992, the Mayan Coordination of the New Awakening (Majawil Q'ij) led Guatemalan participation in debates over whether to celebrate or lament Columbus's regional claims. In 1994, over 150 Mayan organizations joined to form the Coalición de Organizaciones del Pueblo Maya (Coalition of Organizations of the Mayan People; COPMAGUA), which made a proposal on behalf of the Mayan peoples to the peace talks between the government and the URNG (Arias 1990; Adams 1994; Otzoy 1996; Warren 1998).

The third form of Mayan organizations, major Mayan cultural institutions, include the Academy of Mayan Languages of Guatemala, chartered by the Guatemalan Congress in 1990 and charged with standardizing the Mayan alphabet and setting up schools for each of the twenty-one Mayan languages.[8] The Mayab' Nimajay "Cholsomaj" (Mayan Educational and Cultural Center) was established in 1988 to promote all aspects of Mayan culture. The Consejo de Organizaciones Mayas de Guatemala (Council of Mayan Organizations of Guatemala; COMG) was established in 1990, seeking to coordinate fifteen Mayan cultural institutions (Adams 1994: 165–66).

Mayan popular organizations were active in the formation, in 1995, of the Frente Democrática Nueva Guatemala (New Guatemala Democratic Front; FDNG), which elected six candidates to Congress (including two Mayan women) and became the principal force of the Guatemalan Left, in spite of continuing repression. In the same campaign, other Mayan groups supported the successful presidential candidacy of the conservative Alvaro Arzú of the Partido de Avanzada Nacional (National Advancement Party) (Otzoy 1996: 35). Arzú during 1996 would finally bring to a conclusion years of peace negotiations between the government and the URNG, begun in 1991 under the terms of the 1987 Esquipulas II Central American peace accord, which included the signing of a statement that committed Guatemala to the principles of a multicultural, multilingual society. This statement was vigorously advocated by Mayan organizations observing the peace negotiations and was not originally a high priority for either the government or the URNG.

Since 1996, Mayan organizations have actively participated in the difficult and halting process of implementation. After much pressure, revisions were proposed in the Guatemalan constitution to acknowledge the principles embodied in the 1996 peace settlement, but these revisions were rejected by a popular vote in 1999, in a referendum characterized by extremely low voter turnout. The transition to peace has set up conflicts among Mayans, especially land disputes, as returning refugees seek to reclaim land now occupied by others (Taylor 1998). Various Mayan and peasant organizations, such as CONIC, have pressed the government to solve these disputes.

In the past thirty years, Guatemala's Mayans have made major advances in their organization and their ability to defend their interests in the political arena, in the context of a durable and widespread insurgency, and in the face of a brutal counterinsurgency program. During this period, the legal political arena was devoid of a left wing and labor and peasant unions were repressed. Some Mayan organizations, such as the CUC, were tacitly allied with the URNG, and Nobel Peace Prize winner Rigoberta Menchú never made a secret of her sympathy for the guerrillas' cause.[9] Other Mayan groups adopted a more conservative stance. Many organizations seemed anxious to avoid open partisan commitments; the dominant approach emphasized cultural interests such as Mayan languages and community autonomy. Economic and political demands tend to be placed within the context of cultural concerns. Because they achieved unprecedented political weight, Mayan concerns became proportionately more prominent in the political discourse of Ladinos, among whom one may note a certain nervousness about the future.

Chiapas, Mexico

On January 1, 1994, as the North American Free Trade Agreement (NAFTA) was going into effect, guerrilla fighters occupied several towns in the southeastern Mexican state of Chiapas and announced a revolutionary movement called the Ejército Zapatista de Liberación Nacional (Zapatista Army for National Liberation; EZLN).[10]

Mexico is a *mestizo* country: indigenous people make up less than 10 percent of its population. The mythology of the revolution includes a strong *indigenista* element that celebrates the Aztec and Mayan heritage, but indigenous people are nevertheless among Mexico's poorest. The Mayans of Chiapas are the poorest of the poor. Land tenure is highly concentrated, and most Mayans are either landless or land-poor. This is the socioeconomic context for political mobilization of the indigenous in Chiapas.

The political context was the clientelistic face of the Partido Revolucionario Institucional (Institutional Revolutionary Party; PRI) regime, which presented Chiapaneco peasants with means to advance their private or community interests by adhering to caciques who were the PRI's leadership at the state and local levels. Whether one sought a land title, a road, or a school, the means to get it was the classic clientelistic exchange—votes for favors. That this set peasant against peasant, and village against village, was part of the system's advantage for Mexico's rulers.

In Chiapas, some communities and individuals resisted the clientelistic game, seeking economic transformation and social justice rather than particularistic advancement. Especially in the 1970s and 1980s, a variety of organizations of civil society emerged to defend community rights and interests. In this they were encouraged by Catholic priests and activists and led by Bishop Samuel Ruiz (appointed in 1960), strongly influenced by the Liberation Theology movement of the 1960s and 1970s. Partially competing, partially cooperating with the Catholics were several organizations of the fragmented Mexican Left, each struggling to organize the population for political resistance and to create the conditions for a mass-based revolutionary insurgency. One such organization was the Fuerzas de Liberación Nacional (Forces of National Liberation; FLN), a Guevarist movement among whose cadres was a man who came to be called Subcomandante Marcos. By the late 1980s, the clandestine FLN gained a substantial political presence in Chiapas and drew together a significant force of potential Mayan combatants.

Up to this point the story of Chiapas parallels quite closely those of insurgencies elsewhere in Latin America, including Guatemala and Peru. As in other cases, the insurgent leadership came from a national leftist movement, not from the indigenous themselves. As in other cases, indigenous leadership was more visible in organizations of civil society, though outside leadership (from the Church or from the Left) was also present in civil society. As elsewhere, important segments of the indigenous population did not adhere to the revolutionary movement.

Surprisingly, though, the FLN leadership of the EZLN did not insist on a class-oriented movement. Rather, starting on the first day of January 1994, they adopted a strong emphasis on indigenous identity and rights. Whereas in Guatemala it was the Mayan intelligentsia, independently of the URNG, that opted to emphasize ethnicity over class, in Chiapas the leftist leadership itself stepped away from a class analysis. Such a step was consonant with Ché Guevara's theory of revolution, which encouraged foci of resistance wherever oppression prevailed. But Ché himself privileged class over ethnicity, like the Left in the insurgent movements in Bolivia, Ecuador, Guatemala, and Peru.

The Zapatistas' behavior after January 1, 1994, is what most distinguished Chiapas from the other cases. Rather than pursuing a prolonged guerrilla war or a nationwide uprising, the EZLN recognized its military weakness and political strength and quickly maneuvered the government into a cease-fire and political negotiations. The negotiations focused on EZLN demands for indigenous rights and agrarian reform, but also on broader demands for comprehensive, nation-wide democratization of the polity and the economy. Marcos and the EZLN proved remarkably adept at public relations on the national and international level, mobilizing support that made it politically costly for the government to repress the movement. They were thereby able, more effectively than other opposition forces, to place on the national agenda indigenous issues, social justice, and the failings of neoliberal economic policy. The election of opposition candidate Vicente Fox in 2000 led to a partial thaw between the EZLN and the new government, but even a spectacular march to Mexico City by elements of the EZLN failed to achieve a settlement of the movement's demands. In response to EZLN pressure, the Mexican government passed an indigenous rights law in 2001, but it fell well short of EZLN demands.

In Peru and Guatemala, committed revolutionary movements fought unsuccessfully for years to bring about revolution. Eventually, after much suffering, they inadvertently promoted the political opening that allowed indigenous political mobilization (in very different forms in the two countries). In Chiapas, the revolutionary leadership seems to have "cut to the chase," using its initial uprising as a springboard to national debate rather than to prolonged insurgency. That the formal negotiations remain inconclusive is less important than that the national debate goes on.

CONCLUSIONS

All five of the Latin American cases examined in this chapter have witnessed an unprecedented emergence of indigenous peoples as mainstream political actors. Because the indigenous majorities have been essential labor forces for each successive economic model in all five cases, the ruling classes needed to control them and exploit them, but not to annihilate them. This lowly but consequential status gave them the means to survive, and half a millennium of experience in managing the managers, in finding the openings, whether through the courts, through protest and pressure, or through political alliances.

The openings were plentiful. Global changes progressively wore away the foundations of Latin America's systems of domination. Reactionary military regimes fell, victims of economic mismanagement of the debt crisis and of the backlash against their repression. The usual International Monetary Fund demand that the state shrink its roles in economy and society had the unexpected effect of promoting popular movements in general, and indigenous movements in particular, because such policies readily provoked popular protest. The end of the Cold War and the collapse of the Soviet Union helped to clear the way for a transition to liberal democracy throughout Latin America (Peeler 1998: chap. 4). That, in turn, provided a much more open political arena for emerging indigenous political actors.

Not surprisingly, the cases examined in this chapter showed considerable parallels in their development during the period. Authoritarian regimes in each country during the 1970s yielded to a transition to constitutional democracy. The negotiation of new constitutions, or major constitutional revisions, provided indigenous movements with opportunities for political victories that enhanced their visibility and political leverage. Under democratic rule, the energies and pressures produced by years of insurgency, counterinsurgency, and economic crisis could be more easily and openly expressed. At the same time, as Yashar (1998) shows, indigenous organizations in all countries had strong incentives to organize as a result of the dismantling of state programs in rural areas in the 1980s and 1990s.

Where histories and social structures are fundamentally similar, the major source of variations between countries would seem to be distinct political environments. For example, many Peruvian indigenous cooperated with the army against Shining Path, while few Guatemalans cooperated with the army except under duress. It is likely that this difference is related to the extremely repressive history of the Guatemalan army and the more reformist history of the Peruvian army. Also, as previously noted, the URNG and Shining Path differed in their characteristic interactions with indigenous peasants: Shining Path tended to be much more violent and uncompromising in its attempts to purge independent local leaders, while the URNG tended to relate more cooperatively with local communities.

Yashar (1998: 31–32) argues that the countries with indigenous movements had diverse experiences of political liberalization, from relatively full openings in Ecuador and Bolivia, to partial opening in Mexico and uneven opening in Guatemala, to growing restrictions and authoritarianism in Peru (notwithstanding its formal transition to democracy after 1980). However, although the Peruvian regime eventually became more restrictive, it started out around 1980 much less repressive than the Guatemalan regime and was certainly no more repressive than Guatemala in the late 1990s.

The five cases here represent different mixes of the approaches to citizenship and justice outlined in the opening of this chapter. In Peru, we find that indigenous intervention in the political process is largely cast in terms of demands for economic advancement, especially through land tenure in the Sierra and collective territorial rights in Amazonia. The right of Andean *campesinos* to have full civil and political rights, while retaining their distinctive language and culture, has long since been accepted in Peru. They are demanding—as a class, not as an ethnic group— the economic and social rights that go with a more radical approach to citizenship. They may be undergoing, as López (1997) argues, a process of *cholificación,* but without giving up their Quechua identity. Peru represents a clear commitment of indigenous people to a strategy of incorporation into the larger society, and of struggle for advancement as citizens within that society. As citizens in the Peruvian context, they are not called upon to abandon their indigenous identity, but it is not their main political focus.

Guatemala represents the opposite case. Even though class-oriented peasant organizations that cut across the Mayan-Ladino divide remain important parts of the political process, what is striking here is the degree to which explicitly Mayan organizations came to the fore. Such organizations use citizen rights the better to make demands for cultural autonomy and acceptance of the principle of a plurinational state—the sorts of demands that are not being seriously articulated in Peru.

Ecuador and Bolivia represent intermediate cases. The tradition of class struggle is very strong in Bolivia and has a well-established organizational base. In the Revolution, indigenous peasants defined themselves as *campesinos,* not Indians. Yet, in the last generation the Katarista movement brought indigenous Aymara consciousness to the center of Bolivian politics, even as minority peoples from the eastern lowlands began to assert themselves. The Bolivian pattern is thus mixed, but it is probably closer to the Peruvian pattern than to the Guatemalan.

Ecuador's case is the one in which explicitly indigenous organizations moved beyond a stage of exuberant proliferation to achieve substantial national unity. CONAIE, with its demands for ethnic autonomy and for the acceptance of Ecuador as a plurinational state, became a major player in national politics. Yet Ecuador also retains a significant element of more class-oriented organizations that make economic demands. Ecuador, then, is also a blend but is perhaps more similar to Guatemala than to Peru.

The distinct outcomes in these four cases are at least partially attributable to differences in levels of repression of indigenous organization and in the paths left open by repressive forces. Guatemala consistently displayed the most repressive political environment, especially toward revolutionary, class-based movements. Guatemala was scarcely friendly to Mayan cultural organizations, but such groups appeared less threatening to the established order than a revolutionary insurgency like the URNG. National Mayan cultural organizations like COPMAGUA thus posed a paradoxical challenge to the established political order, simply by seeming to be less threatening than the rebel URNG.

Many of the cultural rights demanded by the Mayans are already recognized in Peru, where there is thus less need for cultural organization and struggle; instead, economic issues come to the fore. Government repression is aimed squarely at class-based revolutionary activity (e.g., Sendero Luminoso, the Shining Path). The approach that remains open in Peru, then, is that of ad hoc struggles of local communities for immediate economic interests.

Bolivia and Ecuador have displayed less consistent, systematic repression since 1980 (in the absence of major insurgencies), strong traditions of indigenous peasant participation in economically oriented *sindicatos,* and the persistence of indigenous identity among peasants. Thus both paths, that of economic demands and that of cultural vindication, are open in Bolivia and Ecuador, and both have been taken.

Not surprisingly, in light of its Mayan heritage, Chiapas bears a strong resemblance to Guatemala in terms of the prevalence there of cultural and ethnic demands over class demands. The Mexican state has been less repressive than Guatemala's, but it has been similarly more tolerant of cultural than of class-based demands. The Mexican state is so powerful, relative to the indigenous movement, that the indigenous cannot hope to change it except in conjunction with many other elements of Mexican society.

Is either the strategy of equality or the strategy of difference likely to attain its objectives? The strategy of equality, with the goal of full economic and social citizenship for all, runs into the enormous social and economic inequalities that still exist in all five societies, inequalities that entrench the powerful. Nothing fundamental has changed in the class structure, which is supported by the global capitalist system. Democracies are vitiated by authoritarianism, corruption, and instability. The line of least resistance for indigenous movements will be to adapt themselves to the economic and political status quo, demanding marginal economic gains in return for playing clientelistic games.

The strategy of difference, of ethnic autonomy and plurinationality, confronts a Spanish-speaking power structure that will resist yielding power and equality to indigenous peoples. However, that ethnic power structure has much weaker international support than does the capitalist class structure. In Guatemala, for example, should the indigenous movement achieve its full potential in terms of unity and political mobilization, it could actually win national political power by electoral means. Since the movement is not explicitly anticapitalist, it might be able to win power without provoking a reaction like that of 1954. To stave off such a result, the present power structure might negotiate an ethnic power-sharing arrangement, institutionalizing the idea of a plurinational or pluriethnic state. Any plan for ethnic power sharing would require intense commitment of leaders on all sides to maintaining the balance—or it could easily break down into civil strife.

Probably, the emergence of indigenous peoples onto the political stage will change little. Ethnic power sharing is less likely to occur than the reimposition of a highly repressive dictatorship to put down a potentially winning indigenous movement. But possibly, the political emergence of the indigenous could change everything.

NOTES

Earlier versions of this chapter were presented to the Northeastern Political Science Association, Philadelphia, November 13–15, 1997; to the Escuela Andina de Postgrado, Centro Bartolomé de las Casas, Cusco, June 10, 1998; and to the Latin American Studies Association, Chicago, September 24–26, 1998. And a version of this chapter is to be published as "Citizenship and Difference in Latin American Indigenous Politics: Democratic Theory and Comparative Politics," in *New Approaches to Comparative Politics: Insights from Political Theory,* ed. Jennifer S. Holmes (Lanham, Md.: Lexington Books, 2003). I acknowledge the very helpful comments of Susan Eckstein and Brian Selmeski.

1. In the Latin American context, one is considered indigenous when one's primary language is indigenous and one participates in the culture of an indigenous people. Many Latin Americans are largely or entirely of indigenous lineage but would be viewed as indigenous only if they also carried out indigenous cultural practices. Because indigenous people, culturally as well as biologically defined, constitute only a small portion of all Mexicans, indigenous movements

there focus on minority rights. In contrast, in Bolivia, Ecuador, Guatemala, and Peru the indigenous populations can aspire to rule as a national majority; as will become clear, the relatively small populations inhabiting the Amazon Basin, as well as other isolated regions, are typically considered distinct from the dense populations inhabiting the highlands of the four countries. The Amazonian populations are always referred to as indigenous, while the highland populations, though culturally and linguistically distinct, sometimes are not referred to as indigenous.

2. Perhaps the most determined effort in the four countries to resist the liberal political economy was mounted by the Conservative caudillo Rafael Carrera in Guatemala. With strong indigenous support, he ruled from 1840 to 1865, acting forcefully as the benevolent *patrón* of indigenous communities. Only after his overthrow did Liberal reform come to Guatemala.

3. The Movimiento Nacional Revolucionario was basically a middle-class reform movement led by Víctor Paz Estenssoro, which allied with workers and peasants to seize power in the revolution of 1952.

4. The Summer Institute of Linguistics is a missionary-linked conservative Protestant organization long active in several Latin American countries, including Bolivia, Ecuador, Guatemala, and Peru. It has faced charges from the Left that it collaborates with the CIA.

5. Evaristo Nugkuag Ikanan provides an example of far-sighted indigenous leadership. As early as 1977 he was involved in founding the Consejo Aguaruna Huambisa (Aguaruna Huambisa Council; CAH). In 1984, he took the lead in establishing the Coordinadora de Organizaciones Indígenas de la Cuenca Amazonas (Coordinating Committee of Indigenous Organizations of the Amazon Basin; COICA). He is also an active leader in the movement for sustainable development, through the Asociación Interétnica del Desarrollo de la Selva Peruana (Interethnic Association for the Development of the Peruvian Jungle; AIDESEP) (Morin 1992).

6. In 1980 there was a Primer Congreso de Nacionalidades Quechuas, Aymaras, y Nativas de la Selva (First Congress of Quechua, Aymara, and Jungle Nationalities), but this attempt to unite Andean and Amazonian peoples was apparently never repeated.

7. As events developed, politics in Santiago Atitlán got uglier. A group of Mayan citizens who accused the town's Mayan mayor of corruption were put on trial on allegedly trumped-up charges. Human-rights observers from the Network in Solidarity with the People of Guatemala (NISGUA), who filed the report on the Internet, "fear that a conviction in this case would be a serious blow to the process of demilitarization and free expression promised in the December 1996 peace accords."

8. The Academy's charge to standardize the alphabet was a victory over the competing plan of the Summer Institute for Linguistics (see note 4, above).

9. See Stoll (1999) for a provocative and controversial analysis of the uses of Menchú in North American scholarship on Guatemala. See also an interview with Menchú by Burt and Rosen (1999) and with Stoll by Dudley (1999).

10. The Zapatista movement has been extensively chronicled since 1994. Particularly useful recent sources include Harvey (1998) and Womack (1999).

REFERENCES

Adams, Richard N. 1994. "A Report on the Political Status of the Guatemalan Maya." In *Indigenous Peoples and Democracy in Latin America,* ed. Donna Lee Van Cott, pp. 155–86. New York: St. Martin's Press.

Albó, Xavier. 1994. "And from Kataristas to MNRistas? The Surprising and Bold Alliance between Aymaras and Neoliberals in Bolivia." In *Indigenous Peoples and Democracy in Latin America,* ed. Donna Lee Van Cott, pp. 55–82. New York: St. Martin's Press.

———. 1996. "Bolivia: Making the Leap from Local Mobilization to National Politics." *NACLA Report on the Americas* 29, no. 5 (March–April): 15–20.

Almeida, Ileana, et al. 1991. *Indios: Una reflexión sobre el levantamiento indígena de 1990.* Quito: Ediciones Abya-Yala.

Arias, Arturo. 1990. "Changing Indian Identity: Guatemala's Violent Transition to Modernity." In *Guatemalan Indians and the State, 1540 to 1988,* ed. Carol A. Smith, pp. 230–57. Austin: University of Texas Press.

Ballón Aguirre, Francisco. 1987. "Política de la supervivencia: Las organizaciones de los pueblos indígenas de la Amazonía peruana." *Apuntes* 20: 105–19.

Berryman, Phillip. 1987. *Liberation Theology.* New York: Pantheon.

Burt, Jo-Marie, and Fred Rosen. 1999. "Truth-Telling and Memory in Postwar Guatemala: An Interview with Rigoberta Menchú." *NACLA Report on the Americas* 32, no. 5 (March–April): 6–10.

Collins, Jennifer. 1992. "Ecuadoran Indians March to Capital." *Latinamerica Press* 24, no. 16 (April 30): 1.

Confederación de Nacionalidades Indígenas del Ecuador (CONAIE). 1994. "Proyecto político de la CONAIE." *Anuario Indigenista* 33: 202–44.

Degregori, Carlos Iván. 1997. "After the Fall of Abimael Guzmán: The Limits of Sendero Luminoso." In *The Peruvian Labyrinth: Polity, Society, Economy,* ed. Maxwell A. Cameron and Philip Mauceri, pp. 179–91. University Park: Penn State University Press.

Díaz Polanco, Héctor. 1997. *Indigenous Peoples in Latin America: The Quest for Self-Determination.* Boulder, Colo.: Westview Press.

Dudley, Steven. 1999. "David Stoll on Rigoberta, Guerrillas, and Academics." *NACLA Report on the Americas* 32, no. 5 (March–April): 8–9.

Dunkerley, James. 1984. *Rebellion in the Veins: Political Struggle in Bolivia, 1952–1982.* London: Verso.

Field, Les. 1991. "Ecuador's Pan-Indian Uprising." *NACLA Report on the Americas* 25, no. 3 (November–December): 39–44.

Fischer, Edward, and R. McKenna Brown, eds. 1996. *Maya Cultural Activism in Guatemala.* Austin: University of Texas Press.

Guerrero, Andrés. 1996. "El levantamiento indígena de 1994: Discurso y representación política en Ecuador." *Nueva Sociedad*, no. 142: 32–43 (March–April).

Gutiérrez, Edgar. 1994. "Rural Upheaval and the Survival of the Maya." *NACLA Report on the Americas* 28, no. 3 (November–December): 34–36.

Haggard, Stephan, and Robert Kaufman. 1995. *The Political Economy of Democratic Transitions*. Princeton, N.J.: Princeton University Press.

Handelman, Howard. 1975. *Struggle in the Andes: Peasant Political Mobilization in Peru*. Austin: University of Texas Press.

Handy, Jim. 1984. *Gift of the Devil: A History of Guatemala*. Boston: South End Press.

———. 1989. "'A Sea of Indians': Ethnic Conflict and the Guatemalan Revolution, 1944–1952." *The Americas* 46, no. 2 (October): 189–204.

Harvey, Neil. 1998. *The Chiapas Rebellion: The Struggle for Land and Democracy*. Durham, N.C.: Duke University Press.

Ibarra, Alicia. 1992. *Los indígenas y el estado en el Ecuador*. Quito: Ediciones Abya-Yala.

Jonas, Susanne. 1991. *The Battle for Guatemala: Rebels, Death Squads, and U.S. Power*. Boulder, Colo.: Westview Press.

León, Jorge. 1991. "Levantamiento indígena en Ecuador: El dilema de la asimilación y del reconocimiento de las diferencias." *Amazonía Indígena* 11, nos. 17–18 (July–September): 33–48.

Lijphart, Arend. 1984. *Democracies*. New Haven, Conn.: Yale University Press.

López, Sinesio. 1997. *Ciudadanos reales e imaginarios: Concepciones, desarrollo, y mapas de la ciudadanía en el Perú*. Lima: Instituto de Diálogo y Propuestas, IDS.

Malloy, James. 1970. *Bolivia: The Uncompleted Revolution*. Pittsburgh: University of Pittsburgh Press.

———. 1988. *Revolution and Reaction: Bolivia, 1964–1985*. New Brunswick, N.J.: Transaction Publishers.

Martz, John D. 1987. *Politics and Petroleum in Ecuador*. New Brunswick, N.J.: Transaction Publishers.

McClintock, Cynthia. 1981. *Peasant Cooperatives and Political Change in Peru*. Princeton, N.J.: Princeton University Press.

———. 1998. *Revolutionary Movements in Latin America: El Salvador's FMLN and Peru's Shining Path*. Washington, D.C.: United States Institute of Peace Press.

McClintock, Cynthia, and Abraham Lowenthal, eds. 1983. *The Peruvian Experiment Reconsidered*. Princeton, N.J.: Princeton University Press.

Menchú, Rigoberta. 1984. *I, Rigoberta Menchú*. London: Verso.

Montejo, Víctor. 1987. *Testimony: Death of a Guatemalan Village*. Willimantic, Conn.: Curbstone Press.

Montejo, Víctor, and Q'anil Akab'. 1992. *Brevísima relación testimonial de la continua destrucción del Mayab' (Guatemala)*. Providence, R.I.: Guatemala Scholars Network.

Morin, Françoise. 1992. "Evaristo Nugkuag Ikanan: Entrevista realizada el 7 de julio de 1992 en Lima (Peru)." *Caravelle* 59: 67–70.

North American Congress on Latin America (NACLA). 1990–91. "Fatal Attraction: Peru's Shining Path." *NACLA Report on the Americas* 24, no. 4 (December–January): 9–39.

Otzoy, Antonio. 1996. "Guatemala: The Struggle for Maya Unity." *NACLA Report on the Americas* 29, no. 5 (March–April): 33–35.

Pacari, Nina. 1996. "Ecuador: Taking on the Neoliberal Agenda." *NACLA Report on the Americas* 29, no. 5 (March–April): 23–32.

Palmer, David Scott, ed. 1992. *Shining Path of Peru.* New York: St. Martin's Press.

Peeler, John. 1985. *Latin American Democracies: Colombia, Costa Rica, Venezuela.* Chapel Hill: University of North Carolina Press.

———. 1998. *Building Democracy in Latin America.* Boulder, Colo.: Lynne Rienner.

Quintero, Rafael, and Erika Silva. 1995. *Ecuador: Una nación en ciernes.* 3 vols. Quito: Editorial Universitaria.

Radcliffe, Sarah A., and Sallie Westwood. 1996. *Remaking the Nation: Place, Identity, and Politics in Latin America.* London: Routledge.

Remy, María Isabel. 1994. "The Indigenous Population and the Construction of Democracy in Peru." In *Indigenous Peoples and Democracy in Latin America,* ed. Donna Lee Van Cott, pp. 107–30. New York: St. Martin's Press.

Rivera Cusicanqui, Silvia. 1991. "Aymara Past, Aymara Future." *NACLA Report on the Americas* 25, no. 3 (November–December): 18–23.

Sánchez, Francisco, and Flavia Freidenberg. 1999. "El proceso de incorporación política de los sectores indígenas en el Ecuador: Pachakutik, un caso de estudio." *América Latina, Hoy* 19: 65–80.

Santana, Roberto. 1992. "Actores y escenarios étnicos en Ecuador: El levantamiento de 1990." *Caravelle* 59: 161–88.

Schoultz, Lars. 1981. *Human Rights and United States Policy toward Latin America.* Princeton, N.J.: Princeton University Press.

———. 1987. *National Security and United States Policy toward Latin America.* Princeton, N.J.: Princeton University Press.

———. 1998. *Beneath the United States: A History of U.S. Policy toward Latin America.* Cambridge, Mass.: Harvard University Press.

Selmeski, Brian. 1992. *Transformational Politics: The Development and Effect of Indigenous Organizations in Ecuador.* Honors thesis, Bucknell University Program in Latin American Studies, Lewisburg, Penn.

Selverston, Melina H. 1994. "The Politics of Culture: Indigenous Peoples and the State in Ecuador." In *Indigenous Peoples and Democracy in Latin America,* ed. Donna Lee Van Cott, pp. 131–52. New York: St. Martin's Press.

Smith, Carol A., ed. 1990. *Guatemalan Indians and the State, 1540 to 1988.* Austin: University of Texas Press.

Stern, Steve, ed. 1987. *Resistance, Rebellion, and Consciousness in the Andean Peasant World, 18th to 20th Centuries.* Madison: University of Wisconsin Press.

———. 1993. *Peru's Indian Peoples and the Challenge of Spanish Conquest: Huamanga to 1640.* 2d ed. Madison: University of Wisconsin Press.

Stoll, David. 1993. *Between Two Armies in the Ixil Towns of Guatemala.* New York: Columbia University Press.

————. 1999. *Rigoberta Menchú and the Story of All Poor Guatemalans*. Boulder, Colo.: Westview Press.

Ströbele-Gregor, Juliana. 1994. "From *Indio* to Mestizo...to *Indio:* New Indianist Movements in Bolivia." *Latin American Perspectives* 21, no. 2 (Spring): 106–23.

Taylor, Clark. 1998. *Return of Guatemala's Refugees: Reweaving the Torn*. Philadelphia: Temple University Press.

Ticona A., Esteban, Gonzalo Rojas O., and Xavier Albó C. 1995. *Votos y wiphalas: Campesinos y pueblos originarios en democracia*. La Paz: CIPCA (Centro de Investigación y Promoción del Campesinado).

Warren, Kay, ed. 1993. *The Violence Within: Cultural and Political Opposition in Divided Nations*. Princeton, N.J.: Princeton University Press.

————. 1998. *Indigenous Movements and Their Critics*. Princeton, N.J.: Princeton University Press.

Wickham-Crowley, Timothy. 1991. *Exploring Revolution: Essays on Latin American Insurgency and Revolutionary Theory*. Armonk, N.Y.: M. E. Sharpe.

————. 1992. *Guerrillas and Revolution in Latin America: A Comparative Study of Insurgents and Regimes since 1956*. Princeton, N.J.: Princeton University Press.

Wilson, Richard. 1995. *Maya Resurgence in Guatemala: Q'eqchí Experiences*. Norman: University of Oklahoma Press.

Womack, John, Jr. 1999. *Rebellion in Chiapas: An Historical Reader*. New York: New Press.

Yashar, Deborah. 1998. "Contesting Citizenship: Indigenous Movements and Democracy in Latin America." *Comparative Politics* 31, no. 1 (October): 23–42.

Young, Iris Marion. 1990. *Justice and the Politics of Difference*. Princeton, N.J.: Princeton University Press.

Zamosc, León. 1994. "Agrarian Protest and the Indian Movement in the Ecuadorian Highlands." *Latin American Research Review* 29, no. 3: 37–68.

Zur, Judith. 1998. *Violent Memories: Mayan War Widows in Guatemala*. Boulder, Colo.: Westview Press.

CHAPTER ELEVEN

The War of the Peace

Indigenous Women's Struggle
for Social Justice in Chiapas, Mexico

JUNE NASH

In counterinsurgency warfare, militarization pervades society, with armed men enacting the roles of police force, judge, executioner, and even social-welfare agent. In this kind of warfare, women are targets of hostility in part because their very presence in the spaces controlled by the military is an assertion of the right to remain there and live. This is itself an act of warfare, punishable by rape or killing. The battlefront merges with community; women and children account for 90 percent of world victims of counterinsurgency and civil wars, partly because militaries abuse women sexually to demoralize them and thereby undermine their claims to autonomy (Nordstrom 1995). Armies extend their fighting force through paramilitary units. The unwritten codes of counterinsurgency warfare foster a climate of fear, as neighbors and relatives become armed paramilitaries carrying out acts of violence against fellow civilians, in violation of international covenants. The ever-present threat of force embodied in an army that takes up residence within communities domesticates the use of violence. By this I mean that armed men are able to assert their claim to the resources, labor, and bodies of a civilian people held hostage in their own communities. At the same time, though, that counterinsurgent armies pervade the most intimate spaces of the society, they threaten the validation of the armed forces as defenders of civilians and of national security. In addition to the body count of those they kill, they may leave thousands of women widowed and hundreds of thousands of children orphaned (Green 1999). In turn, debts incurred by counterinsurgency wars deprive states of resources to address poverty alleviation.

Counterinsurgency warfare formulated in the U.S. invasion of Vietnam was introduced into Central America during the Cold War climate cultivated by the Reagan and Bush presidencies in the 1980s. Public outrage instigated congressional cutoffs in military aid to Central America, often leading to low-intensity versions of counterinsurgency warfare that attempted to minimize the body count even as the military maximized the disintegration of the fabric of civil society. Mexico shunned involvement in the U.S.-instigated militarization of the region until neoliberal policies, promoted by the Salinas and Zedillo governments from 1988 to 2000, threatened semisubsistence cultivators by eliminating land grants and social subsidies, and by promoting hydroelectric power and oil and lumber enterprises in indigenous territories.[1]

Incorporation of populations into global flows on unequal terms promoted resistance movements and rebellions among internally dominated ethnicities. Indigenous mobilizations, in Oaxaca in the 1970s and in Guerrero and Chiapas in the 1990s, were rebellions of those who were marginalized in the institutionalization of the victories of the 1910–17 revolution. These included mobilizations of Indians who never had received title to the lands they colonized, and women whose voices had been silenced in the institutionalization of revolutionary victories. Their protest and resistance provoked the Partido Revolucionario Institucional (Institutional Revolutionary Party; PRI) to militarize. U.S. military aid to Mexico in the "War against Drugs" provided what became an army of occupation in the conflict area, with sophisticated surveillance technology, Blackhawk helicopters, and automatic weapons. Mexican military officers followed their peers from Central America to gain counterinsurgency training in the School of the Americas in Georgia.

Indigenous mobilizations of the 1990s differed from guerrilla operations of the past that threatened to seize power from incumbent governments. The Ejercito Zapatista de Liberación Nacional (Zapatista Army of National Liberation; EZLN) rose up from their base in the colonized settlements of the Lacandón rain forest to demand democracy and representation in government. In their attempts to forge a new social contract in the nation in which they were subordinated, Mayans of the state of Chiapas appealed to modernist ideals qualified by their own historical experience. They called for equality but with the recognition of difference, liberty now expressed as autonomy with pluricultural coexistence, and fraternity equated with collective ownership of the means of production. They encountered military opposition to their claims for autonomy. The violence and terrorism carried out by paramilitaries who had long been present in the area escalated after government troops invaded the Lacandón rain forest on February 9, 1995. Although army harassment of the indigenous populations of Chiapas decreased after the victory of Vicente Fox in the presidential election of 2000, tensions persisted because Fox failed to resolve the issues that had sparked the uprising.

As the group most involved in production for basic subsistence, small-plot cultivators, women above all, were particularly threatened by the militarization of the region. Against this backdrop, Zapatista men fought for undelivered promises of the past revolution. Zapatista women, in addition, sought an end to all forms of hierarchy, including male dominance in the home. Women demonstrated that there could be no social justice in society without an end to their subordination within the home. In demanding autonomy they broadened the declarations of the EZLN to include the personal right to full citizenship in civil society as well as in village culture. With their diverse demands, Zapatista women tended to be the most persistent opponents of the military in the counterinsurgency struggles.

Below I address how the militarization of society related to the weakening of populist national institutions that for decades had favored men. In particular, I analyze how a diminution in official support for the patriarchically biased land reform, rooted in the early-twentieth-century revolution, related to the militarization of the state, and how and why men and women, in turn, responded differently to the changed context. With a drop-off in government suport for *campesinos,* small-plot cultivators, young men became demoralized about their future prospects. Women responded, in contrast, by intensifying their involvement in commercial artisan activity. As a consequence, their contribution to the household economy increased relative to men's (Nash 1993). This generated gender hostilities.

I shall argue that the failure of the PRI to respond both to women's demands for social justice and to the *campesinos'* demands for settlement of *ejido,* communal land claims, ended the hegemonic control of the party that assumed power in 1929. Indigenous women's rejection of gender subordination was made explicit with the announcement, in January 1994, of the New Law of Women in the ranks of the EZLN. The rights they claimed—to participate in revolutionary struggle, to work and receive a just wage, to decide the number of children they will have, to participate and hold office in their communities, to receive medical attention and education, to choose their partners, to not be abused or raped, to hold military rank, and to enjoy all the rights and obligations of the revolutionary laws—challenged the hegemonic alliance of indigenous men with power brokers in the PRI party. In reaction to women's demands for a new subject position in society, indigenous men—particularly youths—joined counterinsurgent military forces in order to reassert their control over women's labor and bodies. As a result, women were the targets of both military and paramilitary violence, and of domestic violence that increased throughout the countryside.[2] I shall address the forms of their protest in the years after the armed encounter of the Zapatistas with federal troops ended with the signing of the ceasefire agreement of January 12, 1994. I shall focus particularly on the paramilitary attacks that followed the breakdown of the San Andrés Peace Accord in August 1996, when low-intensity warfare aggravated latent discord within indigenous communities, thus enabling the government to further divide their ranks. This persisted even after the defeat of the PRI in the federal and state elections of 2000 and the withdrawal of more than half of the armed forces from the Lacandón and highland Chiapas conflict area where Zapatista power is concentrated. Zapatistas and their supporters then tried to consolidate their position as autonomous entities responding to new codes of behavior in the home and wider society.

THE 1910 REVOLUTION AND THE CONSOLIDATION OF PRI HEGEMONY

A brief review of the Mexican development process will shed some light on the conflict early in the new century. The revolutionary government's programs engaged men in an alliance that undermined the balance of complementary gender roles in indigenous society. Inspired by *indigenismo*, the ideology that promoted Indian cultural roots while denying their autonomous expression in the political life of the nation, the PRI relied on the institutionalization of force exercised by males over females and by a *mestizocracia* (mixed-blood elitism) over Indians. We can evaluate this extraordinarily convoluted power structure since it has come apart.

The success of the military campaigns in backing the *campesinos'* demands for land validated force and the use of violence by men in their communities and homes. Although considerable variation existed in the degree to which indigenous people participated in the revolution, some of the ideology regarding the construction of gender roles associated with military combat began to pervade their communities. In Morelia, peasants attracted by the Plan de Ayala that supported collective small-plot cultivation joined the campaign of Emiliano Zapata. Pedro Martínez, an infantryman in the Zapatista ranks in the early decades of the twentieth century, reflected on the response of *indígenas* like himself to the behavior of troops in the campaign: "The Zapatistas were well liked in the village, because, although it is true they sometimes carried off young girls, they left the majority of women in place. And after all, everyone knew what kind of girls they took. The ones who liked that sort of thing!" (Lewis 1964). Reflecting on this passage, Stern (1995: 48) points out, "By dividing the 'good' women from the 'bad,' the army served to validate men's right to categorize and exploit the female population in these earlier wars." This is a valid point, underlining the construction of gender hierarchy. Yet it is important to recognize that women did not readily accept male violence, even during this popular revolution. Pedro Martínez's wife, Esperanza, who supported the aims of the Zapatistas, makes it clear in her chapter in Lewis's editing of the family autobiography that she did not share the indulgent view expressed by men toward the Zapatista army's violation of women. She says:

> The government soldiers, and the rebel soldiers too, violated the young girls and the married women. They come every night and the women would give great shrieks when they were taken away. Afterward, at daybreak, the women would be back in their houses. They wouldn't tell what happened to them and I didn't ask because then people would say, "What do you want to know? If you want to know, let them take you out tonight." (Lewis 1964: 92)

Esperanza agreed with her husband that the government troops did the villagers more harm than the Zapatistas, but this was with reference to soldiers stealing their food supplies. She was like the other women left behind by men who joined the Zapatistas, who had to support their children by their own efforts and to defend themselves without weapons against both armies. Distraught, they rejected male abuse. Her voice, like that of women who joined the Zapatistas, was silenced in official versions of revolutionary history. Unlike the contemporary EZLN forces, women who marched with the early Zapatistas were written off as camp followers until scholars influenced by feminist history revealed their participation as soldiers in the armed struggle (Turner 1967).

In the northern provinces of Mexico and in the central plateau, the support among indigenous and *mestizo,* or mixed-blood, *campesinos* for the military action of the old Zapatista forces fostered male hegemonic control over women. The "domestication of violence" promoted by militarism is exercised in the *descarga* (literally, "unloading"), as Stern (1995: 48) explains it, the unleashing of male violence against females as men impose their power over women in an apparently random or arbitrary fashion, thus keeping them in their place. This became a way of life, justified by revolutionary military action and perpetuated in the institutionalization of the revolution that followed.

In Chiapas, indigenous people evaded both armies in the revolutionary wars of the early decades of the twentieth century. In what Jan Rus (1994: 265) calls "a civil war between an occupying federal army, the Carrancistas, and bands of local, counter-revolutionary landowners who fought them for control of the region between 1914 and 1920," Indian women were raped and men were forcibly recruited as burden bearers, their lands turned into battlefields, their food and animals seized. Juan Pérez Jolote, whose autobiography was set down by Ricardo Pozas (1947), was taken from jail, along with other prisoners, and forced to enlist on the side of federal troops. When he returned to his natal village of San Juan Chamula, his father told him that the neighbors said, "See, there goes Juan. They say he walks killing people; he walks very *ladinoized*" (acculturated to non-Indian ways). Far from enhancing masculinity, as occurred in the central and northern armies of Mexico, indigenes of the highland communities of Chiapas felt that the military path dehumanized those who participated in it (Gossen 1996: 534).

In Amatenango del Valle, the revolution confirmed the worst fears of indigenous people's myth-based notion of cosmological destruction. In their beliefs, the "Father Sun" (Tatik K'ak) and "Grandmother Moon" (Me'tikchich u) become jealous when humans carry out sexual acts in the milpa. This causes them to remain stationary in their orbit, with the result that the Sun burns up the crops or the Moon allows too much rain to fall by not giving way to the Sun (Nash 1970). These beliefs were confirmed by drought-linked crop failure that followed after troops of both armies had raped women in the milpas and stolen crops and animals as they swept through the countryside. Indigenous people held both the federal troops and the rebel bands responsible for the famines that followed (Nash 1997b: 353–54). Myths found in indigenous communities retain notions of the balance of male and female power that is needed to preserve balance in the cosmos.

In the seven decades of PRI monopoly of power, from 1929 to 2000, *ejido* land grants were made to male heads of families, although women could benefit as wives and as mothers of boys fourteen years of age or older. The vote was restricted to males, and even though women were granted suffrage in 1950, indigenous women in traditional communities never voted until the Zapatista uprising of 1994. Male youths constituted the vast majority of students in the boarding school initiated by Lázaro Cárdenas in the 1930s. Men were trained as promoters of health and education programs of the Instituto Nacional Indígenista (National Indian Institute; INI). Male priorities were reinforced in development programs of the 1970s and 1980s that enriched an elite of male caciques. These are the local officials who became strong adherents of the PRI, delivering 90 percent of the vote of indigenous men to the party. Indigenous women did not vote even after the 1950 suffrage law went into effect, nor did they receive assistance in marketing artisan products until the 1970s, when the government was looking for low-capitalized ventures for indigenous communities. They did, however, benefit from medical programs introduced into highland communities that were successful in reducing death in childbirth and infant mortality. Colonizers of the Lacandón rain forest received none of these benefits. Thus women were not tied as much as men were to paternalistic structures of the PRI government.

ECONOMIC CRISIS AND THE WEAKENING OF PRI HEGEMONY

Women's resistance to male hegemonic practices institutionalized by the PRI began in the 1970s but increased during the economic crisis of the 1980s. Women in households in highland indigenous communities expanded the production and marketing of their pottery and weavings. Aided by the INI, in the 1970s women formed cooperatives, low-capitalized ventures, for the purchasing of raw material inputs and the marketing of their crafts. With UNICEF as well as government agency funding, they began to produce and sell not merely traditional artisan products but also new tourist items. INI promoted a pottery cooperative in 1971 that enabled women to market their goods directly, to improve their earnings by avoiding merchant middlemen. Six years later a private weavers' production cooperative, Sna Holobil, began to market finer products overseas.

Women's expanded income-earning activity generated unintended noneconomic consequences. Contacts both with government and with nongovernmental organizations (NGOs) through the cooperatives led women to participate in widening political arenas. But so too did the activity increase women's workload. Women remained responsible for social reproduction in the home. In some communities the hard-working income-earning women began to challenge male authority. Men resented this, and responded with stepped-up wife abuse. Threatened by the loss of control over their wives' movements, men were quick to intervene, ordering their wives not to attend meetings out of town. Some men beat their wives if they ventured into the cities to sell their goods or to attend meetings, despite the fact that the family's survival depended on them (Nash 1993; Eber 1998; Hernández Castillo 1998). Antagonized by their loss of control over income earned by women's artisan production, Amatenango town officials hired a man to kill the president of the cooperative.

The debt crisis of the 1980s resulted in conditions imposed by the International Monetary Fund (IMF) that were detrimental to *campesinos*. *Campesinos* broke from the Confederación Nacional de Campesinos (National Confederation of Campesinos, CNC) when PRI officials failed to address their demands for settlement of land claims and assistance in marketing their crops (Collier with Quaratiello 1994; Harvey 1994). Their alienation from the PRI became ever more apparent from 1988 to 1994, during the presidency of Carlos Salinas de Gortari. In 1991 Congress voted to reform Article 27 of the 1917 constitution, to end community land claims. A desire for land rights had drawn Chol, Mam, Tojolobal, Tzeltal, and Tzotzil colonizers to the Lacandón rain forest. Meanwhile, trade liberalization with NAFTA, initiated in 1994, threatened small local corn and coffee producers. For decades tariffs had shielded them from foreign competition. With their livelihood newly threatened, settlers mobilized against the PRI. Men and women of the many different language groups that had colonized the rain forest staged an uprising.

Left out of the co-optive channels of the PRI, women—particularly those who were widowed, separated, or never married—were drawn to alternative political and religious movements in greater numbers than were men. The colonizers of the jungle, particularly women but also men, were mobilized in cooperatives and literacy classes promoted by Samuel Ruiz, bishop of San Cristóbal from 1962 to 1998 (Kovic 1995; Womack 1999: 298). Along with women in highland townships, they were the core of the Comunidades Eclesiales de Base (Christian Base Communities) that promoted the education and politicization of indigenous women. Women in both areas were also the instigators in conversion of their families to Protestantism as well as to liberation-theology Catholicism, in part to avoid the pernicious effects of alcoholism and the abuse they suffered from men. Residents of scattered hamlets that were included in municipalities dominated by caciques were breaking from the PRI and joining opposition parties. These countermovements provoked the caciques to expel dissidents, who fled to the urban barrios of San Cristóbal. In their urban setting they turned to the opposition Partido Revolucionario Democrático (Revolutionary Democratic Party; PRD) or to Protestant sects, since PRI officials ignored their plight as exiles. The colonizers of the Lacandón rain forest, who rarely received government assistance in any form and who never voted (since ballot boxes weren't delivered to the settlements until 1994), were not dependent on government largess. As a result, they were freer to protest the PRI's departure from support programs for the small-plot agrarian sector. Lay deacons spread the doctrines of Liberation Theology, sponsored by Bishop Ruiz, promoting an awareness of social-justice doctrines and the human rights of women as well as of men.

Women joined with men in the regional organizations of *campesinos* that were breaking away from the CNC. They participated with men in the massive protest march from the Lacandón colony Marqués de Comillas in 1991. Like their husbands, they were jailed by PRI officials of Ladino-dominated *cabeceras,* or town centers, that contained the colonized settlements, and they were among the thousands of indigenes who marched into San Cristóbal de las Casas on Día de La Raza, or Columbus Day, on October 2, 1992, protesting five hundred years of oppression. As women gained increasing autonomy within these organizations, they formed independent sections that challenged male dominance.

WOMEN IN THE EZLN UPRISING

The success of the EZLN's brief military encounter galvanized the energies of highland communities. Women constituted 30 percent of the new Zapatista army's combat ranks, and half a dozen or more were included in the high command. Zapatista women participated in the twelve days of active combat. In January 1994, shortly after the uprising, they included the Women's Bill of Rights in the New Revolutionary Law of the EZLN, in which they called for democratic changes to abolish all forms of hierarchy, including male dominance in the home.[3] Their distinctive presence as women and mothers in these public arenas, from which they had been restricted in their communities of origin, served as a critique of assumptions about femininity and masculinity. As women they had experienced humiliation and cruelty inflicted on them by Ladinos in the plantations from which they migrated with their husbands (Olivera 1979).

The presence of indigenous women in leadership roles of the EZLN inspired many indigenous women throughout the highlands. Women insisted on presenting an independent voice and presence in the Asemblea Nacional por la Autonomía de los Pueblos Indígenas (National Assembly for the Autonomy of Indigenous Pueblos; ANIPA), which held the First National Meeting of Women in December 1995 (Hernández Castillo 1995, 1998: 132). From these first encounters, indigenous women critiqued practices, such as alcoholism and mistreatment and abuse of women, that were extolled as indigenous traditions but often represented intrusive values of the *mestizo* society.

Inspired by the Zapatista women's Declaration of the New Law for Women, indigenous women linked the demands for cultural autonomy to self-determination and the rights of women. This translated into demands for the right to communal and private lands after divorce, to choose their own husbands, to have the number of children they wish, and to be respected and not subject to abuse by lovers, husbands, and other family members. Women's subordination to men had been condoned as "tradition" in most indigenous communities. Laws that had granted women suffrage in 1950, and that had allotted specific land claims to women, were ignored in local custom.

The women of highland villages participated in the massive marches calling for peace and the withdrawal of the army that took place in 1995. On March 8, the International Day of Women, women organized a march for peace that culminated with a meeting in the Plaza of San Cristóbal, in which women protested the invasion of the Lacandón rain forest by federal troops and defended Bishop Ruiz. It was an extraordinary sight for me to see indigenous women of Amatenango, who never participated in public demonstrations of any kind when I lived there in the 1950s and 1960s, and who rarely ventured outside the boundaries of their community, shouting for peace and urging the government to withdraw troops from the Lacandón rain forest. Contingents of Amatenango women who had reorganized the pottery cooperative in 1995, with the assistance of PRD women, joined the security belts along with other indigenous women and international peace observers when the Zapatistas negotiated the San Andrés Peace Accord with the government in April 1995.

Although there were wide differences in the level of feminine consciousness among women in the ranks of Zapatistas and their supporters, they began to formulate common demands, all based on their experience of subordination in the domestic economy and their greater sensitivity to neoliberal attacks on sites of production and reproduction (Olivera 1995). They had experienced in their own lives the reduction of medical services for parturition and postpartum patients, even while the government was mounting a huge campaign for birth control in the 1990s (Freyermuth Enciso 1998). Because of government neglect of the colonizers' health needs, particularly those of women in the rain forest, where there were no obstetricians, maternal death rates were six times the norm for the country. After the outbreak of hostilities, the incidence of children dying from curable diseases, and of infant mortality—in 2002 estimated at 150 per 1,000 live births—increased. In this "silent war" (Freyermuth Enciso 1998), the Mexican government carried out a vigorous campaign for limitation of birth but did little to promote maternal and infant health, and did virtually nothing to this end in the jungle.

In the new Zapatista revolution, men focused on the rights of the settlers to the gains of the first revolution—the entitlement to communal land and the right to the vote that had been denied to the colonizers of the Lacandón rain forest because voting booths had not been installed for them during elections. Women went beyond this, calling for dignity and challenging the male hegemonic controls institutionalized by the PRI in the name of social justice. Zapatista women demanded the right, along with men, to plots of land and to redress other inequalities (Plataforma de las Mujeres para el Diálogo 1995). Most importantly, they redefined the meaning of democracy in personal as well as political terms. The women's *mesas* (tables) in the national and international conventions called by the Zapatistas in 1995 and 1996 were the only groups to critique the demand for autonomy of traditional cultural practices. They condemned the patriarchal "traditions" of wife abuse and prohibiting women from taking political office, or even voting, that were characteristic of traditional communities. As Comandante Trinidad, a grandmother in her sixties who represented Zapatista women in the May 1995 negotiations with the government, said, "We want them to respect us, because they have not taken us into account" (Rojas 1995: 26).

The push for women's political participation in public arenas where they previously had been excluded occurred at the very moment when Mexico turned from postrevolutionary corporatist democracy to neoliberalism, a change predicated on elimination not only of land rights but also of smallholder subsidies, and cutbacks in social welfare provisioning (Collier with Quaratiello 1994; Nash 1994; Stephen 1994; Har-

vey 1994). As a result of their primary responsibility for social reproduction, women were aware even more acutely than men were of the
implications of what they saw as an attack on the right to live. Thus they
were in the vanguard of protest against the militarization of intimate
spaces of community and family in the rain forest and in highland communities.

DOMESTICATING MILITARY VIOLENCE

In the thirteen days of military confrontation following the January 1,
1994, armed uprising, two to three thousand Zapatistas confronted a
force of twelve thousand federal troops. In the year after the cease-fire,
the military increased its presence in the towns surrounding the conflict
zone in the Lacandón rain forest to an estimated thirty-seven thousand,
which rose to a force of sixty thousand during and after the invasion on
February 9, 1995. Without any acts of aggression by the EZLN, the government continued to augment the numbers of soldiers throughout
Zedillo's presidency to an estimated seventy thousand, with increasing
air surveillance and numbers of armed tanks and Humvees. The invasion of the Lacandón rain forest by federal troops on February 9, 1995,
curbed the restitutive land actions of Zapatista supporters. Confrontations between the army and indigenous communities began to take place
within colonized settlements, including within the intimacy of the home.
Even before the uprising of January 1, 1994, federal troops were building up in Chiapas, including the 1988 expansion of Nuevo Rancho, a
major military base twelve kilometers from San Cristóbal de las Casas.
Since then, and until President Fox took power in 2001, massive military
forces countered protests by *campesinos* over the government's failure
to grant titles to lands promised to the colonizers and their systematic
withdrawal of support services for small-plot cultivators who were encouraged to raise cash crops, especially coffee.

Women's challenge to the domination of the state over ethnic groups,
and to that of men over women, subjected them to violence on two military
fronts. The first front was in the Lacandón rain forest. There, an army
estimated at 40,000 to 60,000 federal troops in 2002, or about one soldier for every two families, was quartered. Already during Zedillo's presidency, soldiers, illegally deployed near settlements of some 250,000 colonizers in the region, engaged in daily troop incursions in Humvees
mounted with automatic weapons, which interrupted the routines of cultivation and social reproduction. Soldiers, for example, regularly inter-

cepted men's trips to cultivate cornfields or coffee groves and threatened children and women as they attempted to carry firewood and water to their homes or to engage in the harvesting and processing of crops.

The second front was in highland villages, where the lines of battle were drawn between kinship and neighborhood connections, as paramilitary troops recruited from among the supporters of the PRI intimidated, harassed, and sometimes killed their neighbors and relatives. In this setting, paramilitaries became an extension of military control. Even after the PRI finally lost the presidency in 2000, after some seventy years of rule, men and teenage boys were still recruited from kin and neighbors, and women often became the central target. The lines of hostility on both fronts thus merged. PRI officials in towns where they still held office dispersed weapons, officially restricted to use by federal armed forces, to their paramilitary supporters. However, the practice of army regulars training youths in tactics that exceed the codes of regular combat was curbed. In these settings, violence became domesticated, with wife and child abuse increasing along with the rape and prostitution that the armed forces imposed. Because of shame women experienced when making public charges against soldiers, the figures of three rapes reported during the uprising and fifty after February 1995 do not represent the extent of male army assaults on women (Rojas 1995).

MILITARY FRONT IN THE LACANDÓN

On February 9, 1995, federal troops invaded the Lacandón rain forest on the pretext that the prosecutor general's office had discovered that "Subcomandante Marcos" was a member of a subversive underground revolutionary order. I had joined Pastors for Peace as they tried to enter the conflict area on February 10, but soldiers blocked our entry, along with that of human-rights organizations from Mexico, France, the United States, Spain, Italy, and Germany. On the next day they were allowed in, along with newspaper reporters, to collect information on what had transpired during the invasion (La Jornada [Mexico City], February 28, 1995). Villagers from San Miguel, La Garrucha, and Lázaro Cárdenas reported that the army had destroyed property, food, and clothing, and had refused to give water to those who stayed in the village. Others reported that the army had tortured some of the people. Global Exchange, a U.S.-based NGO that organized study groups and tours to the conflict area, reported in a press conference that the army had entered the Calvary in Ocosingo and poisoned food, stolen machetes and hatchets, killed chickens, and stolen everything of value (Global Exchange 1997). In short, the army was following strategies laid out in the manual for low-intensity warfare, cutting people off from their subsistence basis and provoking fear and disorientation.

The army succeeded in their objective of disrupting the daily life-work of social reproduction. Settlers who had fled to the canyons as the army invaded on February 9, 1995, returned, after days of near starvation, to find their houses burned and their food stores sprayed with pesticides, animals stolen or killed, tools destroyed, and personal belongings thrown out and defiled. The army had violated international covenants regarding combat: they had occupied hospitals, schools, churches, and private homes, and had vandalized potable water supplies and food stores that are specifically prohibited as military targets. The army then proceeded to set up military barracks in nearby villages, contrary to the Mexican constitution's regulations on the deployment of troops (see newspaper reports in *El Financiero* [Mexico City], February 26, 1995: 26–27, March 13, 1995: 17, and March 17, 1997: 45; *La Jornada*, February 28, 1995, March 8, 1995: 13, and March 13, 1995: 8). Military helicopters and reconnaissance planes inspired fear with their low-level flights over villages. Foreigners were intercepted in their visits to the "peace huts" that had been set up for observers in the jungle posts.

Over a hundred thousand Mexicans reacted strongly against the invasion, filling the *zócalo* (central plaza) in Mexico City with demonstrators calling for justice. The mixed group of supporters chanted in unison, "We are all Marcos!" (*La Jornada*, February 12, 1995: 1), a reference to the specious claim on the part of the government that they intended only to apprehend the "terrorist leader," eventually identified as Rafael Guillén. In the Lacandón rain forest, women were more forceful than men in denouncing the invading forces. Although this is often explained as a result of the lesser probability that women would be killed, these women in fact were often threatened with having their children taken away (Rojas 1995).

In an attempt to refurbish their image, the Secretaría de Defensa Nacional (Secretary of National Defense; SEDENA) aired television spots on government-controlled news channels showing the activities of teams of "social labor": carrying out dental dispensaries; distributing food; helping with family planning, cutting hair, and medical consultations; and distributing candy to children. The generals told reporters that they could not leave the rain forest "because the people need us" (*El Financiero*, March 17, 1995: 45). What was not shown was the army's refusal to allow access to NGOs with supplies and to Doctors without Borders (*Cuarto Poder* [Tuxtla Gutierrez], February 28, 1995). Nor did controlled TV stations show the rejection of army services by the settlers. In Patihuitz, a Zapatista hamlet in the Lacandón, I saw women on Mother's Day, in May 1995, refuse to pick up the packages thrown from army patrol cars. Alternative media video cameras showed the women menacing the soldiers with sticks and stones. Newspaper articles reported that the women refused handouts of much-needed food and even medical supplies and attention, telling the soldiers to go. These protests by unarmed women belied the army's attempts to validate their presence as protectors of the security of civilians.

Despite the army's public-relations overtures, the people viewed the army as one of occupation. The women complained that soldiers forced them to wash clothes, kill their chickens, and make tortillas to feed them. They also reported that the soldiers harassed the men when they tried to go out to cultivate the milpa. Soldiers took over the school in Santa Elena as their barracks, bathed in the drinking water, and often entered houses with their weapons raised. All of these acts, the women said in their complaints, were in direct violation of international covenants on warfare (*La Jornada,* March 13, 1995). After the invasion, women addressed collective letters of protest to the president, deploring the army's practice of busing in prostitutes and even entrapping women in the profession. At the state convention of Xi' Nich, a coalition of indigenous organizations, held shortly after the invasion, women constituted a Committee of Defense of Indigenous Liberty "to resolve our problems and those of the Union of Communities of the Chiapas selva" (author field notes, February 1995). In their declaration the women linked the presence of the army with the rise of domestic violence and control by men within their families.

The everyday violations committed by soldiers escalated as they entered into the intimate spaces of the rain-forest settlements. Human-rights advocates denounced these violations in international arenas (Global Exchange 1997; *El Financiero,* March 13, 1995: 17, 42, March 17, 1995: 45; *La Jornada,* March 8, 1995: 13, March 13, 1995: 8). As the protest against the military presence rose, the Mexican army carried out what they called a program of "social integration," following a tactic used by the Guatemalan army in the Ixcán. They returned twenty-six thousand colonizers who had voluntarily left their homes in the rain forest shortly after the uprising, locating them in the homes of those who had been routed by the army in the invasion. This divide-and-conquer strategy often turned indigenous people against each other, ensuring the continuation of conflict (*La Jornada,* February 28, 1995; Rojas 1995: 8).

Protests eventually forced the government to send its representatives in the Comisión de Concordia y Pacificación (Commission of Agreement and Pacification; COCOPA) to meet with the mediating team for the Zapatistas, the Comisión Nacional de Intermediación (National Commission of Mediation; CONAI), headed by Bishop Ruiz. After two abortive meetings in the spring of 1995, the negotiating teams reached a tentative agreement in the September 1995 dialogue that was ratified on February 16, 1996, at San Andrés Larrainzar (Nash 1997a). But for five years the government failed to fulfill even the most minimal objectives of the accord. In the first year of President Fox's presidency the Congress passed a revised Law of Indigenous People that gutted autonomy provisions of the San Andrés Agreement of February 1996.

The undeclared war in the final four years of Zedillo's term of office, between 1996 and 2000, took on a new and more insidious form as civilian PRI supporters carried out attacks on neighbors and family members. This was particularly marked in the northern region of the state, where the paramilitary group Paz y Justicia (Peace and Justice) had been disrupting village life in Sabanilla, Tumbala, Tila, and Chilom ever since the January 1, 1994, uprising (author interview with Pablo Romo, director of the Center for Human Rights, Fray Bartolomé de las Casas, March 1998). Taking their name from slogans of civil-society protest groups, these bands developed a model of combat that was copied by other paramilitary groups in the region, such as the Chinchulines and the Alianza San Bartolomé. Repeated calls of alarm from the Center for Human Rights throughout the spring and summer of 1997 failed to gain government attention to the gathering storm in Chenalhó. Internal conflicts between a faction dominated by bilingual indigenous schoolteachers and officials of the PRI grew with the contest for government funds. These came to a head in the fall of 1997, when the leader of the opposition to the PRI-dominated town hall disappeared. A newly formed paramilitary group in Chenalhó, inspired by the Paz y Justicia and calling themselves Mascaras Rojas (Red Masks), began torching houses belonging to the opposition group that called themselves Las Abejas (the Bees). This harassment, along with death threats posted by the Mascaras Rojas, forced the opposition to seek asylum in Acteal, a remote hamlet.

Acteal became the site of the most notorious massacre in the undeclared civil war in Chiapas. On December 22, the Mascaras Rojas, the indigenous youth-based paramilitary group, entered a compound in Acteal. They killed forty-five, including pregnant women and children. The armed men ripped open the bellies of the pregnant women and killed the fetuses. Two of them playfully tossed the fetuses, yelling, "Que se matan la semilla!" (Let them kill the seed!) as they engaged in this extreme violation of women's reproductive being. As part of their training, the young armed civilians were shown pornographic videos, with live models performing the on-screen acts, and were provided with drugs (Monsivais 1998: 13).

The story of the massacre spread throughout the world. Eyewitnesses testified that the men, armed with rifles issued only to federal troops, were members of the local PRI party. State police standing nearby did not intervene as the massacre progressed (Comunicación Popular 1997). The federal attorney general resisted investigation of the incident, attributing the attack to political and economic conditions internal to the region (*New York Times*, December 25, 1997: A1, A7, and December 27, 1997: A45). None of the paramilitaries was detained or disarmed in the first week (*New York Times*, January 1, 1998: 2). However, worldwide attention led to the forced resignation, on January 7, 1998, of Governor Julio César Ruiz Ferro for his failure to respond to urgent pleas for protection of the population against the armed gangs (Julia Preston, "Mexican Governor Resigns in Aftermath of Indians' Massacre," *New York Times*, January 8, 1998). In mid-January, federal prosecutors accused a state police commander of helping the PRI cacique of Chenalhó, Jacinto Arias Cruz, to arm the paramilitary gunmen with AK-47 combat rifles and other sophisticated weapons restricted for use only by the army. The full story of the massacre came out five months later, when the PRI government detained a retired federal army general and a Tzotzil-speaking sergeant of the National Security Forces who were accused of training and overseeing the operation (*La Jornada*, April 3, 1998: 3). Relatives of the victims rejected the five thousand U.S. dollars the government offered as indemnity (*New York Times*, March 6, 1998: A8).

By focusing on the incidents in which women were the principal targets, I do not want to underestimate the harassment and killing of the male population. In the overall military strategy, the attacks on women and children were demoralizing to men, augmenting the terror experienced by all indigenous people. Such acts were relegated to paramilitary bands, with attempts made to conceal their connections to military strategy. In contrast, the army and state security forces were directly involved in attacks on male leaders. On June 10, 1998, government troops attacked a group of *campesinos* meeting in El Bosque, a hamlet of Unión Progreso, killing one and taking seven into custody. Two days later members of the National Commission on Human Rights delivered eight bodies, with clear signs of torture and abuse, to the community. The community considered that the abuse and killing of the men, whose bodies were beaten and disemboweled, were executions committed while they were in custody of government security forces (*La Jornada*, June 14, 1998: 1–14). This time the army could not pass the event off as paramilitary or internecine struggle; instead the government chose to inculpate the Commission on Human Rights that had taken on the task of delivering the bodies, apparently to avoid a blood bath.

The warfare waged in indigenous pueblos was directed at destroying the social reproductive base of the local society. It was played out on three military fronts described in the Mexican army's *Manual of Irregular War: Counterguerrilla Operations or Restoration of Order,* published by SEDENA in 1995 (cited in Center for Human Rights 1997). The first of these was the response to strictly military activities in which the armed forces were enjoined not to cause undue pain to the civilian population. Another front was military institutions and their civilian auxiliaries, whose objective was to recruit civilian support for counterinsurgency measures. Finally, SEDENA listed a public-opinion front that required manipulation of the army's public image and denigration of the enemy. The first two fronts applied to the incidents in the Lacandón rain forest and the highlands, where the army was charged with "defending the frontier" (and not the rich oil deposits that coincidentally had been discovered there), while the paramilitary discouraged the spread of the rebellion in the highlands and into neighboring states. The government clearly was losing the battle on the third front, their interface with the media, as the 2000 election of the opposition party proved.

In perfecting their own model of low-intensity warfare, the Mexican army developed elite forces, special commando operations, and rapid deployment units. The increase in civilian forces eventually under the command of the army complemented the strategy (Center for Human Rights 1997: 160 ff.; *La Jornada,* April 3, 1998), acting outside of the law, controlling and fictionalizing organized civil society and rebelling indigenous communities. In contrast to the paramilitary forces that had always operated as the armed force of the ranchers and large landowners (*La Jornada,* October 29, 1997: 11–12), the armed bands were recruited from within the communities where they operated and were direct extensions of federal forces.

We can gain a clearer understanding of the changing constituency of these paramilitary groups from the analysis of Andrés Aubry, an anthropologist and historian based in San Cristóbal, and Angélica Inda, director of the historical archives at the diocese of San Cristóbal. These researchers documented the existence of 246 paramilitary group members in Chenalhó, the municipality in which Acteal is located (Aubry and Inda 1998). Those who participated in these paramilitary groups were almost exclusively young men frustrated by having no land and being unemployed. The long-standing crisis in agrarian reform, coupled with demographic growth, had created a predicament for the young men, who were married, had families, and were often forced to wander in search of work. For the fourteen- and fifteen-year-olds who were also recruited, this left them with little hope for their own future, as they survived on their wits, occasionally stealing food and animals from neighboring farms. Because they owned no land and had no reliable means of subsistence, they were forced to live outside the law. Their dislocation from community life also meant that they had no reason to attend assemblies and thus had no part in communal decision-making processes (Aubry and Inda 1998). As members of paramilitary groups, these young men collected a "war tax"—a personal income—from compatriots who were supporters of the Zapatistas and/or opposition parties. This kind of harassment forced members of the community who supported the opposition party and the Zapatistas, such as Las Abejas, to seek refuge in Acteal. One can imagine that the frustrations of these youths in the economic arena contributed to their sexual frustrations, since they were unable to save enough money to pay the betrothal price to obtain a woman in marriage. The pornographic videos and drugs used in their training exploited these frustrations, converting pent-up emotion into violent behavior such as that exhibited in Acteal.

With the assistance of these armed civilians, the army attempted to disarticulate organized sectors of the growing opposition to the PRI. Propagandized as internal conflicts based on religious differences or land problems, the armed forces and the paramilitary groups disrupted the economic and social fabric of local society. Violence was coordinated with events that might have alleviated the crisis. The Acteal massacre, for example, occurred just as the coffee harvest was coming in with the promise of higher prices for the crop than in previous years. Paramilitary attacks throughout the spring of 1998 disrupted the cultivation cycle in the growing area of conflict, and armed civilian patrols attacked squatters who had seized unsettled land claims to cultivate their crops, burning houses and threatening the *campesinos* in conflict regions throughout the state. These kinds of attacks occurred, for example, in August 2002, in Ocosingo, when four Zapatistas were killed, twenty wounded, and hundreds displaced (Solidarity Network, September 2002).

ETHNICITY, CLASS, AND GENDER IN THE MILITARIZATION OF SOCIETY

Internationally, incorporation of indigenous populations into the world economy coincided with increased militarization (Rosh 1988: 68). In counterinsurgency warfare waged against civilian populations, soldiers were often pitted against their own ethnic groups (Enloe 1980, 1983). The armed forces of any nation reflect a limited segment of the population. Their lower ranks are composed of predominantly male youths from the poorer classes, and the elite officer's corps is made up of somewhat better-off, educated men whose families lack the capital to launch them into other professions (Gil n.d.).

In Mexico, 70 percent of army recruits were between seventeen and twenty years old, most were poor, and many were of indigenous origin. Each day, as they were on patrol, their masculinity and their very life were challenged, particularly when they threatened young women and found themselves threatened by women. "The frustration to the soldiers is the lack of a battlefield and of a clearly defined enemy," Miguel Badillo, a reporter for *El Financiero,* pointed out, "but at the same time they are afraid because they know that in front and on the sides and behind, the battle can be initiated at any moment" (*El Financiero,* March 26, 1995: 13). The insecurity and frustration of indigenous soldiers in battle against their compatriots may have led them to commit such atrocities as those at Acteal.

The soldiers' identification with the civilian population they were forced to fight had a class as well as an ethnic basis. But whereas their ethnic identity may sometimes have led them to abandon the army when forced to fight, class position had a mixed impact. Lacking the minimal resources to achieve mobility—or even to survive, given the high unemployment rates in developing countries—recruits could seize the opportunities advertised by military recruiters and justify their choice to enlist in terms of necessity (Green 1995; Aubry and Inda 1998; Gil n.d.).

The army learned to distance soldiers from their civilian targets by offering them higher wages and better conditions than they otherwise would earn. Prior to the massive injection of military aid extended to Latin America from 1970 to 1990, armies were as poorly clothed and quartered as their groups of origin. The new generation of soldiers could envision a better life in the army, where they ate more than the civilian population and had superior weapons that enhanced their chances of conquering the populations they were forced to fight. The living quarters for married couples in the armed forces were far better than those of most indigenous people, and they had the security of medical care and pensions. These advantages reinforced class division between soldiers and the impoverished *campesinos* whom they had to confront, thus ensuring a more committed armed force than in the past, when rebels and federal forces had been more evenly matched.

Militarization of civil society in Chiapas sharpened gender dichotomies, in that women became the target of male soldiers who took out their frustrations against society on them. Very few women could (or, possibly, would if they had the opportunity) enter the mobility channels offered by military service. Indian women, in particular, accepted the major responsibility of maintaining ethnic culture. This responsibility encumbered women's autonomy in wider political and economic circuits at the same time that it released men from the constrictions of ethnic-group identification, permitting them to advance their position in regional and national organizations such as the military.

Yet some indigenous women in the Lacandón joined the rebels' armed forces. Their experience in settlements cut off from traditional communities led to their choice of an alternative, unconventional destiny that was one of the most challenging aspects of the rebellion. Since the early mobilization of the Zapatista movement, women linked the fight for respect for indigenous culture and for women in the home to the struggle for economic and political rights. They publicly stated their positions in state and national conventions, claiming "the right to fight together with men in a relation of equality" (Declaration of the State Convention of Chiapas Women, October 3, 1994). As a result of their own refusal to identify with the subordinate roles imposed by centuries of colonization and independence, these women were most aware of the need for translating democratic principles into everyday behavior. At the 1995 State Convention of Chiapas Women, in San Cristóbal, held only two days after the February 9 invasion, participants signed a declaration that identified the war with "the most brutal expression of a patriarchal regime, characterized by hierarchy, authoritarianism, discrimination, and repression, which exists in our country, whose consequences affect the entire Mexican pueblo." The declaration went on to say that "women, historically discriminated against, have seen how our vulnerability has increased, with the sexual aggression and violations that the army and the white guards have committed against women since they ordered the militarization of Chiapas" (from a photocopied leaflet distributed at the convention). That they faced this aggression and violation in their own homes put them in the tragic dilemma of choosing autonomy at the risk of losing family and children.

As the group most committed to subsistence activities, the concerns of small-plot cultivators in the domestic economy, particularly women, were most threatened by the militarization of society (Smith 1990; Nash 1993). As such, they were often the most consistent opponents of the military in counterinsurgency wars.

CONCLUSIONS

The contradictory trends of globalization in the capitalist economy and culture and the emergence of multiethnic separatism promoted indigenous social movements throughout the hemisphere. Women in ethnically distinct societies bore a double contradiction when they were forced to break the boundaries that circumscribed their lives, at the same time that they tried to fulfill their traditional obligations in the realm of social reproduction. They had to pit themselves against armed soldiers who threatened and harassed them as they carried out the daily chores, and they had to contest their husbands' control over their movements when they attended meetings or went out of the community to sell their handmade products. In order to do this they had to use the collective strategies that were still operating in indigenous communities to mitigate the state's military-based manipulation of gender and ethnic identity.

On the one hand, the domestication of violence through the long-term cohabitation of the military with indigenous populations held hostage in low-intensity warfare cultivated opposition, as civilians resisted its expansion. In its breakdown of the mythical dichotomy between home front and battle front, the army undermined its own mission of protecting national sovereignty and ensuring social tranquillity. On the other hand, the long-term coexistence of army and ordinary domestic life encouraged opportunistic adaptation, on the part of indigenous people, to the presence of the military. The militarization of the internal life of communities eroded civilian authority, as officials abandoned their functions to military authorities. Alcoholism rose, as new *cantinas,* bars, catered to soldiers, in violation of EZLN prohibition of alcohol. Prostitution increased, as truckloads of women arrived in the rain forest. Thus, Zapatista women feared the long-term effect on their children of having army barracks in their midst. Yet like Mother Courage, some complied with militarization by taking advantage of the commercial opportunities offered by the army.

The most unsettling impact of the militarization of Chiapas was the threat to collective strategies that have sustained Mayan cultural resistance in the five hundred years of colonization and conquest. The military and paramilitary intervention into community social organization and cultural practices undermined a sense of trust among community members that would have long-term consequences for the reconstitution of a democratic indigenous civil society. The PRI succeeded in dividing communities within the Lacandón rain forest and in highland communities by channeling funds to its supporters and giving arms to local officials to massacre ordinary people. Gender antagonism increased, as men opposed women's participation in political actions. Women, as a result, were forced to assert their autonomy in the home as well as in civil society. The memory of Acteal was still alive and the survivors maintained a watchful vigil. They and other indigenes still lived in what one activist called "the war of the peace," as they lived in exile from their townships or feared going out to cultivate their fields.[4]

Yet there was a great deal to hope for in Mexico. Mexico traditionally has been less dependent on the military than other Central American countries have been, and the stability of the PRI in its seventy-one years of rule drew upon co-optive approaches rather than military solutions to civil problems. Mexico had resisted Washington-linked militarization of the region in part because regimes since the consolidation of the revolution had prioritized political autonomy from the country's neighbor to the north—that is, until neoliberal policies during the presidencies of Salinas and Zedillo eroded nationalist priorities. The enormous reaction by Mexican civil society against the militarization of the conflict in Chiapas led to the electoral defeat of the PRI in 2000. In the first year of the new millennium, the indigenous people waited with hope and trepidation to see whether President Fox would fulfill his promises to reach a peaceful settlement and implement the San Andrés Peace Accord. Soon after his inauguration he withdrew four of the seven regiments quartered in the Lacandón rain forest, and he repeatedly promised to resolve the differences with the EZLN. However, in 2002 there were still over 40,000 soldiers located in the conflict area, with 187 permanent installations; and when paramilitary attacks were made on the autonomous indigenous settlements, the military still did not intervene. Most disturbing was Fox's failure to mobilize his party behind the San Andrés Accord.

Accustomed to the failure of presidential election promises, the Zapatista communities attempted to realize autonomy in their political and economic practices. They developed their own forms of cooperatives and sought markets abroad through their links with NGOs. They also forged new forms of social relations, working toward autonomy and equality for all members of their communities. And the greatest basis for optimism rested in the resistance movement of indigenous women, whose historical condition as repositories of distinct traditions fostered an inalienable sense of autonomy that was rooted in their culture. Women's participation in the ranks of the Zapatistas transformed the guerrilla movement from a bid for power to an attempt to broaden the democratic base for the entire society. In demanding equality within their ranks as well as in the national society, women broadened and deepened the meaning of democracy in ways that exceeded the boundaries defined by past revolutions, which excluded women, blacks, and servile labor from their utopias.

NOTES

This chapter is a revision of a paper I presented at a session of the 1998 Latin American Studies Association annual conference, which was organized by Helen Safa and myself, in commemoration of the twenty-fifth anniversary of the first conference on gender in Latin America, and entitled "Feminine Perspectives on Models of Latin American Society." My paper reflected on my critique of "dependency analyses," a quarter of a century earlier, for their failure to consider the corrosive effects of dependency relations in domestic and marital relations. I have expanded this thesis to show how women's struggles for autonomy in the Zapatista uprising are broadening and deepening the meaning of equality and liberty. I am grateful to Stuart Plattner, who encouraged me to undertake the Research Experience for Undergraduates field-training project in Chiapas, funded by the National Science Foundation, and to the John D. and Catherine T. MacArthur Foundation for a grant that allowed me to spend six months in Chiapas in 1995. My research on the contemporary Zapatista movement is based on my firsthand observations at the demonstrations, dialogues, and conventions that took place from the years before the uprising and in subsequent years up to 1999. It also draws on interviews with long-term friends in Amatenango and San Cristóbal, as well as on documents distributed at meetings I attended, press releases of the Center for Human Rights "Fray Bartolomé de Las Casas," Global Exchange, Pastors for Peace, and communiques from the Lacandón rain forest published in Chiapas newspapers and *La Jornada*. The superb reporting of that daily newspaper, as well as that of *El Financiero* and the weekly journal *Proceso*, provided multiple perspectives on the developments throughout the state. I have benefited from the insights of Susan Eckstein, Cynthia Enloe, Michael Kearney, and Jan Rus, whose comments on an earlier version helped me to clarify some notions about the social consequences of militarism. I am most indebted to the careful editing of Susan Eckstein, who forced me to clarify my argument and draw significance out of the chaos of events that had inundated me in the field. My understanding of the gender dialectic in the Chiapas conflict owes a great deal to the collective work of the Center for the Social Anthropological Investigation of Society (CIESAS, in San Cristóbal de las Casas) on the precedents and aftermath of Acteal (Hernández Castillo 1998), and especially to the contribution in that anthology by Anna María Garza Caligaris and Rosalva Aída Hernández Castillo. The courage that members in that center demonstrated by publishing such a sharp critique of the PRI government's actions is a tribute to anthropological investigation under fire.

1. Carole Nagengast (1994: 110) points to over fifty such ethnic conflicts that have erupted since the fall of the Berlin Wall in 1989. Her exhaustive analysis of the outbreak of ethnic violence throughout the world is an essential handbook for analyzing new forms of multiethnic relations in the process of globalization.

2. Hernández Castillo (1998) assesses the significance of the New Law of Women in her analysis of demands formulated, and its relevance to the Acteal massacre of 1998. These demands are apparently so minimal—"the right to marry whom we choose, the right to have only so many children as we choose, the right access to health clinics that attend to gynecological problems, among others"—that it seemed to some analysts almost absurd that it required a rebellion to bring them to the attention of authorities. Womack (1999: 252) states that the " 'Women's Revolutionary Law,' for women's rights, actually guarantees (on paper) no more than existing law does (on paper)." The only exception, he maintains, is the right to bear arms. Yet, the women's statement of their rights addressed their experience of being denied these rights in their communities. Like most analysts who have not lived with indigenous people, Womack is not attuned to "traditional" customs that relate to indigenous behavior. Zapatista women were addressing these customs, which have little relation to national laws. On June 10, 1995, at the National Democratic Convention in San Cristóbal, women introduced the Women's Bill of Rights. This followed some of the proposals in the Zapatista women's declaration of rights, but with an additional proviso that women ought to have equal presence and participation in civil organizations, in legislative offices, and in municipal, state, and federal government. The women concluded with a call for democratic practices in "intimate" relations.

3. Threatened by the loss of control over their wives' movements, men were quick to react, ordering their wives not to attend meetings out of town and ha-

rassing unmarried women who were active in the cooperatives. Christine Eber (1998) found that women who were engaged in a bread-making cooperative in Chenalhó also had to contend with men's interference with their activities even though they shared the same objectives as members of the Zapatista support group. Rosalva Aída Hernández Castillo (1998: 137) recounts how a Tzotzil woman from Jitotol, who participated with her husband in the political activities of the Central Independiente de Obreros Agrícolas y Campesinos (CIOAC), paid with her life for her growing leadership responsibilities in organizing the State Convention of Chiapas Women in 1994. Jealous of her growing involvement, her husband killed her with his machete. Just as in the case of the Amatenango pottery cooperative leader, she did not receive any support from her companions when her husband began to beat her, and many stopped going to meetings after she was killed.

4. "The war of the peace" was a phrase of an artist who had joined a caravan to the peace camps in the Lacandón, quoted by Hermann Bollinghausen when he interviewed the group ("Despojados, humillados, los pobladores que escaparon de Guadalupe Tepayac," *La Jornada,* March 8, 1995, p. 13).

REFERENCES

Aubry, Andrés, and Angélica Inda. 1998. "Who Are the Paramilitaries in Chiapas?" *NACLA Report on the Americas* 31, no. 5 (March–April): 8–9.
Center for Human Rights, Fray Bartolomé de las Casas. 1997. *Ni paz ni justicia.* San Cristóbal de las Casas: Fray Bartolomé de las Casas.
Collier, George, with Elizabeth Lowery Quaratiello. 1994. *Basta! Land and the Zapatista Rebellion in Chiapas.* Monroe, Oreg.: Institute for Food and Development Policy.
Comunicación Popular Alternativa Grupo de Trabajo. 1997. "Cronología de una masacre denunciada: Acteal, 22 de Diciembre de 1997." San Cristóbal de las Casas: Comunicación Popular Alternativa Grupo de Trabajo.
Eber, Christine. 1998. "Las mujeres y el movimiento por la democracia en San Pedro Chenalhó." In *La otra palabra: Mujeres y violencia en Chiapas, antes y después de Acteal,* ed. Rosalva Aída Hernández Castillo, pp. 84–104. San Cristóbal de las Casas: Centro de Investigaciones y Acción para la Mujer.
Enloe, Cynthia H. 1980. *Ethnic Soldiers: State Security in Divided Societies.* Atlanta: University of Georgia Press.
———. 1983. *Does Khaki Become You? The Militarization of Women's Lives.* Boston: South End Press.
Freyermuth Enciso, Graciela. 1998. "Antecedentes de Acteal: Muerte materna y control natal, ¿genocidio silencioso?" In *La otra palabra: Mujeres y violencia en Chiapas, antes y después de Acteal,* ed. Rosalva Aída Hernández Castillo, pp. 63–83. San Cristóbal de las Casas: Centro de Investigaciones y Acción para la Mujer.
Garza Caligaris, Anna María, and Rosalva Aída Hernández Castillo. 1998. "Encuentros y enfrentamientos de los tzotziles pedranos con el estado Mexicano: Una perspectiva histórico-antropológica para entender la violencia en

Chenalhó." In *La otra palabra: Mujeres y violencia en Chiapas, antes y después de Acteal,* ed. Rosalva Aída Hernández Castillo, pp. 39–61. San Cristóbal de las Casas: Centro de Investigaciones y Acción para la Mujer.

Gil, Leslie. n.d. "Creating Citizens, Making Men: The Militarization of Masculinity in Bolivia." Unpublished ms.

Global Exchange. 1997. "Emergency Response Human Rights Delegation to Chiapas." San Cristóbal de las Casas. Summer press release.

Gossen, Gary. 1996. "Maya Zapatistas Move to the Ancient Future." *American Anthropologist* 98, no. 3: 528–38.

Green, Linda. 1995. "The Paradoxes of War and Its Aftermath: Mayan Widows in Rural Guatemala." *Cultural Survival Quarterly* 19, no. 1 (Spring): 73–75.

———. 1999. *Fear as a Way of Life: Mayan Widows in Rural Guatemala.* New York: Columbia University Press.

Harvey, Neil. 1994. *Rebellion in Chiapas: Rural Reforms, Campesino Radicalism, and the Limits to Salinismo.* Transformation of Rural Mexico 5. San Diego, Calif.: Ejido Reform Research Project, Center for U.S.-Mexican Studies, University of California.

Hernández Castillo, Rosalva Aída. 1995. "Reinventing Tradition: The Women's Law." *Cultural Survival Quarterly* 19, no. 1 (Spring): 24–25.

———. 1998. "Construyendo la utopía: Esperanzas y desafíos de las mujeres Chiapanecas de frente al siglo XXI." In *La otra palabra: Mujeres y violencia en Chiapas, antes y después de Acteal,* ed. Rosalva Aída Hernández Castillo, pp. 125–42. San Cristóbal de las Casas: Centro de Investigaciones y Acción para la Mujer.

Intifada Indígena. 1998. Web site, http://serpiente.dgsca.unam.mx/jor/ (January).

Kovic, Christine Marie. 1995. "Con un solo corazón: La iglesia católica, la identidad indígena, y los derechos humanos en Chiapas." In *The Explosion of Community in Chiapas, Mexico,* ed. June Nash, pp. 109–19. Copenhagen: IWGIA.

Lewis, Oscar. 1964. *Pedro Martínez: A Mexican Peasant and His Family.* New York: Random House.

Monsivais, Carlos. 1998. "La teología solo puede ser de liberación, no de esclavitud ni de violencia, a menos de que sea paramilitar: Obispo Samuel Ruiz." *Proceso,* no. 127 (June 7): 6–15.

Nagengast, Carole. 1994. "Violence, Terror, and the Crisis of the State." *Annual Review of Anthropology* 23: 109–36.

Nash, June. 1970. *In the Eyes of the Ancestors: Belief and Behavior in a Mayan Community.* New Haven, Conn.: Yale University Press. 2d ed. Prospect Heights, Ill.: Waveland Press, 1986.

———, ed. 1993. *Crafts in the World Market: The Impact of Global Exchange on Middle American Artisans.* Albany: State University of New York Press.

———. 1994. "The Challenge of Trade Liberalization to Cultural Survival on the Southern Frontier of Mexico." *Indiana Journal of Global Law* 1, no. 2: 367–95.

———. 1995. "Power of the Powerless: Update from Chiapas." *Cultural Survival Quarterly* 19, no. 1 (Spring): 14–18.

———. 1997a. "Fiesta of the Word: Radical Democracy in Chiapas, Mexico." *American Anthropologist* 99, no. 2: 261–74.

———. 1997b. "Gendered Deities and the Survival of Culture." *Journal of the History of Religion* 36, no. 4: 333–56.

Nordstrom, Carolyn. 1995. "Introduction to Women and War." *Cultural Survival Quarterly* 19, no. 1 (Spring): 3.

Olivera, Mercedes. 1979. "Mujeres acasilladas en las fincas de Chiapas." *Cuadernos Agrarios* (Mexico City).

———. 1995. "Práctica feminista en el Movimiento Zapatista de Liberación Nacional." In *Chiapas: Y las mujeres que? Colección del dicho al hecho*, ed. Rosa Rojas, vol. 2, pp. 168–89. México, D.F.: Editorial La Correa Feminista, Instituto de Investigación y Capacitación de la Mujer.

Plataforma de las Mujeres para el Diálogo. 1995. In *Chiapas: Y las mujeres que? Colección del dicho al hecho*, ed. Rosa Rojas, vol. 2. México, D.F.: Editorial La Correa Feminista, Instituto de Investigación y Capacitación de la Mujer.

Pozas, Ricardo. 1947. "Juan Pérez Jolote: Biografía de un Tzotzil." *Acta Antropológica* (México, D.F.) 3, no. 3.

Rojas, Rosa. 1995. *Chiapas: Y las mujeres que? Colección del dicho al hecho.* Vol. 2. México, D.F.: Editorial La Correa Feminista, Instituto de Investigación y Capacitación de la Mujer.

Rosh, Robert M. 1988. "Third World Militarization: Security Webs and the States They Ensnare." *Journal of Conflict Resolution* 32, no. 4 (December): 671–98.

Rus, Jan. 1994. "The 'Comunidad Revolucionaria Institucional': The Subversion of Native Government in Highland Chiapas, 1936–1968." In *Everyday Forms of State Formation: Revolution and the Negotiation of Role in Modern Mexico,* ed. Gilbert M. Joseph and Daniel Nugent, pp. 265–300. Durham, N.C.: Duke University Press.

Smith, Carol A. 1990. "The Militarization of Civil Society in Guatemala: Economic Reorganization as a Continuation of War." *Latin American Perspectives* 17, no. 43: 8–41.

Stephen, Lynn. 1994. *Viva Zapata! Generation, Gender, and Historical Consciousness in the Reception of Ejido Reform in Oaxaca.* Transformation of Rural Mexico 6. San Diego, Calif.: Ejido Reform Research Project, Center for U.S.-Mexican Studies, University of California.

Stern, Steve J. 1995. *The Secret History of Gender: Women, Men, and Power in Late Colonial Mexico.* Chapel Hill: University of North Carolina Press.

Turner, Frederick C. 1967. "Los efectos de la participación feminista en la revolución de 1910." *Historia Mexicana* 1: 602–20.

Womack, John, Jr. 1999. *Rebellion in Chiapas: An Historical Reader.* New York: New Press.

CHAPTER TWELVE

Reflections on Remembrance

Voices from an Ixcán Village

BEATRIZ MANZ

How does one remember events so traumatic that forgetting them seems an act of redemption? How does one recall the past, when powerful social institutions, individual actors, and the fallibility of memory itself conspire to redefine what took place? The scale of the violence in Guatemala in the 1970s and 1980s was truly of horrific, epic proportions, increasingly documented in devastating, indisputable detail. The most comprehensive analysis of this savagery, the report of the Comisión para el Esclarecimiento Histórico (Commission for Historical Clarification; CEH),[1] concludes that 200,000 people were killed or disappeared, 93 percent at the hands of state forces and related paramilitary groups (1999a: 18, 20).[2] During the most intense period of the military onslaught, from 1981 to 1983, as many as 1.5 million people were displaced internally or had to flee the country, including about 150,000 who sought refuge in Mexico (1999a: 30). "The massacres, scorched earth operations, forced disappearances and executions of Mayan authorities, leaders and spiritual guides," the Commission forcefully charged, "were not only an attempt to destroy the social base of the guerrillas, but above all, to destroy the cultural values that ensured cohesions and collective action in Mayan communities" (1999a: 23).

In this chapter, I explore forces that shape memory among the inhabitants of a remote village in the Ixcán region of Guatemala, a place I first visited in 1973, shortly after it was settled. I focus on military efforts to reshape both individual and community memory: army strategies that subjected villagers to a culture of fear and atomization.

This village was an ambitious attempt of land-starved peasants from the highlands and Catholic clergy to colonize the nearly inaccessible rain forest along the Mexican border. With few resources, in the face of an unforgiving environment, these courageous, optimistic settlers succeeded: growing food for themselves, marketing cash crops, organizing cooperatives, setting up a school and a church; in short, establishing a vibrant community. While it took a decade of determination and backbreaking work to establish the village, the army decimated it in a matter of hours in February 1982, in the midst of the worst violence wracking the country. As a column of soldiers slowly approached, the terrified villagers fled to the surrounding rain forest, scattering in every direction. The troops torched the dwellings and massacred a group of fourteen women and children they encountered huddled in the jungle. The troops likely would have butchered the entire village had they found those who eluded them. After several months in hiding, over half the families made the arduous and emotionally wrenching journey to find refuge in Mexico, where they stayed for over a decade. The army eventually placed those who remained behind under military control, literally on the ashes of the original village, and brought in new peasants to occupy the lands of those in refuge.

The purpose of the terror in this and countless other villages, the Comisión para el Esclarecimiento Histórico maintains, "was to intimidate and silence society as a whole, in order to destroy the will for transformation, both in the short and long term" (1999a: 27). Without question, the army's horrific actions ripped deep psychological wounds into the consciousness of the inhabitants of the village. In the aftermath of this trauma, the military sought to suture the wounds by establishing a new version of the past that portrayed the army as the peasants' savior from the guerrillas, rather than as the perpetrator of unspeakable criminal acts.

What the army has done on a national level—and what many Guatemalans perhaps unwittingly accept—is delay a fuller interpretation of the conflict, one that might produce a moral and political regeneration and thus a greater and broader justice (Corradi 1992: 285). Given the weakness of the insurgents as an armed force, it is apparent the army was not militarily threatened by the rebels (Comisión 1999a: 22). What threatened them and the elites was the mind and actions of the Mayan peasantry. Therefore, they went after that population to bring them, dead or alive, under army control, and then they attempted to defeat the hearts and minds of the survivors.

Was the army successful in redefining recollections of the past? The theme of recalling the past is complex; it is rooted in the nature of memory as well as in the experiences of the individuals and community involved. There are no universal villages in Guatemala (Smith 1990; Warren 2001)—all are rooted in unique circumstances—but the inhabitants of this unique community grappled with more generalized themes: the forces that define the way the past is recalled. A broad divide exists in this village between those who remained under military control and those who fled either to Mexico, the rain forest, or to join the insurgents.[3]

Today, the collective memory of the community is in transition, fashioned not only by the legacy of military action but also by the return of the refugees and a more open national dialogue. Refugees had become more politicized, and many returned with a deeper awareness of their rights. The more open national dialogue came in the wake of negotiations between the military, the government, and the Unidad Revolucionaria Nacional Guatemalteca (Guatemala National Revolutionary Unity; URNG), the principal umbrella group of the insurgents. These negotiations led to the December 1996 peace accords, an amnesty, and a broader national desire, at times hesitant and still fearful, to come to terms with the past.

THE LITERATURE ON MEMORY

Many scholars see the necessity of recovering the memory of the Mayans' situation in the war and interpreting it (Wilson 1991, 1995, 1997; Warren 1992, 1993; Hale 1997a, 1997b; Green 1999; Nelson 1999). "*La violencia* gives a shape to memories and to later experiences of repression," Warren observes (1998: 86). Another scholar notes, "The entire history of *la violencia* can be read as a war against memory, an Orwellian falsification of memory, a falsification of reality" (Zur 1998: 159). Montejo (1987), Falla (1994), the Equipo de Antropología Forense (1997), and others have produced detailed, moving accounts of the experiences of villages during the terror in the 1980s.

When researchers ask survivors in Guatemala's rural areas to recall the violence, these witnesses commonly respond quite specifically to what may be called "fixed events": the number of people killed, dates and times, villages destroyed, kidnappings, and so on, and they overwhelmingly identify the army as the culprit. Underscoring the claim is "hard data," such as mass graves, names of relatives, evidence of a village's destruction, missing persons. When asked why the conflict happened or to explain their own involvement or opinions about it, the responses are much less assertive, more conditional, dubious, and at times shifting. When respondents make statements recalling the past, several considerations shape the dynamics at play: individual and collective memory formation, personal background, experiences since the time in question, apprehensions about speaking frankly, and outside forces influencing the discussion about past events.

On one level, memory reflects the struggle of an individual to deal with the past. The villagers' more conditional answers are rooted in the fact that, as Primo Levi tells us, "human memory is a marvelous but fallacious instrument" (1988: 23); it is in a constant state of adding and subtracting, neglecting, refining and rearranging its silhouette. In the aftermath of major social and political upheaval, events are reorganized even more rapidly. Those who lived in militarized villages may not be distorting the past consciously, in their minds, but history is a remarkably heavy burden to come to terms with. Some "lie consciously, coldly falsifying reality itself," Levi observed, "but more numerous are those who weigh anchor, move off, momentarily or forever, from genuine memories, and fabricate for themselves a convenient reality. The past is a burden to them; they feel repugnance for things done or suffered and tend to replace them with others" (1988: 27). Over time, if not challenged, the distinction between the early and the later remembrance "progressively loses its contours" (1988: 27). It does not take much to reshape a suggested image: an omission here and some embellishing there, until a new picture emerges that fits more favorably with the current context and, over time, barely resembles the original.

On another level, memory is collective and socially formed. "Collective memory is biased towards forgetting that which is negative," Halbwachs suggests (Marques, Paez, and Serra 1997: 258), and painful or shameful events are even more difficult to handle. Halbwachs's main contribution to understanding the molding of collective memory is to formulate its shifting and fluid nature, to identify the collective interest of a group in recalling their common past in a selective, acceptable, and partial manner.

Collective memory, by definition, is a social product, but individual memory also flows from social context. In formulating an account of what took place, individuals tap their own recollections, based on their relation to major events and on discussions with each other. These perceptions of the past are inevitably filtered not only through their own experiences in the interim period, but also through the social arena in which these events are interpreted and understood by society as a whole.[4]

What is this social context? Nietzsche writes that "everything that exists, no matter what its origin, is periodically reinterpreted by those in power in terms of fresh intentions" (1956: 209). Connerton reinforces the point by emphasizing that social memory consists of "images of the past that commonly legitimate the present social order" (Connerton 1989: 3). A Guatemalan military officer observes, "There is a historic truth in Guatemala, which is a truth from the perspective of power, and that is the one that we know and accept" (Cifuentes 1998: 89). One way of legitimizing the present is by denying the past or, if faced with factual truths, by rationalizing the terror that took place. Nonetheless, as Arendt puts it, facts possess "a strength of [their] own: whatever those in power may contrive, they are unable to discover or invent a viable substitute for [them]" (1968: 259). Unfortunately for those who seek to deny or reshape an uncomfortable past, "facts assert themselves by being stubborn" and are, ultimately, "beyond agreement, dispute, opinion, or consent" (1968: 258, 240). Nonetheless, this tension between interpretation and reality is the terrain on which memory is constituted and to which the analysis now turns.

RETELLING, TRUST, AND INTERPRETATION

Social scientists doing research among populations subjected to terror and fear may ask: what is one to do with the recollections people provide? More than usual, it is important here to decipher or decode the meanings in people's stories, to distinguish between the public voice and the concealed unspoken thoughts. It is not simply a question of truth versus untruth, but what is said and what is unsaid. That which remains purposefully unspoken can be more significant, as it connotes agency, defiance, resistance, control, autonomy, contestation, resilience. The aim of a social-science researcher is to uncover the hidden voice, the double meaning, that which resides "between the lines."

In Guatemala the act of remembering, let alone the act of retelling, is a highly charged, politicized event, fraught with danger. Not surprisingly, people tend to give partial information and often misinformation—especially if related to political opinions—until trust is established and it becomes clear what, if any, consequences could befall the respondent. As Warren found in San Andrés, "It is as if denial and a low profile would bring protection from a world that merited greater distrust than ever" (1998: 93). As in a puzzle, a few letters are given and the rest are left blank until confidence allows a fuller picture to emerge.

A respondent's perception of the researcher influences what is said. Javier, a villager, became confused at my persistent questions, apparently reflecting a position contrary to the one he assumed I held. At one point, he blurted out: "You mean, you don't care what my position is, what I think, you don't care if I am for the army or the guerrillas, it doesn't matter to you? You want to hear what I really think?" (interview with author, 1997). It seemed to him that my purpose for writing about the village was to gather documentation and opinions to buttress my point of view. He wanted to show his appreciation for me by telling me what I wanted to hear. He confided:

> When someone we don't know asks a direct question, the first thing we think about is, who is he? Why is he asking this question? What is behind the question? What are the consequences of my answer? We try not to give a direct answer until we figure out where the question is coming from. Then we respond accordingly. For example, if I know you are Catholic I give one type of answer, if I know you are Evangelical, then another. The same, and even more so, politically. (interview with author, 1997)

Villagers, isolated and in this context fearful, have preconceived, stereotypical notions about outsiders. "We tend to trust a Canadian, or someone from Sweden more than we would a German or [someone from England]," Javier explained, "and of course least of all a *gringo*—an American." I follow up by questioning why *gringos* elicit the least trust. "Well, you know, they work together with the army, they send funds for the army, the CIA and all that," he matter-of-factly responded (interview with author, 1998).[5]

A key element of establishing trust was the relationship built up over almost three decades of interactions (Manz 1988a, 1988b, 1988c, 1995). Trust is what distinguishes ethnography from simply careful observation. To interact as well as observe requires a level of confidence that grows unevenly and over time. Often it develops in increasingly personal interventions, sharing the jokes and gossip of everyday life; at other times it is reflected in insights about sensitive matters where a chance comment could damage or destroy a person's life. Trust deepens with patience, often requires restraint from overt judgments, and is defined when one is repeatedly called on to be a mediator. Year after year these villagers afforded me hospitality and exceptional confidence. At the height of the militarization and violence during the early and mid-1980s, they confided their collaboration with the insurgents and divulged the details of what took place. I often feared for them as well as myself to know about their activities, such as relatives in the guerrilla forces coming to visit them secretly in the village. Confidences, familiarity, arguments, and disagreements over many years laid the basis for discussions that could be open, at times painful.

RECOVERING THE PAST

Given the apprehension peasants feel, the challenge for a researcher is to discover what people were thinking when the events unfolded, and to understand what factors have molded current memory. In many Guatemalan villages, diverse, often contradictory, memories coexist concerning relations with the insurgent forces, and the community I studied is no exception. While the entire village provided at least tacit support to the guerrillas, people recall that collaboration differently. Some remember their involvement with the guerrillas as a conscious decision, fully voluntary, and are proud of their actions, even in the wake of what occurred. They blame the army for the massacres, terror, and destruction. Others admit to having provided support but in retrospect feel they were deceived. One villager accused the guerrillas of provoking the massacres and destruction—a rare position.

What dynamics shape and reshape these multiple narratives? Over time, memories of the same events sometimes evolve into mirror images of each other when viewed from the recollections of many inside and outside the country. Consider two individuals who offered diametrically opposed recollections: Gustavo, who was in Mexico from 1982 to 1994, and Nicanor, who spent these years in the militarized settlement. Prior to the destruction of the village in February 1982, Gustavo and Nicanor were indistinguishable politically and both were supporters of the insurgency. Gustavo is a Mayan; Nicanor is one of the few Ladinos in the village, but this distinction does not appear important in this context. I asked Gustavo in 1997 to tell me how many people had collaborated with the guerrillas in the village and to define their involvement. He readily answered:

> At the end everyone collaborated in various ways. The least [involvement] would be helping to give information or to keep the secret [of the involvement of the others]. In either case there was the belief that there would be a

victory soon, due to the explanations [the guerrillas] gave us. It also had to do with the attitude of the army. We hated the army. People understood quickly what the guerrillas said because they explained the situation well and the objectives that they were seeking. (interview with author, 1997)

Between 1979 and 1981, Nicanor had been among the most enthusiastic members of the Fuerzas Irregulares Locales (Local Irregular Forces; FIL), the basic unit of the insurgents. "You should have seen him," a villager recalled. "He marched with gusto during training drills, he carried an old weapon, he was committed, he liked being in the FIL" (interview with author, 1997). In his early twenties at the time, his brother was the first person in the village to join the insurgency. Asked the same question in 1997—why did people join the guerrillas?—Nicanor responded quite differently, offering one of the harshest critiques:

People joined because the guerrillas manipulated the people and said they had to go with them.... The army became angry [when they destroyed the village] and had to do what they did. The people joined because in those days we did not know anything about politics, from one group or the other, you were just an individual. So [the guerrillas] took advantage of us by talking with one and then another without people realizing what was going on. Then when we all became aware, everyone was involved. (interview with author, 1997)[6]

Gustavo and Nicanor reflect a broader divide in the village. Everyone, of course, was not affected by the violence equally, and presence in either the militarized villages or the refugee camps is not the only determinant of how the past is recalled. Nonetheless, Gustavo's position tends to be held by those who fled the borders and sought refuge in Mexico or otherwise escaped the army's authority. Nicanor's position, though not necessarily as harsh a critique, tends to be shared by people who remained under military control.

Outside the country, refugees talked openly, freely, and, in fact, incessantly about what occurred from the moment they crossed the border. NGOs, the United Nations, churches, and international delegations provided the context for the refugees. As Montejo found, "the refugees have chosen exile as a form of resisting and avoiding military repression in Guatemala" (n.d.: 115). In the process, "the refugees have become politicized as they have questioned their social relations in Guatemala" (n.d.: 179). Another group outside military control, excombatants with the insurgent forces (a more extensive involvement than that of Nicanor), are likely to have similar interpretations: mistakes are recognized but they are more inclined to feel their participation was necessary and worthwhile. "It was worth it" is a common expression. Or they'll affirm their contribution: "I gave my grain of sand." Some even feel defensive, if not offended, by the idea that they were duped. I asked José, a former combatant, if he and his wife had been manipulated into joining. He answered emphatically, slowly, almost chewing on every word: "Voluntarily, with my five senses!" (interview with author, 1998). I had the feeling that he had heard the terms "manipulated and tricked" too many times and was somewhat annoyed by my question.

The military subjugated the rural population who stayed in Guatemala (the more prevalent type in the country as a whole) to a widespread military-sponsored "reeducation" and psychological campaign. The army and its related institutions, in addition to exerting physical control in even the most distant villages, sought to retrieve the past in support of their political dominance of the present. The army went beyond separating the villagers from the guerrillas; it sought to atomize the social bonds of the villagers themselves. Those who stayed avoided speaking about what happened even among themselves and were even more reluctant, out of fear, to discuss the past with outsiders. For many years, the military was the only authority and patron for those who remained.

THE PSYCHOLOGICAL WAR:
RESCUE THE MINDS OF THE MAYANS

The version that the army relentlessly promulgated was that the guerrillas stood for violence, hate, destruction, deceit, and lawlessness, while the army represented peace, happiness, development, truth, and law and order—in short, the opposite of the guerrillas.[7] This message, however, collided with a searing reality: the army had committed heinous massacres throughout the Ixcán and had reduced the village I studied, among others, to ashes. Prior to the massacre the army had kidnapped, assassinated, tortured, and raped individuals.

The army's psychological operations sought to reconcile this horrific reality with its desired message by convincing the villagers that the guerrillas had manipulated the people and provoked the army. Now, the army and the people needed to be united to rid themselves of evil; the army builds, the guerrillas destroy; God is on the side of the army; the guerrillas are akin to the devil. The message became more convincing to some not simply through endless repetition, but because the army physically dominated their world, and, as a result, alternative explanations were dangerous if not fatal. Under these circumstances, language shapes the way people think and recall the past. What the villagers may earlier have recalled as a collaboration with the insurgents evolved into having been manipulated into giving aid.

The contextual framework of the army's exhortations is pivotal in understanding the influence of the military campaigns. The villagers had lost everything and suffered tremendously while hiding for months in the jungle. They viewed their own survival as a miracle in the midst of massacres, plunder, and destruction of entire villages. In the aftermath of such horror, survivors were completely dependent on the army for their life and well-being. They found themselves interned physically and vulnerable psychologically. These were the conditions under which they assessed their situation.

Prior to the terror of 1982, had the army attempted the same psychological approach in this village, it would likely have fallen on deaf ears. Considering the tight physical control the army exercised over the village, its influence was not nearly as enduring as I would have initially thought. As several villagers have told me, "One can say many things, but what one feels in the heart is another thing" (interview with author, 1999).

In the mid- to late 1980s, the period of the worst atrocities, the military employed a perverse variant on the Socratic method. The army raised provocative questions and then provided self-serving answers to engage the population in reflecting on why the terror had erupted: What brought on this "situation"? Were you not living peacefully until the guerrillas came to bother you? What did they falsely promise? The army introduced a Cold War framework stressing that the guerrillas tended to be "outsiders and non-Mayan," that they were people from the city, that they had foreign ideologies, underscoring the role of Cuba, Nicaragua, and Russia.

I asked Ramón in the mid-1980s, "What does the army tell you about what happened in the village?"

> They said that the guerrillas burnt our houses, they came to destroy all our possessions. Why? Because they are people from other *aldeas* or countries who only want to destroy communities. They are people who do not want development and only want to destroy, and so that this will not occur again you must comply with your obligations. The guerrillas burned our houses and killed all our animals. The guerrillas are bad people, with bad thoughts. (interview with author, 1987)

Stunned by hearing the army's contention that guerrillas burned the village, I wondered to what extent these lies had seeped into his consciousness. I then asked him specifically, "But who burned the village?" He answered calmly: "Well, the army [actually] burned it, but as they said, it was the guerrillas' fault, they provoked the army" (interview with author, 1987).

Curious about my own standing, I then asked him what was being said about me and my frequent visits to the village. "Well, it is said that you were with the guerrillas, that you were possibly a *guerrillera*" (interview with author, 1987). Another villager said to me at a public village meeting in 1987 that "there are rumors that you are the head of the guerrillas." Humorous moments appeared in the midst of personal threats and fear. One Q'eqchi' villager,[8] a former soldier who began spreading the rumors about my association with the guerrillas, said, when confronted about it while drunk, "But look, you know, if you come to visit again, my house is your house" (from Myrna Mack's field notes, April 23 to May 6, 1987; Mack was in the village during this phase of my research).

CIVIL PATROLS: THE INSTITUTIONAL FRAMEWORK IN THE COUNTRYSIDE

During the murderous Ríos Montt regime in 1982, the military expanded the Patrullas de Autodefensa Civil (Civil Self-Defense Patrols; PACs) to extend military control of the countryside and sever contact between the guerrillas and the civilian population. By the following year, the civil patrols enlisted over a million Mayan men, however unwillingly, into around-the-clock unpaid shifts, as often as once a week (Americas Watch 1986; Manz 1988a; Popkin 1996). These patrols comprised a key dimension of the army's counterinsurgency operations, providing an institutional framework for the psychological efforts. As the Commission for Historical Clarification noted, the civil patrol's objectives were to "control physically and psychologically the population" and to "influence the population psychologically," so that villagers will "repudiate the guerrillas and create a unity between the army and the people" (Comisión 1999b: 26, 29). One villager in the civil patrols who had previously supported the guerrillas recalled, "The army told us, you yourselves must guard your families, your houses, your land, because the army alone cannot do it" (interview with author, 1989). The military explained that they "do not have sufficient soldiers to do it [themselves] because Guatemala is big and the army does not have sufficient personnel to guard the whole country. So in order for you to live in peace you have to be alert so that what happened in '82 does not happen again" (interview with author,

1989). In interview after interview, respondents (even Nicanor, who had told me in 1987 that the civil patrols were voluntary) reported that they were compelled to go on sweeps, sometimes alone, sometimes ahead of an army column or interspersed among the soldiers. Villagers were ordered to be vigilant and to inform on unusual activities, meetings, "strangers" passing through, conversations overheard. If villagers spotted guerrillas they were to immediately inform the army and then a civil patrol would lead a special army unit to that location.

The civil patrols were effective in two broad respects. First, they kept the population militarized and under control. The village, in effect, became an intelligence unit for the army. As Montejo observes, "The civil patrols were the most effective instrument used by the army in maintaining control and creating fear in Mayan communities" (n.d.: 93). The PACs were compromised by their very involvement with the army; they were compelled to report. The system worked so well that an information overload soon developed—a commander in the massive nearby Playa Grande military base recalled—forcing the army to concentrate on defining broad patterns. Second, the PACs became local reconnaissance units for the army, spread out over the entire counterinsurgency area. The local patrols knew the terrain better than even the guerrillas, and could move undetected and unrecognized, all at no expense to the military.

The benefit of the civil patrols to the army became apparent during several of my stays in the Ixcán. When the guerrillas encountered a patrol, ironically they were often not able to tell friend from foe. Nor could they afford to start antagonizing the local population. After the mid-1980s, when the army consolidated control of the Ixcán and the former irregular units of the guerrillas were now civil patrols, it was only a matter of time until the insurgent war was over. Rather than having their irregular units organize the collection of food in the village, the guerrillas in the Ixcán were reduced to stopping vehicles on the road—the famed Northern Transversal Strip—to buy food.

In the militarized context, Nicaragua appears to have been at the top of the civic education curriculum by the mid-1980s.[9] One villager, who had joined the guerrillas as a combatant in the early days, reflected in 1989, after having been named a military commissioner by the army: "The military tells us that the army and the people have to work together to save the fatherland. They told us about Nicaragua, Cuba, and Russia. Those are communist countries and you know what happens in those countries? They make pants for everyone, lots of them, and give them to the people, all the same color, olive green."

I could not resist asking: "Same size?"

"All the same."

"What if they don't fit? Look at me, what would I do?"

He grinned. "I don't know, they don't care if it fits or not, all have to be the same.... There is no freedom there. They work together, they call it collectivism, all have to work and there are no wages. The army says we have to see that that does not occur here and for that the PACs must cooperate with the army" (interview with author, 1989).

Nicanor, the former FIL member and, in 1987, a PAC chief, also brought up Nicaragua: "Look what happened in Nicaragua. Thank God that didn't happen here."

I asked, "What happened in Nicaragua?"

"The officer at the base told us that in Nicaragua everyone dresses the same. You cannot have a wife, no religion is allowed, all the harvests go to the state, you cannot own land, anything. Thank God that didn't happen here" (interview with author, 1987).

I looked at Nicanor, sitting by me, in amazement. Very thin, with his front upper teeth missing, though he was only in his early thirties, he wore torn pants and old shoes with holes in them. He was putting endless hours into the civil patrols and he was risking his life without pay—all of which, of course, negatively affected his family.

A decade later, in 1997, after the civil patrols had been dissolved in the aftermath of the peace agreements, I asked him whether the patrols had been voluntary or obligatory. "Voluntary," he answered without hesitation. When hearing this, I reflected upon the impact his incarceration at the military base in 1982 may have had on him. What else could have made him so bitter and cynical? What effect did it have on him when his wife left him with her parents for the refugee camps and he had to raise their two sons alone? What role might guilt have played? Surely, personal circumstances have played a role in changing attitudes and one should not overstate the army's influence.

CHANGES OVER TIME

In the most recent interview (April 1999), I asked Nicanor again if the civil patrols had been voluntary or obligatory, and the answer this time was more nuanced. "They were forced and voluntary," he responded.

Could he explain this paradox, if not contradiction, that they were both "forced and voluntary"? He said they were voluntary in the sense that the guerrillas once fired at the center of the village and people wanted to protect themselves.

I asked why the guerrillas did that.

"Because the army was here." He said the villagers did not want the guerrillas to come into the center of the village, although "it was OK for them to be in the outskirts of the village."

Then I said, "So that is the 'voluntary' part, as far as you are concerned; what is the forced part?"

"The forced part is that if you didn't do the PAC service, the army would punish you."

"What type of punishment?" I asked.

"Let's say they would make us work a day at the army base."

When discussing controls, Nicanor mentioned that the army counted the peasants' tortillas as they went to the fields to work. When asked why the army would do that, he answered with a grin, "Because they suspected we were taking food to the guerrillas." He gave many examples of control, and with each he said it was done because the army did not trust the population.

Some of his answers were not too different from those he had given years earlier. "Why wouldn't the army let the villagers work in their fields in 1983, the first year, when you returned to the village?" I asked him.

"Because those from the mountains, the guerrillas could grab us, so it was preferable that we not go there."

"Why would they grab you?"

"To take you, that is what they said."

I then asked, "Tell me, why do *you* think the army would not let you go to work on your parcels?"

"Ah, because [the army] did not trust us. They thought we would go talk to [the guerrillas]." As a result, the army would only let them work in groups of ten or twenty men and only in the fields closest to the village center.

Moving to another subject, I asked why the village was burned. "It was burned so we wouldn't have anything, no place to return to," he replied, "so we wouldn't have a house, nothing."

Regarding the massacre of women and children, he said: "Well, [the army] was not just looking for those that were armed, but whoever they found. The orders were to kill anyone they found. It didn't matter."

I asked him once more about his views of the guerrillas. "The army said that we should not let ourselves be deceived by the guerrillas again," he responded. "They only bring problems to the people, they are terrorists."

I then asked him, "When you heard that, what would you think?" I followed the question by probing more personally: "Given your past collaboration with the guerrillas and that your brother was the first in the village to become a combatant, was the army describing your brother when they talked about terrorists?"

There was a long pause. Then he said, "Well, when they would say that, one would know what they were doing, that it was a lie, of course, that they were saying that only to deceive the people themselves."

I asked for clarification: "Who used to say that?" He answered, "The army. They would say [the guerrillas] were terrorists, but the truth is that the whole world knew that was not so" (interview with author, 1999).

AFTEREFFECTS OF MILITARIZATION

Militarized daily life, so radically different from normal community life, mutilated the village and left lasting scars on the population. When asked about the 1996 peace accords, many villagers revealed skepticism that slid into cynicism, reasoning that deep down little had changed—an interpretation that feeds demoralization, paralysis, and hopelessness. Even peace is meaningless, in this view. Corruption and abuse exist everywhere and forever. One conclusion reached by soldiers at the nearby Playa Grande military base, and repeated by some villagers, is that all the suffering was borne by the Indians on both sides and now the big shots are sharing the spoils among themselves. The lessons to be drawn from this are: stick to yourself; never trust anyone, and especially not an outsider or a politician; don't again provoke the massacres of 1982. The political apathy is evident in the lack of political participation at the polls.

The army's extensive psychological interventions provided a framework for thinking about the conflict. The explanations sought to provide justification for the unjustifiable: the army's massacres and wholesale destruction. Moreover, the old stereotypes could remain in place: Indians are stupid, easily manipulated politically, incapable of bettering themselves. They are either victims to be pitied, if one is generous, or they are to be feared and despised, if one is more typically racist. (It should be noted that the idea of manipulation was not used for the guerrillas and their supporters in Nicaragua or El Salvador, but it became an article of faith to understand the collaboration of Mayans in Guatemala.)

This framework negates the ability of Mayan peasants to become actors and shapers of their destiny, a characteristic neither the army nor the elites are comfortable with. For some fearful and defeated peasants, these interpretations seemed to resonate, particularly since alternative explanations remained dangerous to embrace. The army reinforced these interpretations, aiming to have them assimilated and internalized as part of the people's own remembrance. The ideological control of the army was not just confined to the rural areas. Urban centers were affected as well, but the countryside remained isolated for many years. People in Guatemala City were not informed about what was happening in the countryside.[10] This was not an accident. It is far more convenient for the military to steadfastly deny their role and avoid responsibility if the society does not demand accountability.[11]

When peasants in the Ixcán village were asked, "How do you see the future?" two types of answers prevailed: those who said they would never let themselves be involved in anything again and didn't want to participate in any political activity, and those who said that, if things didn't change, the next generation would have to struggle again. The first response generally came from people who experienced daily life in a militarized village, the second from people who fled.

Former refugees from the village seemed to exhibit more pride and assertiveness. They were less likely to feel either guilt or shame, to feel apologetic or pessimistic, or certainly not to the degree that others interviewed reflected these attitudes. While many of the refugees were deeply disappointed and negative about the guerrillas with whom they once collaborated, the prevalent view they expressed was not that they were duped. They listed mistakes, abuse, and arrogance, but admitted supporting the insurgents after giving it serious thought and coming to believe that it was the right, necessary, and just thing to do. That is, they were able to differentiate between a negative evaluation of the guerrillas today and their own memory of why they decided to collaborate at the time. Villagers tended to make a distinction between the regional guerrilla units, the mistakes these units committed, and the villagers' own self-esteem and pride despite their side's failure to attain the desired goal. The villagers viewed themselves as actors, not simply as subjects.

Among those who remained in the militarized village, some fused military explanations with their own pessimism. The guerrillas' failures—

overemphasized by the army—and their own frustrations spilled into the same defeat. When I asked them whether they would be saying the same thing had the guerrillas won, they stopped to think for a while, as if this possibility was now beyond rational hypothesis, and then responded: "Well, of course, then I would think differently."

"What about deception?"

"No, then I would not feel I was deceived."

"So," I asked, "your feelings and memory have more to do with who won and lost than with the way you were treated?"

"I guess that could be so" (interview with author, 1996).

The refugees tend to trace their political participation to a more enduring foundation: the new church or peasant leagues, education, cooperative organizations, communication. They feel much was gained politically even if militarily and materially they were defeated. They can also see their participation in the future. The refugees had been able to talk about the atrocities in a more open and supportive environment, receiving solidarity from Mexicans and from the international community. They had not feared reprisals; they had felt defiant. Later, as a result, they were organized, proud to have survived the army's onslaught. They did not feel judged, morally questioned, or lectured. They did not feel personally defeated. They felt more angry than depressed. While they may not have many good things to say about the guerrillas, they certainly never identified with the winners—the army.

The opposite was sometimes true, at least outwardly, in the militarized village. Among those who stayed, some stated that, in the future, "we are not going to let anyone use us again." The lesson repeated and underscored by the army was that Indians should remember never to trust anyone (except the army). The best thing for Indians, in this view, was to keep their noses to the ground, till their corn fields, and maintain an atomized existence distrusting everyone, especially outsiders who bring ideas that challenge the status quo. In essence, the aim appears to be for the Indians to accept the proposition that their involvement in an insurgent movement stemmed from stupidity, manipulation, and deceit.

On one level, those who stayed and those who fled have converging perspectives. When people were asked in 1998, "Who won and who lost?" a common answer was: "The army won militarily, but the guerrillas won politically...[though] the power is still in the hands of the powerful." When asked who represented their interests at the negotiating table, a common answer was "the URNG" (the main umbrella group of the insurgents). Not a single person replied that the army represented their interests. One man known for his stubbornness and his dislike of the guerrillas said, "I don't know."

I asked a twenty-seven-year-old, soft-spoken man, who became a combatant in 1987 at the age of seventeen and stayed until the demobilization in 1997, "What would happen if the accords were not implemented?" He answered, "We would have to struggle again, but this time with our voice" (interview with author, 1998).

Moreover, the youth are much freer from the experiences and interpretations of their parents in both groups, based on their own experiences and outlooks. About one hundred students are studying with scholarships at the university and at professional schools. One law student at San Carlos University—the only survivor, at the age of six, of the 1982 massacre of fourteen women and children—expressed a prevalent view: "We have always thought that we should help our community." He thought that one way to help future university students was "to contribute ten or fifteen percent of our salary." Another student stated, "All of us together are establishing peace among ourselves." The feeling of giving back to the community is recurrent. A young woman finishing her teaching credentials said, "With the education we are receiving we can understand things better, and that is helping us to prepare ourselves for a variety of service-oriented jobs." She added, "I must do something for the community. We all feel the obligation to respond to these concerns" (interviews with author, 1999).

CONCLUSIONS

The Ixcán village is rather typical in terms of the fear and mistrust that Mayan peasants feel toward outsiders as a result of the violence. The methodology a researcher employs in a conflict zone must emphasize the trust that is needed to conduct research under such conditions. Long-term familiarity with an area and with the people are especially valuable to evaluate and interpret responses as well as silences.

Research in this village over almost three decades indicates that understanding the context in which memory is shaped is fundamental in understanding what is recalled. Villagers who spent twelve years under military control were subjected to psychological operations aimed at changing their political views. Those villagers who fled to Mexico went through a radically different process: they organized themselves, recounted the army's horrors, analyzed what occurred and their relation to Guatemalan society, and were exposed to the Mexican peasantry as well as a wider world. Those who remained in Guatemala are more critical of the insurgents and are politically more apathetic; those who fled stress the military terror and are more active and optimistic. As the villagers came together in 1994, the divergent positions began to converge, but the scars were still palpable.

Reconciliation is complex and takes place in the context of the larger society as well as the village. Guatemala is characterized by deep, rigid power relations, pernicious racism and discrimination, mutual social unease, mistrust, and hostility. The role of the powerful in shaping the public rhetoric of the subjugated—and the evasiveness of the hidden discourse—is especially important, though mutually unacknowledged.

In a post–peace accords period, as a new understanding of Guatemala's violent past begins to emerge—one that resembles the multiple experiences by villagers—more Guatemalans will express themselves openly and a different version of the past will likely emerge. There has not yet been a full recognition, a validation in the appropriate historical context, of what happened.

Ultimately, a pivotal question remains: will Guatemala deal with the human-rights violations of the past and set the stage for reconciliation and a degree of justice? Violence can overwhelm facts in the short term; it cannot replace them. Arendt eloquently states, "Conceptually, we may call truth what we cannot change; metaphorically, it is the ground on which we stand and the sky that stretches above us" (Arendt 1968: 264).

NOTES

An earlier version of this chapter appeared previously as "La importancia del contexto en la memoria," in Beatriz Manz, Elizabeth Oglesby, and José García Noval, *De la memoria a la reconstrucción histórica* (Guatemala City: Asociación para el Avance de las Ciencias Sociales en Guatemala, 1999); and portions of this chapter appeared in "Terror, Grief, and Recovery: Genocidal Trauma in a Mayan Village in Guatemala," in Alex Hinton, ed., *Annihilating Difference: The Anthropology of Genocide* (Berkeley: University of California Press, 2002).

1. The Comisión para el Esclarecimiento Histórico, a United Nations project, was established through the Accord of Oslo on June 23, 1994.

2. See also Oficina de Derechos Humanos 1998a, 1998b, 1998c.

3. Mario Payeras (later known as Comandante Benedicto), one of fifteen combatants who entered the Ixcán jungle of Guatemala on January 19, 1972, wrote about those early days. A brilliant writer and poet, he details how they got lost looking for the village I am writing about. Once they had located it, they bought enough corn, salt, sugar, and cigarettes to allow them to go as far as the

Chixoy River (Payeras 1980: 32–35). In those early days, as Payeras describes, the guerrillas and the people in this village used precaution and secrecy. He says that when they were purchasing the food, they pretended that the transaction was forced, for the benefit of potential army spies. When the army came to investigate, all the tracks had been covered. Three years later, after having attracted recruits and support in several villages, these combatants would become the Ejército Guerrillero de los Pobres (Guerrilla Army of the Poor; EGP).

4. See Halbwachs (1980); Pennebacker and Banasik (1997); Baumeister and Hastings (1997).

5. In my own research, two factors laid the basis for establishing trust. First, I was born and raised in rural Chile, which provided elements of a shared framework concerning Latin America; second, I first went to the village shortly after it was settled, and since 1985 I have been going at least annually, often far more frequently. Moreover, I have interacted with villagers in the refugee camps in Mexico in 1982, 1984, 1987, and 1989, as well as with those scattered in the United States. Javier implied that being from Chile made me accessible and familiar to villagers, yet at the same time distant enough not to have a historical point of reference for them.

6. Segundo, Nicanor's brother, gave an interpretation at odds with Nicanor of why he joined the insurgents. Interviewed in a guerrilla camp not far from the village in 1987, he explained why he became a combatant with the EGP in 1976. "I thought about it for about two months after the guerrillas talked to me. I did not join because I was looking for adventures, or because I was disillusioned, or because I was looking for something without values; it was not because of that; I thought about it a lot." Several years later he reflected again on the first steps that led him to become a combatant with the guerrillas. It was a slow process, beginning with books he was given to read; then several months later those readings were discussed. The guerrillas "first would ask me questions, What did I understand? And then they would broaden on the themes and issues" (interview with author, Santa María Tzejá, Guatemala, 1998).

7. For this section's focus, see Cifuentes (1982, 1998); Ejército de Guatemala (1982, 1987). I will focus primarily on the army's impact on this village after 1982. The guerrillas' (EGP) activities and influence on this village I explore elsewhere as part of a broader treatment of this community. Nor do I dwell on the social and political context of refugees in Mexico and the influence on their way of thinking about the violence here.

8. This individual, along with some fifty families—overwhelmingly Evangelicals—came to the village under the sponsorship of the army to occupy the land left behind by the refugees in Mexico. In 1994 they left the village and the returnees received back their lands. It is the first and still the only village where a successful reintegration of the returnees, and resettlement of the occupiers, has occurred.

9. The Frente Sandinista de Liberación Nacional (FSLN) took power in Nicaragua in 1979. The Sandinistas were defeated in elections in 1990.

10. During the 1980s, it was mainly foreigners who conducted research in the rural areas. Among the first Guatemalans to do fieldwork in the late 1980s was the anthropologist Myrna Mack. She was an exceptional researcher not only

because of her abilities as an anthropologist and her commitment to human rights, but because she could bridge various sectors of Guatemalan society and receive the heartfelt trust of the Mayan peasantry (see AVANCSO 1990, 1992). Myrna Mack was assassinated on September 11, 1990.

11. For recent publications on the Guatemalan military, see Aguilera Peralta and Romero Imery (1981); McClintock (1985); Sereseres (1985, 1992); Aguilera Peralta (1988, 1989); Jonas (1991); Gramajo Morales (1995); Arévalo de León (1998); Kruijt (1998); Schirmer (1998).

REFERENCES

Aguilera Peralta, Gabriel. 1988. "The Hidden War: Guatemala's Counterinsurgency Campaign." In *Crisis in Central America: Regional Dynamics and U.S. Policy in the 1980s,* ed. Nora Hamilton, Jeffry A. Frieden, Linda Fuller, and Manuel Pastor, Jr., pp. 153–72. Boulder, Colo.: Westview Press.

———. 1989. *El fusil y el olivo: La cuestión militar en centroamérica.* San José, Costa Rica: Departamento Ecuménico de Investigaciones (DEI) and Facultad Latinoamericana de Ciencias Sociales (FLACSO).

Aguilera Peralta, Gabriel, and Jorge Romero Imery. 1981. *Dialéctica del terror en Guatemala.* San José, Costa Rica: Editorial Universitaria Centroamericana (EDUCA).

Americas Watch. 1986. *Civil Patrols in Guatemala.* New York: Americas Watch Committee.

Arendt, Hannah. 1968. *Between Past and Future: Eight Exercises in Political Thought.* New York: Penguin Books.

Arévalo de León, Bernardo. 1998. *Sobre arenas movedizas: Sociedad, estado, y ejército en Guatemala, 1997.* Guatemala City: FLACSO.

AVANCSO (Asociación para el Avance de las Ciencias Sociales en Guatemala). 1990. *Assistance and Control: Policies toward Internally Displaced Populations in Guatemala.* Washington, D.C.: Hemispheric Migration Project, Center for Immigration and Refugee Assistance, Georgetown University.

———. 1992. *¿Dónde está el futuro? Procesos de reintegración en comunidades de retornados.* Guatemala City: AVANCSO.

Baumeister, Roy F., and Stephen Hastings. 1997. "Distortions of Collective Memory: How Groups Flatter and Deceive Themselves." In *Collective Memory of Political Events: Social Psychological Perspectives,* ed. James W. Pennebaker, Dario Paez, and Bernard Rimé, pp. 277–93. Mahwah, N.J.: Lawrence Erlbaum Associates, Publishers.

Cifuentes H., Juan Fernando. 1982. "Apreciación de asuntos civiles (G-5) para el área Ixil." In *Revista Militar* (September–December): 25–72.

———. 1998. *Historia moderna de la etnicidad en Guatemala. La visión hegemónica: Rebeliones y otros incidentes indígenas en el siglo XX.* Guatemala City: Universidad Rafael Landivar, Instituto de Investigaciones Económicas y Sociales.

Comisión para el Esclarecimiento Histórico (CEH). 1999a. *Guatemala: Memory of Silence: Conclusions and Recommendations.* Report of the Commission for Historical Clarification. Guatemala City: Oficina de Servicios para Proyectos de las Naciones Unidas (UNOPS).

———. 1999b. "El involucramiento de la población civil en el enfrentamiento armado." Compact disc.

Connerton, Paul. 1989. *How Societies Remember.* Cambridge: Cambridge University Press.

Corradi, Juan E. 1992. "Toward Societies without Fear." In *Fear at the Edge: State Terror and Resistance in Latin America,* ed. Juan E. Corradi, Patricia Weiss Fagen, and Manuel Antonio Garretón, pp. 267–92. Berkeley: University of California Press.

Ejército de Guatemala. 1982. *Plan nacional de seguridad y desarrollo.* Mimeograph.

———. 1987. *El retorno de los refugiados.* Huehuetenango, Guatemala. Mimeograph.

Equipo de Antropología Forense de Guatemala. 1997. *Las masacres en Rabinal: Estudio histórico de las masacres de Plan de Sanchez, Chichupac, y Río Negro.* Guatemala City: Equipo de Antropología Forense de Guatemala.

Falla, Ricardo. 1994. *Massacres in the Jungle: Ixcán, Guatemala, 1975–1982.* Boulder, Colo.: Westview Press.

Gramajo Morales, Héctor A. 1995. *De la guerra...a la guerra: La difícil Transición política en Guatemala.* Guatemala City: Fondo de Cultura Editorial.

Green, Linda. 1999. *Fear as a Way of Life: Mayan Widows in Rural Guatemala.* New York: Columbia University Press.

Halbwachs, Maurice. 1980. *The Collective Memory.* New York: Harper and Row.

Hale, Charles R. 1997a. "Consciousness, Violence, and the Politics of Memory in Guatemala." *Current Anthropology* 38, no. 5: 817–38.

———. 1997b. "Cultural Politics of Identity in Latin America." *Annual Review of Anthropology* 26: 567–90.

Jonas, Susanne. 1991. *The Battle for Guatemala: Rebels, Death Squads, and U.S. Power.* Boulder, Colo.: Westview Press.

Kruijt, Dirk. 1998. "Reflexiones sobre Guatemala." In *Sobre arenas movedizas: sociedad, estado, y ejército en Guatemala, 1998,* ed. Bernardo Arévalo de León, pp. 9–36. Guatemala City: FLACSO.

Levi, Primo. 1988. *The Drowned and the Saved.* New York: Vintage International.

Manz, Beatriz. 1988a. *Refugees of a Hidden War: The Aftermath of Counterinsurgency in Guatemala.* SUNY Series in Anthropological Studies of Contemporary Issues. Albany: State University of New York Press.

———. 1988b. *Repatriation and Reintegration: An Arduous Process in Guatemala.* Washington, D.C.: Hemispheric Migration Project, Center for Immigration and Refugee Assistance, Georgetown University.

———. 1988c. "The Transformation of La Esperanza: An Ixcán Village." In *Harvest of Violence: The Maya Indians and the Guatemalan Crisis,* ed. Robert Carmack, pp. 70–89. Norman: University of Oklahoma Press.

———. 1995. "Fostering Trust in a Climate of Fear." In *Mistrusting Refugees,* ed. E. V. Daniel and J. Knudsen, pp. 151–67. Berkeley: University of California Press.

Marques, José, Dario Paez, and Alexandra F. Serra. 1997. "Social Sharing, Emotional Climate, and the Transgenerational Transmission of Memories: The Portuguese Colonial War." In *Collective Memory of Political Events: Social Psychological Perspectives,* ed. James W. Pennebaker, Dario Paez, and Bernard Rimé, pp. 253–75. Mahwah, N.J.: Lawrence Erlbaum Associates, Publishers.

McClintock, Michael. 1985. *State Terror and Popular Resistance in Guatemala.* Vol. 2 of *The American Connection,* by Michael McClintock. London: Zed Books.

Montejo, Victor. 1987. *Testimony: Death of a Guatemalan Village.* Willmantic, Conn.: Curbstone Press.

———. n.d. "Mayan Exile." Unpublished manuscript.

Nelson, Diane M. 1999. *A Finger in the Wound: Body Politics in Quincentennial Guatemala.* Berkeley: University of California Press.

Nietzsche, Friedrich. 1956. *The Birth of Tragedy and the Genealogy of Morals.* Trans. Francis Golffing. New York: Doubleday.

Oficina de Derechos Humanos del Arzobispado de Guatemala. 1998a. *Nunca más.* Vol. 1, *Impacto de la violencia.* Guatemala City: Arzobispado de Guatemala.

———. 1998b. *Nunca más.* Vol. 2, *Los mecanismos del horror.* Guatemala City: Arzobispado de Guatemala.

———. 1998c. *Nunca más.* Vol. 3, *El entorno histórico.* Guatemala City: Arzobispado de Guatemala.

Payeras, Mario. 1980. *Los días de la selva.* Havana: Casa de las Américas.

Pennebaker, James W., and Becky L. Banasik. 1997. "On the Creation and Maintenance of Collective Memories: History as Social Psychology." In *Collective Memory of Political Events: Social Psychological Perspectives,* ed. James W. Pennebaker, Dario Paez, and Bernard Rimé, pp. 3–20. Mahwah, N.J.: Lawrence Erlbaum Associates, Publishers.

Popkin, Margaret L. 1996. *Civil Patrols and Their Legacy: Overcoming Militarization and Polarization in the Guatemalan Countryside.* Washington, D.C.: Robert F. Kennedy Memorial Center for Human Rights.

Schirmer, Jennifer. 1998. *The Guatemalan Military Project: A Violence Called Democracy.* Philadelphia: University of Pennsylvania Press.

Sereseres, Cesar D. 1985. "The Highlands War in Guatemala." In *Latin American Insurgencies,* ed. Georges Fauriol, pp. 97–130. Washington, D.C.: Center for Strategic and International Studies, Georgetown University.

———. 1992. "The Guatemalan Counterinsurgency Campaign of 1982–1985: A Strategy of Going It Alone." In *Low-Intensity Conflict: Old Threats in a New World,* ed. Edwin G. Corr and Stephen Sloan, pp. 101–24. Boulder, Colo.: Westview Press.

Smith, Carol A. 1990. *Guatemalan Indians and the State, 1540–1988.* Austin: University of Texas Press.

Warren, Kay B. 1992. "Transforming Memories and Histories: The Meanings of Ethnic Resurgence for Mayan Indians." In *Americas: New Interpretive Essays,* ed. Alfred Stepan, pp. 189–219. New York: Oxford University Press.

———, ed. 1993. *The Violence Within: Cultural and Political Opposition in Divided Nations.* Boulder, Colo.: Westview Press.

————. 1998. *Indigenous Movements and Their Critics: Pan-Maya Activism in Guatemala*. Princeton, N.J.: Princeton University Press.

————. 2001. "Telling Truths: Taking David Stoll and the Rigoberta Menchú Exposé Seriously." In *The Rigoberta Menchú Controversy*, ed. Arturo Arias, pp. 198–218. Minneapolis: University of Minnesota Press.

Wilson, Richard. 1991. "Machine Guns and Mountain Spirits: The Cultural Effects of State Repression among the Q'eqchi' of Guatemala." *Critical Anthropology* 11: 33–61.

————. 1995. *Maya Resurgence in Guatemala: Q'eqchi' Experiences*. Norman: University of Oklahoma Press.

————, ed. 1997. *Human Rights, Culture and Context: Anthropological Perspectives*. London, Chicago: Pluto Press.

Zur, Judith N. 1998. *Violent Memories: Mayan War Widows in Guatemala*. Boulder, Colo.: Westview Press.

Contributors

SUSAN EVA ECKSTEIN, professor of sociology at Boston University and former president of the Latin American Studies Association, is the author of *Back from the Future: Cuba under Castro*, as well as *The Poverty of Revolution: The State and the Urban Poor in Mexico* (also in two Spanish editions) and *The Impact of Revolution: A Comparative Analysis of Mexico and Bolivia*. In addition, she is the editor of *Power and Popular Protest: Latin American Social Movements* (also in a Spanish edition); coeditor, with Timothy P. Wickham-Crowley, of *Struggles for Social Rights in Latin America*; and the author of more than sixty articles on Latin American social, economic, and political developments. She is currently working on a book on Cuban-American/Cuban transnational ties.

TIMOTHY P. WICKHAM-CROWLEY is associate professor of sociology at Georgetown University and an executive member of the Center for Latin American Studies there. He is the author of *Exploring Revolution* and of *Guerrillas and Revolution in Latin America*, as well as of several articles on related issues; and coeditor, with Eckstein, of *Struggles for Social Rights in Latin America*. In recent years he has been working on the explanation of different trajectories in comparative historical development within the Americas since the conquest.

MARC W. CHERNICK teaches in the Department of Government and the Center for Latin American Studies at Georgetown University. He previously taught at the Johns Hopkins School of Advanced International Studies, where he served as the acting director of the Latin American Studies Program, and at Columbia University, where he served as assistant director of the Institute of Latin American and Iberian Studies, and he has been a visiting professor at the University of Los Andes and the National University, both in Bogotá. He has worked as a consultant to the World Bank on issues of peace and rural development in Colombia, and for USAID on issues of democracy and human rights in other Latin

American and African countries. He holds a Ph.D. in political science from Columbia University and has written widely on drug trafficking, political violence, and negotiated settlement to armed conflict in Colombia and in the Andean region. He is currently completing a book on the Colombian peace process.

LISA HILBINK is Wilson-Cotsen Fellow in the Society of Fellows and lecturer in the Woodrow Wilson School of Public and International Affairs at Princeton University. Her doctoral dissertation, upon which the article in this volume is based, won the 1999–2000 Best Dissertation Award from the Western Political Science Association. She is currently completing a book entitled "The Politics of (In)Justice in Chile, 1964–2000," and has recently begun a new project on the origins and impact of "Judges for Democracy" groups in southern Europe and Latin America.

TERRY LYNN KARL is professor of political science and director of the Center for Latin American Studies at Stanford University, where she has received multiple awards for teaching excellence. She has published widely on comparative politics, with special emphasis on new democracies, the politics of oil-exporting countries, and contemporary Latin American politics. Karl has done field research in Venezuela, Mexico, Central America, Cuba, Chile, and South Africa. She has published over fifty scholarly articles, and her recent books include *The Paradox of Plenty: Oil Booms and Petro-States,* a comparative study of Venezuela, Algeria, Nigeria, Indonesia, Iran, and Norway; and *The Limits of Competition,* a volume written with the Group of Lisbon.

BEATRIZ MANZ is associate professor of geography and ethnic studies at the University of California at Berkeley and was director of Berkeley's Center for Latin American Studies from 1992 to 1997. She has conducted research in Guatemala and written extensively on that nation since the mid-1970s. She is currently working on a book on the same village in the Ixcán that is discussed here.

JUNE NASH is distinguished professor emerita at the City University of New York. She has done anthropological research among the Mayans of Chiapas, Bolivian tin miners, and General Electric workers in Pittsfield, Massachusetts, on themes of industrialization, economic restructuring, and indigenous social movements. Her book *Mayan Visions: The Quest for Autonomy in an Age of Globalization* was published in 2001.

PHILIP OXHORN is associate professor of political science and associate dean of graduate and postdoctoral studies at McGill University. He is the author of *Organizing Civil Society: The Popular Sectors and the Struggle for Democracy in Chile,* as well as coeditor of *What Kind of Democracy? What Kind of Market? Latin America in the Age of Neoliberalism* and *The Market and Democracy in Latin America: Convergence or Divergence?* His chapter forms part of a larger comparative research project examining the role played by civil society in mediating the social and political effects of economic change in Bolivia, Chile, and Mexico.

DAVID SCOTT PALMER is professor of international relations and political science at Boston University and was chair of the Department of Political Science from 1998 to 2001. His research interests include U.S.–Latin American relations, democratization, insurgencies, and boundary disputes. He has written extensively on Peru over the years and has served there as a Fulbright Senior Researcher/Lecturer (1998), an OAS Election Observer (1995, 2000), and a Peace Corps volunteer (1962–64).

LEIGH A. PAYNE is professor of political science at the University of Wisconsin-Madison. She is the author of the recently published *Uncivil Movements: The Armed Right Wing and Democracy in Latin America,* as well as of *Brazilian Industrialists and Democratic Change.* She is the coeditor, with Ernest Bartell, of *Business and Democracy in Latin America.* Her forthcoming book is titled *Unsettling Accounts,* which deals with the political impact of confessions made by perpetrators of state violence during authoritarian rule in Latin America, South Africa, Yugoslavia, and Rwanda.

JOHN A. PEELER is presidential professor of political science at Bucknell University. He is a long-time student of the comparative politics of democracy in Latin America and is the author of *Building Democracy in Latin America.* He has been working on issues of indigenous political mobilization in recent years.

ANÍBAL PÉREZ-LIÑÁN is assistant professor in the Department of Political Science at the University of Pittsburgh. His research focuses on the presidency and the role of political institutions in Latin America. He is the author of "Neoinstitutional Accounts of Voter Turnout: Moving beyond Industrial Democracies," *Electoral Studies* (March 2001); and "¿Juicio político o golpe legislativo? Sobre las crisis constitucionales en los años noventa," *América Latina, Hoy* (December 2000).

SYBIL DELAINE RHODES recently received her doctorate from Stanford University and is now assistant professor of political science at Western Michigan University. Her research interests lie at the intersection of democratic theory, interest representation, and public policy, particularly technology policy. Her Ph.D. dissertation was entitled "The Privatization of Public Utilities and the Rise of Consumer Movements in Latin America, 1985–2000: A Case Study of Telecommunications."

Index

Note: *Italicized page numbers indicate tables and figures.*

Abente-Brun, Diego, 109
Abregú, Martín, 181n10
Academia Judicial (Judicial School;
 Chile), 83–84
Academy of Mayan Languages of
 Guatemala, 272, 280n8
Acción Democrática (Democratic Action;
 AD; Venezuela), 101, 103, 116
Adriazola, Raúl Morales (senator, Chile),
 91nn22,25
Africa, poverty in, 138
agency: centrality of, 41; of Mayan peo-
 ple, 328; mediation through, 5
agrarian reform: in Chile, 70; in
 Colombia, 197; in Ecuador, 260; in
 Guatemala, 260; in Mexico, 289, 293,
 303; in Peru, 268
agriculture: cash crops in, 296; develop-
 ment and, 145–46; labor-repressive,
 141–42; monocultural crops in,
 143–44; subsistence, 287; violence
 linked to certain areas of, 195–98.
 See also land
AIDESEP. *See* Asociación Interétnica del
 Desarrollo de la Selva Peruana
Alape, Arturo, 211n14
Alarcón, Fabián (president, Ecuador), 106
Alexander, Leslie (U.S. ambassador to
 Ecuador), 106

Alfonsín, Raúl (president, Argentina), 12,
 160
Alianza Popular Revolucionaria Ameri-
 cana (American Popular Revolutionary
 Alliance; APRA; Peru), 259
Alianza San Bartolomé (paramilitary;
 Mexico), 300
Allende, Salvador (president, Chile): ac-
 cusations against, 90n21; coup against,
 75; economic intervention under, 70;
 judiciary under, 66, 73–75; socialist
 government of, 44
Altamirano, Carlos (senator, Chile), 72–73
Álvarez, Oscar (judge, Chile), 74
Alves, Rosental Calmon, 119
Amazonian people: Andean people compared with, 268–69; displacement of,
 235, 270; as indigenous, 279–80n1;
 reserves for, 267
Americas Watch, 180–81n7
AMIA. *See* Asociación Mutual Israelita
 Argentina
amnesties: for confessions, 160, 166,
 169, 173–74, 176, 178; court rulings
 on, 80–83, 85; Fujimori's demand for,
 124; for guerrillas, 186–87, 190; injustice fostered by, 204–8; list of, 206; for
 military, 187; in return for truth,
 182n19; as social, 79; tax, 227

Text: 10/13 Sabon
Display: Sabon
Compositor: Impressions Book & Journal Services, Inc.
Printer and Binder: Edwards Brothers, Inc.